Wendy Anne Paterson, PhD

Unbroken Homes
Single-Parent Mothers
Tell Their Stories

"As a f
teacho
in Women's   _ vften
lamented the scarcity of texts that
combine feminist critical theory
with solid and meticulous research.
Unbroken Homes is such a text. As a
model of engaged scholarship, Paterson's book combines deft qualitative research—in-depth interviews
as a participant-observer—with rigorous analysis of a daunting amount
of data. In so doing, she deconstructs the modern myth of the
single-parent home as always detrimental to the scholastic and social
achievement of its children.

The immediacy of the intermay make the readers feel as
           know (or perhaps are)
           such as Judith, Kathleen,
           Lyn, and Sarah. Nevertheerson avoids constructing
           hs or romanticizing her
           , the result of a critical
stance all too rare in avowedly 'interested' feminist texts such as this
one. It should go on your shelf
with Carol Gilligan's *In a Different
Voice,* Mary Field Belenky et al.'s
Women's Ways of Knowing, and
right next to Stephanie Coontz's
The Way We Never Were."

Gail Corrington Streete, PhD
Associate Professor
of Religious Studies;
Chair, Women's Studies Program,
Rhodes College,
Memphis, Tennessee

More pre-publication
REVIEWS, COMMENTARIES, EVALUATIONS . . .

"Across the world divorce has become a significant, frequent, and more predictable life event. One universal outcome of divorce is the rise of single-parent families headed by women and the important social, psychological, and economic consequences of this phenomenon. In this compelling book, Wendy Paterson weaves a beautiful tapestry of the intimate lives of five single-parent U.S. mothers and their struggles to achieve better lives for themselves and their children. Their growth, resilience, and independence contradict the stereotypes of the research literature that labels their families broken and deficient. Their stories bear testament to the explosive growth of new family forms not only in the United States but all over the world.

Read this important book not only to understand family transformation through the candid voices of single-parent mothers, but also for an excellent example of well-documented qualitative field research in a feminist critical theorist tradition where family life is demythologized and the cloak of the impartial observer is dismantled. The struggles and successes of Paterson's families make a strong case for how we need social policies to support rather than penalize the choices of divorced and single-parent mothers."

Joy K. Rice, PhD
Author of *Living Through Divorce: A Developmental Approach to Divorce Therapy*

The Haworth Press, Inc.

Unbroken Homes
Single-Parent Mothers Tell Their Stories

HAWORTH Innovations in Feminist Studies
J. Dianne Garner
Senior Editor

New, Recent, and Forthcoming Titles:

God's Country: A Case Against Theocracy by Sandy Rapp

Women and Aging: Celebrating Ourselves by Ruth Raymond Thone

Women's Conflicts About Eating and Sexuality: The Relationship Between Food and Sex by Rosalyn M. Meadow and Lillie Weiss

A Woman's Odyssey into Africa: Tracks Across a Life by Hanny Lightfoot-Klein

Anorexia Nervosa and Recovery: A Hunger for Meaning by Karen Way

Women Murdered by the Men They Loved by Constance A. Bean

Reproductive Hazards in the Workplace: Mending Jobs, Managing Pregnancies by Regina Kenen

Our Choices: Women's Personal Decisions About Abortion by Sumi Hoshiko

Tending Inner Gardens: The Healing Art of Feminist Psychotherapy by Lesley Irene Shore

The Way of the Woman Writer by Janet Lynn Roseman

Racism in the Lives of Women: Testimony, Theory, and Guides to Anti-Racist Practice by Jeanne Adleman and Gloria Enguídanos

Advocating for Self: Women's Decisions Concerning Contraception by Peggy Matteson

Feminist Visions of Gender Similarities and Differences by Meredith M. Kimball

Experiencing Abortion: A Weaving of Women's Words by Eve Kushner

Menopause, Me and You: The Sound of Women Pausing by Ann M. Voda

Fat—A Fate Worse Than Death?: Women, Weight, and Appearance by Ruth Raymond Thone

Feminist Theories and Feminist Psychotherapies: Origins, Themes, and Variations by Carolyn Zerbe Enns

Celebrating the Lives of Jewish Women: Patterns in a Feminist Sampler edited by Rachel Josefowitz Siegel and Ellen Cole

Women and AIDS: Negotiating Safer Practices, Care, and Representation edited by Nancy L. Roth and Linda K. Fuller

A Menopausal Memoir: Letters from Another Climate by Anne Herrmann

Women in the Antarctic edited by Esther D. Rothblum, Jacqueline S. Weinstock, and Jessica F. Morris

Breasts: The Women's Perspective on an American Obsession by Carolyn Latteier

Lesbian Stepfamilies: An Ethnography of Love by Janet M. Wright

Women, Families, and Feminist Politics: A Global Exploration by Kate Conway-Turner and Suzanne Cherrin

Women's Work: A Survey of Scholarship By and About Women edited by Donna Musialowski Ashcraft

Love Matters: A Book of Lesbian Romance and Relationships by Linda Sutton

Birth As a Healing Experience: The Emotional Journey of Pregnancy Through Postpartum by Lois Halzel Freedman

Unbroken Homes: Single-Parent Mothers Tell Their Stories by Wendy Anne Paterson

Transforming the Disciplines: A Women's Studies Primer edited by Elizabeth L. MacNabb, Mary Jane Cherry, Susan L. Popham, and René Perry Prys

Unbroken Homes
Single-Parent Mothers Tell Their Stories

Wendy Anne Paterson, PhD

The Haworth Press®
New York • London • Oxford

The Haworth Press, Inc., 10 Alice Street, Binghamton, NY 13904-1580

Cover design by Jennifer M. Gaska.

Library of Congress Cataloging-in-Publication Data

Paterson, Wendy A.
    Unbroken homes : single-parent mothers tell their stories / Wendy A. Paterson.
        p.   cm.
    Includes bibliographical references and index.
    ISBN 0-7890-1139-5 (hard : alk. paper) — ISBN 0-7890-1140-9 (soft : alk. paper)
        1. Single mothers—United States—Case studies. 2. Divorced mothers—United States—Case studies. 3. Single-parent families—United States—Case studies. I. Title.
HQ759.45 .P37 2000
306.85'6—dc21

00-031927

This work is dedicated to my son, Eric,
without whom it would have no meaning

and

to the five outstanding women who trusted me
to sew this quilt from the fabric of their lives.

ABOUT THE AUTHOR

Wendy A. Paterson, PhD, received her doctorate in elementary education from the State University of New York at Buffalo. She is currently an Assistant Professor of Elementary Education and Reading at Buffalo State College, Buffalo, New York. She has more than two decades of experience teaching children and adults at all levels from grade school through graduate school, and has been a frequently invited presenter on the topic of parents and schools over the course of her educational career.

Dr. Paterson is a single mother.

CONTENTS

Foreword

Witnessing with apprehension the immense changes in family life and form in the United States and around the world, we are likely to question the fate and well-being of families as we once knew them. We ask, Where are the fathers? What is happening to the welfare of our children? How can lone mothers cope with the harsh demands of being both breadwinner and single parent?

Understandably, our response is one of fear. It is easy to blame society's multiple ills on the rise of single-parent families, these so-called "deficit" family units that we label and think of as inadequate, flawed, or "broken." With more compassion we may see the mothers and children as victims, but rarely as success stories. Some public policymakers also bemoan these trends, viewing the rise of divorce and women's economic gains and independence as the antecedents of the breakdown of the traditional family; they try to shape welfare benefits and family policies to encourage marriage and deter divorce and single parenthood.

These concerns and efforts are understandable when one considers the potential cost of divorce to the stability of society and to the welfare of its children, as many researchers have documented. Despite the lack of public support and despite economic hardship and social discrimination, many single-parent families are managing to succeed, yet the personal voices and narratives of these women are rarely heard or documented.

This book provides us with a much-needed counterpoint and testimony to the resiliency of single-parent mothers and their families, as shown in their revealing stories of their personal transformations. These women, sometimes with much reluctance or little awareness of their courage and individual strength, draw on their inner resources and become, by necessity, more independent, adaptive, competent, and satisfied with themselves as persons and parents. Indeed several, because of the difficult process of divorce and the necessity of individuation, grow developmentally and become persons in their own right for the first time in their lives. In this way they mirror the voices of other single-parent women who have assured their interviewers that, despite the many personal and financial difficulties they faced, their lives improved after their divorces. They forged new identities and changed in ways they had not thought possible. As Wendy Paterson notes in the summary of her book, those who ascribe to the stereotypes of the overly stressed, burdened, and isolated single parent and the neglectful, incompetent lone mother, will assuredly be "off the mark" when they meet women such as Judith, Kathleen, Shawna, Lyn, and Sarah.

These women describe their lives as journeys still in progress and work hard to overcome the heavy stigmas they feel the outside world places on them. They openly discuss their weaknesses and defeats, their emotional ups and downs; however, what comes through so clearly in their stories is how they feel they have succeeded and improved. They balance their many responsibilities, stretch finances, learn to value themselves accurately, and reject the unconscious repetitions of inequitable gender roles and intergenerational family interaction patterns. In important ways, they try to impart their new knowledge and openness to their children and to support other divorced and single-parent women in their communities.

Wendy Paterson uses a rich ethnographic approach in presenting the various case studies, giving us an excellent example of well-documented, qualitative field research in a feminist critical theorist tradition. Here, family life is demythologized, and the cloak of the impartial observer dismantled. She creatively employs the feminist metaphor of a quilt that simultaneously embodies unification and diversity in each person's story and change. Each story is part of the quilt, but we can also view how these single-parent mothers weave together the many responsibilities, changes, and roles of their lives as they fashion their own life narrative, their own "quilt." The quilts are skillfully "stitched together" by the author, becoming a rich tapestry, colorful and changing as it is seen in different lights and airs.

The intimate lives of these five single-parent mothers and their struggles to achieve better lives for themselves and their children testify to the explosive growth of new family forms not only in the United States, but all over the world. It is important for clinicians, policymakers, and laypeople to begin to view these new families not as broken, but as alternatives. As we hear their voices, listen to their stories, and appreciate the tapestry of their lives, these single-parent mothers tell us that, like women across the world, they want change and equality. A strong theme in the journeys of the women in this book is their rejection of marital oppression and domestic battering, and their rebellion against the myths of motherhood and the stigma of being a single parent. I have noted how divorce may be considered a form of resistance to the oppression of women in families, and the stories of these women also support that interpretation. As partners and parents they are no longer willing to tolerate abusive relationships or to be silently oppressed in unhappy marriages.

The struggles and successes of Paterson's mothers make a strong case for family social policy that supports rather than penalizes the choices of divorced and single-parent mothers. The rise and success of single-parent and other alternative families across the world demonstrates to us that the family is not dead, but it certainly has changed. Responding progressively and compassionately to such change calls for policy that addresses the feminization of poverty, guarantees the best interests of children psychologically and economically, and ensures a collective sense of responsibility for all mothers and children regardless of their family status or role.

Joy K. Rice, PhD
Clinical Professor, Department of Psychiatry
University of Wisconsin Medical School;
Emerita Professor, Department of Educational Policy Studies
University of Wisconsin—Madison

Acknowledgments

I am indebted to many people for encouraging, supporting, and sustaining me throughout the research and writing of this book. I am deeply grateful to all of them, for they are an invisible, but invaluable part of this work.

To my parents, Donald and Edith Paterson, who raised me to believe that I could accomplish any goal I set for myself and who gave me a nurturing family life that helped to make that belief my reality. To my grandmother, Winifred Bissontz, whose strength and will helped her survive as a single mother in an unkind era. To my sister, Gail Corrington Streete, the finest scholar I have ever known, an inspiration and model for me since childhood. To my son, Eric, who at fourteen is a sensitive, loving, kind young man who took responsibility for himself without complaining when I was working late hours, who expressed his love for me when I most needed it, and who gave me wonderful back rubs when I spent too much time at the computer.

To Holly Clements, my friend for tea, tears, and laughter. To the wonderful women whose lives are displayed in this tome and whose camaraderie I treasure.

To my professors at SUNY Buffalo, especially, Dr. Patrick Finn, a truly wonderful teacher and scholar whose substantial and expressed support laid low what sometimes seemed to be insurmountable hurdles; Dr. James Collins, whose observation about my "passion for research" encouraged me to pursue my interests with renewed energy; Dr. Thomas Frantz, Chair, Department of Counseling and Educational Psychology, whose gentle guidance I was grateful to secure; Dr. Michael Kibby, Chair, Department of Learning and Instruction, who taught me true scholarship and who kept doors open that others tried to close; Dr. Suzanne Miller, Associate Dean of the Graduate School of Education, and Dr. Renee Parmar, who gave me both the passion for and ability to do qualitative research.

To the incomparable Joy K. Rice, Professor, University of Wisconsin, Madison, a visionary whose seminal article inspired this work and whose personal encouragement has helped me to bring these women's stories to the public eye.

Introduction

This book is a "story quilt" of personal narratives constructed from in-depth case study interviews of five single mothers, the results of a qualitative research study that I conducted in 1997. The book's title affirms these women's triumphant revelations that their homes are not "broken" simply because they do not conform to the two-parent model socially promoted as the ideal American family. The book chronicles their journeys as mothers, daughters, and women, in relationships and in solitude, displaying their stories in their own words, like squares of a multicolored quilt. To provide "the stitching between the squares," I add pertinent information drawn from family, educational, and women's studies research to extend what the women themselves reflect is significant in their lives and in the lives of their children. Finally, readers may stand back and view the quilt in its entirety, as I piece the stories together by discussing the common threads that emerge.

The women range in age from late twenties to early fifties and are ethnically diverse, college-educated, middle-class professionals who have one or two children (both girls and boys). Four became single parents through divorce, while the fifth, the youngest, chose not to marry the father of her daughter. Each woman testifies to the creation of a new, but decidedly "unbroken" home in which personal and parenting successes heal the wounds of self-doubt deepened by their dysfunctional couple relationships. Kathleen* describes her life today as cushioned by a "feeling of euphoria." Judith attests that she is finally "getting my life back" and "learning to enjoy my own company." Lyn looks forward to constructing "a new narrative" for her life, imagining herself "alone in a beautiful place." Shawna exults that she and her daughter nurture each other: "We both pro-

---

*The women's names and all names of persons mentioned in the narratives have been changed.

vide happiness in our lives." Sarah, whose childhood and marital histories almost destroyed her self-esteem, is proud of all she has achieved as "more than a survivor."

WHY DO WE NEED THIS BOOK?

I am the single mother of a fourteen-year-old boy. Divorced in 1988, I have been raising my son as a single parent for the past thirteen years. When the time came for me to pick an area of particular and compelling interest worthy of a doctoral dissertation, I was naturally drawn toward investigating the single-parent household, an increasingly common, but poorly understood, family type. In my doctoral studies, I met many middle-class professional women similar to me who were pursuing terminal degrees while earning a paycheck and raising one or more children alone. We shared our stories of role confusion, guilt, frustration, and self-doubt while bolstering one another's self-esteem, serving as confidantes and counselors, laughing about our shared parenting traumas and applauding our successes.

At the same time, I continued to read newspaper stories in which the term *broken home* was liberally used with regard to all types of criminal or deviant behaviors. The lives I and my single-mother friends and colleagues knew seemed to be in stark contrast to the serious deficiencies attributed to the single-parent homes that spawned archcriminals such as Timothy McVeigh, the convicted Oklahoma City bomber. I was completely taken aback when I read one of the series of articles on New York State's new, "tougher" learning standards and assessments, a personal crusade of State Education Commissioner Richard P. Mills. In a speech explaining his rationale behind issuing "report cards" to schools to hold them accountable for their students' academic performance, Mills deviated widely from his topic and confused family structure with economic factors influencing schoolwide performance: "When they're out of school, no employer is going to say: 'Do they come from a broken home? We'll cut them some slack.' They won't cut them some slack. They'll tell them: 'We don't have a job for you'" (Simon, 1996, p. A1).

In my role as an assistant professor of elementary education and reading, I often read student essays that are diatribes blaming single-parent families for the demise of children's values and naming them as the cause of students' poor academic performance. I respond to these misinformed meanderings of popular prejudice with the "helpful" suggestion that the student authors do a little research before making such sweeping generalizations, but each time I read some poorly written argument—published or student authored—I realize that single parents are rarely seen as individuals, even though they represent a diverse, growing, recognizable social collective. I believe it is time to encourage single mothers to tell their largely unchronicled life stories.

THE REST OF THE STORY

Are there compelling reasons why even erudite educators so readily accept the popular image of the single mother as a pariah? Perhaps one reason is that in most social science literature, single parenting is a phenomenon devoid of personality. Even a cursory review of social science and education research reveals a trend toward considering the single parent as a demographic phenomenon. Researchers use huge samples of students, such as 8,266 children in the Search Institute report (Benson and Roehlkepartian, 1993); 4,573 high school senior females in the High School and Beyond Study (Karraker, 1991); and 24,599 eighth graders in the National Educational Longitudinal Study for 1988 (Peng and Lee, 1992).

Such studies derive conclusions from secondary sources, data already gathered through questionnaires and surveys, such as the High School and Beyond Study, the National Educational Longitudinal Study (1988), U.S. Census data; the Panel on High-Risk Youth of the National Research Council; A Comprehensive Longitudinal Study of Young Children's Lives, conducted by the National Institute of Child Health and Human Development (1991-1995); the *Kids Count Data Book,* a yearly publication produced by the Center for the Study of Social Policy (1993); and the National Survey of Family Households data (1987-1988).

States and counties interested in trends affecting local school districts also sponsor studies to assess risk factors in school achievement, such as those done in North Carolina (Dulaney and Banks, 1994), Tennessee (Obiakor, 1992), Ohio (Emery, 1993), Wyoming (Wyoming State Department of Education, 1993), California (Sullivan, 1994), and Pennsylvania (Cooley, 1993), to name a few. In all of these studies, the "single-parent family" category is used almost exclusively as a demographic factor in association with other indices of social deviance.

Studies such as these, which use aggregate data, give the impression that single-parent families are most easily studied as members of a uniform group, rather than as a multiplicity of individuals whose widely diverse cultural backgrounds, social strata, economic resources, family composition, living arrangements, and levels of education can be fairly represented by measures of central tendency.

LABELING AND DEVIANCE

What damage is done when single parents are "blamed" for social disintegration? In sociology, labeling theory explains how the labeling of a social group may result in prejudicial assumptions regarding that group. The term *primary deviance* involves whatever behavior a person is engaged in that causes others to identify or label him or her as a deviant. Thus, by simply labeling a certain behavior as deviant from social norms, generalizations and stereotypical associations of other types of deviance often become associated with it (Stark, 1989). According to sociologist D. Stanley Eitzen, the act of labeling any member of a social group as a deviant does not occur randomly; it involves a "systematic societal bias against the powerless" (1988, p. 211).

Many research studies suggest that living in a single-parent family contributes to many factors associated with societal dysfunction: delinquency (Rankin and Kern, 1994), dropout rates (Zimiles and Lee, 1991), teenage suicide (Hirsch and Ellis, 1995), drug abuse (Van Stone, Nelson, and Niemann, 1994), child abuse (Sullivan, 1994), psychiatric disorders (Blum, Boyle, and Offord, 1988), emotional and behavioral problems (Lee et al., 1994), obesity and nutritional disorders (Wolfe, Campbell, and Frongillo, 1994), lower grade point average (Coffman and Roark, 1992), decreased creativity and divergent thinking (Jenkins, Hedlund, and Ripple, 1988), and teenage pregnancy (Cooper and Moore, 1995).

Single-parent homes frequently top the list of at-risk factors among the indices of child and adolescent health, education, and socioeconomic status. For example, in the *Kids Count Data Book* annual report (Center for the Study of Social Policy, 1993), the percentage of children living in single-parent families was listed with the following other factors placing children at risk for impaired growth: low birth weight, infant mortality, child death, graduation from high school, juvenile violent crime arrest rates, teens not in school or at work, teenage violent death rate, percentage of births to teenage parents, and poverty.

It is not unusual for single-parent homes to be singled out as a primary factor placing students at risk for academic failure. The questionable conclusion that the single-parent home is a *causative,* rather than *associative,* factor for risk can easily be seen in the way results from research on problem youngsters are reversed. Studies that focus on children who are already identified through problems they exhibit in school, when such children's social demographics are listed, reveal that large percentages of these children come from single-parent homes. Researchers often turn these results around to support the assumption that since so many of these children are from single-parent homes, that environment must be a factor in their failure. What such researchers often fail to point out, however, is that a large percentage of successful children are also from single-parent homes. In fairness to these researchers, what seems an obvious oversight is most often the result of their singular focus on the problem group (Davis and McCaul, 1991; Peng and Lee, 1992).

The "Inevitability of Damage"

Some researchers are unreserved in their conclusion that, where single parenting is concerned, correlation does indeed point to causation. Citing a study by the National Association of Social Workers, Mintzies and Hare (1985) identify fifty barriers to excellence, including single-parent families with teenage suicide, emotional problems of the gifted, special educational needs of the emotionally disturbed, dropout rates, sexuality, immigration, child abuse and neglect, and latchkey children in a list of some human and social factors that may interfere with attainment of excellence.

Even more emphatic, the Research and Policy Committee of the Committee for Economic Development accepts the inevitability of damage in their 1991 policy statement, which details how social change, particularly the increase in single-parent families, has resulted in more children being born at risk of school failure.

Even research that is obviously limited in scope or blatantly poorly constructed is often cited as "proof" that single-parent homes are bad for children. In 1986, William Shreeve and co-authors claimed that the results of their study of a single sample of 201 students in secondary schools in a single rural school district in Washington State dramatically confirmed that single parenthood adversely affects children's school achievement. Their emotional title, "Single parents and students achievements—A national tragedy" *[sic]* presages their conclusion that "single parenthood itself may be the deciding factor in school success for many students" (p. 175). They base this sweeping generalization on the fact that in their sample, for all but one case, children from single-parent homes scored lower on achievement tests and had lower grade point averages than their two-parent counterparts (p. 182). Readers are left wondering how these researchers, working with such a limited population, could isolate a single variable such as family type from all the other variables complicating typical human behavior so convincingly that it alone emerges as the cause for academic failure.

Blaming the Victim

Regardless of a study's questionable validity, strong negative assertions in research that the single-parent home is one of the "most important factors *harming* children" (Galston, 1993, p. 52) contribute to the shaping of public opinion, subsequently affecting policymakers and building a national agenda that includes political pressure to return to "family values." According to Eitzen (with Baca Zinn, 1988), a "blaming the victim" ideology is "a *prevailing* view in American society" (p. 209) (emphasis added). Such a mentality assumes that school failure, for example, may be "blamed" on a defect in children and their families. Eitzen warns that such an interpretation of data "frees the government, the economy, the system of stratification, the system of justice, and the educational system from blame" (p. 207).

When New York State Education Commissioner Richard P. Mills issued his statement about school accountability, he apparently could not resist equating school failure with family structure, even when focusing on the schools' failures to produce well-educated children (Simon, 1996). Mills is not the only educator who promotes the blaming of single parents for educational inadequacy. In the lead article of the summer 1996 issue of the *American Educator*, the professional journal of the American Federation of Teachers, author Barbara Lerner encourages teachers to maintain academic rigor to help troubled students "transcend the self and its sorrows" by "losing [themselves] in learning" (pp. 6, 7). In the leading paragraphs of her argument, she, too, reflects a general acceptance of "broken homes" as a cause of children's sadness, along with the usual litany of factors contributing to childhood deviance. In the first paragraph, she likens modern teachers to Arthurian legend's Merlin, the magician who helped young King Arthur focus on learning despite his troubles. Making no apologies for the fictional account on which she bases her analogy, she reflects, "Many of Merlin's students were troubled kids from broken homes, kids who had experienced rejection, neglect, and worse. Kids who were menaced by the promiscuity and violence all around them" (p. 4).

Murphy Brown and the American Family

A behavior is not considered deviant or nondeviant until conventional and conforming members of society *interpret* such behavior as deviant (Glaser, 1974). This was played out on national television when sitcom character Murphy Brown decided to become a single mother; this decision became one of the great debates of the Bush/Quayle administration in 1992. The concept of single parenting as an alternative family structure so challenged the traditional concept of the American family that then Vice President Dan Quayle made a highly publicized and widely supported speech denouncing Murphy Brown as a "poor role model" and praising the two-parent family as a more effective vehicle for modeling positive moral and social values.

The popular press followed suit. In *Mademoiselle,* B. G. Harrison (1992) cautioned that the issues pertaining to family values are too intimate and complex to be judged by politicians or influenced significantly by a TV sitcom, while conservative periodicals such as *Christianity Today* (Sidey, 1992) were quick to "quote" research: "Statistics indicate that single-parent families (most headed by mothers) face growing economic and social problems. Fatherless children are more likely to drop out of school, face physical and mental illness and become caught in a cycle of poverty" (p. 18). In *Time* magazine, Margaret Carlson (1992) agreed that Quayle was right to denounce Murphy Brown, stating, "Children can thrive in many situations, but coming into the world with one parent is a handicap, no matter how mature and wealthy the mother may be" (p. 30).

DEFINING FAMILY

The "family values" debate was not unique to the popular press; researchers also struggled with definitions. Just what does constitute a "family"? Studies of extended families, with grandparents; stepfamilies, also called "reconstituted families" (Coffman and Roark, 1992); single-parent households with varying living arrangements, with or without grandparents (Solomon and Marx, 1995); cohabiting couples (Pearson and Sessler, 1991); as well as lesbian and gay couples (Bumpass and Raley, 1995) served to intensify the debate. Some studies cautioned that definitions of single-parent homes should be based on living arrangements, rather than marital status (Bumpass and Raley, 1995). Others (Coffman and Roark, 1992) designated groups as "intact, single-parent or reconstituted families" and contrasted intact with reconstituted families or grouped single-parent and remarried families (Zimiles and Lee, 1991). Still others distinguished between "traditional" and "nontraditional" families by grouping single-parent biological, one-parent biological with live-in mate, stepfamilies, and guardianship families together to compare them with "traditional" two-biological-parent families—no mention is made of adoptive families (Lenhart and Chudzinski, 1994). These various views of the single-parent family in contrast to other types of families result in inconsistent ways of grouping data, which then can be manipulated easily to conform to theoretical or tacit assumptions about the effects of family structures on the experiences of children.

What we do know, however, is that 45 percent of all children born since 1970 will spend an average of six childhood years in a single-parent home due to divorce (Kurtz, Derevensky, and Tarabulsky, 1993), and information from the U.S. Census Bureau reports that 27.3 percent of households with children under eighteen are single-parent households (Casper and Bryson, 1998). Despite the relative prominence of this family type, both researchers and the public maintain significant negative expectations and erroneous assumptions about the single-parenting experience and its effect on children.

THE IMPORTANCE OF THEORIES AND INTERPRETIVE FRAMEWORKS

With the inconsistencies in defining family, it is important for readers of research to consider the historical and tacit assumptions at work in formulating research questions and choosing methodologies for investigating the effects of family structure on children. LeCompte and Preissle (1993) suggest that "[t]heory is embedded in human thought," and that the purpose of theory is to "help us sort out our world, make sense of it, guide how we behave in it, and predict what might happen next." Even more than scholarly philosophical frameworks, tacit theories—lay theories that derive from our own cultural, academic, and personal experiences—"constitute significant sources of researcher bias" (pp. 117-121).

Readers must be critically aware of the influence of both formal and tacit theories on researchers' choice of interpretive frameworks. Such theories are applied to organize and interpret data, to derive conclusions and/or make predictions. For example, researchers who apply sociological frameworks focus on attachment (Mitchell, 1994), adult-child solidarity (White, 1994), mobility (Astone and McLanahan, 1994), and cost-benefit analysis (Coughlin, 1988). Interpretations employing psychological frameworks lead to the consideration of dysfunctionality (Bayrakal and Kope, 1990), attachment (Rankin and Kern, 1994), loving actions and warmth (Parish and Necessary, 1994; Howe, 1994), adolescent anger (Coffman and

Roark, 1992), quality of relationship (Demo, 1992; Aquilino, 1994), support (Van Stone, Nelson, and Niemann, 1994; Jing and Mayer, 1995), suicidal tendencies (Hirsch and Ellis, 1995), and child psychiatric disorders (Blum, Boyle, and Offord, 1988; Swanson, Holzer, and Canavan, 1989).

Only *one* of the resources I found by scanning three databases (Social Sciences, Education, and the Educational Resources Information Center [ERIC] indexes) used feminist theory to critique the deficit comparison model at work in family life cycle studies of single parents. This study offered a new action theory of resistance and change, deconstructing the notion of family (Rice, 1994). Unlike some positivist theoretical frameworks that strive for a "God's Eye" that seeks to reveal an absolute-truth perspective (Smith and Heshusius, 1986), feminist theory represents one of many qualitative approaches to "ways of knowing" that attempts to "do justice to the complexity, tenuity, and indeterminacy of most of human experience" (Lather, 1988, p. 570). It is appropriate, then, for readers to consider feminist theory as an important framework for constructing and interpreting studies on single mothers.

A DIFFERENT SIDE OF THE STORY

The advancement and support of negative stereotypes by researchers using demographic correlations to draw questionable cause-effect conclusions or poorly constructed surveys to make sweeping generalizations from selected research populations needs to be reconsidered, for a growing body of qualitative and quantitative data supports a different side of the story.

Asmussen and Larson (1991) studied the "quality" of family time using pagers and daily reporting of activities, companionship, and subjective experience to observe the overall patterns of time use and subjective experiences in differing family types. They observed similarities among differing family types reorganized within family subsystems.

Richards and Schmiege (1993) interpreted data from telephone interviews using a dynamic systems theory framework, which posits that "persons create institutions," and described the family unit as a changing and morphogenic entity, rather than a static, circumscribed social phenomenon whose main purpose is stability. They investigated the parents' own perceptions of their strengths and weaknesses and presented a personal view rarely glimpsed behind aggregate data.

In fourteen case studies, Lewis (1992) used semistructured interviews of high school students who had lost parents to death or divorce to determine how schools could provide support. Though the association of death and divorce is derived from a value system that considers them equally emotionally destructive events, the use of interview data allowed Lewis to observe that the students wanted to be accepted and considered no different from before.

Banyard and Olson (1991) used structured interviews, rating scales, and daily diaries to assess the recollections of fifty-two low-income single mothers regarding their own childhood and their mothers' ability to care for them. They attempted to determine if mothers' perceptions of their ability to cope with the stress of being a single parent living in poverty reflected their own mothers' abilities. They found that mothers with recollections of good coping strategies had more confidence in their own abilities than did mothers who recalled negative childhood stressors.

Alessandri (1992) interviewed mothers from low-income, single-parent families and their ten- to twelve-year-old children to assess the effects of mothers' work status on the children's perceptions of self, family, and school achievement. Children of employed mothers had higher self-esteem, perceived greater cohesion, and were better able to predict their mothers' beliefs than were children of unemployed mothers.

Van Stone, Nelson, and Niemann (1994) used structured interviews of forty-six poor, single-mother college students to obtain their views of factors that influence academic success. Participants attributed their success to four social support factors—other students, family, faculty, and university services—and four psychological factors—personal ambition, prior knowledge and experience, effort and discipline, and self-confidence.

On the whole, however, aggregate data studies still outnumber those employing case studies, interviews, and qualitative analyses. A few aggregate studies indicate positive results. Using a sample of 4,516 young adults, Aquilino's 1994 study on the implications of childhood family disruption for parent-child relations found that young adults from single-parent families had quite positive relations with their parents even into adulthood.

In a reversal of stereotypical assumptions, Barnes, Farrell, and Banerjee (1994), in a sample of 699 adolescents and their parents, found that black families, with a higher percentage of single-parent households and lower family incomes, had higher alcohol abstention rates and lower rates of abuse and deviance than did the families of white adolescents.

Demo (1992) reviewed a number of studies on parent-child relationships and concluded that children and parents are largely satisfied with their relationships, and that the effects of maternal employment, divorce, and single-parent structures have been exaggerated. He advised researchers to investigate economic hardship and marital and family conflict as "processes more directly influencing children" (p. 104). Finn and Owings (1994) did exactly that in analyzing data from the National Educational Longitudinal Study and discovered that controlling for race and socioeconomic status for single-mother families eliminated the strong effects that seemed evident for alternative family structures.

Kennedy (1992) used the Life Roles Salience Scales to evaluate the responses of 656 young adults from intact, single-parent, and stepfamilies concerning positive expectations of adult life roles. He found that students from single-parent and stepfamilies scored significantly higher on the Occupational Role Commitment Scale than did children from intact families and suggested an overall positive picture for young people entering adult life.

Investigating the effects of work-family conflict, Duxbury, Higgins, and Lee (1994) found no difference in levels of overload and interference from family to work between single-parent and married-parent subjects.

INVESTIGATING THE LIVED EXPERIENCES
OF SINGLE MOTHERS

Given the conflicting and confusing evidence, what are readers to believe? How can the lived experiences of single mothers be honestly and fairly presented? When I constructed this study to investigate this question, there were many puzzles to negotiate. First, what constitutes a family? From a sociocultural stance, multiple family types exist in many cultures, not all of which consider a two-biological-parent, patriarchal structure the paragon of normalcy. I found it necessary to deconstruct the notion of an "ideal" in favor of new, viable, and flexible definitions of family that may present a framework for understanding single-mother-headed families more expansively.

A second concern was the effect of my choice of interpretive framework on the results of my case studies. Traditional theoretical explanations of family life were inadequate for studying single-parent families, since many of the more popular theories, such as family life cycle theory, favor a single family type over many others. Unquestioning acceptance of normative models against mounting evidence that such models may produce more social harm than good must be challenged. Indeed, the research agendas, questions, and methods applied to build and test such theories and models must now make room for a new program of family studies that might explore family choice and definition, "demythologizing family life and recognizing the impact of gender, race, and class" (Rice, 1994, p. 578).

METHODOLOGY

The case study approach was chosen because it is a phenomenological methodology aimed at understanding the particularities of different family types, with the intent to *explore*, rather than *compare*, family formation and definition. It answers Joy Rice's (1994) call for a new research agenda on families that emphasizes "the creative or productive element of individuals in families and the choices they make, the structures they conceive, and the resistance they effect," and that considers the family as "a social-cultural production whereby one looks to the lived culture of the individuals in families as they create it" (p. 579).

The use of qualitative methodology to understand the culture of single parents focuses on the particular experiences and perceptions of diverse families, rather than on statistics describing their occurrence in the population. The intent of this research is to provide impetus for social change and to better inform educational policy-making. The power of stereotypical concepts about single-parent families "exclusively ruled by mothers" (Lund, 1995, p. 43) extends to the labeling of children from such families as "at risk." This affects educators, whose attitudes and expectations for classroom activities may be based on the acceptance of a value system that strongly suggests that any child from a single-parent home is automatically "needy." Such teacher prejudices may indirectly produce effects that inhibit children from developing to their full potential.

By using in-depth phenomenological interviewing (Seidman, 1991), single mothers' own narrations and interpretations of their families' lives and their observations about their children's personalities and behavior in school may help educators, policymakers, and the public better understand the *particular* dynamics of *particular* single-parent families. In reading the stories of the five women represented in this study, readers will learn about the personalities behind the numbers. I sincerely hope that single mothers who read this book will strongly identify with these women and learn through them the value of their lived experiences.

How Do We Know These Stories Are True?

How does the reader know if the participants in this study have actually spoken the truth? This question cannot be answered through traditional scholarly means—rigorous method, scrupulous reporting, thick description, or even triangulation. It can only be answered with another, even more difficult question: "Whose truth is of interest?" Feminist researchers are quick to critique traditional notions about the nature of truth that favor what Bernstein (1983) calls "Cartesian Anxiety," or the "lust for absolutes, for certainty in our ways of knowing" (as quoted in Lather, 1988, p. 570).

Riger (1992) explains that feminist researchers present women's perspectives by "identifying ways women create meaning and experience life from their particular position in the social hierarchy" (p. 734). Case study proponents such as Robert Stake (1994) admit that "[w]e cannot be sure that a case telling its own story will tell all or tell well," but it is also true that the object of case study is to "seek out emic meanings held by the people within the case" (pp. 239-240). Such a phenomenological perspective is most interested in the "ways that the life world—that is the experiential world every person takes for granted—is produced and experienced by members" (Holstein and Gubrium, 1994, p. 263).

In defending interviewing as a data collection technique, Seidman (1991) responds directly to the question, "Are the participants' comments valid?" He replies that the three-interview structure (employed in this study) contains some inherent checks and balances that enhance trustworthiness: it places the participants' comments in context; it spaces the interviews to allow for idiosyncracy and to check for internal validity; and, in interviewing a number of participants, it allows us to connect their experiences and to compare one to another. Ultimately, however, the goal of interviewing in qualitative research is to "understand how our participants understand and make meaning of their experience" (p. 17).

As a collection of case studies analyzed from the constructivist, feminist, critical theorist perspective, this book attempts to present to the reader an accurate representation of its participants, to allow the reader to hear in the women's own voices their own experiences as they remember and interpret them, without, as Michelle Fine (1994) cautions, "romanticizing of narratives and the concomitant retreat from analysis" (p. 80). With this in mind, it is not necessary to establish an external system for verifying their truth. In these cases, the interest of the study is not in how others may see these mothers, but in how they see themselves. That there is more to know is always the case. That other members of their contexts— ex-husbands, children, and teachers, for example—may represent events differently is certainly likely, but the purpose of this study is to learn *about* single mothers *from* single mothers. The reader must judge the value and credibility of this study, not by searching for some external verification of these women's stories, but by appreciating the insights and observations of the single-mothering experience as lived by the participants whose stories are faithfully represented here.

PRESENTATION OF THE BOOK

Following this introduction, Chapter 1 explores the question "What is family?" in depth, using a feminist interpretive framework to critique some staunchly held myths about families. Chapters 2 through 6 present the five stories of the women who participated in the research study, as told by them. To provide a unifying as well as explanatory metaphor for these chapters, I borrowed from Whitney Otto's (1991) novel, *How to Make an American Quilt* and Jane Anderson's (1995) screenplay adaptation. As I watched the movie adaptation of this novel, based on a collection of women's stories about love and life, I was struck by the power of the quilt metaphor to depict a sewing together of the fabric of these women's lives. As Anderson's (1995) master quilter, Anna, explains:

> The challenge with a quilt like this is that each of these squares is made by different hands, so I have to bring them altogether in a balanced and harmonious design. First we have to find a theme. . . . You have to choose your combinations carefully. The right choices will enhance your quilt. The wrong choices will dull the colors and hide their original beauty. There are no rules you can follow. You have to go by instinct and you have to be brave.

Bravely, then, and with an eye to the careful stitching together of each narrative, I weave throughout these chapters my interpretation of their stories in connection with the themes suggested in Chapter 1. Each woman's story is related as her particular square of the quilt, each with her own predominant theme and subthemes. By presenting their stories in the participants' own words, I have tried to array the squares and preserve their colors with respect for their "original beauty."

The job of the master quilter is not finished with gathering together the many quilters whose work is featured in the quilt; "it is not simply the color and design, but the intricate stitchwork involved that brings the many pieces together" (Otto, 1991, p. 48). Therefore, in Chapter 7, "Viewing the Quilt: Patterns and Themes," I "bind the entire work together both literally and thematically" (Otto, 1991, p. 86). The successful result of this artistry can only be judged by the reader.

WHAT CAN BE LEARNED FROM ONLY FIVE WOMEN?

In the introduction to her book *Engendered Lives: A New Psychology of Women's Experience,* psychologist Ellyn Kaschak (1992) answers this question well:

As a clinician I am aware of the dangers of generalization. In a very real sense, each woman's story is her own. As a feminist, I am equally aware that no woman's story is just her own. . . . Each woman leads a particular life determined by her own talents and proclivities, her abilities and experiences, her ethnic and class membership. Yet all these experiences . . . are organized by gender, so that each woman's story is also every woman's story. (p. 8)

It is not the aim of this book to represent itself as containing information that pertains to "every woman's story." Perhaps the metaphor of the quilt can help us answer how these particular results may contribute to our understanding of *other* single mothers and their children *not* represented here. The quilt itself is made from "many different hands," and yet, when all of these individual and unrelated pieces are sewn together, the resulting quilt is an entity that exists as a whole, not just the sum of its parts. The quilt constructed in this book is not one with consistent patterns whose perfect symmetry gives the eye a singular picture. It is a "crazy quilt" of many fabrics, shapes, colors, and textures, meant to be appreciated as an asymmetrical collage, each piece drawing the eye and concentration of the beholder, giving the overall impression of diversity *and* collectivity. Reflecting on the tendency of researchers and politicians to consider the single-parent family as a category and to treat all persons fitting this description as if they had no other distinguishing features, the main purpose of my study was to give voice to these women's stories with "sufficient descriptive narrative so that readers can vicariously experience these happenings, and draw their own conclusions" (Stake, 1994, p. 243).

Chapter 1

What Is Family?
Mothering, Fathering, and Being Single

I didn't want to be a statistic. I didn't want people to say, "See. She's divorced. Look at her kids. They're not doing well in school." . . . I just didn't want to have my kids at any disadvantage, so I probably put in more than most parents, as if there were two parents in the house.

(From Kathleen's narrative, Chapter 3)

Successful single-parent households challenge the notion that the healthiest family structure requires two parents. Faced with a preponderance of research and popular rhetoric that elevates the two-parent home to an American ideal, mothers facing single parenting cannot avoid being influenced by the stigma associated with their family structure.

Reflecting on the "family crisis" platform of political campaigns in the 1980s and 1990s, historian Stephanie Coontz (1992) maintains, "Families have always been in flux and often in crisis; they have *never* lived up to nostalgic notions about 'the way things used to be'" (p. 2). The weight of an idealized image, however, has such a great impact that even the personal experiences of real families often fall short when measured against the myths that define families, gender expectations for mothers and fathers, and the onus of being a single woman in a "couples" world.

This chapter lays the groundwork for the narratives of the women in this book. Having conducted the interviews of the women before doing most of the library research for this study, I was surprised by how the women's narratives and reflections paralleled so many of

19

the discussions about women and single mothers in a variety of texts, especially those which quote other single-parent women. The themes organizing this chapter are echoed strongly within the women's narratives; thus, I refer to resources cited in this chapter within the interpretive "stitching" that connects sections of each woman's monologue. These topics are also revisited in Chapter 7, which presents unique and common themes drawn from the women's stories.

This chapter summarizes and discusses pertinent literature on five major topics. The first and primary area for consideration is defining the term *family:* How is a family constructed in the sociopolitical context? How does history trace its development? How do normative expectations shape our concept of what is a "deviant" family? The second and third topics focus on gender, tracing the American cultural understanding of parenting and child rearing and our expectations about motherhood and fatherhood, adding important information about gender role ascription and transmission. The fourth section concentrates on divorce, contrasting the arguments of experts who focus on the damaging effects of divorce on partners and children with those who see divorce as liberation for women and a necessary end to chaotic marriages. Finally, feminist psychology provides an additional perspective on the female experience in American culture, especially the experiences of "single" women.

DEFINING FAMILY

The Way We Never Were: Myths and History

For her provocative and thorough treatise on the American family, historian Stephanie Coontz (1992) chose the title *The Way We Never Were* to summarize the history of families in American culture. Tracing its development from the early colonial period to the present day, Coontz depicts the way the family has become more legend than reality, more myth than truth.

Sociologists agree. Five of these common family myths are especially helpful in framing the research of sociologists, psychologists, and historians who investigate questions associated with each myth.

What emerges from such investigations is the contrast between these commonly accepted myths and the lived experiences of real families. I have used these myths as a framework for discussing the phenomenon of single-parent families:

1. *The myth of the harmonious family of the past:* History was once witness to a "golden age of the family," and returning to such a model would solve the problems that beset modern families.
2. *The myth of separate worlds:* The family is "a refuge from a cold and competitive world," assuming that the family can be separated from the social forces that surround it.
3. *The myth of the monolithic family form:* The "typical American family" includes mother, father, and children, primarily found in children's books, the media, and political platforms.
4. *The myth of the undifferentiated family experience:* All members of a single family have common needs, experiences, and interests, and the healthy family serves all members equally well.
5. *The myth of family consensus:* Families are successful if harmonious and loving. (Baca Zinn and Eitzen, 1990, pp. 7-21)

What Golden Age?

To the first myth, historians respond that no historic golden age of the family ever existed (Baca Zinn and Eitzen, 1990; Coontz, 1992; Demos, 1986). In a misguided attempt to find solutions to problems that reside in a combined social, political, cultural, and economic context, family "reformers" look for traditional models from past history, but such models either never existed or existed in a totally different context. Instead, such models are amalgamations of "scripts" from a number of different times and locations (Coontz, 1992).

Even the indices of "decay" traditionally used to trace social disorganization have no consistent or reliable interpretation. Data on historical families are available, but some data collection methods and operational definitions associated with recorded data have changed over time. For example, divorce rates predating current court-reported divorce proceedings never reflected the desertions that constituted many divorces before legal records were kept. Increases in child abuse reporting rates may reflect changing attitudes toward child rearing; for example, "Spare the rod, spoil the child" has completely changed from a warning against permissiveness to grounds for social service intervention. High school dropout rates were actually higher before 1940, when less than half of those students who made it as far as secondary education actually finished. Measures of youth violence in pre–Civil War statistics name New York City as the "most dangerous place in the world," and higher youth homicide rates in the 1930s compared unfavorably to those as recent as the 1980s. In the 1820s, per capita alcohol consumption was three times higher than it is today, and the major drug epidemic of the 1800s included opium, cocaine, and morphine (Coontz, 1992).

There is no real value in attempting to locate any single ideal family form in American history, since all forms can be disputed. Family historians agree that "there is no one family form that has ever protected people from poverty or social disruption" (Coontz, 1992, p. 5). The colonial family, for example, often selected as a model of discipline and the Puritan ethic of hard work, was predicated on an all-powerful father who literally owned his wife and children and could use or abuse them, with the blessings of both church and state (Demos, 1986). The intact nuclear family was nonexistent in this era, which witnessed one-third to one-half of all children in colonial families deprived of at least one parent before the age of twenty-one (Coontz, 1992).

The Victorian ideal depicted in serene images of mother, father, and children around the family Christmas tree was really built on the child and female labor of the working classes. In fact, prior to the 1900s, the concept of holidays such as Thanksgiving and Christmas presenting warm opportunities for family bonding was not yet developed, and not even close to the emotional intensity of the current era. Conditions in child labor sweatshops spurred turn-of-the-century reformers to cry for a "return to the traditional family" of the antebellum period. During this time, a new division of labor by age and sex and the segregation of work outside the home from domestic work within the family led to unprecedented gender role divisions, establishing gender-based disequilibrium that persisted beyond its historical antecedents (Coontz, 1992).

Nostalgia for the family of the 1950s, persistently the object of conservative political acclaim, is symbolized almost universally in the literature as the Ozzie and Harriet caricature. The much celebrated nuclear family of the 1940s and 1950s actually represented an "aberrant period" in the history of the family (Stacey, 1990). During this time, unlike previous trends in the American family, women became mothers at an earlier age; fertility increased, with teenage pregnancy more than doubling for white women; divorce rates declined; and women's educational parity with men dropped. The extended family of the depression era, romanticized in the television series *The Waltons,* was abandoned in favor of a "new" isolated middle-class family with strong democratic values and equally strong expectations for attaining both material wealth and perfect familial harmony, a life shared by few 1950s families. Trying to live up to the image, rather than accept their own reality, sent middle-class women to psychotherapists in unprecedented numbers, where they were prescribed tranquilizers, whose manufacture and sale, along with alcohol consumption by women, skyrocketed (Coontz, 1992).

The much touted prosperity of this era was not idyllic for the 25 percent of its families who were considered poor, the 33 percent of its children living in poverty, and the 60 percent of its senior citizens whose yearly income was less than $1,000. Minority families were virtually excluded from the benefits of middle-class prosperity, with 50 percent of two-parent African-American families considered "poor." Women were "forced" from jobs held before World War II, encouraged to "choose" domesticity and child rearing, and punished if they remained employed through demotion to lower-status and lower-paying jobs (Coontz, 1992, pp. 23-30). However, despite one-fourth to one-third of all marriages contracted in the 1950s ending in eventual divorce, this time period fostered a "particularly distorted impression of normalcy and timelessness of the modern family system" in the baby boomers who were raised by its parents (Stacey, 1990, p. 9).

The Nuclear Family in the Nuclear Age

The genesis of the second myth of the family as protection from the world may be attributed to the post-Civil War reformers who reacted to the difficult industrial conditions of an increasingly urban population by forging campaigns to "save the children" of the working and largely immigrant classes. Political attention to these issues led to the enactment of legislation that supported the nuclear family, prohibiting child labor and enforcing female domesticity by giving the government power to regulate work hours and tasks for women. This had an invasive, rather than protective, effect for families—mostly the poor and working classes—whose family functioning did not fit the "model of the true home" (Coontz, 1992, p. 133)

Predating post-Civil War courts' actions regulating marriage, birth control, and criminality by minors, antebellum courts had already adopted the white, Northern middle-class family as the privileged model, and those unfortunate citizens whose families "failed" in comparison were sometimes institutionalized, giving the government the power to act in loco parentis (Coontz, 1992).

Direct government interference, however, was only one force shaping the destiny of families. Historically, "the family was as much acted upon as it was an actor in its own right" (Demos, 1986, p. 18). Economics, social welfare agencies, and psychological, sociological, and educational agencies intervened directly in the functioning of families. Throughout history, the relationship between the family and other institutions has been complicated by many factors—such as workers' pay, hours, and conditions; neighborhood dynamics; schools and other social agencies—taking active roles in defining and setting limits on family time, space, and even daily living conditions (Stacey, 1990). In a dichotomy of evasion and invasion, whereby the state has moved to "protect" family privacy, it has also allowed, and in some cases encouraged, business practices such as forced transfers, layoffs, long work hours, restricted health benefits, and the lack of parental leave policies to manipulate the home economically (Coontz, 1992, p. 146).

Social reform often meant enforcing norms. The Social Security Act of 1935, hailed as family protection, in effect solidified the gender lock on work, enforcing the stereotype of male as breadwinner through whom the female would receive benefits. State intervention in family life escalated with the welfare system and a continued emphasis on the state role in "managing" marriage and family functions. Economics and morality became mixed, indistinguishable from each other, with white, middle-class Protestant values becoming the touchstone by which all families were measured for "worthiness" to receive aid. Historian William Graebner (1987) called it "democratic social engineering," a system of state regulation of families whose purpose was to preserve economic inequality and conservative social control (as cited in Coontz, 1992, p. 140).

Even the rise of therapeutic intervention in social work and psychology made the forces outside the family ever more controlling of its members. Throughout the 1960s, 1970s, and 1980s, continual additions to legislation regulated internal family affairs, from domestic violence to parenting to sexuality. The state itself became the sole mediating body in marital disputes (Coontz, 1992, pp. 137-140). Nowhere, however, is the interplay between outside forces and the family better illustrated than in the family of the 1950s.

Reiterating the assertion that the family of the 1950s was "a historical fluke," Coontz (1992) explains that it was literally "created" in response to "a unique and temporary conjuncture of economic, social and political factors" (p. 28). Home and hearth became the symbolic defense for the cold war that raged outside, and the family was heralded as the first line of defense against the communist threat. Fear, popularized by the McCarthy trials and escalated by nuclear arms proliferation, contributed to the inward turning of the family, which sought escape in "domestic bliss" from an ever uncertain future (Stacey, 1990, p. 10). The children of the 1950s family often engaged in projecting an image of their family's health when, in reality, families were not without problems. The family members of the 1950s were more interested in "preventing the outside world from [seeing] the harsh realities of family life" than they were in promoting world peace. Popular plays of this time by Tennessee Williams, Eugene O'Neill, and Arthur Miller depicted the degradation of families and revealed the explosive emotions that seethed not too far below the surface of the image (Coontz, 1992, pp. 33, 34). In 1990, Benita Eisler wrote, "Behind the hedges and driveways of upper-middle class suburbia were tragedies of madness, suicide, and chronic and severe alcoholism" (as cited in Coontz, p. 34).

Capitalism was perhaps the major creator and supporter of the 1950s nuclear family unit, but it was also the source of its eventual dissolution. From the subsidizing of single-family homes to the heavy marketing of home products and the deliberate promotion of the "American Dream" (single-family home, two parents, two cars, two kids, and economic self-sufficiency), the commercialism of the "boom time" led to the absolute necessity for two wage earners in the family and the subsequent influx of women into the workforce. Commercial ventures capitalized on the consumerist mentality they helped to create, focusing marketing strategies on women and children. Widespread support for education encouraged the upward mobility of youths raised in the 1950s, and baby boomers carried the increased materialism far into their adulthood in the 1980s (Coontz, 1992, pp. 38, 171).

Coontz (1992) sums up the curious dichotomy between family illusions of privacy and state incursions into family affairs:

> neither the family nor the state is unitary, and relations between them are far more complicated than this. In the final analysis, the entire notion of the state undermining some primordial family privacy is a myth, because the nuclear family has never existed as an autonomous, private unit except where it was the synthetic creation of outside forces. . . . The strong nuclear family is in large measure a creation of the strong state. (p. 145)

The image of "the family as refuge" persisted in the late twentieth century, and many families expected home life to offer "buffering or at least relief against the demands and pressures of society at large." The inward turning of the family in opposition to the outside world left us a nation of people "who find it hard to care very much or very consistently about other people's children," fostering individual competition in the name of "taking care of one's own" and "may the best man win" (Demos, 1986, p. 39).

The cliche "Each man's home is his castle" enforces the notion that the family is somehow an inviolable bastion against outer forces, and yet the lived experiences of real families often sharply contrast with this image. The metaphors we use to describe the world outside the home have changed to reflect workers' alienation and automation. Working people adopt Upton Sinclair's vision from *The Jungle* (1906) when they refer to "the jungle out there." The world of work has truly become a "rat race," but the home has also metamorphosed from a quiet sanctuary for recreation and re- pose to a private entertainment industry where modern families may expect excitement in contrast to the dehumanizing jobs that seem beyond their control.

Rather than a comfortable escape from the jungle's dangers and uncertainties, modern men, particularly, refer to wives and families as a constraint to individual freedom, a form of "bondage" (Demos, 1986, p. 35). Nowhere is the contrast between the differing images of the family—as a stabilizing force and as a constraint to free- dom—more obvious than in premarital rituals. Women who are engaged to be married are joyfully ushered into their new family lives by other females who "shower" them with gifts to supply their new homes. Most of these gifts are consumer-based reinforcers of domesticity or provocative lingerie, a not-so-subtle reminder of the wives' sexual duty to their husbands. Men awaiting marriage are supported by their unmarried and married "mates" who set up elab- orate "stag parties" to mourn the passing of a good bachelor. Party favors and decorations at these events include the "ball and chain," to symbolize the loss of personal freedom, and sexually explicit movies or exotic dancers provide the unfortunate male with the opportunity to sublimate his sexual energies while mourning the imminent loss of his sexual freedom.

Monoliths and Modern Family Structures

The third myth, the existence of a single family form against which all others should be measured, provides the backdrop for a discussion of how American society determines deviance, and for considering the absurd resilience of this myth in the face of major trends in the lives of real families. At the end of the nineteenth century, conditions faced by a new wave of immigrants prompted middle-class reformers to call for a strengthening of the family image most antithetical to the working class: a single, insular family unit in which the "women and children [are] totally divorced from the world of work" (Coontz, 1992, p. 13). This, then, became the popularized image against which all families were measured. Developing concurrently were starkly delineated gender role divisions of labor that culminated in the "traditional family" of the 1950s (discussed in the next section, Male Instrumentalists and Female Expressives: Gender Roles Defined).

Although the concept of the family as a father-mother-children unit was operational in turn-of-the-century literature, the term *nuclear family* was introduced by G. P. Murdock in 1949 as an organizational concept for the social unit "characterized by common residence, economic cooperation, and reproduction" (as cited in Rice, 1994, p. 574). It assumed a "socially approved sexual relationship" between the adults sharing the residence and at least one child, adopted or biological. In 1951, sociologist Talcott Parsons firmly established the family as the basic social structure of society and solidified the concept of its function as the main socializer of children, a mechanism for reproduction, and the "stabilizer" in adult development (as cited in Rice, 1994, p. 575).

Thus, the "standard American family" became defined by three features: a nuclear unit; mother, father, and children; and a gendered division of labor (Baca Zinn and Eitzen, 1990, p. 14). Such a conception excludes couples who have no children, older couples whose children are grown and gone, and extended families, which include more than one single-family unit residing in close proximity.

According to the U.S. Census Bureau, the family definition used for all demographic information in census counts through the 1980s was "two or more persons related to each other by blood, marriage or adoption who live together" (Rice, 1994, p. 574). This, of course, excludes same-sex couples, common-law marriages, and other group-centered arrangements (Carter and McGoldrick, 1980). Such restrictions produce operational definitions at the foundation of research based largely on census data, perpetuating conceptualizations of family as related by blood and marriage, essentially ruling out choice, bonds of affection, or substantive commitment, family concepts that are more difficult to incorporate into quantitative research. As Rice (1994) points out, "It is convenient to treat marital status, marriage, etc., as clean demographic variables that can be quantified. Then we can also correlate other events like delinquency, school dropouts and achievement scores with those social markers as though they were the cause" (p. 579). Historian John Demos (1986) agrees: "No two families, no two lives, can possibly be the same. . . . The task, therefore, is one of averaging, of finding what statisticians would call a central tendency. But this in turn is frankly discriminatory: cases that lie far from the average will be poorly represented, or not represented at all" (p. x).

Regardless of census definitions or researcher convenience, "[t]here is a striking gap between the monolithic family and the reality of family formation in this society," resulting from a "false universalization" of a minority of families sanctified as the cultural ideal when, in essence, diversity in families is the *only* major trend (Howe, 1972, p. 11). Regarding case studies of single women, psychologist Lucia Bequaert (1976) adds that "textbook definitions from the literature on marriage and the family lag behind social realities" (p. xiii). Even the white middle-class mythical ideal does not *really* exist in the white middle class. In fact, the middle-class nuclear family—father at work and mother at home, raising their 2.5 children—accounts for fewer than 10 percent of all American households (Wattenberg and Reinhardt, 1981; Baca Zinn and Eitzen, 1990). Psychologist Ellyn Kaschak (1992) agrees that the recent idealization of the nuclear family is curious: "The fact [is] that this family structure is of historically recent origin, is even now very much in the minority in this country, is not functioning optimally at all, and has never characterized the family structure of many people of color or non-Western families" (p. 116).

Family scholars and therapists lack agreement on what constitutes a "normal" family, and many prefer to maintain a sort of "groundlessness" or "normlessness" to allow for individual differences to take precedence over the anticipated and often value-laden judgments of family service practitioners. According to Bennett, Wolin, and McAvity (1988), "There are as many family identities as there are families, making a typology a contradiction in terms" (p. 213). Scanzoni and Marsiglio (1993), promoters of New Action

Social Theory, prefer to treat the family as a "social arrangement that is constructed" (as cited in Rice, 1994, p. 577).

Sociologists Baca Zinn and Eitzen (1990) are unequivocal in refusing to offer a singular definition of the American family: "the first thing to remember about the American family is that it doesn't exist. Families exist . . . in all kinds of economic and marital situations" (p. 15). Bernardes (1993) also refused to attach a singular or collective definition to family because "it simply does not exist and the very act of defining it is normative" (as cited in Rice, 1994, p. 575). Cheal (1993) takes a pluralistic view, recognizing the historical fluctuations in family and understanding the "postmodern family" as a "fundamental cultural shift in Western society" that is neither temporary nor disorganized (as cited in Rice, 1994, p. 576). Gergin (1990) believes that the old ways of defining family served researchers, reformers, and politicians who used such definitions to predict and explain the phenomena associated with families, but such linear conceptions do not serve the "new life paradigms" of real women, men, and children who currently live in a multiplicity of family structures. Psychologist Kaschak (1992) enumerates some of the many viable child-rearing arrangements in today's families: joint custodial divorced parents, single-mother-headed families, single-father-headed families, as well as blended, extended, lesbian, and gay households. She states that "the majority of the children growing up in these settings are developing psychologically . . . much as do those who grow up in traditional nuclear families" (p. 117).

Rice (1994) suggests that a new research agenda on the family needs to adopt a "socio-cultural production model where one looks to the lived culture of the individuals in families as they create it" (p. 579). Ethnographic researcher Judith Stacey (1990) agrees. In her book *Brave New Families: Stories of Domestic Upheaval in the Late Twentieth Century,* Stacey prefers to remain mindful of a context offered by anthropology, that the family "is a locus not of residence but of meaning and relationships" (p. 6). She elaborates:

Today even happy families no longer are all alike! No longer is there a single culturally dominant family pattern to which the majority of Americans conform and most of the rest aspire.

Instead, Americans today have crafted a multiplicity of family and household arrangements that we inhabit and reconstitute frequently to changing personal and occupational circumstances. (p. 17)

The myth of the undifferentiated family experience, which maintains that the healthy family serves all members equally well, and the myth of family consensus, which assumes that families are successful if harmonious and loving, will be considered in connection with the literature on gender roles, including concepts of mothering and fathering, and the large body of information on women in families in the following section, Male Instrumentalists and Female Expressives.

Deviance and Defiance

Regardless of the family definitions offered to replace the "traditional" model (quoted as in popular parlance because historians have soundly disputed the existence of any one traditional model), critics agree that structuralist assumptions about the nuclear family as *the* normative model place all other family forms outside of it, assuming that one model is "better for society" and that the alternatives to it lead to social disintegration (Rice, 1994, p. 577). This "deficit comparison model" leads social researchers to label families that do not conform to the two-parent nuclear unit as broken homes, disintegrated families, or deviant families. Such labels ignore the diversity of families that characterizes the mainstream—no longer the margins—of society (Bequaert, 1976, p. xiii).

Sociologist Edwin Schur (1984) explains that deviance is not intrinsic, but acquired, and that "a general conception of deviance as a social construction developed by those in power and employed as a means of social control" explains much about the marginalization of minorities and women (p. 239). Once labeled as deviant, the person, or persons, can be treated in ways that focus on "correcting, punishing, or isolating" that deviance. This often has an even more insidious effect on the persons thus stigmatized, who "have themselves been socialized to accept the beliefs and values on which the stigma is grounded" (p. 38).

A notion of deviance or brokenness reflects a problem-centered approach that stresses mostly negative outcomes of what are often personal choices. This is true for same-sex couples, those who are voluntarily childless, divorced couples, single parents, and those who are single and childless. The most potent destructive force of the deficit comparison model has fallen directly on minority families, particularly the black family. Baca Zinn and Eitzen (1990) state, "Misconceptions about family lives of people of color are insidious and deeply entrenched in popular thinking" (p. 69). As with all American families, the diversity of black families defies generalization, but should black families attain majority status in American society and white families become the minority, the intergenerational, multiple kinship networks of many African-American communities might be considered the norm for American families. Compared with that model, the isolated, nonextended white nuclear family would be considered pathological (Rice, 1994, p. 562).

The Black Family

The infamous Moynihan report of 1965, *The Negro Family: The Case for National Action,* reported in almost every piece of literature on families since that time, described blacks as "less likely to marry, more likely to divorce, more likely to have illegitimate children, and more likely to live in single-mother headed families" (Walker, 1988, p. 87). A white, middle-class, value-laden interpretation of the survey data in the report "ignited an acrimonious and deeply sexist debate over the crisis in African-American families" (Stacey, 1990, p. 12) and popularized the image that the black family was so badly dysfunctional that it could be considered a "national tragedy." Family reformers issued a "call to action." Deviance from the nuclear family norm, in this case, was considered the cause of the many disadvantages blacks have suffered.

Research reports and texts based on the family life cycle theories of Duvall (1957) and Hill (1970) treat the multiproblem poor black family as an artifact of slavery, yet historical records soundly contradict this assumption (as cited in Rice, 1994, p. 569). Despite the blaming of social ills on blacks, in general, historian Coontz (1992) protests that "there is nothing in the rich history of African-American families and kinship . . . to mandate the outcomes that so many commentators blame either on black family traditions or on the lack of such traditions" (p. 250). Herbert Gutman's (1976) *Black Family in Slavery and Freedom* clarified some misconceptions asserted in the Moynihan report. First, contrary to the belief that slavery routinely split up families and led to the matriarchal structure of a "father-absent" black family, two-parent homes were more common than not, both during slavery and following emancipation, and the black family showed remarkable resilience and adaptability, considering the enormity of the stressors placed upon it.

Even the figures used to support the disintegrated black family are misleading. Before 1950, two-parent households were recorded for 65 percent of blacks. In "Black-White Differences in Marriage and Family Patterns," sociologist Henry Walker (1988) disputes the interpretations of data accepted by researchers since the Moynihan report. Walker states that reliance on separate data for black-white comparisons overemphasizes black trends away from marriage because it fails to account for similar trends in white families. Researchers examining historical data must remain mindful of the fact that data collection and accuracy change over time, making longitudinal comparisons difficult, at best. Atypical trends in history, for example, such as the anomalous 1950s, registered shifts in patterns of marriage and the family for *both* blacks and whites (pp. 87-112).

The equating of marital dissolution and instability in the black family is not accurate either. Data on the dissolution of marriage are often contaminated by widowhood, an especially important consideration given the higher incidence of black male mortality than white. Walker (1988) asserts that, rather than simple comparisons of differences between black and white aggregate data, *rate* of change must be examined. For example, the rate of births outside of marriage has climbed for both races, and the racial differences in marital dissolution over the long term are not very great. In all indices of family change, the white population has exhibited the same trends as blacks, but perhaps because of the smaller numbers of blacks than whites in statistical comparisons, the magnitude of these changes appears greater for blacks than whites (p. 108).

Though marriage and birth statistics for blacks and whites do differ, the explanations usually offered for the differences present problems. Statistics on female heads of household indicate a higher percentage for black families than for white, but the stereotypical image of the absent black father does not typify relationships among black parents. As Barbara Omolade of the Sisterhood of Black Single Mothers points out, "the lack of a wedding band, or even of cohabitation, doesn't mean a woman is estranged from her baby's father" (as cited in Levine, 1992, p. 104). Representing the black father as an "endangered species" is more of an attempt to stigmatize and discredit him than it is a conclusion supported by numbers. "As late as 1970, more than two-thirds of black fathers were living with their kids" (p. 104).

Figures on marital age, divorce, and birth outside of marriage indicate that blacks, in general, marry later than whites, have higher rates of marital disruption, and have lower rates of abortion and adoption. According to Baca Zinn and Eitzen (1990), "for black women, the birth of a first child and the beginning of marriage have become two quite separate events" (p. 120). In effect, the coparenting strategies of extended families may be "a protective strategy against the uncertainty of a relationship based on sex" (p. 120). Lower abortion and adoption rates tend to support the celebration of children in the black community and a willingness to raise the children in an extended family (p. 120; Coontz, 1992, p. 252).

Some theorists have attributed the high proportion of single-mother families in black communities to the drop in the marriage and remarriage rates and the declining availability of black men (Coontz, 1992, p. 251), but the element of choice may offer another explanation. Levine (1992) and Walker (1988, p. 109) hypothesize that marriage may be less central to the family lives of black Americans than it is to whites. Conventional marriage has fewer benefits for women than men in general (Bernard, 1975; Grove, 1976), but for black women, given a generally lower earning power for both sexes, compared with white males, and the black female's tradition of economic independence, marriage may not be economically advantageous either. Urbanization has yielded greater job opportunities for black women, as has the rise in white-collar jobs. Steadily rising salary rates for college-educated African Americans following affirmative-action initiatives have resulted in less disparity between black women and men than between white women and men. Thus, the loss of a second salary through divorce or elected singleness has a lesser impact on black female-headed families than on the celebrated white nuclear families with stay-at-home mothers.

Since the 1960s, it has been legally and socially more acceptable to leave or forgo an unhappy marriage, supporting a strong tradition of economic independence and collective child rearing for black women (Coontz, 1992, p. 252).

The interactions between race and class, which are often poorly controlled in many comparative studies of blacks and whites, should be considered. The tremendous effect of poverty on all races is often the mitigating factor in reports of social dissolution and may be particularly overshadowing in families headed by a single wage earner. Inevitable poverty is a "flaw" often attributed to the female head of household, even though the effects of poverty on two-parent families in the same community are equally devastating. Class differences may also be reflected in the overrepresentation of black women in the working class and their underrepresentation in the middle class, where the idealized nuclear family encourages women to stay home (Walker, 1988, p. 109). Research on black families has failed to account for systems of labor control that have inordinately impacted minority populations and played a part in the functioning and adaptation of the family to the consequences of systematic economic and political prejudice (Baca Zinn and Eitzen, 1990).

Not all black families are poor. The image of the "multiproblem poor black family" contrasts sharply with the lives of increasing numbers of college-educated, middle-class African-American professionals, whose stories are of little interest to researchers following a problem-oriented agenda. The strength of the black family includes extended kin networks, pooling of community resources, effective use of such institutions as the church and social organizations, racial solidarity, and a tradition of survival in adversity (Baca Zinn and Eitzen, 1990).

The Single-Parent Family

According to demographers Norton and Glick, in 1986, fully 40 percent of all children in the United States under the age of eighteen were expected to spend part of their childhood living with a single parent, usually a mother. The 1998 census figures showed that 27.3 percent of all families were headed by single parents. Historically, during wars and in many non-Western cultures, single parenting was considered a normative and fully functional family structure. Therefore, the "disempowered status" of the twentieth-century, mother-headed American family is not a universal phenomenon (Kissman and Allen, 1993).

Curiously, problem-oriented research focuses on the "father absence" of the single-parent home and not the "mother presence," keeping the focus negative, rather than positive, and situating the problems with the mothers (Bequaert, 1976, p. xiii). In 1978, Shinn reviewed studies investigating the effects of father absence on children's cognitive growth. She chose studies for review that had only nonclinical populations, included control groups of "father-present" children, and controlled for socioeconomic status (SES). Only twenty-eight of fifty studies met these criteria. Even of the sixteen studies that passed through a second round of filters for characteristics of father absence, effect sizes were small and not statistically significant for all subgroups (reported in Marsh, 1990, p. 327).

As early as the 1960s, a comprehensive review of the literature concerning divorce, by Herzog and Sudia (1986), concluded that the persistent myth about divorce as damaging for children was less viable than statistics supporting the conclusion that bad and chaotic marriages were far more damaging (pp. 177-182), the same conclusion reached thirty years later by Amato and Keith (1991), from a meta-analysis of 100 studies on children and divorce. Marsh (1990) studied high school students using the High School and Beyond Study from the National Center for Educational Statistics to examine the effects of family configuration on high school students in their sophomore to senior years. Comparing two-parent and single-parent families using multiple regressions with a number of control variables, he found "remarkably little variance" in the diverse set of academic and personal outcome variables between two- and single-parent families. In all twenty-two regressions, no more than half of 1 percent of the variance was attributable to family configuration (Marsh, 1990, p. 331).

Psychologist Ellyn Kaschak (1992) criticizes research on single parents as "replete with methodological problems and buried epistemological biases, so that little is added to our knowledge of what actually occurs in these family constellations" (p. 122). Psychologist and researcher Joy Rice (1994) critiques the discourse at the heart of studies on the adjustment of single parents and children because much of it adopts a problem orientation that focuses on difficulties. She, too, cites methodological problems, such as small samples with sweeping generalizations; confounding factors of SES, ages of the children, unexplained circumstances, as well as personal and cultural differences; clinical samples with prior histories of mental health problems, resulting in effect sizes larger for clinical populations than for community samples; few control groups composed of intact families; little, if any, before and after divorce comparisons; lack of consistency in claims of impaired adjustment for children; and failure to account for threats to validity, such as self-fulfilling prophecy resulting from the social expectations and prejudices of researchers. Herbert Marsh (1990) agrees that "serious methodological problems in studies of family configuration effects have not been adequately addressed" (p. 328). He states that controlling for SES is not enough, that process variables are unaccounted for, and that longitudinal studies comparing families before and after changes are virtually missing.

Rice (1994) critiques the foundation of many research efforts on single-parent homes that assume a family life cycle (FLC) orientation (Duvall, 1957, and Hill, 1970, explicated by Carter and McGoldrick, 1980). Similar to the life stages developmental theory of Erik Erikson (1963, as cited in Carter and McGoldrick, 1980), FLC stipulates that all families must undergo "stepwise successive changes in development and stages in the life cycle" (Rice, 1994, p. 569), articulating tasks for successful completion before proceeding to the next stage (see Table 1.1). When considered using this model, single-parent families are cited as "badly off-schedule" and "fractured," experiencing life cycle squeeze" and "structural disorder" (Rice, 1994, p. 570).

According to this normative model, single-parent families do not follow the FLC progression and must "reorganize" themselves to "normalize" as soon as possible. Rice (1994) shows, through reviewing the work of many FLC researchers, that in case studies such as those of Minuchin and Nichols (1993, as cited in Rice, 1994), case selection of *only* nuclear families overemphasizes a reliance on the nuclear family form for insights and hypotheses on "normal" family development, placing the single-parent family, by

TABLE 1.1. The Stages of the Family Life Cycle

Family Life Cycle Stage	Emotional Process of Transition: Key Principles	Second-Order Changes in Family Status Required to Proceed Developmentally
1. Between families: The unattached young adult	Accepting parent-offspring separation	a. Differentiation of self in relation to family of origin b. Development of intimate peer relationships c. Establishment of self in work
2. The joining of families through marriage: The newly married couple	Commitment to new system	a. Formation of marital system b. Realignment of relationships with extended families and friends to include spouse
3. The family with young children	Accepting new members into the system	a. Adjusting marital system to make space for children b. Taking on parenting roles c. Realignment of relationships with extended family to include grandparenting roles
4. The family with adolescents	Increasing flexibility of family boundaries to include children's independence	a. Shifting of parent-child relationships to permit adolescents to move in and out of system b. Refocus on midlife marital and career issues c. Beginning shift toward concerns for older generation
5. Launching children and moving on	Accepting a multitude of exits from, and entries into, the family system	a. Renegotiation of marital system as a dyad b. Development of adult-to-adult relationships between grown children and their parents c. Realignment of relationships to include in-laws and grandchildren
6. The family in later life	Accepting the shifting of generational roles	a. Maintaining own and/or couple functioning and interests in face of physiological decline; exploration of new familial and social role options b. Support for a more central role for middle generation c. Making room in the system for the wisdom and experience of the elderly; supporting the older generation without overfunctioning for them d. Dealing with loss of spouse, siblings, and other peers and preparation for own death; life review and integration

Source: From Carter, Betty and McGoldrick, Monica. *The Changing Family Life Cycle: A Framework for Family Therapy,* Second Edition. Copyright ©1989 by Allyn & Bacon. Reprinted by permission.

definition, well outside the norm. Indeed, FLC researchers include single parents in segregated chapters, along with such other "deviant" groups as low-income families, poor black families, families of alcoholics, and gay and lesbian families (Rice, 1994, p. 572). Marsh (1990) agrees: "Most research was implicitly designed to test or at least has been interpreted in relation to the family deficit model. . . . Family configuration effects are small and much less pervasive than frequently assumed" (p. 328).

Although emotionally inflamed rhetoric based on demographic studies persists in highlighting the many dangers to children associated with single-parent homes (Whitehead, 1993), an increasing number of studies refutes results based on a deficit comparison model. As early as 1976, case studies of twenty-two single-mother-headed households, done by the Women's Research Center, a group of women clinical workers and sociologists, indicated that "the one-parent home can be a healthy alternative rather than a deviant or trouble-ridden 'broken home' " (Bequaert, 1976, p. 25; Santrock, 1972). In 1982, Cashion's research presented evidence that "the majority of single-mother headed families are as successful as two-parent families when compared on measures of emotional adjustment and scholastic achievement" (as cited in Kissman and Allen, 1993, p. 3). A National Association of Social Workers preliminary report to their 1986 Conference on Women's Issues cited single mothers' lack of conflict in child-rearing decisions, family harmony, strong support networks, and increased independence for both parent and child as notable strengths (Kissman and Allen, 1993).

Economics, too, play a role in unfavorable comparisons of single-parent families and two-parent families. As with race, poverty is often used as an indicator of the social liability of single-parent families. In 1978, sociologist Diana Pearce coined the phrase *feminization of poverty,* a description that appears in almost every treatise on single mothers since that time. Implicit in its legitimate critique of the unequal distribution of resources between genders is the assumption that "poverty for many women begins with single parenthood," a concept that suggests an inescapable correlation (as cited in Weitzman, 1985, p. 348). Yet, Kissman and Allen note that fully half of all single-parent families live *above* the poverty line (1993, p. vii).

Although it would seem that the single-income family would necessarily fare worse than the two-income family, the two-parent normative model (not always a two-income family) offers no guaranteed escape from poverty (Baca Zinn and Eitzen, 1990, p. 118). In fact, Coontz (1992) presents historical evidence based on medical records that shows women and children in poor families bore the brunt of poverty in two-parent households, since they were more likely to be malnourished than the male head of household (p. 4). Despite the popular conception that welfare roles are predominantly occupied by single-parent families, especially blacks, no causal relationship exists between welfare and single-parent families. In a longitudinal study of the welfare system from 1955 to 1972, William Darrity and Samuel Myers (1984) found an inverse relationship between welfare benefits and rates of female heads of household (higher benefits correlated with lower rates of female heads of household). During the period between 1972 and 1980, even when the number of female heads of household increased, the awards from Aid to Families with Dependent Children (AFDC) maintained the same level or dropped for black children.

Pathologies and deviance attributed to the single-parent family form may also be closely allied to mother blaming and antifemale backlash (Bequaert, 1976; Faludi, 1991; Kaschak, 1992; Levine, 1992). This is treated more thoroughly in the section Parenting: Sainted Mothers and Disappearing Fathers, under Motherhood: Beatification and Blame, later in this chapter. Levine (1992) suggests that "overt moral opprobrium or social ostracism of the single mother" virtually disappeared in the 1990s, with the sensationalism of the "stylish single mom" in the media and the familiarity of virtually all persons with at least one single mother in their social circle. Still considered an iconoclast, however, the media-hyped single-mother image offers these mothers little practical help (p. 103).

Summary

What is family? The mythologies surrounding the family provide such a potent framework for conceptualizing the family that, from a sociopolitical perspective, when Americans experience economic prosperity and peace, we thank the family, but when the times are turbulent or uncertain and economic recession and unemployment prevail, we turn to the family for both blame and remedy. In Michael Lerner's (1988) article "Fix the World, Fix the Family," he criticizes the assumption that family change will have any great impact on a world in which working conditions have a much greater cause-effect relationship with social problems: "The idea that people can simply rearrange their family forms and thereby escape the massive impact of the rest of the society is naive" (as cited in Baca Zinn and Eitzen, 1990, p. 13). Images of the American family as an "endangered species" are not only popular with the press but have become accepted assumptions in the research and subsequent therapeutic and policy responses of psychologists, sociologists, educators, and child activists alike (Rice, 1994, p. 561). Demos (1986) summarizes our fervent expectations for the family:

[The family is supposed to] supply what is virtually needed, but missing, in social arrangements generally. It must protect its individual constituents against imminent and mortal danger or it must fill a void of meaninglessness. To put it another way: the family is not experienced in its own right and on its own terms, but in relation to outside circumstances and pressures. It is for this reason that we have become so extraordinarily self-conscious about family life—and more, have broached it for so long from an attitude of crisis. (p. 38)

From this discussion, the complexity of the researcher's problem raised in this chapter—"What constitutes family?"—may be fully appreciated. The dangers of privileging one family form over another—whether that form is based on historical antecedent or idealistic fabrication—preclude any singular answer to this question. In harmony with the constructivist paradigm that guides the current study, I prefer Rice's (1994) fluid definition, based on the lived experiences of diverse persons in myriad social arrangements, which allows the participants of any prospective "family" to define their own model as they produce it. Multiplicity allows the examination of such models for viability or dysfunction, as does the single-model typology, but begins, not with what *all* families *should* be, but with what *each* family *is,* so that the family itself can determine what it hopes to become.

MALE INSTRUMENTALISTS AND FEMALE EXPRESSIVES: GENDER ROLES DEFINED

Women Re-Create Men

In the 1950s, sociologists Talcott Parsons and Robert Bales solidified the division of roles in the family along gender lines, attaching a pseudobiological determinism to the rapidly diverging labor division of the American family, developing since the early twentieth century (Boss and Weiner, 1988; Rice, 1994; Baca Zinn and Eitzen, 1990). They advanced the notion that the home needed to be a place where the American working man could receive necessary re-creation after battling the increasingly alienating world of American industry. Thus, the "complementary" role divisions of labor that assigned women the duties of nurturers and caretakers at home and men the rigors of work outside the home became justifiable as a means of sustaining the productivity of the American worker.

It was easy to reverse the direction of this association to conclude that women functioned "better" as nurturers and caretakers because they were "naturally" well suited for it, given their biologically determined reproductive capacity; thus, women's roles were termed *expressive*. Men, in turn, were better suited to the workplace because they were biologically free from reproductive responsibility and were thought to be physically and emotionally better suited to the harshness of the working world; thus, men's roles were labeled *instrumental* (Baca Zinn and Eitzen, 1990, pp. 128-129).

This gender-locked role theory did not consider the many economic differences between classes, nor did it particularly care about the power differentials it created within families. In fact, the term *family* itself originally meant "a band of slaves," an ironic commentary on the power relations now masquerading as bonds of love (Coontz, 1992, p. 43). Theorists made the erroneous assumption (see myths 4 and 5) that good families were the sites of love and harmony, and that such families functioned equally well for all members, somehow ignoring how the husband's role gave him access to power and prestige, while the wife's role produced no exchangeable commodities, making her economically dependent on her husband. Her isolation from the power endowed in the production of marketable goods and services gave her a lower social status as well (Baca Zinn and Eitzen, 1990, pp. 7-21, 129-130). This ideal-ized arrangement made men resent their obligations and women resent their dependence. Indeed, the cost for women was great. "Expected to subordinate her own needs and aspirations to those of her husband and children," the 1950s "housewife" turned to tran-quilizers, alcohol, and, increasingly, divorce. Women who failed to fulfill the idealized obligations to their husbands were often abused (Coontz, 1992, p. 36).

Mothers Go to Work?

Despite economic realities of increased consumerism, growing clerical and service job opportunities, and skyrocketing inflation—all of which increased the participation of mothers in the workforce by 400 percent between 1940 and 1960—political theorist Susan Okin (1989) notes that "most Anglo-American theories of justice—not to mention most arrangements of work and education—have been about men who have wives at home" (cited in Coontz, 1992, p. 59). In fact, in 1950, 23.5 percent of all wives worked; in 1970, that number had risen to 40.8 percent; and by 1985, fully 54.2 percent of all wives had entered the workforce. The economic disparity between male and female workers, however, undermined women's hard-won entry into the spheres of economic power and perpetuated gendered work expectations at home: "The one who contributes less in the labor market is expected to contribute more at home" (Davis, 1988, p. 83).

The magical importance of traditional family values (which usual-ly means stay-at-home mothers) to American social well-being is so appealing that a "return to the stability of marriage and family" rhetoric has been *central* (Clinton versus Bush, 1992), or at the very least *included*, in every political campaign since the 1950s and into present-day politics. Indeed, "when commentators lament the col-lapse of traditional family commitments and values, they almost invariably mean the uniquely female duties associated with this doc-trine of separate spheres for men and women" (Coontz, 1992, p. 40).

The realities of women's "choice" to conform to this model were far from the popular imagery that is still maintained in the media. During the 1950s, 40 percent of black women and children worked, and 25 percent of black women headed households. Women of the

1950s were often forced from jobs they held during the war. Those who resisted were blamed for male unemployment and called "castrators." Women were systematically denied equal rights that implied economic parity with men, such as credit cards, contracts, home ownership, and even jury duty. Women who chose not to be mothers were social pariahs, and most women—even those who worked—defined themselves first as wives and then as mothers (Coontz, 1992, p. 32). According to a study of schizophrenic women hospitalized in the 1950s, women were sometimes institutionalized and subjected to shock treatments if they rebelled against their husbands' dictates or wanted abortions (Warren, 1987, as cited in Coontz, 1992, p. 32). A 1957 Smith College survey of its graduates found that homemakers "resented the wide disparity between the idealized image held of them as housewives and mothers and the realities of their daily routines" (Coontz, 1992, p. 164).

Self-Made Men and True Women

Coontz (1992) points out the paradox in the assumption that a strong family organized around dependence and personal needs was the mainstay of the capitalist/democratic American tradition that vigorously defended "rugged individualism," independence, and equal rights. The desired balance between private advancement and individuality encouraged in the male-dominated workforce and the "nurturance, mutual support, and long-term commitment" available in the home was primarily dependent on women continuing to "compensate for, rather than challenge, the individualism in our larger economy and policy" (pp. 40-41). In fact, family crisis rhetoric worries more about the changing roles of women than those of men. In effect, the celebrated "self-made man" of American legend required the cooperation of a "true woman" whose assigned role of compassionate caregiver "softened the effects [on men] of untrammeled individual competition" (pp. 45-53).

Gender role assignments designed to benefit capitalism soon became wildly romanticized. Biologically determined sex roles became blurred with socially determined gender roles. Men, by *nature,* were assigned "ambition, authority, power, vigor, calculation, and logic." Women, by *nature,* were assigned "gentleness, sensitivity, expressiveness, altruism, empathy, tenderness, piety, purity, submissiveness, and domesticity" (Coontz, 1992, p. 58). The complementary illusion of these assigned roles became a sort of yin and yang that encouraged American couples to feel incomplete without "the better half." One reason why sex-role boundaries are resistant to change is the mistaken belief that there are indispensable advantages to symbiotic and complementary roles that draw the sexes together, and that tampering with these potent mechanisms will threaten the psychological benefits of sex itself (Dinnerstein, 1976, p. 88). No confirmable or indisputable evidence shows that this fear is justifiable or has immutable biological origins.

I Want a Wife

Studies of personal well-being indicate decidedly unequal distributions of benefits from marriage for men and women. Though, statistically, women generally enjoy a longer life span than men, several texts cite surveys attributing the advantage in marriage to men because married men enjoy better physical and psychological health, greater economic security, and more freedom to focus on productive work, as compared to single men (Bernard, 1975, and Grove, 1976, cited in Llewelyn and Osborne, 1990; Kaschak, 1992; Rice and Rice, 1986). Women, on the other hand, pay a hefty psychological and economic price when they marry, as they subordinate self-identity and financial independence to achieve a oneness with their husbands. It is not unusual for women (see Chapter 6, "Sarah"), especially working women, to offer the lament, "What I need is a good wife!" In 1972, Judy Syfers (now Brady, since Mr. Syfers left) first published her classic essay, "Why I Want a Wife" in the first edition of *Ms.* magazine. It has since been reprinted over 200 times in at least ten different countries. The following are excerpts:

> I want a wife who will work and send me to school. And while I am going to school I want a wife to take care of my children. I want a wife to keep track of the children's doctor and dentist appointments. And to keep track of mine, too. . . . I want a wife who will take care of *my* physical needs. I want a wife who will keep my house clean. . . . I want a wife who cooks the meals, a wife who is a *good* cook. . . . I want a wife who will

take care of the details of my social life. . . . I want a wife who is sensitive to my sexual needs. . . . When I am through with school and have a job, I want my wife to quit working and remain at home so that my wife can more fully and completely take care of a wife's duties. My God, who *wouldn't* want a wife? (Brady, 1990, p. 17)

Though many baby boomers born in the 1950s learned the gender roles expected of that generation, inflation in the 1970s made necessary two incomes; economics—not feminism, which is usually blamed—led women to leave behind the "ideal of motherhood." During the 1960s, divorce rates increased, especially in families whose children were grown and gone, and as women moved steadily into the workforce and benefits increased, dependence on male breadwinners became an embarrassment, rather than an inescapable reality (Coontz, 1992, pp. 55, 167). Yet the gendered nature of child rearing remained unchanged. Family therapists Rice and Rice (1986) indicate that "[t]he gender gap is historical and cultural and likely will not be closed in one or two generations" (p. 13).

The mythological power of the mother-nurturer role as the natural purview of women and the breadwinning superiority of the "mostly absent" father remain entrenched symbols, transmitted across generations, that limit our own self-definitions (Dinnerstein, 1976). In her provocative book *The Mermaid and the Minotaur*—much quoted in feminist literature—psychologist Dorothy Dinnerstein (1976) maintains that people consent to intolerable and unequal gender arrangements, not because of the dictates of biology, but because these roles are learned and reinforced socially. Because the dominant male-female gender role definitions are socially rather than naturally constructed, they are mutable, but such change will be difficult because roles are "interlocked and symbiotically interdependent" (Dinnerstein, 1976, p. 55). The polarization of those who remain in their assigned roles and those who do not fit them makes life difficult for nonconformists.

Rigidly differentiated gender roles (often confused with sex roles) were also thought to help male and female children develop healthy personalities (Boss and Weiner, 1988, p. 238). Girls are taught to base their self-esteem on their success in relationships, and boys are taught to seek self-worth in public work (Kaschak, 1992). Role modeling has become the vehicle by which many gender-locked characteristics are transmitted, and worrying about proper role models of both sexes for children—or lack thereof, as in the case of mother-headed families—has become a primary concern for critics, therapists, *and* mothers (Bequaert, 1976; Carter and McGoldrick, 1980; Dornbusch and Strober, 1988; Kaschak, 1992; Llewelyn and Osborne, 1990).

Even Carol Gilligan's 1982 landmark work, *In a Different Voice*, has come under fire from feminists who suggest that her theories of women's moral development inadvertently reinforce the notion that women are, by nature and *choice*, other-centered, rather than self-centered, and that women conceptualize morality around their understanding of responsibility and relationships (p. 19). Her assertion that women feel responsible for "a life lived in relationships," superseding "selfishness," and that women "realize that the self and other are interdependent and that life . . . can only be sustained by care in relationships" advances the notion that women actually choose caring as an "anchor of personal integrity and strength" (p. 171). This further suggests that the gendered division of responsibility is a moral construct as well as an economic one.

Kaschak (1992) disputes this assumption. She states that men are not less, but differently, relational than women. In viewing the context of relationship, Bernard (1975, cited in Kaschak, 1992, p. 127) found that men seem to "require relationship for survival" and are indeed dependent on women as wives, lovers, and assistants. Though women often do define themselves in terms of the failure of their relationships or their sensitivity to the needs of others, it is not a question of who "mothers" and who does not, but of *how* both women *and* men (and sometimes older siblings) parent, that will set the tone for children's learning about becoming men and women, and their subsequent focus on the well-being of their relationships (p. 117). Kaschak cautions that we should carefully examine the ways girls and women in nuclear families are encouraged to view themselves as relational by nature: "We may lead them as women to attend to interpersonal cues and to the relative (or illusion of) safety in a relationship, particularly when the main value imparted to women [is the importance of relationship,] especially with men and children" (p. 114). It is entirely possible that boys would become equally relational to girls if their fathers exhibited the same nurturing and caring behaviors in their socialization, but the crux of difference would remain in the valuing of men over women, even if they act in identical manners (p. 121).

Summary

The defining of gender roles is dependent on the many social, cultural, economic, and political forces that shape the lives of persons regardless of their gender. The relationship between the genders is concomitantly dependent on the perceptions that each partner has of his or her role in same-sex or heterosexual relationships, especially those involving the raising and socialization of children. Historically, gender roles have tended to be shaped by, rather than shapers of, the social context. Thus, equity or inequity among people may be reflected in, rather than caused by, gender role definition. Rigid gender role assignments may indicate the pervasive inflexibility of a particular historico-cultural era, whereas fluid gender role boundaries may signal a climate conducive to change and forward momentum.

PARENTING: SAINTED MOTHERS AND DISAPPEARING FATHERS

In a chapter titled "Toxic Parents, Supermoms and Absent Fathers: Putting Parenting in Perspective," Stephanie Coontz (1992) echoes the voices of thousands of modern parents: "American parents get it coming and going" (p. 207). Lack of parental influence or interference in children's lives is thought to be the cause of most social ills. According to Coontz, "modern discussions of maternal employment, day care, divorce, and single-parenthood are distorted by the myth that parents can or should be solely responsible for how their children grow" (p. 210). Yet, parenting "experts" such as John Rosemond and Christopher Lasch blame everything on overly permissive parents who have "failed to instill guilt, discipline or a sense of limits" in children of the 1980s and 1990s (cited in Coontz,

1992, p. 208). In fact, two specialists in the "at-risk" industry, Herbert Gravitz and Julie Bowden (1987), have made the incredible announcement that 96 percent of the population comes from dysfunctional families (as cited in Coontz, 1992, p. 208).

The pronouncements of experts on parenting, however, have varied over time as much as cultural ideals about child rearing. Historical and cross-cultural records reveal a tremendous variety of parenting arrangements, and an equal number of different ways to transmit role socialization:

> The tremendous variety of workable childrearing patterns in history suggests that with a little effort, we should be able to forge effective new institutions and values. Instead, however, many commentators seek out every scrap of evidence they can find to "prove" that all innovations are bad. . . . By heaping more and more guilt on individual families, they make childrearing even more difficult than it already is in today's changing society. (Coontz, 1992, p. 215)

Gender-specific expectations for mothering and fathering in American society have thus resisted even historical retrospection.

Motherhood: Beatification and Blame

Motherhood is a concept built on folk expectations and imbued with sacred awe. Many women and men alike are fervently devoted to keeping the sacred and mystical scripts of the mother-child bond intact. Dinnerstein's (1976) philosophical argument that motherhood is more magical than practical begins with the assertion that a serious and (she believes) pathological imbalance exists in the mother-child-father triangle that is difficult to disentangle from its "powerful evolutionary and biological" roots in the human instinct to protect an infant to guarantee the survival of the species. This, she notes, has taken on "wildly disproportionate psychological weight" in trying to change gender roles in child rearing (pp. 77-78).

The veneration of motherhood, however, is a powerful force against the liberation of both men and women. One reason it is so easy to depersonalize women is the concept of mothers as "superhuman." Schur (1984) asserts that "fear of the dominance of mother-

hood" is what threatens males and supports gender role socialization practices that devalue women in an attempt to reduce that
perceived omnipotence (p. 44). Dinnerstein (1976) cautions, however, that "it is one thing to want to change the educational, voca-
tional, and legal status of women, it is quite another thing to start
tampering with Motherhood" (p. 76).

Biological determinism maintains that women's desire to have
children is instinctive, but studies of women have demonstrated that
choices are constrained and constructed by psychological and social
considerations more than some kind of mysterious hormonal yearn-
ing called "baby hunger" (Chodorow, 1978; Eichenbaum and Orbach, 1982). For most women, the issue of motherhood can become
"one of the most central themes of life," but a woman's freedom to
choose whether to become a mother is largely controlled by cultural
expectations (Llewelyn and Osborne, 1990, p. 124). "We live in . . .
a pronatalist society which stresses women's reproductive and
mothering functions to the exclusion of virtually every other function" (Llewelyn and Osborne, 1990, p. 129). Schur (1984) notes
that violation of these norms, including intentional *nonmotherhood,*
unwed motherhood, and *unfit* motherhood, means that women are
punishable along the entire continuum of child care: from not having them, to having them under the wrong circumstances, to not
caring for them adequately (p. 81).

Even those women who adopt the "do-both" mentality of what is
often called the "superwoman complex" (see Chapter 3, "Kathleen") are trapped by conflicts between their dual roles in the workforce and the home (Blake, 1974; Coontz, 1992; Gimenez, 1984;
Llewelyn and Osborne, 1990). Therapists who specialize in women's
issues often see clients who are "torn apart by their responsibilities
as mothers, guilt-ridden about not living up to their own idealized
images of what motherhood should be, and yet desperate for some
time to be themselves" (Llewelyn and Osborne, 1990, p. 160).

Farrell (1972) calls the "myth of motherhood" an amalgamation
of many others: an assumption that all women have maternal instincts; the notion that women cannot be fulfilled without children;
the "fact" that a mother's constant attention to a child is irreplace-
able and beneficial; and the tacit acceptance of "proof" that the

absence of the mother from a young child is irreparably damaging. In reality, mother myths become more popular when the market is highly competitive and jobs are few. During wartime, mother mythologies are rarely enforced, but afterward (as is evidenced in the 1950s), the home lovingly managed by Mother is once again glorified (p. 108).

Underlying theories of child rearing is an "assumption of the existence of 'motherlove' (note not 'fatherlove' or 'parental love') which continues to be biologically defined" (Llewelyn and Osborne, 1990, p. 160). As early as 1916, in her article "Social Devices for Impelling Women to Bear and Rear Children," Leta Hollingworth warned that evidence supporting a notion of innate maternal instinct was lacking, a notion often used as a means of social control (as cited in Schur, 1984, p. 81). The national horror engendered by Susan Smith's intentional drowning of her two children in 1995 is continuing evidence of our obsession with the inviolable nature of "motherlove" instincts (Mones, 1995). The socially acceptable form of aggression and anger expected for women is the "mother bear" fiercely defending her offspring. Behavior to the contrary completely overthrows our deep conviction that mothers have such an innate tendency (Levine, 1992, p. 16). Levine (1992) and Dinnerstein (1976) attribute the repugnance of women's anger to the mythological power of the mother-nurturer image. Women's acceptance of "parenting permanence" is so strong because the number of women who abandon their children is small compared to the number of fathers who desert their families entirely (Kaschak, 1992).

Our culture teaches both women and men that the instinct for parenting is uniquely feminine, thus discouraging the active promotion of any other model (Farrell, 1972). Sacred as it may seem, this assumption is questioned by studies such as Rutter's (1977), which showed that "under appropriate conditions, children can form satisfactory attachments to a number of caretakers, none of whom need be the biological mother" (Llewelyn and Osborne, 1990, p. 160). Others indicate that bonding to caregivers other than the mother leads to healthier child development (Kagan, 1984). Oakley (1986) points out that even the early mother-baby bonding thought to be so important has been medicalized, and, thus, the mother-child relationship is not even fully controlled by the mother herself.

Despite these observations, popular and sensationalized studies such as Belsky's, in 1986, concluded that mothers who return to work too early place their children at risk for "insecure attachments," and conservative research groups such as the Rockford Institute on the Family continue to fund studies devoted to proving the damaging effects of maternal work on children (for critiques of these studies, see Coontz, 1992; Milne et al., 1986; Mischel and Fuhr, 1988). Dinnerstein (1976) adds that technological advancements have freed women from sole charge of infant and child care, and that other quite efficient societal arrangements, such as extended family and close-knit communities, can call upon the "village to raise the child" (p. 26). For example, in tribal societies such as the !Kung (Lee, 1979, as cited in Kaschak, 1992), the primary responsibilities of child socialization and care fall on the older children and the men.

Even in our own history, child rearing has not always been the primary responsibility of the mother. According to Hollon (1974) and Demos (1986), the colonial father was attributed the stronger parental role, since he was given divine providence over his wife and children. Mothers were thought to spoil their children, and men were considered the better role models for both sexes. In fact, during that era, *all* adult men were expected to become fathers (Demos, 1986, p. 39). During nineteenth-century industrialization and the "wrenching apart of work and home-life," the mother became the primary parent, since she could remain isolated from a hostile world of avarice and immorality and was somehow considered to be more "pure" (p. 51).

A critical asymmetry of child care responsibility is the root of the persistent sex role patterns and expectations maintained into adulthood and recycled through generations (Dinnerstein, 1976, p. 40). In contrast, Farrell (1972) states that "balanced parental care means balanced children," but this "collides head-on" with the "Myth of Mom" (p. 108). It is hypocritical to expect equality in gender role socialization as long as "each man has one whole woman to cook and wait on him" (p. 114). Farrell warns that men are casualties of motherhood myths as well (p. 143). Since the interaction of socializing forces of parents, peers, media, and institutions such as schools and churches creates and perpetuates self-fulfilling parenting myths, reification of the assumptions composing such mythologies is transmitted vertically across generations. Our culture "teaches women" and "discourages men" and then claims the instinct for parenting is unique to women (p. 109).

That same veneration of motherhood, and the subsequent one-sidedness of child-rearing responsibility, however, allows inordinate attribution of blame to the mother whenever problems arise with the children, the family, and—by extension—the world (as evidenced in the folk admonition "The hand that rocks the cradle rules the world"). Boss and Weiner (1988) note that "even in animal studies, monkey mothers are written about less negatively than human mothers" (p. 237). The assumption of the primacy of nurturance enforces the expectation that women should be caring and nurturing, and that if those functions do not promote smooth functioning in families, mothers are at fault. Boundaries between a mother and her family are unacceptable. The myth of the "total mother" asserts that motherhood is a woman's absolute realm, and, thus, any behavioral abnormalities in her child must be attributable to *her* behavior. The father is viewed as only a "transient" whose functions outside the family have little or no impact on the children (pp. 236-237). However, after children enter school, they spend most of each day away from *both* father and mother (Kaschak, 1992, p. 116).

Simone de Beauvoir (1949) presented the psychoanalytic perspective that since bodily life comes through women, so also comes fleshly corruption, and women are thus condemned for their original sin: "From the day of his birth, man begins to die: this is the truth incarnated in the Mother" (as cited in Dinnerstein, 1976, p. 127). Thus, loving the flesh that woman represents includes an "ashamed love" for something that is actually loathed. Dinnerstein (1976) adds, "Woman, who introduced us to the human situation and who at the beginning seemed to be responsible for every drawback of that situation, carries for all of us a pre-rational onus of ultimately culpable responsibility forever after" (p. 234).

The weight of this guilt is evidenced in every research study that emphasizes the mother's role in "producing" harm for her children, an effect particularly obvious in the literature on single mothers. Psychology and psychiatry have not been kind to mothers. "Pathological mothers" are blamed for being either too rejecting, too overprotective, or both; held responsible for neuroses and psychosomatic disturbances in their children; and attributed with the resultant homosexuality of their boys if they prove themselves domineering or "smothering" (Llewelyn and Osborne, 1990, p. 164). Descriptors of mothers in family therapy literature include "schizo, engulfing, enmeshing, smothering, castrating and controlling" (Boss and Weiner, 1988, p. 238). Van Wormer (1989) believed that women's overdeveloped sense of responsibility for the mental health of their families leads them to attempt to "control" their families, when in essence they lack such power (see Chapter 2, "Judith"). Such attempts are alternately viewed as laughable or pathogenic. The most popular pseudopsychological diagnosis in common parlance in the 1990s is *codependency,* a strange pejorative once used solely to describe alcoholic families, but now generalized to blame mothers for "doing just what is required of them" (Kaschak, 1992, p. 157).

Despite advances in theoretical understanding about the complexities of family functions in child development, many child health and mental health professionals hold the tacit belief that *mothers* are responsible for their children's emotional and physical welfare. In their 1993 publication for social work practitioners, *Single-Parent Families,* Kissman and Allen cite Caplan and Hall-McCorquodale's 1985 review of the literature that found no fewer than seventy-two different psychological disorders attributed to mothers' failings; they warn therapists that "persistent mother blaming in traditional therapeutic encounters" exacerbates the powerlessness such women already feel (Kissman and Allen, 1993, p. 4).

Few, if any, research studies associating single parenting with deviance in children and young adults studied father-headed single-parent families along with mother-headed single-parent families. Rice (1994) observes that there is a "paradox in family research which assumes that women have a greater readiness and aptitude for childrearing, but when they do it alone, it is not good." The very labeling of families as "female-headed" or "mother-headed" eclipses the role of the father and associates problems and solutions solely with the mother (p. 566).

Divorce research is particularly guilty of mother blaming. Wallerstein and Kelly's (1974, 1975, 1976, 1980) often quoted research on the effects of divorce on children attributed developmental disruptions in children to the fact that mothers leaving for full-time work made children experience a "double loss," and they called the single-parent model one of "diminished parenting." Hetherington, Cox, and Cox's (1978) longitudinal studies on the effects of divorce and single parenting on children suggested that single mothers suffer from "task overload," with a resultant "increased difficulty in parenting their children with confidence and enjoyment" (as cited in Llewelyn and Osborne, 1990, p. 210).

Those who take a less retributive stance—such as Dornbusch and Strober in *Feminism, Children, and the New Families* (1988), Weitzman in *The Divorce Revolution* (1985), and Carter and McGoldrick in *The Family Life Cycle* (1980)—still resort to a rhetoric that clearly overemphasizes single mothers' inabilities and weaknesses. Even Farrell (1972), in making a case for the "re-education" of men toward more balanced parenting, engages in mother blaming, especially of single mothers, when he criticizes mothers for producing abnormal effects in male children:

> The mother-dominated boy is not only excessively passive in many cases, but develops many of the very traits of traditional femininity, such as lack of self-confidence, which we are suggesting is harmful to either sex. . . . When this is compounded by the domination of just one parent it adds problems of over-attachment to one sexual role to the problems of inability to extricate oneself from that attachment. (p. 111)

The Disappearing Father

In contrast to the well-documented historical consideration of motherhood, a paucity of information exists about fathers: "Fatherhood does have a long history, but virtually no historians," comments Demos (1986, p. 39). The information we have on men's participation in child rearing comes mostly from women's history, but previous to a resurgence of interest in "better fathering" in the 1990s, research has shown little interest in investigating men's private lives. Farrell (1972) criticizes research on parenting for one of its "fundamental fallacies," an "almost total focus" on the mother as socializing agent, which he believes has hurt men (p. 31). Levine (1992), too, wonders about the strange penchant of researchers to study father absence rather than father presence: "A review of the academic psychological literature on families from 1929 to 1956 found only eleven articles about the father-child relationship compared with 160 about mothers and children" (p. 189).

Historically, as with motherhood, fatherhood has changed in the context of social and cultural forces that shape the family and define the roles of its members. The colonial father, as described previously, was invested with the most central role in the family. The powers to grant or deny in matters of courtship, decision-making authority, and child discipline were solely his. He was expected to control his children and prevent them from their "sinful passions," something their mothers—whose penchant for sinning had biblical foundations—could not do well. The activities and domination of the father made him the predominant parent (Demos, 1986, p. 35).

In the nineteenth century, with its many changes in work and home, the role of the father also changed. A nostalgia for the past, curiously similar to that of the 1990s, was precipitated by the uncertainty and vast changes in the outside world, and the family was expected to defend and support what were considered strong family values. Marking the passage of the nineteenth century was a "massive system" of sex role stereotyping resulting from the widening rift between work in and out of the home. As the father became the provider, he also separated from his children and was increasingly absent from his family. The father's life outside the family became mysterious to his wife and children, and his ability to do battle in "the jungle out there" elevated him to positively heroic proportions. The family became his place of repose, and children were expected to leave him alone so that he might become rejuvenated and concentrate on work and public affairs, leaving domestic and parenting responsibilities to the new primary parent, the mother (Demos, 1986).

The father maintained his ultimate power in discipline ("Wait until your father gets home!") and his moral guardianship, but his role in the family as an occasional playmate, a detached listener, and an audience for other family members to entertain started his descent into part-time status. During this era, the courts legalized the primacy of the mother: in 1847, a New York court ruled, "All other things being equal, the mother is the most proper parent to be entrusted with the custody of the child" (Demos, 1986, p. 58). It was during this stage that the (in)famous "Victorian patriarch" became the symbol of fatherhood. This powerful image has maintained its venerable stature and presents a curious icon, inspiring even twentieth-century images of fatherhood.

The rise of the suburbs and the continual distancing of the working world from the home made Father a "Sunday" phenomenon, a curious and bumbling incompetent who was "cajoled, humored, and implicitly patronized by long-suffering wives and clever children" (Demos, 1986, p. 61). This was reflected in the many father caricatures in 1950s and 1960s sitcoms, such as Ward Cleaver in *Leave It to Beaver,* and Archie Bunker in the 1970s sitcom *All in the Family.* As the family borders were pulled in ever tighter, the "father as provider" became monolithic, and the father participated unevenly in a sort of self-conscious "chumming" with his children (p. 62). The notion that father was for "play" and mother was for nurturance became entrenched in children's conceptions of their parents (Dinnerstein, 1976). Studies from the 1970s described fathers' interactions with their children as more play than caregiving (Belsky, 1979; Clarke-Steward, 1978; Kotelchuck, 1976; Lamb, 1976, 1977; cited in Kaschak, 1992, p. 121). However, since the father was still the most powerful member of the family, he would maintain his right to discipline both children and wife, a function upheld by the courts (Farrell, 1972).

Two significant events in recent history have had a profound impact on this long-term image of fatherhood: the entry of women into the workforce and the growing incidence of divorce. Farrell (1972) believes that the seeds of divorce were laid in the fractured division of labor, whereby men and women inhabited different worlds and developed different interests, a sort of "psychological divorce training" (p. xxvii). However, when women entered the workforce, the world outside the family was no longer mysterious to them, and as work became the responsibility of both parents, so, women thought, should parenting. Even fathers separated from their families by divorce were paradoxically forced to enlarge their duties during the time they were fully responsible for the children. This closing of the "gulf between the experiences of men and women" has presented a dark side as well. As some fathers increase their commitment to child rearing, others, grappling with the role change, avoid or abandon parenting altogether (Demos, 1986; Coontz, 1992).

In her investigation of man hating in American culture, *My Enemy, My Love*, Judith Levine (1992) characterizes some men as "abandoners" who "see little or no relation between begetting and supporting" (p. 103). Citing Dinnerstein's psychoanalytic perspective on the antipathy of men and women, Judith Levine adds that "[m]an-hating is born in the predominant quality of Western fatherhood: absence" (p. 4). Levine believes that new no-fault divorce laws assert the automaticity of women's ability to support themselves and raise their children successfully, while absolving men from their responsibilities in pregnancies and fatherhood, making women "no less vulnerable than they were before, only differently so" (Dinnerstein, 1976, p. 104).

Weitzman (1985) agrees. In critiquing no-fault divorce laws for reinforcing gender inequalities, not eliminating them, she notes that "postdivorce equality between the sexes will remain an impossibility. For without equality in economic resources, all other equality is illusory" (p. 378). Basing her claim on her study of 2,500 court dockets over ten years and interviews with 228 families, plus family law attorneys and judges in California, she adds that the new laws give fathers a choice that mothers do not get: "The current laws, in effect, provide that divorced fathers *may* participate more in the lives of their children if they *choose* to do so, but they need not so choose," but that mothers who may *not* choose whether they wish to work must at the same time accept responsibility for parenting. She calls for the courts to become sensitive to this unequal burden and asks that they should demonstrate a "willingness to require fathers to shoulder their responsibility for their children" (pp. 377-378).

Sex role modeling is a preoccupation of some researchers who worry that single mother-headed families do not allow male children, especially, to interact with "good" male role models as frequently as their two-parent counterparts. Yet, some critics of role modeling see inherent dangers in too much gender typing. Farrell

(1972) outlines the problem thus: "Men are not born with masculine values, they are taught them" (p. 16), and "[t]he stereotype of masculinity is imposed upon a boy from the day he is born" (p. 31). At a very early age, boys and girls who observe male role models see aggressive wealth seeking, control of emotions, reverence for strength and leadership, rugged independence, and sexual domination. Women's socialization, by contrast, reinforces domestic skills, nurturing, dependency, modesty, coyness, deviousness, warmth, and emotionality. The media continue to depict men who do women's work in mocking ways, and even those television families whose wives work show both husbands and wives performing traditional gender-associated chores in the home, even if they do them badly, (e.g., Tim and Jill Taylor on *Home Improvement*). Hattley (1959) claims that boys who learn stereotypical behavior tend to maintain it in adulthood and that children's concepts of male and female roles largely conform to societal definitions of those roles.

Studies indicate that fathers are much more upset than mothers when their children deviate from proper sex role behavior, and they are particularly concerned that sons learn to act "like men" (Farrell, 1972; Levine, 1992). Chodorow and Contratto (1976) claim that the boy's sex role identification with his father is "positional," in that the boy emulates the masculine role he "assumes his father plays— rather than a close-up personal identification with the ways and values of the man himself" (p. 92).

Unlike mother blaming, the term *father blaming* is almost nonexistent in the literature. Father absence might actually be considered a convenient excuse, since it implies that the father cannot be blamed for children's delinquencies because he is not even there. In contrast to this assumption, Chinn's 1938 study of 1,000 delinquents indicated that problems with the father were twice as important in "producing" delinquency as problems with the mother (pp. 78-85), but such studies are atypical. Homosexuality and sexual adjustment problems attributed to counterbalancing a mother's domination in a father-absent family reveal the tendency to associate the boy child's deviance with an overbearing mother, rather than blaming the father. A study by Bieber and colleagues in 1962 is often cited to "prove" the mother's culpability in "producing" homosexual sons. In this study, the statistical association between

the presence of a "superheterosexual father" who pays little attention to his son and an overattentive mother and boys who are homosexual was significant at .001 (as cited in Farrell, 1972, p. 111).

However, both Herzog and Sudia's (1973) and Shinn's (1978)
reviews of multiple studies on the effects of depressed child functioning due to father absence found numerous methodological problems. Herzog and Sudia (1973) concluded that "the evidence so far
available offers no firm basis for assuming that boys who grow up
in fatherless homes are more likely, as men, to suffer from inadequate masculine identity as a result of lacking a resident male model" (p. 184). Even researchers who overemphasize the importance
of sex imprinting through role modeling admit that the effects of
father absence do not seem to be associated with long-term developmental problems (Krantz, 1988). Kagan and Moss's (1962) study
of academic achievement and gender roles indicated that neither
high-achieving boys nor girls adopted traditional sex roles.

In fact, father absence is almost expected. Even in intact families,
the gradual disappearance of the father in child rearing has led to a
sense that even when present in the family, he is often engaged in
another world, focused on his job outside the family, and only an
occasional "visitor" at home (see Chapter 3, "Judith"). Levine (1992)
claims that father absence is not considered a social aberration, but
a "foregone conclusion," in "normal" American homes: "Even if
the Father's body entered the front door at 5:30 sharp every evening, he was, in a vast majority of cases, an emotional phantom"
(p. 190). In their study of father-daughter incest, Herman and
Hirschman (1981) claimed that "[i]f paternal neglect is a problem,
then most children suffer from it" (as cited in Levine, 1992, p. 214).
Girls are harmed by missing out on the meanings of masculinity and
femininity gained through observation, and boys socialized with
this model often "become" the fathers they idealize. Girls, however,
also idealize the father. According to Dinnerstein (1976), fathers
become "glamorous" to little girls because they provide a type of
"vicarious access" to the powerful world of men that their mothers—especially stay-at-home mothers—do not (p. 52).

Just how do fathers begin to break free from the powerful intergenerational socialization that has defined their roles for at least two
centuries? Historian Demos (1986) offers hope: "[R]eceived mod-

els of fatherhood are not writ in the stars or in our genes. . . . Fatherhood, history reminds us, is a cultural invention" and is therefore mutable (1986, p. 64). Psychologists Farrell (1972) and Dinnerstein (1976) have taken on the challenge of reacquainting fathers with themselves. Farrell (1972) writes that men must become involved in breaking out of the "straitjacket of sex roles," especially for the sake of the next generation (p. 11).

Legendary feminist Betty Friedan (1981) believes that men's choices are the key to change: "The solutions [to problems of gender inequality] will come about only because more and more men demand them, too—not to help the women, but because of their own new problems and needs and choices as fathers and for themselves as men" (p. 121). Farrell (1972) agrees that fathers will not demand equal responsibility for child care until men consider child rearing to be a role that gives them a chance to liberate themselves from the alienating self-definitions they obtain from their work (p. 11). Dinnerstein (1976) sees the task as reconnecting the male with his child as soon as possible after his or her birth: "[Men] need to find ways of making their actual contact with the very young as intimate as women's." This is not to say that the qualitative differences between parents should be wholly changed since paternal passions for babies have their own merits (p. 81).

Kaschak (1992) is more skeptical. Assuming we can equalize parenting experiences in fathers and mothers is assuming that fathers and mothers are already equally valued in society and that women are equal to men as parents, except perhaps in contact time. She cautions against assuming that the "reintroduction" of the father into primary parenting "will create symmetry when there is asymmetry in virtually every aspect of male and female relationship" because such logic ignores the sociocultural context in which parenting takes place. The fact remains that male parents relate to their children differently, and the way males are evaluated and esteemed continually places them in a superior position to female parents (p. 128). For example, when male and female parents read studies reporting that children are damaged because mothers work, "mothers reading popularized versions of these studies develop a guilt complex if they work, while fathers can get away with giving lip service to a desire to spend more time with their children" (Farrell, 1972, p. 32).

Kaschak (1992) cautions family therapists who focus on strengthening the father's role or, in some cases, reintroducing the father into the family that "if men matter more than women do, making them matter even more and women even less in one more arena will not only not solve the problem; it will exacerbate it" (p. 130).

Parenting Partnerships

Levine (1992) is optimistic about changes in parenting and changes in gender roles in the next generation:

Theoretically, an adult of either sex can be the first caregiver, and either can provide a haven from this omnipotent figure. . . . Cross-cultural studies and modern life show that biology can be relegated to playing a minimal role in parenting. And increasingly, the hegemony of the two-parent, split-role family is being challenged by sexually egalitarian parenting. . . . What may be most interesting to observe as these kids grow up is how, and if, they divide the parental roles if their parents don't, how they shed infantile dependency if it is not decisively embodied in one primary caregiver, and independence is not represented by a more distant other parent. (p. 194)

DIVORCE:
A BATTLEGROUND FOR GENDER WARS

"No aspect of marriage and family life has invited so much scrutiny or provoked so much controversy as has divorce" (Bequaert, 1976, p. 21). In fact, according to recent statistics, two-thirds of all first marriages dissolve (Rice, 1994, p. 560). Critics sound alarms about "the disease of divorce" as "the central cause of our most vexing social problems" (Whitehead, 1993 as cited in Rice, 1994, p. 560), but feminist literature heralds it as "a creative rather than destructive act[, an] orderly instrument of change" (Bequaert, 1976, p. 25) describing it as "resistance to the oppression of women in families and a marker of societal and historical transformation" (Rice, 1994, p. 560). The voluminous literature on divorce merits nearly its own section in libraries and bookstores.

In considering the history of marital law in the United States, Weitzman (1985) states, "A divorce provides an important opportunity for a society to enforce marital boundaries by rewarding the marital behavior it approves, and punishing that which violates its norms" (p. xv). Divorce laws did not exist in England until 1857 because the state assumed that marriage was a holy matter, an indissoluble union sanctified by the church. To restrict divorce was to protect marriage, and soon the state joined the church in "forcing" married couples to "take it seriously," an attitude currently making a comeback in the United States (e.g., Governor Terry Branstad's campaign to tighten divorce laws in Iowa). A curious mixture of "hands on and hands off" laws governing marriage involves the state in mediating marital disputes both in and outside of marriage. For example, although the state may force a divorced couple to pay for a child's college education, it cannot force a married couple to do so. Even custody decisions that favor women but allow men to "walk away" from economic liability for their children, through poorly enforced support laws, uphold traditional gender role expectations (Coontz, 1992, p. 142).

Weitzman (1985) further explains that rules on the division of property contain messages about the relative worth of each member's contribution to the marriage. Though traditional marital law based court decisions on the assumption that the man had a duty to support his wife and enforced the wife's responsibilities to home and children, it was assumed that both spouses were engaged in a joint enterprise and should share equally in the fruits of their endeavors. However, the introduction of an adversarial stance, whereby one member of the couple—the one assuming the "innocent" position—must accuse the "guilty" other of some "unholy" act that would justify the dissolution of the marriage (grounds for divorce), created lawyer-fought court battles in which bargaining and legal punishments became dramatic charades.

As summarized in the book's introduction, there is certainly no lack of information offered by studies condemning the negative effects of divorce on children, especially with regard to behavioral disorders and depressed school achievement. Critics of this literature, however, point out methodological flaws such as limited sample sizes, lack of comparisons with intact families, and contradictory evidence (for a thorough critique of this literature, see Rice, 1994). The effects of divorce on women are also documented, but experts are divided between those who believe it victimizes them and "feminizes poverty" and others, particularly those who analyze case studies, who show its many benefits for women's development and self-esteem. The lopsided focus on mothers in the treatment of parenting is true also of the treatment of divorce; the effects of divorce on men are not as well documented as those on women. Statistically, women are more likely than men to sue for divorce, a fact that may not be surprising, given that women do not benefit from marriage as much as their male partners (Llewelyn and Osborne, 1990). Some analysts of divorce offer the observation that because marriage benefits men, divorce is only a temporary stop on their way to remarriage: five of six divorced males remarry (Baca Zinn and Eitzen, 1990). Men report fewer psychological gains than divorced women (Rice, 1994, p. 564), but studies of divorce settlements provide evidence that the standards of living for divorced men either stay the same or are enhanced, thereby implying that divorce, similar to marriage, has more positive consequences for men than it does for women (Weitzman, 1985).

It is literally impossible to make statements about the effects of divorce on men, women, and children without adopting some philosophical stance that invariably attaches a positive or negative value to the phenomenon. Therefore, this review will present both sides. I will reserve my own observations about the effects of divorce on the women in this study for Chapter 7.

"Divorce Is As Bad As It Looks"

Family studies base claims about the negative effects of divorce on the assumption, held by Carter and McGoldrick and other family life cycle theorists, that, similar to the effects of death, divorce, single parenting, and remarriage are "special issues that interrupt the developmental course of the family life cycle" (Carter and McGoldrick, 1980, p. 15). They assume that a deviance from the path of "normal" development in families requires major effort and energy to "restabilize" the families so that they may then move along the regular life course.

The research studies of Wallerstein and Kelly (1974, 1976, 1980) and Wallerstein and Blakeslee (1989) are often cited as the basis for claims that children suffer long-term adjustment problems from their parents' divorce. Even preschool children will experience developmental delays. The "Wallerstein reports" catalog "severe disruptions in their development" for two-thirds of all of the children they studied over the course of five years (Krantz, 1988, p. 257). Hetherington, Cox, and Cox's 1977 longitudinal study on divorced families with young children is also widely cited to support the contention that mothers who must return to full-time work after divorce cause disruptions in children, who feel "doubly deserted." Father absence studies, such as those reviewed by Shinn (1978), are often quoted to claim that depressed cognitive performance on IQ (intelligence quotient) tests and poor school achievement are the result for children in families without fathers present in the home. Nelson and Maccoby (1966) attribute depressed school achievement to stress, lowered quantity and/or quality of interaction with parents, especially single mothers, and a decrease in parental control.

Even in their text that claims to be written from a "structuralist, feminist, humanist viewpoint," Baca Zinn and Eitzen (1990) argue that "both partners in a divorce are victims," but that "the negatives of divorce clearly outweigh the positives for most women" (pp. 366-367). Divorced women are quoted as feeling helpless, experiencing a loss of identity as the result of the break with their husbands, overwhelmed by the demands of full parenting and economic survival, and increasingly socially isolated, cut off from the outside world because of time constraints and locked into the world of their children (p. 368). Their financial situation is even more grim. Jencks' (1982) and Duncan's (1984) reports on the "feminization of poverty" accelerated an increasingly popular conceptualization of women's dire straits from severely reduced financial circumstances, an automatic handicap as they begin their lives as single parents (as cited in Baca Zinn and Eitzen, 1990). Weitzman (1985) adopts a legal metaphor, calling this effect "sentencing [the women and children] to periods of financial hardship." Her evidence that women experience a 73 percent decline in standard of living in the first year after divorce is widely cited (p. xiv).

The introduction of "no-fault" divorce laws in California in 1970 led to the adoption within the ten years following of some form of no-fault legislation by all but two states. These laws, notes Weitzman (1985), had the undesirable effect of reinforcing the very gender inequities they sought to tear down, or, more accurately, to ignore. Though these reforms were thought to reduce the "blood sucking" of rich men's wives, and to preserve the family by reducing the harmful effects of long acrimonious legal battles, both conservative and liberal supporters failed to acknowledge the inevitable consequence, that the "equitable" division of marital resources would likely harm the economically weaker party, which was almost always the wife. As Levine (1992) states, "Able they may be as people, but enabled by social and economic conditions, they are not" (p. 110).

Weitzman's (1985) argument is compelling. She points out that women who may have given up developing career opportunities to focus on making a marriage successful are unprotected by the new laws, which make a unilateral decision to divorce by one spouse the only necessary condition. "Today the marriage contract can be broken, and the spouse who has abided by its terms is not entitled to any damages or compensation at divorce" (p. 25). The subsequent division of the marital property and reduced alimony awards were evidence of the court-enforced expectation that the divorced woman must become self-supporting in short order; they failed, however, to account for her economic handicap as she emerges from a marriage, having given up critical career development years to parenting or having sacrificed education or social standing in favor of her husband's career aspirations (p. 25).

In addition, even under the new laws, 90 percent of the divorcing couples in the United States during Weitzman's (1985) study agreed to let child custody reside with the mother. Thus, children, too, become the unwitting "victims" of the reduced circumstances of their mothers. Custody awards do little to offset this effect. In Weitzman's study, the typical support award was less than one-half of the estimated cost of raising a child, and noncompliance orders ranged from 60 to 80 percent of all court awards (p. 321). Levine (1992) adds that of the twelve million children whose parents divorce each year, fully 30 percent receive no child support from their fathers and only half of the men are ordered to comply fully (p. 110). With even feminist writers asserting the victimization of women by divorce, it is not surprising that public and political figures have capitalized on the notion. In a message dramatizing the helplessness of women and the cruelty of men, Representative Dan Coates of Indiana painted the popular picture when he delivered a speech about divorce and single mothers before the 1983 Congress:

We see a picture of single mothers struggling to enter and make their way in a marketplace in which many lack the necessary training and experience to successfully compete. The burden of those mothers in providing economic and emotional security for the family is nearly an overwhelming task, but even more complicated when they don't receive adequate child support from the fathers. (cited in Weitzman, 1985, p. 322)

Even self-help books for "women alone" inadvertently emphasize problems and failures, offering advice on coping with loneliness and suffering, suggesting that women should rebuild "shattered lives" by returning to a rich social life as soon as possible, with the objective of finding a new mate (Bequaert, 1976). Jackie Burgoyne's (1987) study of single mothers concluded that indeed, a great deal of time and energy is spent by single parents on returning to a "decent" standard of living and in "normalizing family life." Hetherington, Cox, and Cox (1977) noted that single mothers suffer from "task overload," described as lack of satisfaction in parenting because of the burdens of survival. They discounted women's reports that they felt "freedom" and "exhilaration" immediately after divorce, claiming that, in the long run, women saw themselves as less attractive, more apprehensive and helpless, and more apathetic and depressed about the future. Carter and McGoldrick (1980) indicated that "social isolation, increased anxiety, depression, and loneliness may serve to foster decreased functioning in a single parent" (p. 256).

Llewelyn and Osborne (1990) present the single mother's life as a Herculean task:

> a struggle to be in at least two places at once; to hold down a job and yet to fetch the children from school; to develop some kind of independent social life and yet to be constantly available to the children; to do the housework and yet to play with the children as much as the children from two-parent families are played with. (p. 209)

"Divorce Is Not As Bad As It Looks"

Bequaert (1976) reflects:

> We know more about the problems of divorce than we do about its benefits; more about the process of separation than about building post divorce lives; and we know little about the women who head more than 85 percent of all post divorce families except that almost half of them are poor and most of them remarry. (p. 21)

Not underestimating the pain of divorce, Llewelyn and Osborne (1990) remind readers that equal, if poorly documented, misery exists in couples *prevented* from divorcing for moral, social, or religious reasons (p. 210). In fact, though money is important, it is not always an *agonizing* problem for single mothers, even when resources are stretched. Hetherington, Cox, and Cox (1977), who were mostly negative about the long-range effects of divorce on children, found no statistically significant correlations between level of income or feeling financially distressed and parent-child interaction patterns.

Citing Herzog and Sudia (1968), Santrock (1972), Nye (1957), and the McCords and Thurber (1962), divorce advocates remind readers that "bad or chaotic marriages are far more damaging to children than divorce itself" (Bequaert, 1976, p. 29). Some studies critical of divorce fail to recognize that children's adjustment to divorce follows the same process of adjustment as most other major changes in their lives. Rice and Rice (1986) cite several studies on postdivorce adjustment to generalize that "the better the adults adjust to divorce, the better their children do" (p. 5). Krantz (1988) adds, "Each child is unique, and so the short and long term functioning of children after a divorce varies widely" (p. 257). An overemphasis on the inevitability of damage leads divorced mothers to self-stigmatize, taking on an almost "mandatory feeling of guilt" (Bequaert, 1976, p. 30). Similar to the mothers in my case studies, one of Bequaert's single mothers declared, "I took all the blame that I'd done this awful thing to my kids" (p. 31).

Researchers who assume divorce inevitably damages children rarely concede that the rift in relationship is primarily directed at the adults, and that neither parent is actually "divorcing" the kids. In fact, Hetherington, Cox, and Cox (1977) found that after two years, fully one-fourth of the fathers in their study and one-half of the mothers reported *better* relationships with their children. Kissman and Allen (1993) warn that family therapists should not interpret an expressed need for parental support in single-parent families as "reflective of women's inadequacy to head families," nor should the reintroduction of the father as a sort of rescuer be encouraged (p. 7). They suggest a holistic approach to family support that recognizes the multiplicity of factors that determines the functionality of families and deemphasizes the importance of the single-family structure.

To reiterate, studies on the depressed functioning of children of divorce often suffer from overgeneralization. Cherlin (1991) and Cherlin and Furstenberg (1989) emphasize that variations in functioning between children from divorced and intact families are often no larger than 3 percent, and that the adverse effects observed in children postdivorce were often present prior to the divorce, a fact rarely mentioned in negative studies. Even the census data that provide the foundation for most of the correlational studies on families and divorce are based on self-reported data from single interviews, leading to questionable accuracy, especially when mothers report the frequency of father contacts.

Rice (1994) details the many problems in divorce literature. For example, Weitzman's (1985) dire conclusions about no-fault divorce were based on a local sample taken almost entirely from Los Angeles, California. Harris and Plog's (1991) conclusions that single mothers suffer emotional problems and parenting deficits are based on only two studies (cited in Rice, 1994, p. 566). Meta-analyses such as Amato and Keith's (1991), Shinn's (1978), and Herzog and Sudia's (1968) find reduced effect sizes and serious methodological deficiencies in the scores of studies claiming negative findings. Indeed, Rice (1994) argues convincingly that any study basing its investigations on family life cycle theory suffers from automatic bias toward a nuclear family, using a deficit comparison model to assess the "impaired functioning" of other family forms (pp. 571-573).

Some studies suffer from sampling prejudices. For example, Krantz (1988) admits that many of the studies using "antisocial behavior" to assess divorce disruption were done on adolescents, and that lowered socioeconomic status and class differences affect children's postdivorce experiences. Others fail to account for the significant effects of parental educational level on school achievement. In fact, many of the studies performed using 1970s census data were based on single-parent homes in which nearly half the parents had never completed high school (Carter and McGoldrick, 1980).

Perhaps the single most compelling refutation of the inevitable ill effects of divorce on children comes from the children themselves. Using questionnaires and interviews, Reinhard (1977), Rosen (1977), and Kurdek and Siesky (1980) found that the children in their studies between ages five and twenty-eight felt that their development was enhanced rather than impaired. They reported increased responsibility, maturity, and interpersonal sensitivity. Kurdek and Siesky (1980) stressed, "Clearly, children's own perceptions tend to modify the crisis-flavored tone of literature regarding the effect of divorce on children" (p. 341).

Bequaert (1976) believes that mistrusting single women is at the heart of studies on divorce that pathologize some single-mother-headed families while ignoring the viability of many others (p. xiii). Rice (1994) maintains that divorce as a female expression of resistance presents a challenge to the traditional patriarchal power structure at the heart of American society (p. 574). Blaming increasing divorce rates on feminism and the liberation of women is naive, according to Coontz (1992), who details how changes in behavior preceded changes in attitude toward divorce. Women's entrance into the workforce, increasing divorce rates, and feminism were concurrent phenomena, not cause-and-effect dualities (pp. 167-168).

In fact, the self-concept of women beyond divorce "belies the social image of the unhappy or bitter divorcee" (Llewelyn and Osborne, 1990, pp. 208-209). Studies on post divorce women show that they are mentally healthier, report greater self-satisfaction and a more positive outlook, are satisfied with their lives, and suffer less depression (Coontz, 1992; Gigy, 1980; Hafner, 1986; Hoeffer, 1987; Loewenstein, 1981). After the initial jolt of loss, most women on their own "develop a range of competencies rarely fostered in married women" (Llewelyn and Osborne, 1990, p. 209). This stands in stark contrast to the popular conception of divorced women as simply "waiting to remarry" (Kissman and Allen, 1993, p. 14).

In Stacey's (1990) case studies of "brave new families," "we observe people turning divorce into a kinship resource rather than a rupture" (p. 16). In their text *Living Through Divorce*, Rice and Rice (1986) suggest that "divorce can be an opportunity for personal and interpersonal growth and development through the enhancement of independence and autonomy" (p. 5). Gray (1978) reported significant gains in measures of mental health and self-esteem (as cited in Rice and Rice, 1986, p. 19). This is nothing new. In other cultures, such as the Crow Indians, divorce is seen as a positive event that enhances self-esteem (Rice and Rice, 1986, p. 4).

When reading studies on individuals who have had a poor adjustment to divorce, it is important to be aware that some may have had psychopathologies present previously. Rice and Rice (1986) explain:

> Adverse effects associated with divorce may actually result from marital and family discord that preceded the divorce. Divorce may act to relieve rather than to precipitate stress. . . . It may be the psychologically healthier individuals in unsatisfactory marriages with high discord who are able to make the break from their spouses. (p. 20)

When comparing self-reported levels of satisfaction in and outside of marriage, data may be affected by cultural expectations that marriage is supposed to be happy. According to Albrecht (1979) and Weingarten (1980), within six months to one year post divorce, the majority of divorced people are "indistinguishable from their married counterparts on a variety of indices of adjustment and reported well-being" (as cited in Rice and Rice, 1986, p. 19). The common misconception that the liberalization of divorce laws poses a threat to the institution of marriage fails to account for the fact that ways to divorce have always existed. However, those ways often involved only the upper classes who could afford them (Rice and Rice, 1986). What increasing divorce rates may reflect is a change in the nature of our expectations for marriage. Now united by love and desire for companionate satisfaction, rather than economic or religious reasons, couples may find such bonds to be "more fragile and harder to maintain" (Weitzman, 1985, p. 375). Regardless of the number of marriages that end in divorce, the heartiest endorsement for the resilience of the institution of marriage is that four of every five women and five of every six men who divorce eventually remarry (Baca Zinn and Eitzen, 1990; Rice, 1994).

SINGLE WOMEN: APART AND TOGETHER

The title of this final section of the literature review is borrowed from Lucia Bequaert's (1976) book detailing her case studies of single women (1976). It represents the third face of the single mother—her womanhood. Though much of the literature on women has already been discussed in the previous sections on families, parenting, and divorce, the information provided by the participants in this study cannot be fully appreciated without an understanding of their identities as women. Thus, the journeys of women through identity formation and social stigmatization are discussed in this section.

The Making of Women

Simone de Beauvoir (1949) stated, "Women are created, not born" (as cited in Rice, 1994, p. 368). The women in this study have not yet completed that task. As with other women socialized by the history, economics, and culture of their time, they continue to evaluate and reevaluate their identities as events and people shape their experiences. Schur (1984) asserts that "[a] woman's development cannot be assessed apart from the contexts in which she has lived" (p. 242). As mothers, they strive to maintain an independent identity, while sometimes intensely aware of the needs of their children. As daughters of their mothers, they grapple with memories—good and bad—of their own childhoods. Conflicting feelings of manipulation or overprotection and nurturing and comfort confuse and may overwhelm, but they may likewise provide blueprints for translating their own hopes and ideals into action (Llewelyn and Osborne, 1990).

Motherhood, too, as described previously, is based on erroneous assumptions that "all women need to be mothers, all mothers need their children, all children need their mothers" (Oakley, 1976, p. 186). In addition to a rebellion against an automatic imposition of motherhood, radical feminist Shulamith Firestone (1971) has even suggested that recent technological developments in reproduction may allow females to become reproductively autonomous, an alarming prediction for the future role of males in families and parenting.

Women in Relationship

Feminist interpretation of family research raises the question, "What do women do for the family, and what does the family do for women or to women?" (Baca Zinn and Eitzen, 1990, p. 130). Women bring their individuality to the mothering experience as they do to their other roles. They are neither *all* good mothers or *all* bad mothers. Instead, a range of mothering concepts is enacted by women with different personalities and needs, from those who look forward to having a baby and adapting their lives to the child such as Sarah in this study, to those who anxiously anticipate a return to work that provides more of their self-definition, such as Lyn in this study (Raphael-Leff, 1985).

Marriage is a prescribed role for women: "It is a sacred script, one we have trouble rejecting because it is so central a part of our socialization and adult expectations" (Laws and Schwartz, 1977, p. 139). Marriageability is a test of attractiveness. Unmarried women are highly stigmatized, and women themselves have grave doubts that singleness is actually their "choice" (Schur, 1984, p. 61). In her famous treatise on the "demise" of feminism, Susan Faludi (1991) claims that women who divorce or choose to remain single too long are told that they will be penalized for their rebellion by infertility, economic suffering, and the unlikelihood that they will be able to marry at all.

Fear of being alone often results from an overemphasis on the total separation of single women from relationship. Such a false sense of aloneness disregards what Bequaert (1976) says is "not ipso facto women without men; there can be and often are fathers, brothers, sons, and lovers in their lives. And it is even less likely that they are alone; there are mothers, daughters, sisters and friends" (p. x). It is absurd to think that women outside of marriage are the only ones susceptible to aloneness. Women within marriages are often alone and function as the heads of their households when the men they live with do not provide substantive companionship. Yet, few women feel comfortable eating in a restaurant alone or going to the movies alone, when this is quite common with men (Llewelyn and Osborne, 1990, p. 199).

The indirect result of women's fear of being "out of relationship" can also keep them trapped in unhealthy relationships. Unable or unwilling to step out of unfulfilling marriages, women sometimes generalize their frustration with a particular male to a hatred of all men. In investigating man hating in America, Judith Levine (1992) discovered that women's economic dependence on men and their distrust of men's violent nature may exact a greater price for speaking up. Women worry that unleashing their own anger and resistance will bring their worlds crashing down around them (pp. 4-16). Man hating, then, is less a function of feminist encouragement than it is a reason for feminism. Levine maintains that neither men nor women perpetuate envy, hatred, and fear of the other sex, but that "gender itself breeds . . . misogyny and misandry, both" (p. 385).

Women Alone

In American society, single women are distrusted, and divorced women are considered threatening and predatory:

Although it is a state which will happen or has happened to virtually everybody, being single is still seen as somewhat abnormal by most people. Women on their own are, on the whole, perceived by others as odd, frustrated, dangerous, unfortunate, to be pitied or to be avoided. (Llewelyn and Osborne, 1990, p. 196)

These negative images are internalized by women who are single and may affect the way they are treated in social, legal, and economic spheres. Women's actual experiences of being single, however, are as different as they are. Still the dangers of aloneness are emphasized in the socialization of little girls, for whom dependencies are endorsed, so that early fears of being alone are perpetuated. Such fears can lead to feelings of panic and impending danger (as with Judith in this study). Kaschak (1992) states that the sense of danger is "ubiquitous" and that even though most women have not experienced male violence directed at them, fear of men manifests itself in their bodies, movements, use of space, and dreams (p. 125).

Gilligan's (1982) conclusions about women's moral emphasis on defining self through relationship may reflect their socialized expectation to be in partnership and concomitant fear of lacking a partner to meet emotional needs, to provide practical help and companionship. Women in general are more likely to try to "fix" relationships in trouble, initiating marital counseling or seeking personal therapy to "work on the relationship," and they are more eager to explore and change their roles than their male partners. Thus, assuming that the failure of a relationship is hers, a woman's self-esteem suffers whenever she attempts to reintegrate (Kaschak, 1992, p. 126). Because of the negative fallout from a relatedness-centered moral paradigm, Kaschak (1992) is critical of relatedness as a positive characteristic of women's moral outlook:

One strategy for remaining unconscious of the destructive and shaming context, that [is] most frequently taught to females, is to remain permeable and to immerse oneself in relatedness. For safety and even survival, women learn to maintain permeable boundaries and to be defined primarily through relatedness to men or through their absence of relatedness to a man or men. The psychological boundaries that women develop subsume their relationships with men and children and are not individual boundaries, but relationship boundaries. For this reason, women often do not feel complete if they are not in a relationship. (p. 125)

Even family therapists who practice within a primarily feminist framework emphasize the importance of supporting single mothers as they develop relationships with men and try to "fit" them into their families (Kissman and Allen, 1993).

Left without a partner, however, a woman can become self-resourceful for confirmatory and validating activities, turning to friends, work, and leisure activities to meet her desire for self-affirmation. "Either by necessity or choice, therefore, the single woman has to develop a stronger sense of self than her married sister" (Llewelyn and Osborne, 1990, p. 201). For some, this is not difficult, since they have clear, strong self-images and find their needs fulfilled in emotionally rich relationships with children and friends. For others, taught to sacrifice themselves for the sake of the "other" and to define themselves as only half of a relationship, this is a difficult task. Social stigma about being single can make a woman feel of lesser importance without a man, for her connection to a man has been clearly marked, from her wedding ring to her title (Mrs.) and the changing of her name (Llewelyn and Osborne, 1990).

In opposition to stereotypes, researchers find single women to be independent, less stressed by the complications of sexual and marital relationships, free to develop in ways not open to women in long-term relationships, less constrained by gender role expectations, and enjoying a richer emotional and personal life based on a secure personal foundation (Bem, 1974; Spence, 1979; Williams, 1984).

I Am My Body/I Am Not My Body

A woman is also encouraged to seek identity in her body. The reproductive functions of her lifetime often assume disproportionate importance. "Every aspect of a female body is considered to say something about a woman's value as a person and as a woman" (Kaschak, 1992, p. 96). She measures herself against the images of female perfection constantly bombarding her from television, magazines, and the cosmetic industry, always coming up short. "As women's bodies are found wanting, so do women find their own bodies wanting" (p. 205).

Eating becomes tied to appearance, self-control, self-indulgence, nurturance, guilt, and shame. It becomes obsessive and can result in disorders such as chronic overeating, bulimia, and anorexia. "Fat women are blatantly devalued," and overeaters may be expressing their rebellion at an imposed body image while at the same time devaluing themselves and lowering their self-esteem (Schur, 1984, p. 72). In a strange, conflicting process of defining her identity, a woman learns to disassociate herself from various body parts, sending herself mixed messages: "I am my figure. I am not my figure." Food assumes a symbolic significance, and hunger remains unsatisfied because the woman remains undeveloped:

> [Women] can be fed until they are physically full but symbolically starved or the reverse. To be full as a person is to be empty, a failure as a woman. If one is starved for basic respect and affirmation for the esteem of others for who one is, but instead is esteemed for who one is not, one remains forever starved. The "not-me" survived and is fed as the "me" remains undeveloped and invisible. (Kaschak, 1992, p. 205)

In a "health- and fitness"-crazed country where abdominal machines, dieting services, and plastic surgery are multimillion dollar industries, it is no surprise that a woman may believe that "the less she can eat, the more of a woman she is . . . self-esteem for women is based on self-denial" (Kaschak, 1992, p. 206; Schur, 1984).

Black Women

Black women, especially, are accused of antimale activities because their matriarchal strength is viewed with suspicion. However, according to the writings of Toni Morrison, Alice Walker, Terry McMillan, or Suzan-Lori Parks, black mothers who carry on with or without men portray less gender enmity than they do "a celebration of women's relationships" with one another. Hortense Spiller notes that "male absence or mutability in intimate relationships is not the leading proposition of a woman's life, but a single aspect of life issues" (as cited in Levine, 1992, p. 108). Mary Helen Washington states that the writings of black women exhibit a process of self-discovery: "They are laying claim to the freedom and triumph that were forbidden little black girls in this century, and in the process, springing from their own heads, full-grown" (as cited in Levine, 1992, pp. 108-109).

The Self

Selfishness is a theme that takes a mostly pejorative tone but exposes the conflicts inherent in a social assumption that women *do*, and therefore *should*, identify themselves through relationship. Barbara Ehrenreich (1983) levels criticism at "the pro-family women's movement," headed by Phyllis Schafly, which directs anger not at men but at women (Levine, 1992, p. 112). Their distrust of an independent woman lies in a fear that "her selfishness will undermine other women's fragile privileges" (p. 147). What is considered "self-actualization" in Maslow's (1970) famous hierarchy of needs is based on values that are more often accepted in males than in females.

Females are somehow caught in between, condemned for movement in either direction. If they are too autonomous, they are considered negatively as self-centered or self-absorbed, and "if they put their needs before their children's they are judged harshly while men are expected to do so." But even though they are encouraged to be dependent and relational, they are "judged immature or even pathological" if they do not exhibit at least some autonomy (Kaschak, 1992, p. 157). Carter and McGoldrick (1980) voice this accusation: "Anxiety, depression, and phobias are characteristic symptoms of women who have not sufficiently individuated from the people whose needs they serve" (p. 265).

In *Labeling Women Deviant: Gender, Stigma, and Social Control*, Edwin Schur (1984) describes the many ways that labels are attached to women's experiences, "to devalue the very condition of womanhood itself . . . controlling women through an imputation of spoiled identity" (p. 235). Men appear to benefit psychologically, economically, and socially from imposing stigma on the experiences of women. By focusing on women, men are excused from punishment for their offenses against women and women can be punished for their "deviance." Women are caught in "deviant-either-way" expectations. If they violate what is considered normal feminine behavior, they are viewed unfavorably as masculine, even though those very traits possessed by a male are valued. In disputing Kohlberg, who based his work on moral development entirely on studies of young college men, Carol Gilligan (1982) claimed that a male paradigm in psychology sets up models of male psychological development as the norm and pathologizes the female when she deviates from them (p. 14).

More pertinent to women's identity formation, however, is the equally "insidious effect that categorical devaluation can have on women's self-conceptions," which includes the incorporation of that stigma into a woman's self-image and "induced passivity" for women who come to accept the beliefs and values others place upon them (Schur, 1984, p. 241). This is particularly damaging for women in abusive situations whose "oppressors have invaded their psyches and now exist within themselves. They are caught in a web of self-defeating behavior" (Daly, 1974, p. 48). Gender role conformity is seductive even for those women who are "proud and adventurous." Guided by some sense of the justice, protection, or comfort in traditional gender role divisions, they maintain a "balance of power" by "losing their identities to the traditional setup" (Dinnerstein, 1976, p. 158).

The Cinderella Complex

The Cinderella complex is the pop psychology term for a woman's total conviction that her most dearly prized life goal is to find the perfect prince and settle into a life of complete dependence on him, losing her identity, living in his castle, maintaining her youthful beauty and devotion, and remaining childlike and passive, so she can live "happily ever after" (Schur, 1984). A well-known fairy tale among little girls from many cultures, the Cinderella image is only part of a woman's general education in romance (Davies, 1993). The broader concept of romantic love owes its origin to twelfth-century France. Once the courtly indulgence of French aristocrats, but never a reason for marriage, the romantic courtier came to symbolize the "ideal of sexual relations in the West" (Holland and Eisenhart, 1990, p. 93).

Studying black and white women in two southern U.S. universities, Holland and Eisenhart (1990) described their participants' firm conviction that even education will not bring automatic success in a hostile market. In a *created* culture of romance and attractiveness, girls use romantic love to shield themselves from the inequalities facing them in the world after college, an immersion that only serves to perpetuate gender inequalities and to "embed them more deeply in the culture of domination and submission, of double work, both waged and nonwaged" (p. 51).

Task Overload versus Multiple Roles

The multiple role juggling of the single mother is sometimes negatively viewed as "task overload" (Hetherington, Cox, and Cox, 1977), but this concept, too, can be conceived differently. In supporting their contention that women can thrive on multiple roles, Baca Zinn and Eitzen (1990) quote an article by David Hellerstein (1987) in *Ms.* magazine titled "Multiple Roles: The Next Stage," in which he extols the "multiple satisfactions" that accompany the "multiple frustrations" of mixed role performance. He calls it both liberating and tyrannical and attributes the lessons learned in "successful multiplicity" to women "who have always known how to do several things at once" (p. 203).

CONCLUSION

In 1979, reflecting on the successes and failures of two decades of the women's liberation movement, Betty Friedan wrote what is still true in the new millennium:

> The great challenge we face in the 1980's is to frame a new agenda that makes it possible for women to be able to work and love—in equality with men—and to choose if they desire to have children. For the choices we have sought in the 70's are not as simple as they once seemed. Indeed some of the

choices women are supposed to have won are not real choices at all. (p. 49)

Judith Stacey (1990) adds that freedom to choose may be a double-edged sword. As women are given the opportunity to make choices for their lives, one of those choices may be to submit to dominant husbands and to return to the safety of religious orthodoxy, effects she observed in her case studies of working-class women (p. 261).

It is hoped, however, that by allowing single mothers to tell in their own voices how they developed their identities, experienced their worlds, and made their choices, we will learn that "singleness is an experience that is by no means unique, or deviant, or accidental; that it can be planned, chosen, survived, endured, and enriched through personal self-directed change and collective action" (Bequaert, 1976, pp. xv-xvi).

SQUARES OF THE QUILT:
SINGLE MOTHERS THROUGH
THEIR OWN EYES

THE STORY QUILT

Slave and pioneer women of America who were not taught to read and write often kept the chronicles of their lives and their families by sewing their stories onto quilts. For these wondrous "books" of personal narrative, they used the bits and pieces, colors and textures that came from clothing outgrown by children, favorite dresses representing special events, blankets that once warmed their loved ones, and whatever remnants of time and memory encoded in fabric they had saved. Each square of a story quilt represented some important event or recollection in the quilter's history (Otto, 1991).

Chapters 2 through 6 may be read like the squares of a marvelous story quilt, made by many hands, but built around the unifying theme *Unbroken Homes*. As with any story quilt, the following chapters invite the reader's eye to consider each texture, pattern, and hue, but they are also meant to be read with fascination and curiosity. Just as the dizzying stitchery of a crazy quilt surprises the viewer when a unifying pattern emerges from a first impression of chaos, as we consider the squares of this quilt, drawn from the many images of each woman's life, common patterns emerge.

THE INTERVIEWS

The focus of this study was how the participants see themselves, their lives, and their children's lives, and the most appropriate choice for collecting such introspective data is interviewing. I. E. Seidman's (1991) in-depth phenomenological interviewing was chosen for its suitability to this investigation. This technique employs open-ended questions, "building on and exploring the participant's responses to those questions" (p. 9).

Participants were interviewed three times. During the first interview, a free-form recollection of life history, the women were asked to discuss themselves, their families, and the events leading up to, during, and following divorce or separation. In the second, they were asked to provide the details of their current life experience. The third interview gave them the opportunity to reflect on the meaning of their experiences.

The interviews lasted from sixty to ninety minutes. Because the participants were already acquainted with me, we had an easy rapport that allowed them to talk freely. Despite the cautions inherent in interviewing acquaintances, the nature of these women's free and continuous monologues was such that my own familiarity with them did not inhibit probing or confirming issues suggested in their narratives. My status as a single mother facilitated what Seidman (1991) refers to as "listening for the inner voice as opposed to the outer, more public voice" (p. 56). And though it was fairly easy with these women to "listen more, talk less," it was also natural for me to participate in conversation with them whenever I felt that a shared meaning or experience would extend or probe some comment or reflection.

The interviews were audiotaped and transcribed verbatim using a transcription machine and a word processor. I did all the transcriptions myself.

THE WOMEN

The five mothers selected for study are middle class, financially self-sufficient (though not wealthy), highly educated (college degree), professional women. Given the preponderance of research grouping single parenting with factors of social deviance, I chose to work instead with mainstream mothers whose priorities are not focused on fighting poverty to survive. By middle class, then, I refer to mothers with an income level for their family configuration that is substantially above the nationally established poverty line, which for a family of four was set at $17,028 in 1999 (census.gov/ hhes/poverty/threshld/99prelim.html). Their salaries ranged from $28,000 to around $80,000, with the exception of Sarah, who was a full-time student currently living off a modest trust fund inheritance. My intent was to focus the study on the family lives of single women and children who are not particularly well represented in the literature, in which the effects of poverty, lack of education and opportunity, and social class inequalities may predominate. Selection was also based on ease of access and convenience within the boundaries of the criteria established. Cases were located through my own professional contacts, and all of the women were previously known to me.

The group is neither typical nor particularly unusual. The women selected represent a broad range of ages, and the group includes mothers of one and two children. Of the five women, two are mothers of boys, and three are mothers of girls. Beyond ensuring that both genders were represented among the children, no particular effort was made to dictate the number of each gender. Time spent as a single mother varied with each woman, ranging from recently divorced to twenty years.

Mothers in the study present diverse circumstances: one remains unmarried, one has a long-term relationship with a male friend, one has a teenage daughter who is also a single mother, one shares her experience as a solely responsible parent *within* her marriage, and one has already "launched" her grown sons and looks forward to a new episode as a single woman alone. One of the cases is African American; the others are Caucasian, including one who spent a portion of her childhood in Asia. No attempt, then, was made to select or screen these cases on the basis of race.

Judith

Judith, in her early forties, is the mother of one son, Ian, age nine. She has been divorced for a year. Judith has a master's degree in education and is a teacher in a public school. She seemed very comfortable with the interview process and laughed often and easily throughout the course of the interviews. She provided a detailed and sometimes painful recollection of events and feelings, but she was also remarkably analytic in her commentary.

Kathleen

Kathleen, also in her early forties, has two teenage daughters, one, age seventeen, who has just completed high school and one, age fifteen, who is in her sophomore year. Kathleen has a master's degree in education and is currently employed as a supervisor at an urban college. She has been divorced for twelve years. She was candid and open, providing me with much detail about both events and her feelings.

Shawna

Shawna, an African-American woman in her late twenties, has a three-year-old daughter. She is the only single mother in the group who chose not to marry. Shawna has completed her master's degree in science and is employed as a computer programmer-analyst at a local college. My interviews with her were lively and full of rich dialogue. Her narrative presents stories within stories, and she framed her reminiscences as if they were conversational scripts. She gave me the impression of wisdom beyond her years.

Lyn

Lyn is in her early fifties. Both of her sons are grown and are currently in college. Although single for almost twenty years, she gave a remarkably detailed and revealing recollection of her divorce, as well as a complete narrative of her parenting experiences, from the births of her sons to their "successful launching" as adults. Lyn, a PhD and professor, has held a number of important positions at a local college. As a marvelous addition to her own story, she also recounted some information about her own mother and grandmother, both of whom became single parents through widowhood. In her narrative, then, we can see the effects of three generations of single mothers. Her background in education and therapy allowed her to discuss families with knowledge gained both from her own experiences and from working with others.

Sarah

Sarah, also in her early fifties, has one nineteen-year-old daughter, who has a young son of preschool age. Her second daughter is seventeen and recently graduated from high school. Sarah has been divorced for six years. Her narrative contains some remarkable information about a troubled childhood, memories of which she can only partially tap because she once spoke a second language that is now lost to her. The most unique aspect of Sarah's interviews was her collage of pictures representing her life. This artistic and unparalleled summary of her life and feelings about herself reaffirmed my decision to use the theme of sewing a quilt to unite the stories in this study.

Chapter 2

Judith:
"Getting My Life Back"

Judith's square of the quilt represents a woman's metamorphosis: a continuing process of self-discovery as she deconstructs the idealized myths that once shaped her self-definition, reestablishes her role within her family, and asserts confidence in her ability to live happily on her own. She expresses it best: "It's really nice to get out in life again, to feel like you've got your life back."

To understand the changes in her life and in her son's life that were precipitated by her divorce and their co-construction of a single-parent family unit, it is helpful to look at the process before, during, and after the divorce. We see her personal growth from a woman who felt "incomplete" without husband and child to a woman confident in her ability to accept *Positive Solitude* (a book she is currently reading, by Rae Andre, 1991). Her story reflects the strong social forces that shaped her gender role expectations, especially those defining what mothering and fathering are supposed to entail, and she suggests how those roles may be challenged and changed to benefit the next generation.

PARENTS AND PARENTING

As she reflected on how she arrived at her parenting style, she remembered the history of her parents' unhappy marriage, her mother's defining herself through her children, and the unequal partnership she found in her own marriage:

As far as my own parenting style, I think that, unfortunately, because I married someone who was semi-irresponsible, that

89

really exacerbated a style that I don't think was a real positive one in the first place for me. . . . I don't mean that in a negative way, I mean being responsible, feeling responsible alone for whatever happened to the child.

When asked, "What do you think contributed to that parenting style of yours?" she described her family history:

Well, I think that comes from original family, and of course that's history repeating itself because you've got an absent father emotionally in the original family and a mother who took complete control, and I'm only saying that in a responsibility sense, not in a bossy or domineering sense, although I fit well into that category too. I think, well, you had a mother who took total charge of the kids because the father wasn't there and was very very overprotective because she was so bonded to the kids that she didn't have a life. And I really did not want that for myself. I wanted to make sure that I had a life, so I didn't do to my children what I felt that my mother did to me, which was really suffocate me and keep me from having lots of experiences that I think are really healthy growing experiences. But they're also separation experiences, and my mother could not stand separating from the only thing that really brought her pleasure in life. So I think that I got a controlling kind of parenting style from her, but I was aware of it, and I tried to fight a lot of the stupid little idiosyncratic things that she did in my own parenting. I'm still actually working at it.

Her perception of herself as a controlling person was a recurrent theme. Blaming mothers for attempting to control their families as they do "just what is expected of them" is a common theme in psychological literature as well (Boss and Weiner, 1988; Kaschak, 1992; Llewelyn and Osborne, 1990). In her first interview, Judith referred to herself often as "controlling" or "overly responsible" and reflects that this may have contributed to a grossly unequal distribution of parenting responsibility that allowed her husband to focus most of his energy on his work, with most of the details of everyday existence left in her "control," including the major parenting responsibility. In her third interview, however, she clarified an important difference between being controlling and feeling talented and competent. In an insightful observation about her interactions with her husband, she stated, "I was trying to change his perception of what life should be to fit more with my perspective of what life should be."

However, the tendency for her to take over the major details of running the family and raising the child was rooted in the unequal distribution of responsibility that she observed in her parents' marriage, and replayed in her own. She described such gender role expectations of mothering and fathering often in her narrative. In the first interview:

> Had I married someone who insisted on being the other half of the parent, I may not have been as overly responsible, and it would've helped me to learn how to share and to let go a little bit and to step back and just let somebody take charge and not feel like I have to . . . the only one who can do anything is me; I'll do it right; I have to do it right myself if it's gonna get done. So I think that that's how it started, and, unfortunately, because of the way Mike is, it just played right into his *childish* behavior and my overly responsible, you know, overresponsible/underresponsible . . .

and again in the third:

> He very much played up being irresponsible. When we were married, the more irresponsible he was, the more responsible I was. So I did everything, and he kind of just put in his time. . . . I'm not saying that my being overly responsible was a good thing. It wasn't a good thing. What I probably should have done was, "You're half of the team here; you have to do such and such. I'm doing 80 percent; you're doing 20 percent. What gives?"

Roles and Responsibilities in the Family

The differences in the performance of their roles as mother and father were not atypical of many two-parent families: defined by social expectations, modeled by their parents, and fulfilled, somewhat unconsciously, in their interactions with each other and with their son. Typically, Judith assumed control of the daily details of parenting, giving attention to her family precedence over her personal agenda. Mike, she felt, defined himself mostly through work and scheduled his days in accordance with his personal "rhythms," as we can see in her description of a typical morning:

> **J:** When [Mike] was at home, he'd be sleeping, and that would really get my goat because I'd be running around trying to get me ready for work, trying to get [Ian] ready for school, trying to do all this stuff, while this other person is lying upstairs in bed sleeping, and it just galled me. It really always put [a] slight damper on the morning. It really bugged me . . . if I was in bed half dead, I could never not see off my family. I would get up, and see off my family, and that always bugged the *hell* out of me that that would not be important to him.

> **WP:** Did you talk to him about it?

> **J:** [Emphatically] Oh God, yes!

> **WP:** What did he say?

> **J:** Well, he just laughed; that was not his body rhythm. He would stay up late because he got most of his work done late at night because that was uninterrupted time. But he also used to watch TV from midnight until one or two in the morning, so he isolated himself. He just wanted the time to do his own thing, and we weren't ever a part of it.

Though she accepted these patterns of behavior as normal, Judith resented that she and her son lived their lives around her husband's schedule:

> It was just such a part of life; I mean, even I accepted it. Now that I look back, I can't imagine how I let this man kind of set our lifestyle like that. . . . Everything kind of revolved around his work. People were coming in and out of our house constantly because he worked out of our house, so I'd come home from work and there'd be all these cars in the driveway and people coming in and out, and the doorbell ringin' and the

phone ringin'. You know, it was just like you were in an office, when you came home from work all day yourself, which is really not a pleasant experience. If you wanted to put your pajamas on or sit around, or look like a mess while you were cooking dinner, you have all these [people] walking in and out of your kitchen to use the bathroom, and it really was not a fun time.

Even though she, too, worked, she accepted more of the responsibility of family life to allow her husband to do his work. She felt that if she supported him in his work by keeping that time uncluttered by the details of family life, he could at least reap the benefits of *her* efficiency, which would in turn make room for them in his life:

> The whole time it was happening, I knew I didn't like it. It didn't satisfy my needs. But I just figured . . . I guess I thought that if I took over more of the other things, that would relieve him of stuff so that he could perhaps devote some time to other things, but it does not work that way.

Judith's husband, whose role during her marriage she describes as "present, but not really there," is an example of the "phantom father" described by Levine (1992). This re-created the "absent father" role she disliked about her own father, a cross-generational gender role for men that allows, or even expects, the father's role to be secondary to the mother's as far as child rearing is concerned (Coontz, 1992; Lamb, 1977; Levine, 1992). She described how this role expectation affected her and how it was also unhealthy for her husband:

> He lived with us, but even when he was with us, he was with us physically and mentally for limited times. When he was with us physically, often he was contemplating other things, especially his work. It was kind of like he was dropping in or kind of putting in his time because he knew that that was what he was supposed to do, but I never really felt that he was all there—wholeheartedly there. So naturally, in order to avoid conflict for me, I just took on all the responsibility and didn't

ask him to be a partner in half of the parenting. I just took on whatever needed to be done. I shouldn't have done that, now as I reflect back, because all that did was cause him to see me as more controlling, to find fault with that, and that really kind of played into his irresponsible behavior even more. So I don't think it really did any good. I should have forced the issue and not made it easy for him.

Mike's patterns of fathering may have generational roots. In her description of Mike's childhood experiences, the repetition of behaviors and expectations is clear:

His father was a workaholic so . . . his memories were very limited of his father. I mean, he remembers things like him coming home late at night from work, coming back from business trips with presents. He doesn't have memories of sitting around on a Sunday reading the paper with his dad. And then his father died . . . and that was the ultimate desertion, and I think that maybe he felt that if he truly loved somebody or if he put everything into that basket, maybe that person would leave. . . . So I think that he never really had a good model there.

Seeking the Perfect Marriage and the Power of the Ideal

She spoke often of measuring her life against some kind of ideal, the image of the perfect family, believing that holidays required family, that she was the "normal girl next door dealing with somebody who was just different." She recalled thinking that all of her other friends had such happy marriages, and she wanted to live in the "ideal world" of being able to work part-time and stay home with her son. The illusion that the perfect marriage actually exists but must be one other than her own is common for almost all couples (Coontz, 1992; Holland and Eisenhart, 1990; Rice and Rice, 1986), but she learned through her divorce:

The thing that I find really interesting is, when you're married, you always think that your relationship isn't as good as so-and-so's, and everybody has perfect marriages except me, and then when you step back and go through the horror of divorce and you start to look around, you realize that many people are settling for relationships that really are flawed, and a lot of people are unhappy in those relationships, and they don't know what to do about it. They're aware that they're unhappy and have *told* me that they're unhappy, but [they] stay in the relationships for various reasons, and it's fascinating because I guess I used to see things when I was younger as black or white, and now I think that things are so complicated that, although my first reaction might be, "Well, gee, they must have a really great relationship," all of a sudden I start thinking there's gotta be gray.

The search for the perfect nuclear family is a strong socially prescribed goal that may cause serious psychological damage to those women who seek this ideal for themselves. Such women risk losing confidence in their abilities as independent individuals through their identification of self as "part of" a couple or a family (Coontz, 1992; Llewelyn and Osborne, 1990). This, explained Judith, is how young women learn to gauge their happiness:

As young women we are brought up to think that we are only complete if we are part of a family. That's how we gain our satisfaction; that's what makes us happy. And I really just bought into that, and I don't know why I did because I always had a career. I mean, I wanted that, too. And it's not that I just wanted to stay home and be Suzy Homemaker, but for some reason, I always felt most complete when I was with husband and child.

The traditional Cinderella myth—a woman needs to be rescued from a life of loneliness and isolation and cared for by a man—is one Judith advises young women to reject (Holland and Eisenhart, 1990; Schur, 1984):

Unfortunately, I think that all of the media just play right into that whole prince riding off on the white stallion and taking you up on his horse, riding away with you and taking care of everything and taking care of you. And I think the whole society is responsible for exacerbating that image, and I think it's a real negative one to do to women because it's hard. I mean, naturally it's easier to say, "Well, all I have to do is just sit around and have somebody take care of me," but most of the people who are in that situation don't feel very fulfilled. You gotta put out the work. You have to work hard and you have to feel pain, but on the other hand, you feel good about yourself once you've done it. I don't know very many women now who are waiting for Prince Charming to ride in and take care of them. I know if I ever had a daughter, I certainly wouldn't have her waiting for anybody.

Social role expectations contain mixed messages. Even though economic necessity made room for accepting women as wage earners, they were still expected not to sacrifice their roles as mothers for the sake of their careers (Blake, 1974; Coontz, 1992; Gimenez, 1984; Llewelyn and Osborne, 1990). To accomplish this incredible juggling act, many women, similar to Judith, relied on husbands for primary support and were comfortable with working part-time and mothering part-time. Judith called it "the best of two worlds because I was with Ian most of the time, but I had a career, too."

She described how painful it was to discover that she could no longer have what she had been socialized to prize:

My whole idea of that traditional family was shattered. And that's what I had spent twenty-five years of my life working at. Half of my life was spent trying to achieve the goal of this perfect little nuclear family because that's the only thing I really wanted. I didn't have that when I was growing up, and I wanted the perfect family in my own marriage.

She reflected that the Ozzie and Harriet family myth of the halcyon 1950s was a similarly potent barometer for her parents. She referred to her mother and father's inability to live up to this image, despite their tenacity in keeping an unhappy marriage together, "for the sake of the children." Judith asserted that this actually harmed both her parents and the children (Herzog and Sudia, 1968; Nye, 1957; Santrock, 1972):

My parents stayed together because they wanted to do right by the children, and I think that they definitely caused four children a lot of harm. I think that when people stay together for those reasons, you're showing children a very poor model of what a relationship should be. And the parents are both totally unhappy, and in my case, my parents both had physical ailments that were really from the stress . . . heart conditions and colitis and, you know, those kinds of things that are made worse in those kinds of situations . . .

Judith mused that her mother was trapped by financial dependence in a marriage that was destructive to her. She stated, "I can't think of anything more destructive to her or those around her than to be in a relationship where two people hate each other because you can't pay the bills." She described the verbal abuse her mother endured from her father and said that she has even talked to her mother about her leaving the marriage, but as Judith noted, her mother is in such a rut, emotionally and financially, that she cannot leave.

Holidays, traditionally hyped by the commercial media as family affairs, are unhappy times when single women such as Judith face their aloneness with regret (Bequaert, 1976; Falicov, 1988). The image of the perfect American family portrayed in the famous Norman Rockwell painting of Thanksgiving became a real expectation for Judith, who, similar to many other women, assumed that an ideal family was better represented by Hallmark than by their real experiences. She mentioned this perception several times:

I remember thinking I would never want to go through holidays without having a boyfriend or a husband or someone to buy me things, and I get a lot of pleasure just with friends and Ian. I mean, I just enjoy the holidays for what they are on my own, and I just can't believe that I could ever have done that.

I used to measure everything, my happiness by *who* I . . . I would think about a holiday and think about what I would be doing with this perfect family unit—you know, plan the whole thing—and now it's really interesting because I find that I'm much happier with much less. I look for the more important things, not the getting presents from the husband. I mean, what's the good of getting presents from your husband when the feelings aren't there?

SENSITIVITY TO STEREOTYPING

Judith, a teacher, admitted that her stereotypical assumptions about divorce, divorced people, and children from single-parent homes have made her feel guilty. When asked if people's opinions of her had changed since she became a single parent, she replied:

> Yes, but I feel it in myself. Part of me feels guilty, and I have to fight this because, of course, being a married person in the past, when I had a student twenty years ago who came from a divorced home, I had this picture in my mind, you know, that they were just second-class citizens or something, and as I got older and started to meet people more, my whole philosophy about that changed. Now, I feel like when I tell somebody I'm divorced, I'm embarrassed because I think, "Oh God, what if they're thinking what I used to think twenty years ago?" I don't like to check it off on the application because I'm afraid people will think less of me, before I realized what kind of people become single parents.

FACING ALONENESS AND FINDING STRENGTH

Judith's reacquaintance with her abilities, strength, self-worth, and confidence outside of her marriage were hard-won. When asked if she had learned anything about herself through the divorce process, she described her painful transition:

> I guess what I've discovered is that I'm really a lot stronger than I ever thought I would be. I remember just . . . my whole world . . . I thought, "I can't get through just one day. How can I live alone? How can I do this alone?" . . . [When I learned about Mike's wanting to leave, my world] was shattered. I thought, "There's absolutely no way that I can do this." And to

find that I have done it, and gone through unbelievably stressful situations because of it, and been able to achieve what I've
achieved through it—I'm quite proud of myself actually.

Judith recalled the emotional and psychological devastation of
anxiety and depression that she experienced during her divorce,
which she tried to control on her own, and offers this advice to other
women facing divorce:

> First of all, I think, because I'm such a control person, I'd
> obviously recommend counseling. I think that's very very im-
> portant. I think that another thing that people should know
> about is that depression manifests itself in different ways. And
> I was very much afraid for two years and tried to avoid taking
> any medication that would help me. I finally came to accept it
> and found that it helped a great deal, but that I could stop it
> successfully. The depression caused me to be always facing
> inward, taking . . . an emotional temperature . . . throughout
> the day. Most of my thoughts centered on how do I feel this
> minute—I'm in pain. I'm scared—all day long, and then forc-
> ing myself to look outward at things to accomplish throughout
> the day.

Judith participated in regular counseling, finally accepted the
medication recommendations of her psychiatrist, and faced the
world again with optimism:

> Now I find myself focusing outward and every once in awhile
> going, "Gee." And then looking in and saying, "Yeah. This is
> really a nice day." It's really nice to get out in life again, to feel
> like you've got your life back, to be on the road again, to be
> happy. Outside the sun is shining, and to just be in a good
> mood. To feel excited . . .

Losses and Changes—Independence and Pride

This same optimism characterizes the outcomes of other substantial changes in her life: the loss of her husband's sizable income, the
selling of her house, having to quit a job she liked, and job hunting

for a full-time position that provided financial independence. When asked to describe the problems facing her as a single parent, she recounted these losses and changes, but mixed into her account were positive assertions of independence and pride:

> I think the biggest one is going from a two-income [household] where my husband made a lot more than me, scrunching down to one income now. That's been a shock. I sold my house and moved into a smaller condominium, about half the size of my original house. It's funny [how] it really frightened me in the beginning, and I just felt, "I hope I like this; it's something that I need to do." I'm really, really excited about it because it's my own, but I guess I could look at it as, "Well, he caused me to give up this style of living, and . . . go into a much lesser, a cheaper house." It's not really that, and I make it sound horrible, but it's not—it's a lovely place—but I mean, I lost my home.
>
> I had to quit teaching part-time and go back to full-time teaching in the public school. I couldn't support myself and maintain a home on what I would have made, and although I loved my job, to be in your forties and go back into teaching full-time and think, "This is an unbelievable way to end my life!" To be in your sixties with these kids cussing at ya and spittin' [laughs], dying their hair green [laughs], you know, it's unbelievable. Part of me tells myself that's what's gonna keep me young, and that's the positive way you have to look at it because otherwise you just think, "Oh my God, what a way to go!" So it was real hard for me to face to the divorce, to face the financial difficulties.

Benefits Beyond the Divorce

Despite the financial difficulties, the feelings of loss, and expressed fear of being alone in old age, the "after" story of Judith's divorce is a much brighter picture than that painted by negative research on single-parent homes (see Mintzies and Hare, 1985; Shreeve et al., 1986; Galston, 1993). Among the benefits she sees in her new family arrangements are the following: healthy communication between herself and her son, increased parental responsibility by Ian's father, more quality time spent by both parents, a realization that separation from Ian is not the specter it once was, a redefinition of self outside of the "ideal," greater understanding of others and the destruction of previously held stereotypes, new and exciting prospects, a strong support network of friends, a move toward independence for both Judith and her son, and a generally better environment for both of them. Studies of postdivorce women report results remarkably similar to hers (Bequaert, 1976; Coontz, 1992; Gigy, 1980; Hafner, 1986; Hoeffer, 1987; Llewelyn and Osborne, 1990; Loewenstein et al., 1981). She stated:

> As far as the marriage itself goes, I think that now that I look back at it, I'm really kind of amazed that I hung in there as long as I did.

She described warm and supportive times shared with her son, though stolen moments in the midst of hurried daily lives:

> I get up about six-fifteen and get ready for work, and then I usually wake him up at seven o'clock, and then . . . we talk. . . . So we chat in the morning, and he'll think of anything to keep me up there, so he does chat away, and then we go downstairs and we do our ritual of getting the lunch money, doing the spelling words, packing the backpack, having breakfast [speaking as if a litany], and we're usually out of the house by seven forty-five, and I drive him to school. And it's only fifteen minutes in the car together, but we usually have a *wonderful* time, and the other morning he went to get out of the car and he said, "You know it was really nice, really nice talking to you, Mom!" [laughs]. And I said, "Well, you know, it was really nice talking to you!" That's the kind of thing . . . I mean, it's really just a wonderful way to start the morning. For me, I love it.

This description contrasts with her previous account of mornings spent in their former two-parent home, where resentment and conflict got the day off to a rocky start.

THE QUESTION OF QUALITY TIME

Previous researchers issued dire warnings about single parents not having time to spend with their children and the harmful effects of this reduced contact time (Baca Zinn and Eitzen, 1990; Burgoyne, 1987; Hetherington, Cox, and Cox, 1977). Judith, however, described how she and her son negotiate their times together comfortably and routinely:

> On a Saturday, he just likes me to be around . . . we might play a game together, we'll snuggle in the morning, maybe we'll play a board game, but he doesn't spend all that much time with me, especially if he's with his friends. I mean, I'm ignored. But when it's getting toward nighttime, then all of a sudden, he wants, especially when it's bedtime . . . then he wants me. That's it. You know, and then he starts the talking, but I'd say probably to devote time to each other in an eight-hour day—I don't know—an hour maybe?

Regardless of the time spent together, the quality of their communications are rich and may be initiated by either Judith or her son.

> Usually there are two times where he initiates them, and those times are often in the car driving somewhere or before bed, *a lot* before bed. He just goes on and on and on. Other times, *I* will initiate, like if it's during the day, you know, like the school conversation this morning, "I'd like you to . . . put more time into your studies" type of conversation . . .

Asked to comment more fully on the way that their unique communication style developed, she explained that, in this case, the son taught his mother:

> *He* has really taught me how to be a better communicator. My family did not talk; they either got angry or withdrew, held everything inside . . . but I've never had a better teacher than Ian because, for some reason, he has the ability. I was criticizing him about his nonserious attitude toward school, and . . . he

basically turned to me in a very calm voice and said, "You're right," and I said, "I can't believe that you could say that, that you could turn around and say, 'You're right,' when I'm saying something very critical to you, and it would be a first human reaction for you to get snippy and defensive." And he said, "Well, you *are* right," and I said, "You know what, I really appreciate that you could say [that.]" You know, it's that kind of a thing with him, where he can step back, and I learned from that because I have a real hard time with that. And with him, I've never been real good at saying, "I'm wrong; I'm sorry," but he has opened that up, and now really I try very hard. I will say, "You know, Ian, that was wrong of me to such and such, or . . . you are right in this or that," but he's taught me a lot about communication.

BEYOND THE DIVORCE: PARENTING CHANGES

Divorce has positively affected both the mother's and the father's parenting by increasing the son's contact time with his father, giving Mike full responsibility for Ian during visitation times and forcing Judith to surrender some control. Despite her emotional involvement in the circumstances surrounding her divorce, she was candid in admitting her tendencies to be overprotective and made an honest assessment of the differences in their parenting styles. She commented that "the whole dynamic is better." She described her husband as being "a much better parent now that we're divorced than he was when we were married because he really does have to take more responsibility for himself." This phenomenon is often reported in research on postdivorce fathers (Hetherington, Cox, and Cox, 1977; Lamb, 1977; Levine, 1992).

In her third interview, she repeated that her role juggling did not change very much. However, her resentment about the burden of too much responsibility experienced during her marriage, which once took up "a lot of emotional space," was now lessened:

Now I don't have that resentment, so I can be better at the role, and it seems like there's a lot of work, but on the other hand, I think that because his father has been thrust into a position of responsibility now, where I'm not doing everything, he has had an opportunity to become a much more involved father than perhaps he would have been if I had maintained all the roles that I had and been resentful at the same time.

When asked if anything had changed in her parenting style since the divorce, she said:

I think it's changed because I was forced by his leaving to give up some of the control and responsibility for Ian. That has been very very hard for me because I have always felt that my way was the right way, and I guess I'm only saying that in comparison to what his way was. He has a much looser philosophy than I do about what's appropriate and what's not appropriate, you know, what he let Ian do, and that kind of stuff. Maybe it's just sex differences there, but he's just a lot freer with Ian than I would be, and that's been very scary for me, but I don't have a choice.

Their differences in child rearing may be affected by the fact that a father who has been accustomed to a peripheral role, whose contact with the child was mostly as "the player" while the mother served as "the comforter," would probably continue to preserve this type of interaction, even though his time alone with his son has increased (Dinnerstein, 1976). In addition to the "goofy things," as Judith referred to them, such as allowing the child to do things that she thinks are socially inappropriate, Judith identified another more pervasive difference between them that survived the divorce:

The challenging part of it is that, of course, you're doing all the running around and the worrying. And, of course, you handle most of the chauffeuring, most of the chores with the school stuff. I'm lucky that his father has as much input. I think I'm unusual because his father sees him a lot, and he also helps him with homework, but he's not . . . he'll put in his [visitation time] and when it's over, and that child comes home, I'm running [errands], organizing his life, and worrying about dentist and doctor and those kinds of things, and with working full-time and having my own life, which is very limited, it's been hard.

When asked which parent has more of an influence in their son's life, she answered without hesitation:

> I do, yeah. I have the majority of the time with him. Our interactions are deeper. His father tends to be the "I'll play with you" relationship, and before bed, I get that special time . . . an unwinding where all the questions come and all the talk comes, and so I get most of that, and that's where you make the greatest impact on a kid, those talks.

The father, then, remains more distant from the child than the mother, even though his contact time is frequent. When asked about this, she reiterated that the nature of mother-son and father-son interactions may be affected by the son's expectations for his parents, patterns laid down too deeply, perhaps, to be changed (Dinnerstein, 1976; Farrell, 1972):

> **WP:** The bond between you and him is forged in many ways that his father is not a participant in or not even aware of?
>
> **J:** I think he's aware of it, and I think it bothers him. . . . I don't know that their relationship is so set that he would get into discussions with his father like he gets into with me. He may, I'm not sure, but he doesn't have those kinds of opportunities.
>
> **WP:** He feels more comfortable doing that with you?
>
> **J:** Yeah. He tells me that his father is more fun for play and I'm more fun for comfort.

To provide balanced maternal and paternal influence on their child, Judith and Mike have agreed to liberal visitation arrangements that acknowledge the importance of the father's influence and contact with the child. Such arrangements mean that divorced mothers, while dealing with the pain of their estrangement from their former life, must also face and accept regular, if temporary, separation from their children, a painful process, especially when negative feelings toward the father have not yet been resolved. Judith found this "loss of control [to be] extremely stressful":

> You know the feeling of loss of control. . . . He's the most precious thing in your life, and you send that child off, and you

have no control over what happens to him when he's in the care of other people, and I find that extremely stressful.

Resisting Codependency

Though researchers warn against the pejorative mother blaming implicit in therapist lingo such as codependency (Kaschak, 1992), Judith acknowledges that even though *she*'s "never faced aloneness before," her son needs to learn how to "be away" from her:

> The thing I'm working on now is being aware that [learning how to be alone] also means Ian, because I don't want to transfer over the need for somebody to him and foster that codependency thing. So just trying to think of ways that he can grow and go off on his own without it hurting me too much [laughs] has been real challenging. . . . I've wanted him to feel real secure [through the divorce], so I haven't wanted to push him out. I think now, as time goes by and we finally get settled, I think once he feels secure, then I'm gonna start introducing situations like sleepovers. He really should start to . . . he has never slept in anybody's house. He's afraid, and I think that he really doesn't want to be away from me, and although that makes me feel real good, it's not good for him.

Such transitions are important as Ian co-constructs his new family with both of his parents.

The Effects of Divorce on Her Child

How has the divorce affected her son? Critics of single parenting and the "dissolution of the family" are quick to emphasize the inevitable damage that divorce does to children. Did the divorce harm Ian? Does Judith think divorce is harmful for children? Judith's answer reflects the contribution of women's self-esteem to the assurance of a happy environment for children, and she believes that parenting *improves* when each parent can concentrate on the quality of his or her interactions with the child:

> I think it's a positive thing that people are thinking more highly of themselves, and that women can support themselves

now and can move out of relationships that are detrimental to themselves and/or their children and have a happier environment for their kids. I still think that it's better for the child if the situation is amicable and the parents, for the child's sake, can talk about the child and not say hateful things to the child about each other. I think that puts the child in kind of an awkward situation. I mean *my son,* who's from a divorced family, has it better than lots of kids who are in traditional families. He spends more time with each of us; we're more dedicated to spending quality time with him. You have two parents who are very conscious of being supportive of each other because you don't want to not be, so it seems to be an ideal situation.

It is interesting to note that she describes her new family arrangement as an "ideal," completely abandoning the fairy-tale family she once thought she needed.

Judith explained how important open and honest communication, already her pattern with Ian, continued to be beneficial in allowing Ian to express his fears about the divorce:

He said, "You know, Mom, I'll never forget when you and Dad called me in to talk to me that day. . . . I was really disappointed because I thought you were raising my allowance!" [She laughs.] But he cried. His biggest fear was that we would make him choose between us, 'cause you see all those movies where the kid has to decide whether he wants to live with the mother or father, and he just kept crying and saying, "I can't choose. I can't choose. I love you both." And once we assured him that he would never have to choose . . .

Perhaps equally important to the child's successful journey through the process of divorce is both parents' willingness to put aside their feelings toward each other, even though wounds are fresh and emotions still volatile (Rice and Rice, 1986):

I made a vow then that I would never speak ill [of] or make him side with me over his father because I didn't think that was healthy for him, and it's been . . . because of [this] that . . . he's done really well. His father does not speak ill of me either, but he has no reason to. I haven't really done anything [laughs]. So, because the thing wasn't my idea, he speaks very highly of me; you know, he thinks I'm wonderful. But it's been very hard for me not to say things to Ian about the cause of the divorce or my feelings about his father, and I have mixed feelings, but Ian has done really well through this thing. He seems to be the same kid.

She explained how difficult it was to suppress her feelings, but in this, she placed her child's feelings ahead of her own:

I think that one of the things that I would recommend is that [if] people want their child to do well with the divorce [then] they need to try. And this is really hard, and it's hard for me, but they need to swallow their hatred, at least in the presence of the child, and don't . . . don't think that turning the child against the other parent is the best for the child because that's exactly what you want to do. And what I have found is that the child is best and happiest if he's free to love both parents.

The Effect of Personality

As Judith answered my questions about Ian, I realized that studies rarely describe children *before* divorce (Cherlin, 1991; Rice, 1994). In responding to my question, "Do you think he's basically the same kid?" she reminded me that the personality of a child will interact with divorce as it does with other life situations. A child's basic personality does not suddenly take a sharp turn simply because the parents divorce, even for older children such as Ian who are fully aware of what is happening with their parents (Rice and Rice, 1986):

He has always been an extremely sensitive child, very articulate with his feelings, very happy . . . you know, joking, laughing type kid, but a worrier, perfectionist, that type of a kid throughout his life.

She described Ian as worrying the most about "doing the right thing," "people loving him—or not loving him," and wanting to please. As she related some events from his early years, it was apparent that all of these worries were present and developing long before his parents lived apart. This is in her description of her son's performance in school:

> He has always been very . . . insecure at school. And what I mean by that is perfectionistic to the point where he drives the teacher insane. You know, the teacher will say, "Hand in your homework." Ian will want to know, "What box do I hand it [in,] in?" . . . From first grade, he has been like that. And in fact, in second grade, he had a teacher who told him to shut up and put his hand down and stop asking questions, and he cried most of the year because she would not let him ask any questions. So I'm working with him toward independence, but that's been his personality all along. I truly don't believe it has anything to do with divorce. Every teacher that we've gone in to see says the same thing.

To be certain that Ian was not harboring some deep distress that he could not express, his parents took him to talk to a child psychologist. In his assessment, the counselor challenged former assumptions about the inevitable connection between the misery of divorce and problems for the children of a divorcing couple, as Judith related:

> We took him to a counselor to make sure he was really doing as well as we thought he was doing, that he didn't have some deep-seated hidden problem, and the psychologist said, "Is he eating? Is he sleeping? Is he acting out in school? Is he doing any of these things?" And it was "No. No. No." He talked to the kid, and he comes out and says, "You know, you guys do a hell of a divorce because maybe you couldn't be married, but you've done right by him in the divorce. He's doing fine."

Perhaps because she is an educator, Judith requested a second observation, this time from the *school* psychologist:

> We had the school psychologist observe him again. We wanted to cover all bases to see if he was indeed doing as well as we

thought he was doing, and she brought him down and she interviewed him, and she went into the classroom and she observed him, and she said he [did] not exhibit what you would call normal behaviors for a kid this age. Like, he would go around and compliment people [laughs], and he went up to one girl and he said, "You know, you're really doing a nice job on that." And she just looked at him and said, "Buzz off." Because they really don't know how to handle that kind of behavior. It's just a foreign behavior. You know, he's gonna have probably a difficult time because kids are mean. But, I think when he gets to be an adult, he's going to be a really nice person. I think that he is a nice person. He does well in school.

The psychologist's observation that Ian did not exhibit normal behaviors for his age may be extended to the many ways that Ian exhibits adult behaviors. Critics of single mothers claim that this "child-parent" phenomenon is unhealthy, but feminists denounce such a judgment as just another way to chastise the mother with social expectations for normative behavior—"Kids should be kids" (Kissman and Allen, 1993; Rice, 1994). On the other hand, in interviews and surveys, single parents themselves sometimes consider their children's adultlike behaviors, such as increased responsibility and independence, not as a debit but a benefit (Kurdek and Siesky, 1980; Reinhard, 1977; Richards and Schmiege, 1993; Rosen, 1977). In Ian's case, it is important to remember that his adult language and his attempts to please others are characteristics he developed long before his parents divorced.

DIVORCE AS LIBERATION

Feminist researchers of single mothers agree that divorce can be a liberating force for women (Bequaert, 1976; Kissman and Allen, 1993; Llewelyn and Osborne, 1990; Rice, 1994). Freed from the stress of having to create the perfect family and her resentment of her husband's "doing his own thing," while she assumed more and more family responsibilities, Judith took pride in her personal growth:

I always felt that I really could do anything. I always felt fairly strong, but at the same time, I always felt complete as a person only as part of a couple. And, now, I mean, I'm still doing the same things I was doing then, but I don't have that kind of fear that I can't do this by myself. I don't know why I had that fear because I was doing the things anyway, but being part of a couple was like a support net, the safety net that a wire walker would have, and the relationship was like that. Even though it didn't necessarily do anything for me, I was doing the tasks myself anyway, but I always felt like if I fall, it'll be there. And now it's amazing that I don't feel at all like I'm missing something or that I couldn't do something. In fact, when I think about doing things that I always put the kibbutz [*sic*] on myself because my spouse would not have liked these things, I feel really almost refreshed that I can go ahead and make the decision that serves my needs because I'm by myself and I don't have to worry about what he would like or what he wouldn't like or how it would fit into his work schedule. . . . The freedom is exhilarating.

Amazed at her self-sufficiency, refreshed, working toward satisfying her own needs, and exhilarated by her freedom, she has redefined herself as a competent, strong person: "for the first time in my life, I have come to feeling I don't need someone else." She is proud of surviving the stressors of divorce and the establishment of a new household and takes ownership of her accomplishments.

Regarding those who say a single mother's feelings of liberation and self-power are a price the child pays (Carter and McGoldrick, 1980), she stated:

Well, I can only answer from my case, and I totally disagree with what they're saying. First of all, I think I make the best of a bad situation. I didn't ask for myself to be put in the situation, or to "take this test," if you will. But since I took the test and *passed*, it really has made me more comfortable with myself. And my son is an extremely perceptive person. He knows by the look on my face if I'm unhappy or if something is bothering me, and because I feel very content most of the time, he seems very content. So I don't think that this feeling of power or whatever has been necessarily anything but a positive experience for him.

Some Advice for Other Women Facing Divorce

In several interviews, I asked Judith what advice she would give to others facing the same situation. Her responses revealed her confidence in the strength of women and the importance of self-actualization:

> Well, I think the positive aspect of being single is that you live your life according to what *you* want, and, especially, women tend to put their needs after spouse, child, parents, employer, whatever, and as a single person, it's kind of neat just to be able to do what you want when you want to do it.

She offered advice to *young* women:

> If I had a daughter, how I would bring her up today? [I would tell her,] "You are you. *You* are an entity in and of yourself. You are strong. You're gonna make it in the world, and if you choose to hook up with somebody, that's just hooking up with somebody, that's not a make-you or break-you type of thing. . . . You go to college." Instead of "You marry a doctor; you *be* a doctor and take care of yourself.". . . I do that with my students all the time. I think being a good woman role model for them is important.

The Element of Choice

The element of choice was important in these conversations. Though Judith stated that her divorce was "not her choice," if she observed behavior similar to her husband's in another person, she would take a different path:

> I was not the one who initiated the divorce, but now that I've worked through the pain of it, I look back and think, "How in the world could I have done this? How could I have lived for [so long with] him . . . *put up with* [his behavior]." I mean, I get little images like that and think, "Oh my God!" [Laughs.] I

would never do that again. I would just say to the guy, "Take me home! You're outta here!" [Laughs.]

She asserted that women's choices are circumscribed by their intelligence and finances, that those who could "opt out of marriages because they wanted to be free" were financially able to support themselves, and that "those who were financially and emotionally dependent on the man stayed and suffered."

An element of choice is evident in her many assertions that she consciously works to "break the cycle" of her family's unhappiness, her mother's overprotective obsession with her children, and the father-to-son transfer of role expectations. She stated that the difference between being alone and being lonely is one of choice. One can choose to be alone, but loneliness comes when one does not want to be alone but is.

The Downside: Loneliness and Reduced Finances

In addition to constant stress in negotiating the differences between her parenting style and her ex-husband's "easygoing" style, which is evident in her descriptions of some of their ongoing conflicts, Judith listed financial worries and loneliness as drawbacks:

> The negative aspects—it's kind of hard to say, right now, other than the financial . . . but I think that probably in the long run, it would get lonely. I really haven't been real lonely yet. I've been so caught up with just trying to make it through this whole transition, the divorce, and the move, and all this stuff, and the jobs, that I haven't had time to really be lonely, but I think the negative thing is thinking about getting old and not wanting to kind of end my life by myself, especially when Ian goes away to school or has his own life, you know, just the thought of me being in a house with a little dog or something [laughs]. I just don't know if that's real satisfying.

Certain fears come from being the primary caregiver and supporter of the family (Kaschak, 1992; Llewelyn and Osborne, 1990). Judith likens these fears to those which men have experienced in feeling pressure to provide for their families:

I guess one of the things that I think is interesting is that being single and sole support of my family [is] a very frightening position. I'm often very anxious . . . "What if I get sick, what's gonna happen? Could I lose the house?" You know, the whole nine yards, and I think that part of me thinks that men have probably felt this for a long time, and it's really too bad that they couldn't sit down and talk about it or even maybe aren't even aware of it, of where their anxiety stems from, or to get a support group where you can talk about it with people and their wives or whatever. Because I think that that's a real fear. And I've gotten a better picture of what it must have been like for a lot of men who are supporting ten kids, or something, and working in the factory, and just petrified that they would drop dead and their kids would be starving, and that type of thing. So I guess I've just become a little bit more sympathetic to that whole thing.

She described grappling with warring "parts of me" as she worked to overcome a lifetime of conditioning to want to be part of a couple. When asked how she would feel if she had a crystal ball and could see that she would indeed be single for the rest of her life, she replied:

J: Well, I guess my first reaction would be fear, and I don't know why. I guess it's again fighting that conditioned response. My second reaction was that I am going to build up a network, starting now, to ensure that I won't be a lonely person and I'll have a full life then.

WP: So you're not so fearful of the future. It's just that there's still some vestiges of wanting to be part of a couple?

J: No. I think it's . . . there's still parts of me that still want love, the experience of sharing, to have shared experiences with someone. You know, when my son goes off to college or goes off to whatever, to be an adult, and I am by myself, I think that even if I'm watching a funny television show, and it doesn't necessarily have to be with a man, as much as I still think it's so meaningful to me to have somebody to share things with. So I certainly . . . if I thought I was going to be by myself for the rest of my life, I would want to be sure that my friends were still of the highest priority, so they would be there.

Social Pressures to Marry Again

Aware of social pressures for her to become part of another couple, she described people's typical response to finding out she is divorced:

> I can't tell you how many people will say, when I tell them I've gone through a divorce . . . , "Oh, I'm sorry, but don't worry. I bet you'll be remarried; by the time you're forty-five you'll be remarried." And it's always, "Well, you're not whole now, but it will be coming soon [laughs] because you have so much to offer." And people think that they're saying the right thing because they're totally conditioned that that's what's supposed to happen, that they want everybody to be in that same mold, too. It's really funny because I was talking to my godmother the other day, and she had lost her husband, my godfather, whom she loved very very much, and she felt totally empty and that her life is ruined. And we were talking about how this has frightened her oldest daughter and [how] she's afraid that she'll never marry. And I said to my godmother . . . I can't believe that I could ever say this—but I wonder now if I even feel that marriage is necessary. Because it's not essential.

Social pressure to remarry may stem from societal expectations that all women should be married and that singleness from divorce is only a temporary state on the way to remarriage (Bequaert, 1976; Kaschak, 1992; Laws and Schwartz, 1977; Llewelyn and Osborne, 1990; Schur, 1984; Stacey, 1990).

Learning to Enjoy Her Own Company

Although strong in her conviction that a woman does not need marriage to be happy, she still hears her own competing voices:

[Referring to the book *Positive Solitude*] Well, they talk about some of the intellectuals of the past having chosen a life that was extremely fulfilling, and half of me, the cynic in me, says, "Oh yeah, it's written by a chick who can't find anybody so she's gotta justify it," and the other half of me thinks, "Oh, this is a wonderful idea!" [laughs], and they're just battling back and forth: "Oh yeah, you couldn't get a date, so you talk about how great it is to be alone." So I'm still fighting a lot of my whole life, of being conditioned to think that it's more fun with people, but I'm learning slowly to enjoy my own company.

This duality is reflected in her comments on the injustice of her husband's quick return to dating. The proud voice of her self-sufficiency is muted by her anger at her husband "messing up her life" while he "just got on with his." Her conviction that hers is the better lot, however, resurfaces:

J: Well, of course, the thing that bugged me was that it angered me to put my life in total turmoil and to see that he was . . . just getting on with his life, and I guess that I still kind of want to see him suffer more. But we were married a long time, and I felt that he didn't give it the time it deserved, to mourn for it or something. He felt he did. I just didn't feel he did, so it bothered me. That's a real touchy subject for me, so I'm learning to deal with it. But it's hurtful to see somebody that you gave your all to with someone else.

WP: When you're not—

J: When I'm not with anybody else? That doesn't . . . part of me says, "I'm smarter than you are because I'm not gonna let anything happen after getting burned like I did, so you're a fool for jumping in something again because you're asking for a whole new set of problems." So part of me feels slightly superior. The other part of me would love to have him just die of jealousy because I know it would bother him when he finally does see me with someone, at least that's what he says.

Dating Again

Though Judith often said that she is not ready to cope with dating yet, she has discussed the possibility with her son. Ian has told her that he "wants her to be happy," "find the perfect man," and "have a boyfriend," and assures her that just because he does not mind when she goes out and leaves him with a baby-sitter, "that doesn't mean I don't love you." She shared the following conversation she had with Ian:

> I asked him in the car when we were driving to my sister's . . . "I'm going out tonight, do you mind?" and he said, "Well, no . . . . Because I've seen you enough and it's okay if you go out . . . . It doesn't mean that I don't love you. I still love you." And I said, "Ian, I completely understand. You can love me and be happy that I'm going out and doing something else because I love you and I'm happy when you're having fun with your friends." You know, so that was kind of an interesting conversation. He said, "Now if you went out a lot more, I might, you know . . . " but since I don't [laughs], since I don't do anything but grade papers right now . . . I don't know how much is too much.

Judith is sensitive to Ian's feelings regarding the possibility of her finding a new relationship. Ian told his mother a story about a "friend" who was worried that his mother might be falling in love with someone, and her son feared she would "leave" him. Because Judith has not had the opportunity to date yet, Ian has no real reason to be fearful, but Judith knows that when it happens, she will have to deal gently, yet directly with Ian's fear of being "replaced" as the sole recipient of his mother's love.

Judith, happy with her social life with friends, described how difficult it would be to fit dating into her schedule:

> I have a rich social life of friends. I don't have any romantic involvement at this point. I can't imagine having time to have romantic involvement. Someone asked me if I was dating and I said, "How could I fit in a boyfriend?" So, that kind of worries me because although I think it might be fun to go out

and do things, I'm not quite sure how it would fit into schedules I have made up for myself.

More vexing than simply finding the time, the inner conflicts between her need to express herself as a woman in a relationship with a man and her dedication to her son may cause great turmoil, though these warring factions have thus far not been put to the test (Kissman and Allen, 1993). A foreshadowing of this may been seen in her explanation of how she would negotiate the possibility of jealousy from Ian when she brings home "the competition":

> First of all, I probably would only bring home somebody who was gonna be kissin' up to him anyway, [who] would be really really nice to him, and I guess I'd probably try to do things with the three of us until he felt . . . comfortable, and maybe try to go out on my own more without that. But I think that I would only feel comfortable—especially in these first experiences that I haven't had in many years—I would only feel comfortable if I knew that it wasn't causing my son pain, 'cause it's gonna be painful enough for me to be dating after so many years.

This is an interesting answer. Instead of focusing on how *she* alone would feel and separating her life as a dating woman from her life as a mother, she makes her son's needs her own, placing his comfort first in helping her to make a choice and suggesting that her dating experiences include her son.

EMOTIONAL CODEPENDENCY WITH HER SON

Judith, in all three interviews, honestly expressed what she calls her "codependency" with her son. Although this term was formerly used only clinically to refer to dysfunctionality in the families of alcoholics, it has been generalized and popularized in recent years to refer to any relationship—especially mother-child relations—in which the members are overly dependent on each other for emotional satisfaction. It connotes an excessive and unhealthy attachment. She explained that it started in response to feeling unloved by her spouse:

J: I think I was always overly dependent on him because I only had one direction for all the love to flow, because it was reciprocated in that direction in ways that I could measure it and feel it. But when I gave the love out in the spousal direction, it was never sent back in a way that I could feel loved back. So naturally I directed it where it would come back freely to me. I think I have always been overly dependent on my son.

WP: How do you judge that?

J: The dependence? I feel much more comfortable. I feel uncomfortable when he is not with me. I don't think that's really normal, you know. I feel very very anxious when I think of him going on a vacation with his father. I mean, some mothers would be like, "Wow! I can do whatever I want! I'm gonna go to New York! I'm gonna go shopping!" and I think, "Oh, I'm not gonna be able to sleep thinking of his little empty bed, and I have to sleep with his teddy bear!" And now that I'm settled, I have to work on that because I don't think it's good for him. I want to encourage his independence from me. He is a momma's boy.

Her honest evaluation of her child-parent relationship is a positive step toward a more balanced and independent coexistence for both of them. Such a maternal reliance on a male child to provide emotional support, however, is one of the "worries" of single moms, a concern exacerbated by stern critics of single parents who proclaim that this Oedipal relationship is unhealthy (Farrell, 1994; Kissman and Allen, 1993).

Reconstructing Gender Roles and Expectations

However, the close relationship between Ian and Judith has a more positive effect. Judith explained how they discuss problems she has at work, with Ian offering some important insights regarding discipline problems with her students. Ian gives solutions to problems, and Judith helps him, in turn, to understand how his teachers may think. Critics would say that she substitutes the child for an adult in a conversation that normally takes place between husband and wife. However, because he is actively included as a full participant in their family, Ian may be dismantling sex role stereotypes:

> I think that, obviously, he'll think that women can do anything. I mean women *can* do anything, be anything. He's just gonna have a very different attitude toward women from the attitude that they're little prissy things who just don't wanna get their dresses dirty. So, yeah, I think that that's gonna be very very different because of who I am and what I've done.

In fact, Judith believes that her son will make someone a wonderful partner (if he chooses to be one) because he does his share of the housework. She believes that because he is already responsible for household chores and is a caring person, he will continue to see himself as part of a "team effort," not offering to do everything for the other person (as she once did), nor expecting that the other person will "put up with you not participating and pulling your weight" (something she regrets). I pursued the idea that a new generation of sons of single mothers may eliminate some previously transmitted gender role expectations for men in marriage (Levine, 1992), and Judith added:

> I think we're breaking a lot of the traditional roles. I mean, I think my son will not think that he's gonna marry someone and take care of her. I don't think that he's going to get together with the guys and say, "How 'bout that sports team, huh?" He will talk about real things and feelings, and hopefully all the other little boys, at least some of them, will be moving in that direction too. I know there are the little men of big men [boys who imitate their fathers] that are stuck with the very conservative behaviors, but there are those boys who are being raised by people like us to be sensitive individuals, and I think that's really starting to change what happens to relationships . . .

She continued with a deeply meaningful reflection on falling in love in which she described her vision for her son, shaped around her hard-won lessons:

> I know one of the things I really want to talk to him about, too, is the idea of love and what that means, and how we have to

move away from [believing that] when you're in love, that's when you get married. I think that Scott Peck, in *The Road Less Traveled,* says that only when you feel out of love with someone and you still want to spend your life with him should you marry that person because the feeling of being in love is a façade. Falling in love is very different from truly loving someone. Ga-ga infatuation stuff is for the birds. It doesn't last, and I think that we need to start to teach our kids that that might be nice and wonderful, but getting past that is the important stuff.

The Importance of Role Models

A patricentric belief cautions that boys may be harmed by the influence of strong women unbalanced by the influence of other men, and that the boys of single mothers are particularly susceptible to all sorts of role confusions, which may eventually contribute to homosexuality (Bieber and Society of Medical Psychoanalysts, 1962; Farrell, 1972). Judith confirmed that her son needs strong male role models, but that, for her, they are "harder to find" than strong women:

J: I think that as a single mother you would probably want to be particularly aware of having your children be around strong role models that are men too.

WP: How do you do that with your son?

J: Well, he's with his father. He sees his dad [a lot]. But, you know, I'll try to point out people and say, Uncle so-and-so is very good at this, but just to let him know that there are men who have qualities that I admire. I think it might be difficult for me if he didn't see his dad as much as he does because I don't see the men in my family enough. I would have to really radically change how I live in order to get him around men who are role models.

WP: Hard to find them, huh?

J: Yeah. I think they're very hard to find—good male role models. Lot[s] of good female role models, but not a lot of good male role models.

However, when asked whether she thought that strong female role models were harmful to boy children, she added that it is not a question of gender so much as a question of personality. A child should not be under the influence of any one major personality type to the exclusion of others. It is better, she stated, to ensure that children are exposed to "different types of men and different types of women."

COMPLETING THE JOURNEY

Judith's journey to single parenthood is complete, though her voyage of self-discovery continues. Navigating unknown and unsought for regions she once feared, she learned to negotiate deep waters of loss, anger, rejection, and depression. To overcome each obstacle she encountered, she drew strength from her inner competence, the support of friends, and intelligent, compassionate therapy. She got her life back.

Her son, too, made the trip, not unaffected by the changes with which he was challenged, but developing and interacting with others according to his personality, as good a student as he was before his parents divorced, and now actively engaged with his mother and his father in constructing two new families.

Chapter 3

Kathleen:
"I Want to Do Everything Right"

Kathleen's square of the quilt is a picture of what it means to be a superwoman of the 1990s. Hers is a story of negotiating multiple roles; of intergenerational changes in defining the roles of women; of the challenges to value systems presented by divorce; of her attempts to juggle, both practically and emotionally, the tasks she faces as woman, mother, worker, supervisor, "wife," girlfriend, and daughter; of trying to be perfect in all of these roles. She provided some important information about relationships: her divorce experience; the benefits of extended family and a support network of friends; her reflections and observations about male-female relationships, destructive and constructive. She also discussed her orientation toward nurturing and facilitating the success of others, such as her daughters and their friends, her co-workers, and her male companion. In commenting on her responsibilities as a supervisor at work, she stated, "I want to do everything right," which emerges as the unifying theme for her story.

Kathleen's story presents a provocative look at different facets of the relationship between school and home: the school's lack of understanding of parents with regard to time and money, the inequities supported and advanced by a peculiar program of privilege advanced by a political agenda, and the many ways that she has supported her daughters' successes in school.

THE DIVORCE EXPERIENCE

Kathleen's divorce process moved from recognition that she was making a mistake in marrying David, through struggles to work two jobs to make ends meet, and eventually to a euphoric feeling about herself, her life, and her children's success. In a loose chronology of events, Kathleen described the reason for her divorce, which began with recognizing that "something was not quite right" with her husband, David:

> **K:** I really think when I was walking down the aisle—I'm a Catholic; you don't get divorced—I knew I was making a mistake. I sensed it. I felt it. It was a beautifully gorgeous day, but, you know, something just didn't seem quite right. So I think from the very beginning and . . . throughout the nine years we were married [I sensed] that it wouldn't last; it just wouldn't last.
>
> **WP:** What made you sense it?
>
> **K:** My husband was into pornography. He would hide books and magazines between the mattresses, and I would go to make the bed and I would find—and they weren't just *Playboy* and that. He was going to those all-night video stores, and he was picking up some pretty raunchy stuff. And I just couldn't stand that type of stuff. . . . So that was very hard for me to take, and then, probably the biggest thing was, after having my second child, he made a comment to me; he said something like, "We could have as many girls as you want because as they grow older, I'll be able to watch them undress." So I knew that for my protection, my daughters' protection, he wasn't good. [And the final straw was when] he enrolled in a camping course or something similar to that. . . . And when he came home after the weekend, I knew something was wrong. I found empty liquor things . . . I guess everybody got totally drunk . . . and I learned that my husband at the time had shared his tent with a female student who was seventeen years old, not even eighteen yet. . . . So that was really the beginning of the end.
>
> It was right after that, that I went to a lawyer friend of the family. . . . My lawyer said to me, "You know, Kathleen, people like him will not change." And I had already met someone who was going through hell in his marriage, and I think it made it easier for me to go to talk to the lawyer and inquire about a divorce. That was in October, and David was out by December,

the end of it, right after Christmas, and that's when I started my job at the university. . . . Well, I think we stayed together to get through the holidays, and he couldn't find a place. I guess there [were no] regrets. He got into drugs after that and all kinds of stuff.

Kathleen's constant fear has been that her ex-husband exhibited signs of recklessness, and she was worried about child-molesting possibilities:

He . . . was a terrible driver. We were paying . . . close to two thousand dollars insuring him because he had three accidents in one week during that one last period of the time he was with me. And I always had a fear of that, and he was a very touchy-feely type of person, which bothered me because he used to tickle his nieces and nephews, and I could see the disdain on his sister's face when he did things like that, and I know that he would tickle his own daughters [in ways I didn't like].

Because of his questionable character, Kathleen accepted a lower child support rate (only fifty dollars per week) and did not use court enforcement when he lost his job and stopped paying (Weitzman, 1985). She stated:

I felt that if he was paying for them, he might feel that he had more vested interest in their lives, and I didn't really want him to be in their lives. After I saw what he was doing, I didn't want him around. If he felt like he was paying me, [he would think] that he should have them, he should be doing things with them, he should be taking them places, and I didn't trust him.

In her third interview, she reflected on the divorce process. She commented on the impersonal treatment of her lawyer and her inexperience, since she was the first of her friends to go through a divorce. She offered the "before and after" perspectives to those who are currently facing divorce:

If I had to do it over again, I would make sure that I had a better lawyer. I felt like . . . I was going through a revolving door. You know, "This is what we'll do." He made it sound so matter-of-fact; of course, it probably was because he does it every day. And I don't think I asked enough questions because I really didn't know what to ask, and I went into it alone [because] in my circle of friends, nobody went through the experience yet. Nobody went to a lawyer, nobody divorced that I knew, so it was an interesting experience, and, you know, I thought he was doing good for me. I didn't know any different. Now I do. . . .

But if I had to sit down with the people that I know who are going through horrendous [experiences], I would say it's so much better. Because within a year . . . you know, the divorce part was so easy, just going to court. The lawyer says to you, "Just say 'Yes' to this question and 'No' to this one." I went alone, and I was nervous and scared, and it was over before it even started. Because I was the first one they called and it was over.

Challenges and Changes

But that lightning-quick ending was not a good introduction to the process of change and adaptation that awaited her. She described the challenges of finding a full-time job, working late-shift hours, taking on extra jobs for extra pay to make ends meet, needing to find child care, relying on the support of her family, and establishing a routine to keep her sane, finally reaching a comfortable level of functioning and acknowledging that she was "better off without him":

Oh God. I remember just sobbing that first maybe six, seven months. Changing jobs, working so far away, having to accommodate for the kids getting to and from school was really . . . oh, I can remember just sobbing! It was like a week after he left, Kim got the chicken pox. And then a week later Terry got the chicken pox. So, thank God my mother lived just a couple miles away. She watched the kids. She even offered to make dinner every night for me when I would come and pick them up because Terry was only going to school a half day and we arranged for the bus company to have Terry and Kim dropped off at the corner near my mother's.

Since we work an eight-fifteen to four-thirty day, and the kids got out and would get home around three or three-thirty, my mother and father would hold them at the house, and I would go home, pick them up, and then feed them when I got home. At that same time I was still working at the community college doing their [college boards] testing program, so there were nights when I would pick them up, take them home, feed them, then take them back to my mother's, and my mother would come over so she could get them ready for bed, and I would go do the testing until nine o'clock, nine-thirty, and then I would come home, and then get up in the morning, and this would go on.

I would test maybe once, twice a week, and then I used to work one night here when we were open in the evening, and when I was low man on the totem pole. . . . So that was brutal; it was just brutal. My brothers and sisters were helpful too. . . . And then my sister Jane was still [in high school], and during the summer, she would come over for the whole day and baby-sit until she graduated and went to college. She even did it part-time then, and after that I had one of the neighbors, a young girl in the neighborhood, to come during the day and watch them. . . .

But it was really hard. I got into a routine . . . which I'm still in now. I would have just died if I didn't get into a routine, and at that time I was making sixteen thousand, five hundred dollars on a grant, so I had to do as many extra little things on the weekends and the evenings at the community college as I could do.

Problems with money inevitably follow the loss of a second income. In addition to that, as a teacher, even in college, Kathleen's earning power was not sufficient to support her home and raise two daughters without supplementing her income (Baca Zinn and Eitzen, 1990; Llewelyn and Osborne, 1990). The conflict between having to work multiple jobs and spending sufficient time with her daughters to feel in control of their child rearing came into focus when her brother commented, "You know, your parents are really raising your kids." As Kathleen recounted:

... at the time when I was doing the testing and I was working, I taught on the weekends for the Teacher Corps, and I did leave my kids with my mother a lot. ... And I think from that day on, I started calling my mother less, tried to do a little more on my own, hired baby-sitters more often than asking [my parents]. If I gave up going out, I'd have pizza in the house or something instead of going out with the kids. Oh, my brother, when he said that, I'll never forget that. And it *hurt!* I mean, maybe there was some truth to it, and even Michael [her male companion] said, "You know, Kathleen, your mother and father are too involved in your kids' lives." And I think they *were* overly involved, you know, looking back now. I think they started, "Well, Kathleen, maybe you should . . . do this instead of this. Maybe they shouldn't go to dance because you can't afford it."

This type of criticism is not unique to single mothers; working mothers are also accused of not raising their own children. Mother blaming is common in the research on gender roles, divorce, and working women (Baca Zinn and Eitzen, 1990; Belsky, 1986) (for critiques of such assumptions, see Blake, 1974; Coontz, 1992; Farrell, 1972; Gimenez, 1984; Kaschak, 1992; Llewelyn and Osborne, 1990).

Managing the Money

After normalizing her life, with only a little borrowing from family for emergencies, by exercising expert money management, Kathleen soon reaped the benefits of her economic good sense. Aside from an occasional contribution from Michael for food or spending money for the girls, Kathleen managed her expenses alone. She paid off her mortgage and employed the lessons in wise saving that she had learned from her parents to finance the many school expenses of her two daughters, even saving for their college education.

K: I paid off my mortgage. It'll be two years in October that I paid off my mortgage, just in time for my daughter to start college. . . . Way back, I socked some extra money we had into

the escrow, and I didn't realize it would make such a big difference because I paid it [the mortgage] up almost two years early.

WP: Michael kind of helps with the expenses, or primarily this
is your money?

K: When it came to the house it was all my money. I paid for
the house. Michael helped with the expenses as far as food and
that, and if the kids needed a couple bucks. . . . When I first got
divorced, they [her new employers] screwed my paperwork up,
and I didn't get paid for three months . . . and I did borrow
money from Michael to pay my mortgage once, and that was it
. . . . It was always . . . I knew it was the second check of the
month. I had to have the money, and luckily, I never had any
problems.

WP: How did you do that? How did you manage your money?

K: I knew almost down to the penny what I had to pay and
when it was due. . . . When I was a little kid, when I had my
first job, my mother would pick me up on payday, drive me
right to the bank, and she always said, "Keep half and bank
half." So I have a credit union account here. I have a bond taken
out of every check, so I always had money. And I used to cash
the bonds a lot, but I don't think I've cashed a bond in probably
seven or eight years. They're all growing and maturing and all.

WP: And that's toward their college education?

K: It will go toward their college education. Kim has a full
scholarship to a small private college, but it's still $5,880 for
room and board.
    . . . So in two years Terry will be starting, so who knows
what's gonna happen then? . . . Every time I get a raise, I put
that raise into the account because I figure I can live on that
money.

Some added expenses were generated from the school's unusual
and, she speculates, politically motivated practice of sponsoring
expensive field trips, such as cruises to the Bahamas and trips to
plays in New York City and Toronto. Through skillful borrowing
and money management, she was able to give her daughters the

chance to go on all scheduled trips, but she wonders how other parents fared, since the number of students on each trip was far below the numbers who were eligible to go:

> **K:** Being a single parent, and even though I have a significant other, you know, I don't ask him for help, as far as when it comes to the kids going on trips and everything. And I always felt [that] for my kids to be up there with the other ones, they had to experience the same thing. And there are a lot of field trips that are offered, and they're not only field trips that are local, like to the show [local theaters] or something; these are things in New York City, Toronto; there was a cruise to Nassau and Mexico. And all these involved a significant amount of money. Of course, when the kids get these things, "Can I go? Can I go? Can I go?" I have to really look at the resources I have, and there wasn't any time that I could not come up with the money for them. But sometimes it was very hard. I had to go to the credit union. I had to take money out, or one time I borrowed money from my mother to pay for my car, and I would say, "Do you mind if I don't pay you this week because I need the money for dance clothes or a trip, or whatever," and those were hard times—those few big trips, like the cruise [that] was over six hundred dollars— I think it was six hundred, ninety-eight dollars. The trips to Florida [were] well over two hundred dollars apiece.

> **WP:** Why did they go on these trips?

> **K:** The trips to New York were sponsored by the music department, and both of the kids are involved in music, so they offer them to the students, and when you go to the train station, you can see there's only about twenty students that go.

> **WP:** Why don't the other ones? Can't afford it?

> **K:** They can't afford it. . . . It's supposed to be a learning experience. They go to the plays; they see three or four plays, they go to the music hall, and it's supposed to be a learning thing.

> **WP:** Do they have scholarships for kids?

> **K:** Not that I know of. [So if your parents can afford it] you get to go. The cruise was Honor Society, so that would be a reward

. . . and they needed *x* number to go, and I know when Kim went, *x* number couldn't go. So what they did was open it up to the seniors, any senior that might want to go, and then if they didn't fill, they probably would have gone to the juniors, so you had to have the money. . . . You would think there would be some money . . . you know, for one [or two] students that can't afford it, or like a scholarship, or pay half.

WP: How does that all get planned? Who encourages that kind of stuff? The school board? Is it the school? The principal?

K: . . . I would say it's got to come down from the top. Because I think they want to make it look like they're competing with the bigger, better school systems in the area, and even though they're ranked way at the bottom, just like [another city].

Kathleen's concerns about footing the bill for school-sponsored events are reflective of her conviction to provide for her daughters. She believes that the expensive field trips are good educational experiences for her daughters, but she struggles to pay for them. Schools assume that such expenses are "optional" and thus do not directly discriminate against a parent who cannot afford to pay. However, as Kathleen's story suggests, when money is involved, the opportunity for all children to participate in enrichment events is hardly equal.

On the Other Side

The divorce is twelve years behind her, and in her second interview, as she described what life is like for her now, she mentioned a euphoria that comes from knowing that she has done well and that her life is happy (Coontz, 1992; Gigy, 1980; Hafner, 1986; Hoeffer, 1987; Llewelyn and Osborne, 1990; Loewenstein et al., 1981):

And I will tell you, for the last two or three years, I get this euphoric feeling. I feel good about what's going on, about my life, about my kids, and I'm so pleased that my daughter is the valedictorian and that she did so well. . . . Because I think I'm a good parent.

PROVIDING EVERY OPPORTUNITY

As Kathleen assumed her role as a single parent, she was sensitive to social disapprobation of single-parent homes and "made sure I did everything" to be certain that her daughters did well in school and had every opportunity to participate fully in school and extracurricular activities such as dance, music lessons, and sports. Her comment that she "didn't want to be a statistic" indicates the power of research to reach and shape the actions and self-esteem of single parents (Kissman and Allen, 1993; Rice and Rice, 1986; Stacey, 1990):

> I didn't want to be a statistic. I didn't want people to say, "See. She's divorced. Look at her kids. They're not doing well in school." And in working at the university and seeing how kids come underprepared for college, I just didn't want to have my kids at any disadvantage, so I probably put in more than most parents, as if there were two parents in the house.

From the added expense of dance outfits and the financing of school-sponsored trips to staying up late to help with homework, Kathleen made an "extra effort." In fact, she admitted that she became "almost obsessive about it":

> From the very beginning, I always went to every parent-teacher conference. . . . I would attend one or two things for each kid every year. I would take a day off. . . . I made sure that the teachers knew me by going to the parent-teacher conferences. I always went on a picnic or something with each of the kids every year. At night, I made sure they got their homework done. If they needed help, I'd either assist them, or if I didn't know something, I'd call a friend. . . I made sure they knew what they were doing. I made sure they had library cards. I made sure I did everything.

> You get them into school—you can see they're doing well—and you get that going. I wanted them to take an instrument or have some kind of music. I continued the dancing. Never had any help. My ex never gave me any money for dance outfits

that could run anywhere from one hundred to two hundred dollars for each of them. The lessons are twelve dollars for each of them per week, so its like twenty-four dollars a week. . . . I never pulled them out of anything. If they had a trip to go on, even though money was tight, I would borrow the money from my mother. I never wanted them not to have the opportunities, and I really think that's why they're doing so well in school. Because education isn't only what they do in the classroom.

I would say . . . that maybe I was even obsessive about it.

In all three interviews, Kathleen spoke of her desire to provide all possible opportunities for her daughters to learn and grow, so much so that it became the predominant theme of her narrative. Though it sounds as if Kathleen may have overcompensated for being a single parent, she explained that these expenses were a natural—and typical—part of raising daughters, similar to the experiences of her married friends with girls. This conscious effort to support her children's success in school was often made at her own expense:

I used to be so tired some nights I would cry. . . . I would get to the point where I would say, "I can't. I can't keep up with all of this."

I made a conscious effort. I knew I was doing it. And there were nights that I stayed up with the kids because of a test or because of a project that wasn't quite done . . . to make sure that it got done and, you know, to have some quality behind it. And in my mind I'm going, "I'm so tired! I am so tired!" And there were times Terry would say to me, "Ma, would you just ask me these questions one more time?" and I felt like saying, "No, I'm tired." But I didn't. My mind was saying, "Kathleen, go to sleep!" and my heart was saying, "I have to ask her."

Has it paid off? If school success is measured by class ranking, it surely did. Kathleen's daughter Kim recently graduated at the top of her class. Because she was valedictorian, Kim earned a full scholarship to college and brought in several other awards to help finance her education. Terry, too, is a good student, although she is quite different from her older sister. Kathleen described how she set the stage for their "good luck":

. . . anything that they have ever wanted to go on that the school has offered, they've gone. I mean, there hasn't been a time that they haven't gone on one of the trips. And they're very lucky, and I think they realize it. . . . The cruise was Honor Society, and I figured that because she has maintained her average . . . I want her to think that it's good to do well. So, she went, and she was only in ninth or tenth grade when she went. . . . And she's a valedictorian. . . . I never ever wanted them to feel . . . I mean, I paid for music lessons, voice and keyboarding, so they sang at the Festival of Lights, and maybe they didn't have the greatest voices, but they've performed in front of people . . . and I think it's so good—reading music, understanding music—and I know they love all music.

REFLECTIONS ON DIVORCE

In her third interview, Kathleen reflected on what she has learned from her divorce. She believes that women often stay in emotionally destructive relationships because of fear, enforced financial dependence, and poor self-esteem (Baca Zinn and Eitzen, 1990; Farrell, 1972; Kaschak, 1992):

It's not easy, but I think too many women are afraid to break the ties even though they're in horrendous . . . I mean, I can think of two people right now that are in marriages that are horrific, and I think the reason they stay with the people is because they are afraid. If they separate, what's going to happen with the kids? And I think they're afraid of being independent because they've been dependent so long. . . . Within a relationship . . . the person makes you dependent on the "What's going to happen if you take the kids and leave? How are you going to pay for it? I'm gonna make life miserable for you." Things like that. Because I know I have a friend who's still in a relationship . . . her husband's an alcoholic, but her kids are older now, and I really think he's just got the hold on her. She wanted to go to Al-Anon, and all kinds of things, with another friend of mine who did leave her husband, had the guts to do it, and she never went through with it. And she's allowed herself to become very heavy. Probably doesn't have a good self-image. Self-esteem is probably very low. And she just lives it. It's sad. It's really sad, and you see cases—Michael's secretary is the same way . . . she says she's afraid that if she leaves him—he doesn't work; he's a loafer—she's afraid if she leaves, he will take part of her salary.

The difficulties posed by divorce are not unique to women, however. Kathleen has had the opportunity to observe the results of a state-enforced moral code dictated by laws that make divorce more difficult, supposedly to protect the marriage contract (Weitzman, 1985). The results of the legal system's involvement in enforcing the sanctity of marriage were felt when Kathleen's partner Michael sued his wife for divorce. Because the woman did not believe in divorce, she contested his claim of "cruel and inhuman treatment." The court denied the divorce because he did not provide sufficient evidence to prove the claim. After many years of living apart, Michael sued again, and he lost again. Kathleen described the absurdity of the situation:

K: They went to their respective lawyers, had an agreement made up, and when it came to signing it, she did not sign it. She decided she'd contest the divorce . . . went to a better lawyer obviously than Michael because the first time around, he lost. They denied the divorce . . . there was no proof that there was cruel and inhuman [treatment]. . . . And the second time around, the same thing—maybe around two years later . . . and he lost again, where he thought and the lawyer thought that he had a real good shot at it.

WP: How does this happen in [this state]?

K: Because in [this state] there's only three things that you can sue for divorce, and the only other thing that Michael could sue for now is adultery. That's it, and I highly doubt that they could prove anything there, and once you sue for divorce under a particular [category], you can't go back and resue under any of the categories. If you lost suing under one thing, you can't go back.

WP: So if one partner refuses, you can't get a divorce?

K: Correct.

WP: Because *he* left *her*, and they've been apart for how many years?

K: Twelve in November. In [this state] there's no law that says if you are separated or anything for seven years, nothing like that, so if Michael wants a divorce, he has to go out of state where there is the uncontested divorces. . . . He has to establish a residence, and that was why he didn't do it now because to do it now, he would have to give up his job. . . . He's trapped. That's more or less it.

The state is not the only institution with a proprietary interest in marriages and families. Churches have stricter tradition-entrenched laws. Uneven obedience by parishioners illustrates the dichotomy between actual behavior and religious codes that propose to regulate it (Weitzman, 1985). Because Michael's wife is a devout Catholic, she contests the divorce on the grounds that it is against her religious beliefs. Kathleen discussed how she has reconciled her divorce with her own religious beliefs:

WP: So how does it feel to be a woman in your situation? Do you feel . . . you're Catholic—do you have any problems with the conflicts in values?

K: I think it's a lot easier now because there are so many Catholics that are divorced and that still participate in their religion. [And I am] very active in my religion. I go to church every Sunday. I have never felt that I shouldn't participate in my religion because of my divorce. . . . I can take communion until the point where I would marry somebody outside of the church. And even that is kind of a gray area because I've talked to people who have remarried, and they are still very active in their religion and they got married outside the church and they talked to a priest and he said, "Whatever you feel is right in your heart, do it." And there are priests who say, "You can't take communion."

WP: And it doesn't cause you any internal conflicts?

K: No, it doesn't. It doesn't at all. Not at all. And I make sure that my kids are brought up in the religion. . . . I think my parents had trouble with it. . . . They felt funny when I was going to communion and everything until I explained to them how it works. The divorce isn't what they get all upset about; it's the marriage outside the church.

Kathleen further reflected on the involvement of church *and* state in protecting marriage:

It drives me nuts to even read it in the paper how certain states are looking to try to get off the books the no-fault divorce laws because people don't have commitment to the marriage and all this crap. To stay in a marriage that's . . . I mean, I don't think anybody goes into a marriage thinking they're going to get divorced—I mean that's crazy—but to stay in a marriage where the love is dead and you can't work together, the kids suffer more that way.

MULTIPLE ROLES AND ROLE CONFLICTS

Changes in gender role socialization for women and the growing percentages of women in the workplace have been the topics of much discussion across academic disciplines (Baca Zinn and Eitzen, 1990; Coontz, 1992; Demos, 1986; Holland and Eisenhart, 1990; Stacey, 1990). Some women try to reconcile their roles as workers outside of the home with their assumption that they are also responsible for domestic duties, a vestige of the home and workplace labor division experienced by women of former generations (Coontz, 1992; Stacey, 1990). In addition to the dual roles imposed by work *in* and *outside* the home, single mothering adds an extra dimension of sole responsibility. Women such as Kathleen find that rather than rearranging their roles to accommodate an increased workload outside the home, they have simply added it onto their domestic responsibilities, juggling both in compressed time (Kissman and Allen, 1993). Referred to by many family researchers and historians as the "superwoman complex" (Baca Zinn and Eitzen, 1990; Coontz, 1992; Llewelyn and Osborne, 1990), this phenomenon resonates throughout Kathleen's descriptions of her daily life and her decisions for labor division in her household. Her daily schedule is a cycle of constant activity—getting her daughters and Michael successfully off to school and work; work at the office, with its weight of responsibilities; preparing and cleaning up after dinner; helping the girls with homework; and chauffeuring them and their friends to events and activities. This was graphically portrayed in her second interview, as she described the successful orchestration of a typical morning:

> Oh, my typical day—I get up at six o'clock, six-fifteen, wash my hair real fast, and then I go out and I make three lunches . . . Michael's and my two daughters—'cause I usually bring something in that's quick [that] I pull out of the freezer. . . . I get dressed . . . and the kids—they're older now—they make their own breakfast. . . . I have to take the dog out, and check, . . . "Do you have everything? Remember your instrument, Terry. Kim, when do you work today? Do you need the car?" That type of thing in the morning. . . . And they get off. Sometimes they forget things, they come back, and then I end up driving them to school if they miss the bus. And that happens [pauses] a lot! [She laughs.] Enough that the day doesn't start off that great. Either Michael or I will take them to school, then Michael usually comes over a little after seven o'clock. . . . He gets dressed at my house, and usually he takes off before I do, and I'm the last one. I make sure the doors are locked, the dog's downstairs. I go from there.

At work she takes the opportunity of an early morning coffee klatch to unwind a little and vent any of the aggravations of the evening or morning. Hers is a full eight-hour day, and "some days are busier than others." After a fairly long commute home, she is instantly launched into the next flurry of events:

> Oh God! The few hours between five-thirty [and] ten o'clock, it's dinner, homework, could be baseball games, it could be practice, it could be something at the school. Those hours go

so fast, and there are some days I don't know how I'm gonna get everything done in the amount of time that I have.

I asked her when she felt the strain of such a schedule most acutely:

Oh gosh, I think when . . . a day that was real hard—when I did a lot [at work] and then I'd go home and the kids would have places to go or they have an assignment that they'd need help with. I can feel my anxiety level, like I want to scream. I don't feel like I can do another thing. Those are days that are killers for me, and they happen quite often. With the two of them, and sometimes they both need help the same night, or they're . . . one's using one computer, and the other's using the other computer, and "Will you read this over, Ma? How do you spell that? I have to go here, and can I use your car?" And I don't feel like getting the dinner ready, and I'm not a late-night person. I have to be in bed by ten, ten-thirty, or I'm dead the next day, and the space between the time I get home, which is five o'clock, and ten o'clock—those five hours—sometimes they can be the most stressful part of the day.

The relationship between gender and her lack of transition from work outside to work inside of her home is evident in her descriptions of her ex-husband's, and now Michael's, after-work behavior:

K: I was thinking, "I don't have time to unwind from work." There's no cooling off when I get home, and I think men tend to deal with that. With my ex and even with Michael—they will come home, eat, remove themselves from the kitchen, watch the news or doze off, where I *never* do that. I clean the table off—the kids will help me—you know, fill the dishwasher up, wash the table down, and by that time, they [the kids] have something for me to do, or I have maybe a load of wash to throw in or something [and Michael's] out watching the news in [his] chair, or taking the dog for a walk.

WP: So you have to attend to all the details?

K: That's right! That's right. You know, not that if I didn't say, "Michael will you help me clean the table?" that he wouldn't.

It's just that, for some reason, I feel that it's my place to clean the table off and do whatever I have to do.

Kathleen expressed a strong gender role orientation in her comment that, "it's my place to clean." When asked why she felt that way, she related the influences of generational gender role socialization and cultural heritage (Coontz, 1992; Demos, 1986) and reiterated her tendency to put her children's needs before her own:

I think it's probably inbred! [She laughs.] With the kids, I would rather see them start their homework, get it over with, so I don't have to stay up or they're not up too late. Even when I iron, I noticed just recently, I iron their clothes first and my clothes last. And I guess that's the way I feel when I do the work in the kitchen and that. I would rather have them do what they have to do and let me do this, so they can get started. So it doesn't set them off.

I guess it's just the Polish [upbringing] in me! [Laughing]

Intergenerational Gender Role Differences

The transmission of gender role socialization from mother to daughter was discussed extensively in Chapter 1. It is important to remember, however, that historical, cultural, and economic forces shape the ways that persons are socialized to gender roles. When the gender-associated roles and expectations of one generation differ from those of the next, intergenerational conflicts between parents and children of the same sex are likely (Chodorow and Contratto, 1976; Dinnerstein, 1976; Levine, 1992). Kathleen's incorporation of her career self with her domestic self shows a transition away from the strict polarization of male and female roles with regard to work inside and outside of the home. Her mother, however, was a stay-at-home mother, a role enforced by her husband's desire that she be one, and by the size of her family (five children), until her youngest child entered school, at which time she took a job to help extend the family finances. A part-time secretary and library aide, Kathleen's mother's jobs were well within traditionally acceptable boundaries for women (Schur, 1984). Kathleen thinks that her mother was "spoiled" in her childhood:

My mom [and] my father always believed in the stay-home mom, until the youngest girl went into—and there's 13 years difference between my youngest sister and myself—when she went into grade school, and I was in high school and my brother was in college, my mother started to work. She was a secretary at a local university . . . and she started working for like six, seven years. She worked as a library aide. So she went to college for only a year. . . .

My mother was not an academic type. I think my mother's bright, but college? She went for a year, or maybe just a semester. I'm not really sure. . . . She's a very talented secretary, but . . . she was the youngest of three, and I think my mother probably was spoiled. And my father was the exact opposite, one of nine, and he had to milk the cows, and he *had* to do . . . and I think there was this age difference between my mother and her sister of eleven years, and my mother had everything she wanted. I see her wedding gown, and I see the wedding that she had, and I think my mother was spoiled. . . .

And my mother, she tells how she used to work downtown in one of the motels making beds. I do think my mother was rather spoiled, and even her sister referred to it. My mother could speak Polish with her mother, and I think my mother is bright, but I don't think she ever wanted to pursue any career path.

Kathleen's mother was proud of being beautiful and socially popular, all images of womanhood commonly held to be ideal in her generation, and even now (Kaschak, 1992; Schur, 1984).

I think my mother was a little socialite because just the other day she was telling Kim, "You know, I went to the prom three times." . . . I think she did do it; she was beautiful.

Kathleen described her mother's attitudes about herself, openness to communication, sex, religion, morality, maternal expectations, marriage, divorce, and child rearing:

My mother wasn't open with us at all. My mother couldn't really . . . she never talked about sex with us. She couldn't. My father told me about the facts of life, not my mother. My mother was a good mother. . . . She wasn't the greatest housekeeper or anything . . . but there were a lot of things that she wouldn't discuss. She's fairly religious. She had us in a lot of religious organizations. Even from the time we were young I can remember a group called the CFM, Christian Family Movement, and she would have the people come over to the house and that, so I think her religion kind of motivated the way she brought us up. She was strict, but she has a hard time [even] now talking about certain subjects.

. . . she knew how to make me feel bad. When Michael and I were starting to go out, she didn't have a kind word to say about anything. She really made me feel like a trollop. "How could you do these things? People are seeing you now when you go out. And he's not divorced." And they had a real hard time, both my mother and father. My father was pretty cool about it because he didn't like my ex-husband, and I think he saw Michael as a better alternative because he was educated and could do a lot and did a lot around my house. . . . But my mother, I'll never forget. Michael took us up to Canada's Wonderland. When we came home, and it was rather late, and I guess my mother was calling every half hour, but we didn't get home until after midnight. And you should hear the guilt trip she laid on me. "What are you doing? What are you showing your kids? What kind of model are you for your daughters?" And all of this stuff. Boy, she made it really difficult.

Using guilt to judge and punish her daughter for deviance from her personal ideals of motherhood and morality alienated Kathleen and made her "feel bad" (Chodorow, 1978; Dinnerstein, 1976). In fact, she did not seek her mother's advice when "things got bad" because she knew she would only say, "See? I told you so. If you did that, I told you so." But when asked how she coped with her mother's open disapproval, she said:

I stood my ground because I knew I had something better. And I must say, after the divorce, I became more independent from my parents. . . . But she knew what strings to pull and how to make me feel bad, and she still does: with my ex, "Oh, I saw

him at the concert and he looked really nice at the graduation."
And you know I don't want to hear those things. When we
were first separated, she was the one who said, "Maybe you
ought to go to counseling." Maybe that her religion [made her
disapprove of] the divorce. [She was embarassed about me,
you know]—"Kathleen's the black sheep in the family"—even
though that didn't come out; she never said anything like that.
I always felt that maybe she thought . . . because whenever
someone would ask her a question about me, she really had a
hard time responding to it. I know she did.

Although she tried not to internalize her mother's opinion of her
"failure," she compensated for it by working hard to make her mother,
especially, understand that she was not only a good worker but a good
person:

I think that's the reason why, when I got that job here, and I got
that award for advisement, I wanted them to see that I am—my
mother especially—that I work hard, I do a good job, and no
matter what happened in my personal life, *I am a good person!*

Turning into My Mother

Psychologists and sociologists maintain that gender roles are
transmitted from mother to daughter, but—a serious message to
women—it is sometimes jokingly implied that a daughter is
"doomed" to "turn into her mother" (Chodorow, 1978; Dinnerstein,
1976; Llewelyn and Osborne, 1990). Kathleen described some very
important differences:

I think that's where we differ. Because when I went to library
school and we had the courses on censorship, I censor very
little for my kids. And I talk to them. I'm constantly, "Do you
understand? Is there anything that you don't understand? Remember this. Don't do this." I think with my mother everything was negative. Sex was always such a negative thing—
"Oh! Kathleen! Ooh!" When I talk to my kids, I tell them it's a
wonderful thing, you know, and it's sharing, responding, coming together, but my mother, Oh! [She laughs.] She couldn't

talk about it. To this day, she couldn't talk about it. She has a very hard time. Other things, too. She couldn't be open, and that's why I always . . . when I had a problem, I always went to my father.

As a sort of "declaration of independence," in the second interview, Kathleen asserted, "I am not my mother." In the third interview, I asked her directly about women's fear of becoming their mothers. She responded that though she recognizes the temptation to parent the way her mother did, using the same words and lessons, she catches herself and refuses to use guilt as her mother and aunt did, to manipulate and perpetuate attachment (Dinnerstein, 1976; Kaschak, 1992):

> I can see! When I look into the mirror, I do resemble my mother, and I can hear myself saying . . . but there are times when I catch myself before I say something because there were things that my mother said to me, or to the kids, that she probably shouldn't have. I never said, "Finish your meal because there's kids in China starving." I never did anything like that, and she did. I know she did.

> I want them to understand. I don't want them to feel guilty, and I think that's one thing my mother was very good at and still is, making me feel guilty about what [I'm] doing. . . . Because maybe sometimes [parents] feel what you're doing is a reflection of them, and they really use it. I may use it too, but not to the extent my mother did, and maybe still does in some respects. As she gets older, I'm wondering how she will be because I see how my aunt was, about the guilt. [She's] totally dependent now, but when she was still functioning, everything was guilt: "You owe me."

Kathleen reflected on the tremendous political and social changes of the 1960s and 1970s and their impact on her expectations for the future:

> When I was eighteen years old, I had already graduated because I left high school a year early—but . . . my . . . I really thought that I might end up like my mother—go to college for

a year or two and find somebody and get married and have a family, which was . . . I think that that was real in my mind, that that would probably happen. But I went to an all-girls school, and I think it really helped because of the competition. And we were in the period of Vietnam and protesting, and there was no such thing as student apathy at that time; the students were so involved. And here was a school of women, protesting the war, and I mean, I did a complete three-sixty [360° turnaround] at this time in my life. I didn't think, "The only thing I want to do is sit at home and bake and cook and be my mother." I [wanted to] do something else. And that's when it really happened. I mean, I became conscious of the fact that there was a lot more out there than being a wife and a mother.

Kathleen offered her observations about the differences between gender role expectations in her mother's generation and those she, her sisters, and sisters-in-law enact. A change from her father's head-of-household management of his wife's choices and the effects of work and education on his daughters are typical of the 1960s generation (Coontz, 1992):

> **K:** We're more independent. A *lot* more independent. I think just the way society is set up today allows us to be more independent. I know my father wanted my mother to stay home and to be a mother and not to even think about working. He *wanted* that. And I can see that some men still do, but not to the extent when my mother was at home. My father would *say* that, "I want you to stay home." And she accepted that. That was her role. . . .
>
> She started working when my sister went to kindergarten because she had time during the day, and, more or less, her job was in the school system and my father worked in the school system. So he knew what the job was and it was okay because it wasn't taking any time away from the kids. Petra was in school, so there was no problem there.
>
> **WP:** And all three of you girls worked, right? Full-time?
>
> **K:** Right. Full-time. Always . . . because my parents gave us the opportunity to have an education. And once you're educated, you want to make the most of your life. I enjoy it. I know my

sisters enjoy working. My brother Charles, the oldest, his wife works, and the only one who's a stay-at-home mother is my brother Jerry's wife, but one of the factors there is Jerry is very well-off. His one income probably would be three or four of [mine], and the necessity to work isn't there. And we want nice things. We want nice homes, and everything, and the fact that the woman is working contributes to the fact that we can get by a little easier in life. The kids can have all that much more . . .

I get a lot out of it. It's self-fulfilling. It gives me a sense of worth, other than my kids saying, "Mom, I love you." And it gives me something else to do, to know that I have a purpose in life.

Our discussion of the contrasts between Kathleen's life as a worker/mother and her sister-in-law's, who chooses a more traditional domestic role, illustrates the transitional nature of this generation's women, from the Donna Reed media-hyped ideal image of womanhood (Baca Zinn and Eitzen, 1990; Coontz, 1992; Demos, 1986; Stacey, 1990) to a new ideal promoting women in the workforce (Bequaert, 1976):

K: [My sister-in-law, Jerry's wife,] Diane's goal was to be an actress. She's very talented in music. She's got an excellent voice and can sing . . . so I think she feels that she is getting what she perceives. You know, it's different than what we were trained for, and she substituted for awhile, but she didn't like it. So I don't think she's missing anything, to be honest with you. I think she's very comfortable, and she's just the type. Other women may not feel that way, but in this particular case, [Diane thinks], she has it all, and I think she's happy with her life the way it is. And she gets to use her talents, maybe not quite the way she wanted to, but she sings.

WP: Do you think she has the perfect life?

K: No . . . looking through my eyes, no. I mean, *I'd* want a little bit more, but I believe that she thinks she has the perfect life because she doesn't have to worry about money, and I know that she probably has enough money in the bank to pay for their kids' education already. I really believe they do. And I think she has the big huge house, which probably takes her the whole day to clean, and she keeps it in perfect condition, and she has a big yard, and she does the gardening, and I think a job would just be in her way. I think she likes it the way it is.

WP: Where does that come from, the big house, big yard, money, lots of clothes?

K: Probably got a lot of that from watching TV and the perfect Ozzie and Harriet syndrome. . . . [laughs] I don't think that ever was or will be [laughs]. No! No! That was just too, dressed all the time, the mother having every hair in perfect place and always having a dress and an apron on, and that probably was the ideal when my mother was young; that's how everybody wanted to be, like Donna Reed. Never showed a woman cleaning the oven out or washing the floor [laughs], but that was the perfect world. I never, never could be like that.

When asked to reflect on the image of womanhood promoted in her generation, Kathleen answered that women are perceived as stronger. She attributed this to the impact of growing numbers of women in the workforce and the importance of a chain reaction effect, whereby these women promote other women, in other words, female mentorship:

I think we're getting to the point where women are perceived as a little bit stronger than they were fifteen, twenty years ago. I think, even when I got married, there was a different perception than there is now . . . and the change has become a little more rapid at this point in time because there are more women in the workforce promoting women. It took awhile to do that because there weren't any women to do something about it, and the women that did get into positions were strong women—the women I knew—and they brought women in, they promoted them, and I think that was good. And I would never be where I am right now if it weren't *for* a woman—she was the mover and the shaker for me. . . . She wanted me because I was a good worker—she could see that—and [that job led into this job]. And my first boss here was a woman who—well, I don't know if she promoted us as much as she could, but it helped, and I can see it now. I can see women in positions where they can do something about it, and that's good.

As a mother of teenage daughters, Kathleen sees even more changes for women of the next generation. She explained that schools are no longer complicit in enforcing the strict gender-associated roles for which they prepared young women of her generation:

> **K:** I think with my girls . . . they don't . . . there was never any, "Well, should I go to college?" They are just *expecting* to go. They don't see any other path. They want to go to college. They have more concrete ideas of what they wanna be. There may be something they will never be, but they think about what they wanna be, even Terry at sixteen. She's talked about becoming a marine biologist. She's talked about becoming an FBI agent [laughs]. I mean, she goes through [stages], but she really knows that she needs—whatever she wants to be—to go to college. And they're pretty strong. [Kim wants to be] something in medicine.
>
> **WP:** Have they ever talked about wanting to be wives and mothers?
>
> **K:** Never. Never. They always talk about career. I mean, they talk about men and all that stuff. If I say to them, "Just think, a couple of years from now, when Kim graduates, we could be talking about Kim getting married." And they both look at me like, "I don't think so!" [She laughs.] They really don't. And they have not had boyfriends per se. They've had friends that were boys, and they've done things, but they have not had any serious relationships at all, and that's something that probably would prevent them from thinking about marriage and kids, but no, they never think about it. . . .
>
> In my age group, and within my peers and as I look around, I see most families that have young women, young girls, that they're going in the same direction. I don't see them . . . we don't prepare our kids to be homemakers anymore. And I think

it was a conscious effort at times to do that. You even see [this trend in] the curriculum—we don't take Home Ec anymore, it's Careers; we talk about careers, and my daughters can't sew worth a darn, yet I could use a machine in seventh grade and in high school I took Home Ec as an elective. . . . They know how to do simple things, but there's no effort to prepare them, and I think we were, in high school and in junior high school, pre- pared for home, to be a housewife; we were taught about things and "This is how you want to make your husband happy!" [She laughs.] That type of thing. It was very much a part of our education, our schooling. I don't see that anymore. . . . Most of the girls are a lot like my girls; they don't want to spend time in the kitchen, or whatever we did.

A Working Mother

Kathleen currently has a comfortable concept of herself as a worker and a mother, but the two roles have not always meshed. She described the process of breaking away from the image of motherhood modeled by her mother, the respect for and tradition of work she gained from her father, the economic necessity that drove her back to the workplace, the way that divorce ended the "perfect solution" of working part-time to leave enough time for mothering, and the support she gained from other female co-workers who successfully dealt with the same stressors:

I think, early on, probably after the divorce, I felt—because I came from a home where my mother was home all the time with the kids, and that's the way it should be was still in- grained in my mind—and I felt bad. I thought working part- time when I worked at the community college was a perfect solution to being a mother and out in the workforce because at age sixteen my father drove me to work . . . the day after my sixteenth birthday, and I enjoyed the working, and after I had the kids, I thought maybe it would be great to have to be a mother at home and stay home, but I don't think I could do it after always working. So I enjoyed working part-time while I was married, teach a course or two. It was really nice. And . . . my husband wasn't making that much money. He was a plant worker, and we'd just gotten the house and the two kids, [and] we needed a supplemental income. . . . But then when I had to work full-time . . . I felt guilty being away because they were still little, I mean, six and four. Terry was not in school yet, so I had to make accommodations, and they went to a Montessori school, day care, and I think the kids learned an awful lot from that. That was a very good experience for them. But after the kids were going to school and I was spending less time [at work], or [it seemed] I was home more with them [in the evening] because they were gone all day and the few hours that even Michael watched them or my parents had them until I could pick them up, it wasn't bad. I felt a lot better. They were in school. I knew where they were. I was working, and their day and my day pretty much coincides, so they saw me in the morning, they went to school, and they were with me in the evening. And I felt a lot better about it as they got older and they were in school for the full day, but early on in, boy, there was a lot of conflicts—quality time versus the quantity of time you spend with them, and everybody's, "Kathleen, it'll work out. It'll work out." And again, like I said, [my girlfriend] Joy . . . had two sons and she had to work, and she used to talk about quality time and . . . it all worked out, and I felt *better* about it. I had a lot of guilt at the beginning when I was leaving them so much. I hated that. And they would say, "Mom, we didn't see you all day." And it hurt!

It is interesting to note that her guilt about leaving her children in day care was offset by her recognition that they "learned an awful lot from that" (Coontz, 1992; Kagan, 1984; Rutter, 1977).

Kathleen even went so far as to say that her children had an advantage over others who did not have the preschool experiences her daughters had:

[If my daughters stayed home,] they wouldn't have had the experiences in the day care centers and the Montessori school, where they were with kids their own age and they learned. I think when they went to kindergarten—they could have skipped kindergarten and gone into first grade because they learned a lot. They could *do* things—[and] some of the kids . . . didn't have that—and they enjoyed it. *They* enjoyed it.

A Question of Time

Time was a theme that appeared in a number of different contexts: compressed time in the morning, time to do homework, time to unwind at work but not at home, time off for school events and doctors' appointments, time for her relationship with Michael, and, finally, time for herself. In the previous discussion, Kathleen introduced the working mother's nightmare—not spending enough time with the children. The argument that women should stay home with their young children rather than leaving them with strangers was advanced in literature critical of working women (Belsky, 1986). Other researchers, however, have established contradictory evidence to support the assertion that the effects on children of mothers who work have been greatly overstated (Milne et al., 1986; Mischel and Fuhr, 1988). An appreciation for the need to use quality of time (in popular parlance, "quality time") to offset the necessary loss of quantity of time seems to have entered the modern parent's ethos (Lamb, 1976).

Lack of time spent with children because of work responsibilities has been a particular criticism of single parents, almost exclusively single mothers. Because the single mother experiences a halving of her income from divorce, has less earning power as a female, and must often work more hours or more than one job just to make ends meet, analysts claim that she experiences loss of time more acutely than two-parent families (Baca Zinn and Eitzen, 1990; Hetherington, Cox, and Cox, 1977; Wallerstein and Blakeslee, 1989; Wallerstein and Kelly, 1974, 1976).

In the earlier discussion of changes following her divorce, Kathleen described her difficulties with working extra jobs and her parents' overparticipation in child rearing because of her work. Later, however, as her income increased and she didn't have to work as often, her daughters' schooling kept them busier, and their schedules finally harmonized nicely. Kathleen's description of her evening activities, her intense involvement in the school and in her daughters' studies and extracurricular activities, her desire to spend weekends and travel *with* her children, and her ability to manage a social life and time for herself would seem to point to a successful manipulation of compressed time without inordinate losses for her children (Kurdek and Siesky, 1980):

> **K:** I think they know that I spend a lot of time with them—and I gave up doing things on the weekends . . . and I like to do things *with* them, take them to the show with me. I always try to involve them. We go out to dinner on Friday night. They look forward to it.
>
> **WP:** So you and Michael involved them in your social life?
>
> **K:** Oh, yes, definitely, but there are times, now that they're older, they don't want to be with us, or we don't want [to be with] them. *We* want to go [to] the show and be alone or to have dinner . . . alone. And that feels good.

Kathleen's comments show that time problems are not the exclusive domain of single parents, and that the *attitude* of the parent, rather than his or her marital status, affects a desire to spend time with the children:

> **K:** And I look at the way some of the other kids are treated and are not treated at all, and the girl that was one of Kim's best friends would spend days with us, and her mother would never call to check on her or anything.
>
> **WP:** Does she come from a single-parent home?
>
> **K:** No. But it is a single-parent home now, for maybe three years, but her parents were together up until maybe three, four years ago. And I don't know what was going on in that house. Both parents did work, but her mother—in the morning the kid would come over to our house and leave in the evening. . . .

Helping with Homework

Actions of social workers and family therapists indicate a tacit acceptance of the assumption that the single mother does not have enough time to spend on such things as helping children with homework, and this somehow explains why her children do less well in school than children from two-parent homes, at least according to certain research studies (Baca Zinn and Eitzen, 1990; Kissman, 1991). In this, Kathleen is certainly a disconfirming case. Her description of homework time with her daughters supports her continual assertions that she "wants them to do well" in school. Regardless of her fatigue and the number of activities she must cram into the five hours between arriving home and bedtime, Kathleen's daughters are her first priority:

> **K:** Homework. My kids are pretty independent, but Terry, more so than Kim, likes me to quiz her, to go over terms, to read the definitions; she tells me a term or I read what the term is. She took Biology last year—a lot of terms, a lot of definitions—so I would go through the notebook [and] the highlighted areas in the book. She seems to learn better when she can . . . she can't read it and get it; she needs to have another [oral] alternative.
>
> **WP:** What do you do with Kim?
>
> **K:** Very little now. Just encouragement. If she has a paper to do, she'll go down on the computer, write it, and then ask me to read it, edit it if it needs it, and sometimes that takes a long time, sometimes it doesn't. But between the two of them, some nights . . . both computers are going. . . . I want them to do well. I want them to get a good grade. If I can make a suggestion to them where the teacher won't take off because of a big faux pas, as far as an incomplete sentence or something like that, then why not help them?

Her story about the "cat project" launched a meaningful discussion of the lack of understanding or regard that schools exhibit concerning how much family time is taken up with homework:

> Oh, the cat story! My daughter's taking advanced placement Biology, and one-third of her grade will be determined by how well she does on a cat skeleton. The cat project, I think, started a couple of months ago [when] they had to dissect a cat. . . . They were tested on each phase of the cat. The final project involving the cat was to get down to the bare bones, the skeletal system. . . . They have to lacquer it and everything. And she has

spent—I was bound and determined I would not help her with this one. I said to her, Michael said to her, "This is ridiculous. You have your grade. You're number one in your class. Don't even bother doing it." But she wanted to do it. And she spent probably from Friday until Sunday this past week, over twenty hours, until midnight. . . . She worked an eight and a half hour shift on Saturday and then came home at nine o'clock and was out until after midnight working on the cat bones, cutting, boiling, putting them in Clorox. Ridiculous. So then, Sunday—it's due Tuesday—Sunday, Michael and I went out and helped her. There's no way she's gonna get it done without our help. It was Father's Day. We came home from a nice dinner at [a restaurant] and we sat outside, whittling away at the bones. We were out there till at least nine o'clock, nine-fifteen, so figure at least another three hours, three people were working on it for about three hours last night, and it's still not to the point where it looks like a nice clean skeletal system.

The "cat story" illustrates how schools expect parents to help with difficult—sometimes almost impossible—assignments. This may promote inequality along class, rather than family structure, divisions. Regardless of the intent, the importance of state exams tempts parents to "help" children do projects they cannot easily complete alone. Rather than encouraging students to be independently "resourceful," they allow parents to help their children do well, leaving those with fewer resources at a disadvantage:

WP: You do a lot of work with your daughters when they have projects.

K: A lot of work because there's no way they can complete them without help. There are things that are dangerous that they have to do, maybe involving electricity, where you don't want them to be fooling around. Michael helped wire lightbulbs for a project Kim was doing with light, and there's no way a fifteen, sixteen-year-old is going to wire light.

WP: Why do you think the school assumes so much about what the kids can do at home? Why do they give them those kinds of projects?

K: Number one, I think they think that these projects are wonderful things, that they learn a lot from them. Knowing the kids that were in the top of my daughter's class—the top five have parents that are teachers. And I think they give them the projects because they know . . . that . . . their parents will help. I think they assume a lot, and they assume they will get back a product from these kids, and I think that deep down inside they know that [the students are] getting help from their parents. Part of the new Regents Exam in Earth Science . . . is a project, fifteen points, and they gave them a list of things to do. There was nothing on that list that we saw that a kid could do without some kind of help. Terry did a solar reflector, and it had to be painted, and it had to have water going through it, so Michael had to bend tubes around and attach the tubes to metal, and that was her project, and the water had to go through the tubes, and there was a list of ten, twelve things, and there was nothing on that list [for] kids to do on their own. The kids have to be resourceful. There are very few kids that end up in the top of their class that don't have parents right behind them, and that's why some kids that may have ability that don't have parents on their tails . . . don't do well. They don't have the opportunities to do well. And I think the schools do it to them a lot.

Being a Good Parent: "The Ultimate Ma"

The treatment of single parents in much of the literature more often than not focuses on their "singleness," rather than their parenting (Bequaert, 1976; Llewelyn and Osborne, 1990). Although all participants freely provided information on their parenting philosophies and practices, I posed the direct question, "What is a good parent?" Kathleen's answer resonates with examples of her convictions. She listed support, affection, setting limits, and encouraging independence and gave many examples of the ways that she embodies these qualities. Though it is certainly a temptation for her to be overprotective, as she perceives that her parents were, she maintains a safe distance, attends to their needs, helps them when they seek her support, and covertly supervises their behavior.

WP: What is a good parent? What constitutes being a good parent?

K: Supporting your kids. I mean really *being there* for them. You know, when they need the hug, giving them the hug. You have to know when to draw the lines, too . . . and you have to know kind of when to cut the cord, too. Let them do on their own. I think my mother and father had a hard time with that, and I'm trying to be better, even though I know I'm probably not.

WP: What makes you say that?

K: Because I worry like you wouldn't believe when my daughter has the car, goes out with her friends, late, now that she's eighteen. I want to say the same things my parents did, "Be in by eleven. Don't drive anybody." All that stuff . . . but I don't. I try to be fair and . . . they sit on the porch and talk and things, the girls at night. But, you know, I kind of look out and make sure they're not foolin' around.

Kathleen's discussion about driving her daughters' friends illustrates how different family arrangements and circumstances within one-parents, two-parent, or even grandparent guardian homes result in different interactions with the children. As a single parent, she is more active in the lives of her daughters and their friends than other single mothers or two-parent homes. This, she noted, results from many circumstantial factors. Unlike the picture of the beleaguered, time-starved, at-risk parent painted by social science research (Hetherington, Cox, and Cox, 1977), Kathleen sees herself as *fortunate:* "I have that much more." In fact, she was paid the ultimate compliment by one of her daughter's friends, who calls her "the ultimate Ma".

I do a lot of driving [for my daughters and their friends]. A couple of them are from single-parent homes where the mother works maybe one or two jobs. Kim has two friends, and one mother has a job at a department store and someplace else, and her friend lives between parents—sometimes she's with her father and sometimes she's with her mother—and they feel more comfortable having me pick them up, than having their parents drive them, or in the one case, her mother works such strange hours that [she cannot do it]. . . . And I don't mind. Class Day [a day of senior parades and celebrations] I was up at four a.m. I picked them up from their homes, and they don't live close; they live downtown. I picked them up and brought them back to my house so they could have the car and experience Class Day with a decorated car and everything. Diana calls me "Ma" because I don't think she ever got whatever from her mother. I know that she's kind of estranged from her mother, even though she does go over there, and she tells me every time she does go over there she ends up fighting with her mother. And Kim says that Diana says I'm the "ultimate Ma," which makes me feel good; I don't know what I've done other than pick her up a few times and let her stay overnight and things like that, but, you know, the kids are good and Terry has a couple of friends, too, and one of her friends lives with [her] grandparents. She's African American, and her mother lives in a bad section, so she lives with her grandparents in a nicer part of the city, and I do the same, drive them, take them to baseball practice, volleyball practice, and I know they can't reciprocate, or if they do, it can't be as often. . . . I figured I have that much more. I have a nice car, I have not always time, but I make the time, and my kids enjoy their company, so they're getting something out of it, too.

Considering the variations in homes she described, I asked her, "What makes a home that works and a home that doesn't?" Given that one major problem often cited for single-parent homes is lack of time for one parent to do all that is needed to successfully raise children, her answer is surprising:

Commitment to it. Time. Putting time into it. I mean, having children is not an easy proposition, and if you don't spend time with the kids, if you don't talk—and again, it doesn't have to be hours and hours and hours. Your children have to know that you love and care for them and you're there for them whenever they need it. And you work with them. You let them know, "This is wrong. This is right." And it takes a lot of hard work.

She added that to be a successful parent, "you really have to want to be one." She described the emotional trauma of once being told that she would be unable to have children:

> You were talking about being a successful parent. I think, for one thing, you really have to want to be one. . . . I went through a time when I thought I wouldn't be able to have kids, which was like the lowest part of my life. I wasn't getting pregnant, and my ex went for fertility tests, and he was told that there would be [a] one-in-a-million chance that I would ever get pregnant. That really, *really* bothered me. And we went to Catholic Charities about adopting a baby, and they told us [that] people that started five years ago are still waiting, and it look[ed] like the situation was really not a good one, and I'm glad we didn't have to pursue it any farther because I did get pregnant. But there was a period of time from November through the following April when I thought I wouldn't be able to have kids. And it was terrifying because I can remember sitting in the counselor's office at Catholic Charities just crying . . .

Feminists are critical of the societal influences that encourage women to base their self-concepts on biological functions such as motherhood. Women can experience grave depression from infertility, and single women are especially vulnerable to unfulfilled "baby hunger," which sometimes pervades their consciousness to the point of obsession and even mental illness (Blake, 1974; Gimenez, 1984; Kaschak, 1992; Llewelyn and Osborne, 1990). Kathleen explained why it was so important for her to become a mother:

> There were five in my family, and I enjoyed my brothers and sisters, and I really . . . I really enjoy kids. . . . If the situation was such that I could've, I would have had more. And I get a lot out of my kids. I mean, my kids make me happy—they make me sad [too]—but I get a lot out of them. They make me a stronger person.

She explained the difference between getting a lot out of her children and living through them:

> I let my children experience their own experiences, and I'm happy for them when it happens, but I don't live for it. I don't demand them to take dance because *I* always wanted to take dance. If they said, "Oh, I don't want to take it anymore" that would be fine with me. But, I want them to be happy. I want to *share* in their happiness. I don't want them to think that I am living *through* them to be happy myself. That's not what it's all about.

TEACHING VALUES

The Murphy Brown incident thrust single mothers into the spotlight and spearheaded the "family values" debate of the unsuccessful Bush/Quayle political campaign (Carlson, 1992). Despite the American voters' rejection of this moralist platform, the issue of family values continues to play a major role in politics. As long as single parenting is considered outside the norm of the two-parent family, single mothers are particularly vulnerable to criticism that theirs are somehow the wrong kind of family values (Rice, 1994). Kathleen disagrees. Relieved when her ex-husband—whose moral character was questionable—was out of the picture, she saw herself as the one who transmitted the values and realized that her children only need the one stabilizing force to move in the right direction:

> I was able to deal a lot better with my children the way I wanted to, and they got the values from me. We talked about religion—I think a religion is an important part no matter what the religion is—and I gave my kids values. And the family values that the Republicans talk about . . . one parent can instill in their children values. They don't need the two parents to do that. . . . I see a lot of single parents who bring up their children to be outstanding kids, people. And it doesn't take two. And in families where there are problems, it's usually . . . you only need the one stabilizing force to move the children in the right direction.

LEARNING ABOUT NEW RELATIONSHIPS: HER SIGNIFICANT OTHER

Kathleen's story would not be complete without considering the effect on her and her family's lives of the male companion who has shared the past twelve years with them. Michael is older than Kathleen and has two grown children of his own. His unusual marital situation was described previously. Kathleen explained how his presence in her life helped her to improve her self-image, taught her about equal participation in a marriage, and gave her a unique opportunity to conceive of herself as both a wife, since theirs is a monogamous relationship, and a girlfriend, since they do not fully cohabit. She described the stresses of his introduction into her already existing family and the ways that he, she, and her daughters negotiate their roles:

K: As Michael became more of a part of my life, where he came over more, he would help me in some respects, as far as watching the kids at night and that, but that didn't happen for a good year and a half because of his situation with his divorce and my divorce. So, I mean, he kept where he was. I kept where I was, and we weren't always together. But then, when he lost, and he said, "Fuck this. We're going to be seen together." And then we started a real relationship from that point on.

The younger one, Terry, [had] no problem at all, very much listened to him, enjoyed him, and he enjoyed her, and still does. Kim was belligerent. . . . Oh, yes, she used to get so mad at him, like he would say, "Why don't you pick up!" [and she would reply] "You're not my father! I'm gonna tell my grandmother you're here!" She knew the right things to say. I mean, she was only seven years old, and she just knew what would get him and what would get me. . . .

I used to talk to her and say, "Michael loves you and he disciplines you for your own good." . . . I think things are so much better now, but I never felt like they ever really bonded. There was always an adversarial relationship. They were always [competing] for my attention, I think, too. And Kim would resent the fact. She would say to me, like if we went out, "Well I haven't seen you for three or four hours, Ma.

You're always with him." But Terry, I think she sees him as her father. . . . I think she realizes more what he has done for her than does Kim. Kim just can't see it. She *knows* it, but she still has that place in her heart for her own real father.

Reorganizing her family meant making adjustments that sometimes put her in the middle, a phenomenon not unknown in blended families (Stacey, 1990).

And there were some days it was very hard. I would sit down and I would argue with Michael. "You gotta understand. She's a child. She doesn't realize." But he would say, "She *does* realize."

WP: Did it cause stress between the two of you?

K: Oh, boy! [She laughs.] You know, you read the books, and the biggest thing in a second marriage or a second relationship [is that] usually problems develop because of the children. And that's for damn sure. . . . There were times . . . when I felt he was putting too much pressure on her. And then there were times when I thought, "Kim, can't you see what he is doing for you and how he bends over backwards?" And sometimes he was maybe too accommodating. That was a hard situation. I still think sometimes it's hard. But . . . now she drives around in his truck, she [accepts] things [from him], she sees him, and she knows . . . [she] was talking to a friend, and she said, "My parents went out to the field day." So she sees it, but I think she feels like she's disloyal to her father, even now after twelve years. Where Terry never, never had that problem.

Kathleen and Michael, however, take good care of each other. She affirmed that their relationship is founded on mutual respect. Unlike in her former marriage, in which issues such as the amount of closet space she was allowed and the amount of money she could spend were battlegrounds to establish her husband's domination over his wife and his living space, Michael's first inclination was to do too much, as she put it, "to pamper me." As the relationship matured, however, they fell into a "comfortable" division of labor that still followed somewhat along traditional gender lines, but one that both partners feel is equitable:

K: I enjoy Michael, too. Michael pampers me. Michael made me see myself different. . . . He does. He takes good care of me—I take good care of *him* though. . . . I'm independent, I will tell him if I think he's doing something wrong, and I can get mad at him, but I think we've learned a lot from each other. And I know that [in] his marriage . . . he used to do so much for her, and I think when he came into my life, he wanted to do so much for me.

He did a lot, and then as I was home more and as we were more comfortable with our relationship, it just evened itself out. I take care of pretty much the house, and he takes care of around the house and anything that should happen to go wrong . . . he's really good with that. . . .

It works very well. He cooks a lot, more since he's home early. Dinner will be ready when I get home. . . . So I think he did a lot of that, where the reverse was true in my situation. I did everything. . . . I think Michael did almost everything for his wife.

WP: So for each other you have that respect?

K: I would say, "Yes."

Kathleen reflected on the unusual nature of their noncohabiting, but marriagelike relationship. Because of her moral reservations and her desire to protect her daughters from confronting a situation that conflicts with their Catholic upbringing, Kathleen and Michael maintain separate residences. Sometimes this marriage without a contract is difficult for her, but sometimes she thinks it is ideal:

K: I can live with it sometimes, and sometimes it really bothers me. Because . . . when I'm happy, I'm really happy and the situation is fine, but when somebody talks about marriage or when his kids get involved with his life in certain ways, and I feel that he's taking time from me, I mean, I get jealous. I wish [at] different times that we were legally married, that we had the time together, and there are nights when I hear noises or something, and I get scared. It would be nice to have a man in the house just to have a man in the house.

WP: He doesn't stay overnight?

K: Never . . . I think because of the girls. Morality, there. And I think at the beginning he really wanted to live together more than he even does now. Because somehow maybe that's part of the good of the relationship, that we have someplace like neutral corners.

I think it has kept the relationship good. Maybe if we did get married at the beginning, we'd be going through another divorce now—I don't know! I don't know, but I think we're good friends as well as lovers, but we have a good relationship. We work together well, and . . . he gives me a lot of space. He really does.

Negotiating a maze of extended family relationships and the legal implications of a common-law situation in which the previous marriage has not been legally dissolved can be a challenge (Weitzman, 1985):

It scares me, I guess, that if something should happen to him, where is my place in all of it? And I explained that to him. I said, "If your family was one hundred percent behind me, there wouldn't be a problem." But they waver day to day, minute to minute, and they are still very friendly with [his ex-wife]. I mean, what would happen there? "I know you have a will, but I'm gonna tell you, she's gonna contest that will no matter what because most of the stuff goes to me." . . . I know what she's gonna say, "Well, I'm still his wife. I'm entitled to . . . " She would. I mean, I can see it being a big problem.

Legal implications and family problems aside, I asked Kathleen if this unique situation gave her a chance to think about the differences between being a wife and a girlfriend. In her situation, she sees herself moving between both roles. Her descriptions of the activities and feelings she ascribes to each role reveal interesting definitions and prescriptions for both women's and men's actions and interrelationships inside and outside of marriage. When asked whether she felt more like a wife or a girlfriend, she replied:

K: It depends on the day. It really does. Sometimes, you know, I am the wife. Sometimes I am the girlfriend.

WP: Which do you like best?

K: Oh, boy! [Long pause] I like the wife part. Yeah, because I think when you're a girlfriend, you're still trying to impress. When you're a wife, you're taken as you are; I mean, you don't have to put on airs. You can put [on] your old Saturday clothes, your ripped underwear [laughs], and not feel so . . . when you're a girlfriend you're still trying to impress.

WP: What are the times when you feel like a wife versus the times you feel like a girlfriend?

K: I think in times of stress. When he's under stress, when I'm under stress, and we are able to talk about it. That's when I feel husband and wife. . . . I feel like a girlfriend sometimes when we go out and we're having a good time; that's the girlfriend time—the courtship part. But, when you're at home and something goes wrong and you have to deal with it and you need the support of somebody, going both ways, that's when it's a marriage. And I've been through some hard times and so has he. And, you know, when you need that hug, not even the kiss, just the hug, the closeness, that's when it's good.

The importance of keeping the courtship alive was reaffirmed in her third interview when we talked again about Michael's unusual nonmarriage/nondivorce:

K: I coped with it. Some days better than others. . . . Maybe because the situation is not a bad situation. Maybe, as I said, if we got married, we would be on our second divorces. I don't know. But we have a good time.

WP: It's like it keeps the courtship up.

K: Yeah. That little spark that you have that you're doing something that you shouldn't be doing is still there sometimes, even though it's twelve years later. But . . . it's a good relationship, and he's good to me and the kids, and Kim wouldn't be valedictorian if she didn't have the support, and I know she would never have gotten the support from her father.

She contrasted her satisfying and ego-supportive relationship with Michael to her destructive relationship with her ex-husband:

My ex didn't support. He didn't encourage. Michael encourages me doing my work. He's willing to help me with my work and, you know, "Kathleen, you can do it. You can do it!" I never got that from my ex. He would rather put me down than . . . you know, maybe because I was more educated than him—I don't know—and he had to make himself feel better than thou.

She also contrasted the two men as fathers:

I think Michael could have . . . if he had the custody, he would have been a good father and worker . . . because . . . he's got a lot of energy, a commitment. He loves his kids. I think, he would not put anything above his children. Where the ex, the least little thing that might be for pleasure for him, he would go for it.

CONCLUSION

As she herself has judged, Kathleen is a good parent. Her description of her involvement with her girls throughout their schooling and their immense successes would seem to contradict some pervasive images of the single mother as so self-involved and time constrained that she cannot function effectively. Her successful parenting, however, has its costs, tricky financial footwork, a sometimes frenetic pace, and emotional strain among them. Such is the cost of parenting itself, which she described as a commitment involving time and focus on the children. Kathleen devotes the same concentration to her family as she does to her job, though her multiplicity of roles often competes for thinning resources of time, money, and personal stamina. She has her "up days," when she exalts in "that euphoric feeling" of well-being, but she has her "down days," too, when responsibilities at home and at work drive her to cry from exhaustion.

As a single mother of two daughters, Kathleen can see the changes in gender role socialization that have progressed from her mother's acceptance of her "place" at home with her children, through her own life decisions shaped by historical events and divorce, to her daughters' focus on careers rather than marriage.

Her male companion, Michael, is indeed a helpmate, very different from the man she once called her husband. Absurd contradictions of social, moral, and political laws concerning marriage and divorce have had a significant impact on their lives, but they have forged, as Judith Stacey (1990) states, a "brave new family," founded on mutually productive kinship, bonded by trust, love, and support, rather than contractual promises.

Chapter 4

Shawna:
"Stand Your Ground"

Shawna's square of the quilt tells the story of her struggles to stand up for her beliefs and to hold her ground against forces trying to control her destiny, to send her in directions she does not choose to go. Shawna mused about passing on her own mother's strong spirit to her young daughter, Tasha, similar to the passing of a story quilt across generations. Shawna is a young woman in her late twenties, but her observations on life and her determination to find her way through the maze of family patterns that shaped the lives of the men and women around her display wisdom beyond her years.

Shawna has seen life as a single mother from three different perspectives: first, as the youngest child in a family of six headed by her divorced mother; then, as a single mother herself who chose not to marry the father of her child; and, finally, as the surrogate mother to her teenage sister's troubled daughter. She offered her observations about parenting from all of these experiences, and it is clear how much she has learned about herself, her mother, and the dynamics of family life in many forms.

A strong value system that includes the desire to help and nurture others and the discipline of athletics, which taught her "you have to be in it to win it," drives her to make a quality life for herself and her daughter.

POWER AND CONTROL:
A QUESTION OF PROPERTY

In the first interview, Shawna related the events that led to her single-parent status. She explained how she had dated a man eleven years older than she, who had been divorced once and had a son from his previous marriage. She hinted at the differences in gender expectations for black men versus black women when she commented, "I always dated guys older than me because I could never find any my age that was mature, which is always a phenomenon for black females." This is probably more of a gender-associated phenomenon than a racial one (Dinnerstein, 1976), but from Shawna's experiences with the men in her life—father, brothers, companions—it becomes apparent that irresponsibility, lack of respect for themselves and women, and relationships maintained by power and control are common characteristics that she must negotiate to assert her identity and to fulfill her needs.

Shawna became pregnant a year after starting to date William, her companion. Although they agreed to live together, Shawna did not want to get married. Once proudly independent, working and involved in the community, Shawna began to see William tighten his control after she was laid off from her job and she became economically dependent on him, and once again after their daughter, Tasha, was born. She likened his domination over her to "slave days":

Well, to begin with, when I was seven months pregnant, I was laid off from my job. . . . When I got laid off, and I wasn't working for like seven months, that's when the problems really occurred. That's when I realized that my daughter's father was really a very possessive individual, and he liked the fact of me not working because that gave him more control . . . he was providing everything, and so I had to be dependent upon him.

. . . I was his woman, and so it was almost like slave days. I had to tell him things that I was going to do. He always had to know where I was. He had to have say in the type of clothes that I wore. I couldn't cut my hair because he loves his daughter's mother to have long hair. If I wore certain things, I'd be questioned about why I was wearing it, and if I had guy friends, that was like a no-no. But prior to that time, I could do all those things—have guy friends, cut my hair, wear anything that I wanted—but it was the fact that I was not working, that I had a child by him, that made him have all this control over me.

So, and in 1993 . . . I decided it was time to go back to work because my daughter was seven months at the time . . . and I was employed at the college . . . which really made for a very uncomfortable environment because I retained some of my freedom and some of my independence because I didn't have any for almost a whole year. When things started working out at the college, he proposed to me . . . but I didn't want to get married because I didn't want him to feel that it was just . . . the right thing to do because we had a child together. It would have been different if it had happened prior to the time I found out that I was pregnant.

So in 1993 we got engaged. . . . I think the reason why he proposed to me . . . was that controlling thing again. You propose, you get married, and then you have that control all over again, for life. So we got engaged, and a couple of months after that, it was that whole controlling thing again, because it stopped for a period of time where he gave me my freedom because I was working. I didn't have to be with him twenty-four hours a day.

Shawna saw William's possessiveness as grounded in his economic control over her, and in her new bond to him as the mother of *his* child:

But, as soon as I found I was pregnant, that's when I saw everything—little by little, though. It didn't happen in the first two trimesters. It was like that third trimester when I was unemployed . . . and I guess that he figured, well, hey, he's providing everything . . . if he wants to come home and holler and raise hell, he can. He's taking care of me and his child, you know, so someone must listen to him bitch and moan.

His regarding her as a possession was evident when she described his attempts to control her by making her happy and to "buy her" with expensive gifts after a fight. She resisted such control and told him so, but he persisted with this behavior:

"I'm gonna do this because it's gonna make you happy, but at the same time I want to control you, but I'm not gonna let you know that I'm doing all this." Because whenever we had a fight, I always got these really expensive gifts. So whenever he did something wrong, I would always get a whole bouquet of flowers. I hate flowers! And a gift! And I would tell him, "You cannot buy me. When you do something wrong to me, you don't have to apologize to me by buying me a gift. Because it doesn't mean anything to me. When you do something and you apologize, don't do the same thing over again." And that's what happened. He kept making the same mistakes over and over again, and he thought that he could buy my love, and you can't buy no one's love.

Although aware that William was using economic necessity and her own motherhood to keep her confined, to her surprise, she surrendered her autonomy, passively falling into patterns that made her feel she had lost herself (Dinnerstein, 1976; Weitzman, 1985):

And because I'm a strong-minded individual, I got to the point where I felt as if my identity was being taken away from me. And I did *lose* it. I will tell you, I lost it for awhile. I lost my own identity. I lost who I was. Because you lose that being in a relationship, but you don't have to lose that totally, and I found out that I lost it totally. I was just very passive. If things weren't right, I wouldn't stand up and say, "Well, no, that's wrong."

Before her relationship with William, she was active in the community and willing to stand up for what she thought was right. Jealously guarding their time together and using the baby as a reason for keeping her at home, William compensated for his own insecurity about himself and her love by draining her of all her energy. She became submissive:

I always enjoyed working with kids and doing a lot of work in the community, but once Tasha was born, I had to cut back on some of my extracurricular activities and then eventually give it all up. But that wasn't my doing. That was his doing. Because it was like, "Well, we don't have any time." He would say to me, "You don't have any time for me because you're too busy." So I figured if I give up this, then we get some more time, but then the thing that I found out [was] that it didn't matter anyway. You know, I had to give up everything, but he didn't give up anything, and that's how it worked. . . . Because it was fine and well if he had to work overtime or if he picked up this side job because he felt that we really needed some money. 'Cause I'm fine with just the baby, but I had to give up everything. You know, I had to sit in the house and take his treats and be this submissive woman. But prior to that time, when I met him, I wasn't submissive, and he knew that, but in order to compensate for his own insecurity, he was draining me of all of *my* energy.

After the baby arrived, however, she, too, became a threat to William, a reaction not uncommon for new fathers. Shawna remembered that William was jealous of the attention and time Shawna spent with Tasha. Similar to many first-time mothers, she felt she must explain her "love affair" with her child (Llewelyn and Osborne, 1990):

He felt . . . after Tasha was born, that I didn't think about anybody else but Tasha. I was spending all this time with Tasha. Like I would get out of bed in the middle of the night and check on her. It put a real strain on our sexual life because if she was crying, I would just stop everything and go and check up on her. And I guess I was kind of selfish because that was my first child. I did give her a lot of attention and give her a lot of time. But I said to him, "You did the same thing with your son, and you have to understand that I was always told that I would never be able to have kids." And I said, "Now that I have one, I don't know if it could ever happen again, so I want to spend as much time as I can with her. And it's not that I'm trying to take away from you or anything like that, but it's just something I guess that females go through when they first have a child." And I went through that for the first year.

This, however, was not the only jealousy that William entertained. The year after Tasha's birth, William and Shawna became engaged, and, "a couple months after that, it was that whole controlling thing again." He became jealous of any attention that she was paid by other men. She wondered why he could not accept her loyalty to him and laughed about men's inability to understand that a woman with a full-time job and a child would simply not have *time* to cheat. However, she was perceptive about possible reasons for this revived possessiveness, his insecurity about their age difference, and his increased drinking:

> Which is a funny thing about men. [She laughs.] I don't understand why they feel that a woman can do something when she's working full-time and has a child. How does *she* have the *opportunity* to cheat on him? And I know that they are insecure about that, and I think a lot of that has to do with the age difference. Of course I look young, and guys would make little comments in front of him, and that . . . teed him off [laughs], and if we went out, guys would try to hit on me or walk by and just stare, so he was jealous, and I knew that that had a lot to do with it. But at the same time, you know, that if you're living with this woman and she's with you, why should you be jealous of everything? But some people are just like that—that's that insecurity thing. . . . A couple months after we got engaged, it winds up being the same thing, but this time it got worse because he started drinking. Once he started drinking, it threw another loop into the situation. He became very abusive, languagewise and emotionwise . . . physically, too, once.

Physical Abuse: Exerting a Hold on Her

In a culminating act of possession and suspicion, precipitated by a bout of drinking, William grabbed and held Shawna and they fought. It began after she returned from shopping—"doing my 'womanly duties,' buying things for the house and the child and for him," as she related with some sarcasm. Incredulous, Shawna faced his jealous rage:

> So, my daughter's godmother, she dropped us off, and you could hear the music down the street, and that was an indication to me right then and there that he was [drunk] because the music was really loud, so she had said to me, "You be careful."

So I walked in the house, and he was ranting and raving about, "You were gone all day. Who were you with? What guy were you with?" And I'm like, "What are you talkin' about? How could I be with a guy and have bags in my hands? I have Tasha." [Sarcastically] That makes it very difficult for you to cheat with a child! [She laughs.] What'd he think? I locked her up in a different room while I take care of business? . . . So he just starts going off.

Exhausted by more than just a day of shopping, she retaliated, no longer submissive, but asserting her place in the household and her right to respect. However, because she has bitter memories of her parents fighting in front of her and her siblings, she stopped the altercation long enough to remove their daughter:

And at that point in time I was tired, and I said, "Look. I'm working just like you are, full-time, and I'm taking care of Tasha and providing some finances for this household. I don't feel as if I have to be questioned about where I go, who I've been with." And I told him, "Enough is enough!" Well, we were both goin' at it. And I said, "Look, I'm not gonna get in no hollering match in front of Tasha because I don't want our daughter to grow up and be nervous and think that this is appropriate behavior." So I got my daughter ready for bed and I brought her upstairs.

I come back down to see if there was things I needed to do in the house. Well, he couldn't just leave well enough alone, so he followed me into the kitchen. I'm washing dishes [and] he's still arguing. So I turned around and I cursed because I was pissed off. I said, "Fuck it! I've had it! I'm leaving you!" You know, period! Well, when I said that I was leavin' him, that's when all hell broke loose! He grabbed me, and I looked at him like he was crazy because never in my life have I ever been grabbed before by no man and no one, so I punched him! And he hit me back. And when he hit me back, Wendy, I will tell you that I lost it. And he knew that I had lost it, and I knew that he was drunk . . . because normally he knows how to leave well enough alone, but that was the straw that broke the camel's back. When he hit me, I would say I was trying to kill him, but I could not do that because he's a bigger person than I am, but I tried to.

So I went upstairs and I got my daughter and I got in my car to leave. He pursued us outside. He's standing in front of the car crying, saying he's sorry, saying he'll never do that again, that he's gonna stop drinkin'. But by that time I was through. I was livid. So I went over to my daughter's godmother's house and called the cops, and they came over. And they basically told me what I needed to do because we had lived together for awhile, and they had this law that, you know . . . you're kind of married, but you're really not.

Shocked into action by the indignity of physical abuse, Shawna galvanized the strength she never really lost. It became her turning point: she knew she must break free and get back in touch with those things which were important to her. The tightness of his physical hold was a tangible manifestation of how he had constrained her life. Her description vividly depicts her outrage at being considered his property:

The turning point in my life was when he hit me, when he grabbed me and I hit him back, and it was a *tight* hold. I mean, it was so tight that my circulation was probably being cut off in my arms. And when I was grabbed like that, I had to look at him and say to him, "Are you crazy? I am not your child! You have not purchased me." . . . And that was a turning point for me.

Breaking Free

So Shawna began the "divorce" process, one that was complicated by legal strictures regarding common-law marriages (Weitzman, 1985). Because they owned a home together and had a child, they had to proceed with the same property and custody resolutions to dissolve the relationship, but because they were *not* married, he was not required to leave their home. As in many situations involving police response to physical abuse, the burden of proof is on the victim of the abuse (Baca Zinn and Eitzen, 1990). Shawna stated, "I had to prove to the court that the living situation that I was in was not conducive for my child and myself because our lives were in jeopardy." This proof was not easy. William went into rehabilitation for a time and stopped drinking. Because he was fighting for custody of Tasha, Shawna had to endure a "long drawn-out fight for a whole year." During that time, she returned to her home, but when William realized that Shawna was standing firmly by her decision to leave him, he made living conditions for both Shawna and Tasha difficult, even unhealthy:

> I moved back into the house. The whole time that we were going to family court, he was still living there with me, which made it really bad, because he would act nice and he would do all these things, but I had already made up my mind that I didn't want to live like that anymore, especially for my daughter. Because that was my real main concern because he was just going back and forth with behavior swings. . . . So, for three months, basically, I think I probably lost like thirty pounds having to live with him, and plus I live in a single home. There's two bedrooms upstairs, and two bedrooms downstairs. My daughter and I were upstairs, he was downstairs, and I'm asthmatic, and my daughter's asthmatic. Up until that time, he would never smoke in our house. He would always go outside and smoke. Well, he figured, since I'm leavin' him, he's just gonna make it very hard for me, which it did. He smoked every single day, had the house filled with smoke. And because of that, my daughter had problems, and it made her allergies really bad because of all that secondhand smoke. And he knows it, but because he was so angry . . . he just didn't care. He figured he was losing everything. What the hell?

His seemingly callous disregard for his daughter's health indicates the depth of his offense at Shawna's move to break out of his control. His sense of property rights was acutely felt when he finally did move out and took everything. Shawna said, "I came home from work one day, and everything was gone!" The reason for this strong conviction of ownership may be William's belief that since he was the provider (though not solely, since she contributed her salary as well), he was the rightful owner of all of the once joint property that "his" money had purchased. Shawna's rights in this case were not protected by marriage, nor by the law (Weitzman, 1985). Even William's family stressed Shawna's obligation to him, but she asserted that the nature of their relationship was private and involved William's volition:

> So his family would come over, and they would talk, and they really got involved with the whole process, which I *did not like* because I figured that was our business. So for three months [after] I filed we were living together. And I told the judge, I said, "I can't live like this anymore. I'm being harassed by his family." If they weren't over there when I came home from work, they were calling, threatening me, asking, "How could you leave my brother? Everything that he's done for you." I was like, "Excuse me! But this is a relationship that involved he and I, not *you*, and if he's done it, he's done it because he *wanted* to."

In fact, his custody suit may have been an effort to maintain control over what he considered his property from the relationship. When he lost that suit, it was soon apparent that supporting and raising his daughter was not the priority it had first seemed. Faced with possible financial hardship, William agreed to leave the house in exchange for Shawna's capitulation on her claim for back support for Tasha. They agreed on visitation around his work schedule, one that was not entirely convenient for Shawna or Tasha:

> **S:** Because of his work schedule—he works four days on and four days off—he could be called into work anytime. I have custody of Tasha. He gets to visit her twice a week, and he gets to get her on his birthday, Father's Day, and every other [meaning alternate] holiday.
>
> **WP:** How do you feel about that? Is that hard for you?
>
> **S:** No, actually I wish he could get her more, and get her on the days that I don't have to work. Because what happens is that he gets her on the days when she has day care, so she's already in an environment where she has kids to play with. There's nobody on the block that she can play with. There's nobody her

age. So the times that he gets her, he's taking her away from her friends. He only takes her for a couple of hours, like he'll go to get her for breakfast or he'll take her out for three or four hours.

Similar to single mothers, once married or not, Shawna must "rebuild and move on":

> So, I had to start all over again. And that was . . . and still is a long continuous fight, because, you know, you are trying to rebuild and move on. But the one thing that I can say is that it made me a stronger individual. I know that I don't have to accept anyone's insecurities. I don't have to deal with any-one's emotional welfare. If you're not fit, then you shouldn't be in a relationship.

Now somewhat philosophical about the failures in their relation-ship, Shawna admitted that William brought some baggage to their relationship that he carried from his first marriage. He would accuse Shawna of being like his ex-wife, and he resented the burdensome financial arrangement to support his ex-wife and their seven-year-old son. At the end of our first interview, Shawna indicated that she and William were working now to break some of these old patterns for the sake of their daughter. Shawna is intent on allowing her daughter to develop a strong relationship with her father, one she was not allowed to develop with her own father:

> **S:** I wanted to get to know [my father] because I never knew him because I was so young, and during that time when they had the divorce, I never really saw him . . .
>
> **WP:** Didn't he have visitation?
>
> **S:** He did not exercise his visitation. Only when I was an adult did I get to know him, and I hated my mother because I thought she kept me from seeing him. And I don't want that for Tasha. I don't want her to grow up and be angry with me and think that I stopped her from seeing her father or I didn't want them to have a strong relationship.

FROM THE OTHER SIDE:
THE CHILD OF A "BAD" MARRIAGE

Shawna provided the unique opportunity to hear the story of a grown child from a single-parent home that was not as successful as she was in providing a nurturing environment for her daughter—the story of her own childhood. Shawna was the youngest of six children, three girls and three boys, who were caught in bitter fights between their parents. Married for thirty years, Shawna's parents divorced when she was seven:

> My mother and father were married for thirty years, and there's six of us, and I got the short end of the stick. My mother and father were separated when I was one, and when I was seven, they were divorced. So, between one and six, I saw many things happen! I saw fights . . . and when I say fights— my mother, she was the type of woman where she would go blow for blow with my father. I mean, she did not hold back. I saw the yelling, the cursing. I saw the works.

Angry, unable to fully understand the reasons for her parents' breakup, knowing only that (unlike her brothers and sisters) her mother prevented her from seeing her father, Shawna acted out in school, the classic "child from a broken home" so often displayed in the literature (Wallerstein and Kelly, 1974, 1976, 1980). As she got older, however, she was able to see her father for what he was and to understand her mother's urgent need to protect her:

> **S:** So when I was growing up, I was a very angry child because I couldn't understand why my parents were going through that, and why my father was doing the things that he was doing. And I always took his side because I was always Daddy's little girl. But then, as I got older, I realized that my father was a dog. He was cheatin' on my mother. He would go off with his women, and that's when I was one [year old], and my mother got to the point where she . . . said [that] she didn't have to take it any- more. . . . And I knew the strain that it caused [in] my life because when I was a child, I was always behind in school, when I was in elementary school, because I was always so

angry. . . . I had to get counseling. I had to, they put me in all these remedial classes because they thought that I was a slow child because I wouldn't participate. I would do all these [bad] things.

WP: Did you act out? Were you a discipline problem?

S: Oh, yeah! I was *very* bad in elementary school, and if any of those teachers are living, they will tell you that they had the time of their life with Shawna Martin!

I was very angry. I was angry because I used to watch my mother tell my father, "No. He couldn't see me," or "No. I couldn't go places." But she would let everyone else go except for me. And I didn't understand why she was doing that, so I was really angry with her. But I didn't know how to express it. And then during the summer months, I was the only one at home, while my brothers and sisters went away with my father, or they went to go and stay with my aunts and stuff on my father's side. So it made me very angry because, up to this day, I just didn't understand why my mom did that, and that she was just using me as a tool.

One of the things that my mother said [about] why she kept me at home was [that] I was also a very sickly child. It's because I was sickly and my sisters and brothers weren't. My younger sister is two years older than me, but basically they [my sisters and brothers] could take care of themselves, whereas I was a sickly child who had to depend on people to help me out with certain things. She said it's because my father . . . liked to hang out and drink his booze. He would just leave them with my aunts, and they would basically be taking care of themselves, and she didn't want that to happen to me.

Shawna later forgave her mother for this seeming lack of sensitivity to her needs. Now that she, too, is a single mother, she realizes the strength it took for her mother to keep her family clothed, housed, and fed:

It took me years because I thought that my mom was a very malicious, mean old woman. But then as you get older, you realize the reasons why your parents did certain things. And I respect my mother utmost because she worked two jobs while taking care of six kids. And when we were young, when I was young, I just thought that she didn't care because she was never around. Because I didn't understand everything. But then as I got older and I started to fall into the same predicament, I realized, no, you have to be a real strong person to work full-time, raise a child, you know, and provide for your child.

She now considers herself "lucky" and can appreciate the fact that her mother's work schedule kept them off social services and allowed her family to have things that other large families did not. Even the onerous cleaning chores her mother assigned, she believes, taught her to respect herself and to be responsible:

I thought my household was bad, but living here, I realize that I was lucky because my mom was never on social services. We always had food. We might not have had all the name-brand stuff, and I always had hand-me-downs, being the youngest, but we *had.* My friends used to always come to our house and say, "Wow! You really have a nice house." And from doing a lot of community work and going into different households as I'm dropping the kids off, it makes me realize that, "Wow! You were lucky!" because our house was never dirty or smelled. Even though we had to clean, it was never dirty. Because some parents . . . won't even force the kids to clean up. Because that teaches them how to be responsible. And that teaches them, "You want to be tidy. You want to respect yourself. This is something you're going to have to do when you get older."

Brothers/Father; Sisters/Mother

Since her father took everything with him when he left, her mother needed two jobs to support the family, leaving little time for her to be at home. Shawna's brothers and sisters contributed to her parenting, much as she later did for her nieces and nephews, born early to her teenage sister: "So I really didn't have a mom because she was always working and my brothers and sisters . . . were basically raising me." Shawna described their different personalities and mused about the persistence of the patterns modeled by her parents. Similar to their father, her brothers exhibit little respect for women, though they loyally defend their sisters against indignities imposed by *other* men. Her sisters, one of whom was a promising student, had children, both within and outside of marriage, with men who resembled their father. Even Shawna chose a man similar to him, despite trying not to do so:

[My brothers and sisters] had their own problems. They were decent students, but they were into other things—because my older brother is forty and back then it was that "live and let live," peace, that whole movement. So, you know, back then he was into the things that everyone would do back in the sixties. He turned out to be a decent individual. My middle and my youngest brother[s]—they're both not married—have a lot of females. My oldest sister . . . is on her second marriage, with two kids, and my middle sister . . . hasn't been married, and she has three kids. She's engaged now to her youngest child's father.

I think what happened was my sisters and brothers, because they [were the] backup for us for a mother and father, and they actually were older and they had to listen to the different stories—where I only heard one story, my mother's story, and she really didn't tell me that much—[they were] very confused. Because my middle sister . . . had a baby as a teenager, and my older sister . . . wound up getting pregnant [in college and] married the baby's father—which I don't know why she did that—but that's another story. And that relationship was just doomed because he was just like my father.

And I think that what happens is that we choose people who have the same traits as our parents, and that was one of the things that I was trying *not* to do, but I think that I did in a sense. I realized that my father was also controlling, 'cause that's what he did with my mother. He wanted to control her, while he was doing the things that he wanted to do. And then, my brothers were like my father. They think that they are just

God's gift to man, especially my youngest brother; he's the biggest dog. I mean, he's just so into himself. And he has no respect for women at all. None of them do. And the reason why I say that is because if you have respect for women, then you wouldn't abuse women the way that they do sexually. How can you have five girlfriends and they all know about each other and don't have a problem? How do you feel about yourself? He doesn't have no problem, but he had a problem when I went through everything that I went through with my baby's father. See, it's all right. What'd they say, "It's all right for the goose but not the gander"?

A Second Marriage Fails

Her mother's remarriage further complicated the situation. Shawna described her anger and resentment toward both her mother and her stepfather. Though she first described him as "nice" because he "didn't cheat" and was a hard worker who was "always there" for her mother, he proved himself to be a "mean somethin'" who "tore up the house" and had a violent temper. Adding the wicked-stepfather ingredient to a volatile mix of personalities did not enhance or enrich their family life. Instead, their mother was caught in the middle, hoping to trust a new man who made her life easier, but finding out that her children suffered from displays of his bad temper. In a hopeless cycle pitting their personal hell-raising against his frustration at not being able to discipline such an unruly mob of kids, he vented his feelings on the furniture and then the children. Shawna resisted him because he was not her father. Her brothers defended themselves and their sisters from physical attack, and, ultimately, Shawna's mother was put in the undesirable position of having to choose between her new husband and her children:

> She was remarried when I was in the fifth grade, so that was only three years since she had that divorce, so I probably figured that she was cheating on my dad. How did she meet this guy within three years? You know, aren't you hurt? Because I know I was hurting. *My* father's not there. My stepfather . . . was really nice. He was a different guy from my father. He was always there. You know, he didn't cheat on my

mother. He worked really hard; you know, they had the business together and like that. But he had a temper!! A temper! My dad didn't have a temper. With his kids, he didn't have a temper. But my stepfather had a temper. He was the type of person that when he got angry, because he couldn't discipline us . . . he used to come home, and if he was angry about something—you talk about punching holes in walls, throwing furniture! And because my mother was never there, it was always our story against his story.

And I think that it's really hard for a person to get married to someone who already has a set family. You're talking about six kids, and we were like *bad* kids [laughs]. So that made it real difficult, and I will tell you that I was the one that was really resistant. I didn't like him because he was not my father, and I didn't feel like I could listen to him, and we all felt that way. So whenever my mother wasn't around, we'd always give him the most hell that we could give him [laughs], which made it real difficult [because] my mother stayed married to him for many years, because they didn't get divorced until I was a junior in high school. You're talking about from fifth grade all the way up until my eleventh-grade year. And I think he had all that he could take!

And it was just getting to the point that it just wasn't working for my mother because she was caught in the middle. It was, "Either my kids or my husband." And she started to believe us when she came home from work one day [on a surprise visit] and she saw how the house was tore up—because he used to tear up the house and put it back together before she would come home, and he knew that he could hit us. Because my brothers . . . were older, . . . when he got angry and he wanted to hit us, . . . they would jump in the middle, and that's what happened. They used to fight all the time. And my mother was like, "We can't have this," so they got divorced. But he was a mean somethin'!

Troubles in School: Triumph on the Track

Shawna admitted that she was "livin' a life" terrorizing her teachers and just being mean. She honestly did not feel that she was "developing as a person," but because of the discipline of sports, a devastating loss by fire, and an unforeseen injury that kept a "cocky something" from expressing the talent of which she was proudest, Shawna learned to prove to herself and others that she had what it takes to be successful:

> I don't think I was developing as a person. It took me years. I think I really became in touch with myself my senior year in high school. Over the years, I found a sport [track] that I really liked. And I started running in seventh grade on junior varsity, so by the time I was in eighth grade, I was running for the varsity because I was really good. By the time I was in tenth grade, I was being scouted by college scouts, so I knew that I had this talent, but I still was a mean person, okay? And that was the problem that I had. I could be coached, but I couldn't be *coached*. Because if my coach did something that I didn't like, I would walk away, or I wouldn't come to practice or wouldn't run up to my potential, and like really [anger] the coach.
>
> . . . by the time I was in fifth grade, I was really a little cocky something, you know. I knew that I was good, and I knew that I was able to give quality, and I knew that I was going somewhere, even though the attitude wasn't great, because that wasn't important to me. Well, by my junior year, I was still doing good. Things were working out, got a little bit more involved in my academics, not that involved, seventy, seventy-five, because I was just "livin' a life"!
>
> Where during my senior year in high school, that was a big turnaround in my life. We wound up having an electric fire in our house. We lost everything. At the same time that that occurred, I found out that I had phlebitis in my left arm because I had minor surgery and I had a reaction from the anesthesia, so I was out of school for three months. And because I was out of school for three months and I could not participate in track, all the scholarships that I was promised—they reneged on it. They were not going to pay for me to come, at least my first year, because I had to prove to them that I still had the speed and endurance that I had . . .

As she had done before in singling out her youngest daughter for protection against the influence of her ex-husband, Shawna's mother taught her a difficult lesson, this time to make Shawna responsible for her own well-being. Unlike her brothers and sisters, who had either gone off to school or were still living off their mother's hard work, Shawna had to go to work, pay her mother rent, and keep up her car insurance. This was a lesson on the scarcity of finances that she would face without a college education, and Shawna knew that college was a way out of the negativity she knew within her family. As an athlete, she had learned to fear failure because it would let the team down, and—as she stated so appropriately—"I was my *only* team":

> Well, . . . I [could not] afford to go to a twenty-thousand-dollar-a-year school because both of my sisters were already in school. My mother was working two jobs just trying to pay for the house, and both of my brothers . . . were deadheads and still living at home. So . . . I wasn't going to go to school, and I was working at Sears. So . . . my mom didn't want me to fall into the same situation that my brothers and sisters were in, so my little job that I had at Sears . . . she made me pay her rent to live at home. . . . Because I thought one hundred dollars was a lot of money back then, she started taking half of my paycheck, and then when I said that I wasn't going to go to college, she said that I was going to have to pay for my car insurance, and that was like my whole check. So I met a man in admissions at the college who accepted me Johnny-on-the-spot. And since then it's been a world of difference.
>
> . . . Because once I got into college . . . during my senior year, I had to bust my butt to get good grades. And I realized that I wasn't the dummy that I [thought I was], because I wind up getting all nineties, to bring my average up to at least eighty-five. So I went away to college because I knew that I had to get away from home. I didn't want to go anywhere that my family could reach me in a short distance, so I decided to go to the college, but by the time I got there, my sister was gone anyway; she was [pregnant]. So once I was here, I knew that I couldn't fail. . . . . I had that fear of failure you develop from being an

athlete . . . and I knew that I couldn't go back home, because if I went back home, I knew what the repercussions would be. And that's how I dealt with it, and I think that's what made me do extraordinarily well in college—because I was afraid to fail, and . . . if I went back home, I knew what was waiting for me.

Mentors and Teachers

Mentors/teachers played a part in Shawna's development. Because her mother did not have the time to spend talking with her or providing the kind of support and attention she craved, Shawna was drawn by the confidence of her sixth-grade teacher, who was able to see past her anger, and by an art teacher, who became "a second mom":

My sixth-grade teacher was very instrumental in helping me develop because she didn't give up on me. She figured that there was something behind all my anger. She'd just sit me down and she would talk to me, and by the time I went to junior high school, I was changing. I found an art teacher I really liked; I will never forget her because she was like a second mom to me. She was my cheerleading coach, and her and her husband . . . spent a lot of time just to take me out. They used to come to my track meets, and, of course, I was also on the cheerleading team and I played soccer. They spent a lot of time . . .

She explained that the mentors who had the greatest effect on her were female, perhaps because even the male coaches she respected were too similar to the powerful controlling males who had made her childhood so difficult (Levine, 1992):

I had mentors when I was in high school too. I had two mentors, and they helped out a lot. And, of course, they were all female. . . . I didn't really get along with my track coaches because they were all male, but I don't have anything against them, though, because they did change my life.

Sports and the Winning Spirit

The lessons Shawna learned from participating in sports had a profound effect on her value system. She came to prize persistence, perseverance, and the desire to be "in the running":

> It's like when you're an athlete, there's things that you learn. You get *trained*. And it trains you to develop a certain way, and to think a certain way, and to run a certain way. So you still have that mentality . . . you know, "Don't give up. Persevere. Keep going. Get your opponent. You gotta be in it to win it. If you give up, you lose, and a loser's not wanted on this team." [These are] the thoughts that you have for the rest of your life because that's how you trained all your life.

These sentiments were echoed in different contexts throughout her interviews. In the third interview, she explained why she urged her daughter to develop her physical abilities, not because she thought making her a tomboy would toughen her up, but because sports had given her strength and a winning spirit:

> **S:** No, not to be tough, because I think the way that I was able to deal with a lot in my life was sports. Sports added to my personality. I'm not gonna say my strong will, but when you're an athlete, you're different from other people, as far as whatever you do. You wanna do well; you wanna win. Okay? And I think that has a lot to do with it because you're gonna persevere. You're gonna keep going at it. You're not gonna give up.
>
> **WP:** And that's what you've done in your life?
>
> **S:** Yep.

Giving Back

Shawna recognizes the importance of early mentoring interactions in the lives of children such as herself, so she volunteers her time to community centers, "giv[ing] back to the community everything [she] received":

It is said that, or research has indicated that, by the time kids, especially black boys, . . . get into third grade, eight years old . . . that would be the turning point in their life. And I'm really interested in working with second, third, and fourth graders because you can have such a dire impact on them. Because things may not be going well in their household, and they might come from a household where the mother or the father's not inputting the time, but they can still walk out of that situation and contribute to society and be emotionally and mentally stable. But you got to get to them early.

HAVING A BABY, NOT A WEDDING

Shawna's pregnancy was unexpected, and as with many young women, it came at an inconvenient time—when she was preparing to go to law school. Choosing between her career aspirations and becoming a mother was not really a difficult choice, though it caused her some internal conflict. She had once been told that she might never be able to have children due to spinal problems, so she decided to redirect her career path and to have her baby. This created some consternation for her mother, whose hopes and dreams were pinned on her last daughter's strength of character; for her grandmother, who was a preacher whose religious convictions denounced children outside of marriage; and, she admitted, for herself—she felt that she had let herself and her family down. She was afraid to tell her mother, even though she knew that she ultimately had to please herself:

> . . . my family's pretty religious, and my grandmother . . . used to be a [pastor], and everyone has career aspirations for you; you know, it's always what *they* want you to do, so you're basically living their dreams. I think when I found out I was pregnant, I was like three months, and I just got accepted into law school. So I had to make the decision if I was going to go to law school, if I was going to have Tasha, and that was a decision both her father and I made. Well . . . I was twenty-five years old at the time, just petrified of telling my mom that I was pregnant, and I'm an adult! [She laughs.] . . . I couldn't figure out how I was going to tell my mom.

I decided that I wasn't going to tell her on the phone because I wanted to be personal. I wanted to see the response on her face because that always means the most. When I told her, Wendy, I swear, my mother just had this blank look on her face. And she couldn't respond to me, and I was upset because at that time I was worried how she felt because I knew that she had these high expectations. I knew that she wanted me to be a lawyer. She wanted a lawyer in the family. But at the same time, I knew that I didn't want to have an abortion, and I had to do what was gonna make me happy.

Her mother's hesitancy at supporting her daughter's decision is not a surprise. From the beginning, her mother had protected her youngest daughter from the influences that made life so unhappy for herself and her other children. She had singled Shawna out for difficult lessons in self-sufficiency. She wanted Shawna to be a lawyer, possibly because Shawna's talent for assertiveness was recognized early by her godfather, who was a judge, but also perhaps because a career in law would give Shawna power, and a way out—out of gender role boundaries, financial hardship, and her social class (Levine, 1992). Instead, she saw Shawna trapped by the same situation that controlled her life and the lives of her other daughters (Holland and Eisenhart, 1990). When she finally responded, she tried to remind Shawna that her life need not be surrendered entirely to motherhood:

It took my mother almost a week to say something positive like, "I'm happy for you." By the time I got to the city . . . she had called to make sure we got home safely, and that's when she told me, "Congratulations. I know you're gonna be a good mom, and what are you gonna do about law school?"

Shawna's response to her mother affirmed that she would continue to work and might postpone the law career, that is, if it was even meant to be. She discussed her internal struggles: feelings of guilt because of her moral convictions; feelings of failure, something that did not set well with her athlete's spirit; and feelings of responsibility for disappointing her whole family, since she was expected to be "the good one." After all, she stated, "We internalize other people's expectations" (Gilligan, 1982; Kaschak, 1992).

S: And I said, "I don't have any answers basically about what I'm gonna do with law school, but . . . I'm gonna continue to work to capacity," because I was working then, "and if it's meant for me to be a lawyer, then that's what I will pursue down the line." But I just don't want to give this up because . . . when I was younger . . . I had scoliosis real bad; there was some doubt I'd ever be able to have a child. And here I am pregnant, past the first three months, and was able to carry a child. And I'm saying to myself, "Well, if I give this child up, and I'm already past the first [trimester], what happens if I can't have another one?" . . . and I want kids.

. . . That was something that it took me awhile to deal with because, I guess, I was disappointed with myself because I wasn't married and . . . well, how could this happen to me, somebody who clears everything and is just on top of everything? And then just getting my mom's reaction was something real difficult for me to deal with. . . . I was always the responsible one out of all her kids . . . it took my whole family by surprise. . . . And my grandmother had to pray for me because having the baby out of wedlock [was] like the worst thing you could ever do.

WP: But you weren't the first one.

S: No, my sister was the first one, but see my sister, the middle child, she has the "devil in her.". . . I was the good one . . . and they thought the devil was just takin' over me.

And even through my whole pregnancy, I was always concerned about my mom and how she was going to deal with it. Because you know how parents are. My mother was always constantly bragging about me, and I'm gonna be this big-time lawyer and all this other stuff. And it was a blow for her, but I had to come to the realization that it was a blow for her because that's what *she* wanted. But this is something that *I* wanted and I'm gonna do, and I really couldn't concern myself too much with how she felt. We have a really close relationship now, and she *loves* her granddaughter to death. But that was another turning point in my life.

PARENTING TASHA

Rather than follow the patterns laid down in her family, where her mother worked too much to have time with her children, where male role models used power, sometimes violently, to control, and where cycles of behavior continued unbroken, Shawna learned to value herself and her daughter and to act in ways that would nurture them both. She stated, "We both provide happiness in our lives."

As with all the mothers in this study, time is a major concern for Shawna, but from her description of a typical day to her skillful manipulation of time to her advantage, Shawna's life stands in stark contrast to the misconceptions so often associated with young single mothers, especially those who are African American (Carter and McGoldrick, 1980; contrast with Gutman, 1976; Rice, 1994). She has time to talk, play, eat, and work with her daughter and to pass on her values of "strong-mindedness" and "standing up for what is right." She volunteers in community service to "make a difference in people's lives." She persuaded William to see how his treatment of his son and daughter may push them into actions that imitate those very characteristics which have brought him so much disappointment (Dinnerstein, 1976; Farrell, 1972). She works to-gether with him to assure their daughter that she has both of her parents' love, a concept that three-year-old Tasha already under-stands well enough to articulate:

> And I don't want my daughter to feel that she has to look for love, she has both of her parents' love, although she only lives with her mom. And she knows that because she'll say, "My daddy loves me and my mommy loves me, and I love my daddy, my mommy, and my brother" [her "brother" is Wil-liam's son from his first marriage, Thomas].

"The Best Mom"

Shawna spoke often of spending quality time with her daughter. In the daily household activities of getting ready for work, driving

Tasha to day care, fixing and cleaning up after dinner, and getting ready for bed, mother and daughter talk, play, and sing together. A typical day begins with listening to stories about Tasha's dreams, preparing Tasha for the day's events, and doing all of those mundane little tasks that become part of their close relationship:

> A typical day consists of getting up at six o'clock in the morning, getting myself ready for work, waking my daughter up if she's not up by that time, then finish getting dressed, getting her ready in the morning, feeding her breakfast, and sitting down [and] having coffee. And we're talking because now she has dreams. She tells me about her dreams . . . and we talk about what's gonna happen during the day, if her dad's gonna pick her up, what's gonna happen in school. Then, we get her dressed and we leave. I drop her off at day care, which is conveniently located right across from work, and I come to work, and sometimes I go over and I have lunch, which is really great, since she's in close proximity. So, we have a really strong relationship. . . . I normally have an hour with her. I give myself an hour and she has an hour, depending on the traffic [laughs]. We do our quality time in the morning.

Shawna does not rely on the morning hour, however. She makes an effort to be involved in her daughter's daily life as much as possible, meeting her at day care, going on field trips with her class. From her narrative, it is clear why Tasha's playmates think that Shawna is "the best mom":

> . . . sometimes if things don't work out . . . if I wake up late or if we can't spend that time together, I'll go over and have lunch with her, which is really good because she likes that, because all the kids in her classroom really like me. They think that I'm like the best mom because I go on their field trips with them. . . . She's popular in class because her mommy's cool. And . . . one of her friends told [her], "My mom can't run. Your mom is nice. She can run!" Three- or four-year-olds are real—they're little adults—and most people don't realize that they're just little people, but they're real smart and they know what they want.

The Ties That Bind: Rituals, Chats, and Stickers

After work they return home, where the chores and rituals of the evening are opportunities for talk and "teaching"—many times daughter teaching mother. It is interesting to note that such simple things as seasonal weather conditions, traffic, and whether they have leftovers for dinner affect the amount of time they have together, sometimes compressing activities into less time, but never causing them to sacrifice important rituals and affectionate contact:

> Then when I get off from work, I pick up Tasha, [and] we go home. . . . I like to cook so that I can have leftovers, so I'm not cooking everyday. I warm up the leftovers or I cook, and while I'm doing that, Tasha is either [inside or outside], depending on the weather. If it's cold outside, she's indoors watching TV or helping me prepare dinner because she likes to watch me do that. And if it's nice outside, she's riding her bike. And when dinner's ready, she comes in, we eat dinner, [and] we talk. Then she either goes back outside or she . . . watches TV, colors, and she has things that she can read, or she is making up her own story as she is reading a book. Once [she's done with that] and dishes are washed, then we spend our quality time together. And . . . when she helps me cook dinner, I consider that quality time because we still have the opportunity to chat.

> . . . we talk about a lot of things, and I told you before about our conversation; my daughter . . . is very curious about a lot of things [laughs]. So that after dinner, depending on the time—if we have leftovers, we normally have a lot of time—we'll do things together like . . . color . . . or [play] games. She has a couple of computer games, and she's learning her letters and her numbers, so we'll play with that. And then we'll get ready for bed.

> And while we're getting ready for bed, we'll sing songs [that] she teaches me . . . because I forgot all the nursery songs. Which is really good because it takes me back to my own childhood, and after I get her ready for bed, then we do the reading. And she always gets a half an hour TV time every night. Because if she doesn't get to watch her cartoons, she gets

very upset. So we definitely do that every day, no matter what
. . . . So normally she's bathed and fed by seven-thirty. During
the summertime . . . I'm home by four-thirty, four-forty-five.
During the wintertime, it's normally five, five-fifteen. So after
her bath, we go upstairs to her room, and depending on the
amount of time, we either play some more—she loves to play—
and then we do stories. We do two stories per night, and it's
normally the same stories over and over and over again. . . . I
like to read different stories, but . . . she likes the same story
because . . . she's . . . memorizing everything in the story, so
[when] her friends are sitting around . . . she [can] read to them.
Some people think she's actually reading, but she's memorized
the whole book.

Then after her two stories, we sing "It's Time to Go to Bed"
over and over and over again. It's a little song I made up for her.
[Singing to the tune of "Farmer in the Dell"] "It's time to go
bed. It's time to go bed. Don't let the bedbugs bite you at night.
I love you in the morning. I love you in the evening. I love you
at night because you're my little angel." . . . We sing and sing
until she's yawning, and then [she says], "Mommy, you have to
give me my kiss and my hug." So we do kisses and hugs. Then
[she says], "I have to go to the bathroom." We do that *every*
night.

Shawna uses positive reinforcement in the form of sticker re-
wards to encourage good bedtime behavior and to foster Tasha's
sense of self-control and responsibility for her behavior:

She gets rewarded if she doesn't cry before she goes to bed or
wants me to read five stories. She gets a sticker each morning,
and [if] she doesn't have any potty accidents in the bed, she
gets a sticker. So each morning, she gets a sticker based on her
bedtime behavior. And at the end of the week, on Saturday,
she's awarded a treat, and it's always Dairy Queen. So every
Saturday, we go to Dairy Queen and she gets a Dilly Bar and
she's gets to hold her own money and ride her bike, and she
loves it.

Child Illness and the Single Mom

A "sickly child" herself, Shawna understands how her daughter's asthma can wreak havoc on their daily schedules, which is an important message for employers of any parent. Beyond the total exhaustion that a wakeful night with a child can mean for a parent, the delicate juggling act between work and family obligations becomes hardest at such times, especially for the single parent. Shawna eloquently described what choice *must* be made:

> Tasha reminds me a lot of myself when I was younger because I was sickly. So we have to stick to a strict schedule with her because she's asthmatic also. And she keeps a lot of colds. Once she gets a cold, the asthma starts acting up, and I have to stay at the doctor's office or the emergency room with that young lady a lot. So I'm really running home sometimes . . . if I have to stay late to complete something, I'm running to get her just so I could stay on that schedule, even if I have to cut some things off. If we have to cut playtime out so we can get dinner ready, get [Tasha] bathed—'cause I definitely like to do the reading every night because she loves that. And *I* do, too, because it builds a stronger bond with her.

> . . . when she gets sick, that really throws in a loop because then you're really juggling. And it's difficult when you're a single mom and your child gets sick because you're only approved sick time for one person, not two. So normally . . . when she gets sick, depending on her father's schedule, if he's off, he'll take her for me, but if he's not off—because he gets called in a lot—it gets difficult. Normally . . . I have to . . . bring her to school and bring her medicine, and you have to get a doctor's note, and then the day care center will start the medicine. But probably for the first two days that she's sick, I normally stay home and make sure she gets her medicine, depending on how bad it is.

> The antibiotics . . . work really quickly, but sometimes, you know, we're up at night if her cold is really bad because she gets really bad respiratory infections, and she's up at night wheezing, running the humidifier, and you have to wake up and

make sure she gets the medicine on time. And that's really hard when you're getting up in the morning because you're exhausted, you know. They slept through the night, but you're just sitting up holding them so they could breathe, and *they're* not tired.

So that's probably the most difficult thing about being a single mom, when your child gets sick, and you're still trying to take care of them, make sure that you're getting your proper rest, that you're able to go to work. No one cares that you're a single mom. It's not your employer's fault that you're a mom. That's your responsibility, so you have to try the best we can to juggle all those responsibilities. And it's difficult at first, and then after awhile you get used to it.

You have to make a decision. It's my child or my job. And for me, it's always my child because I know that my child will always be there, but my job might not be. And to me, that's the most important thing because my child adds something to my life that my job doesn't offer. . . . My child loves unconditionally.

Passing on Values

Shawna is passing on the strong moral conviction that her mother instilled in her:

I was still strong because I saw how hard my mom was working, and she [has] instilled certain morals in us, and that's the same thing I'm trying to do with my daughter because my mother always told me, and I'll never forget it to this day, "If you know you're right, no matter what anyone else says, you stand your ground. Even if there's one hundred people against you and you know you're right, you stand your ground." She said, "You don't give in because as soon as you give in to pressure, that's when you become a follower. . . . You want to lead by example." And that's what I tell my daughter all the time. But in different words, though.

In all three interviews, Shawna described her daughter with great pride and discussed the values she promotes through example and encouragement: the "stand up" philosophy of her own mother, independence and strong-mindedness, honesty, and a confidence in her ability to reach goals. From the first interview:

> My daughter is very independent. She expresses herself well, I think, for three years old. She's not a follower, and she will tell you how she feels . . . and if something's not right, she will tell you that, and that's one of the things that I think that my mom did do. She always told us that if you're right, you stand up to whoever it is that's doin' the wrong, and you don't back down, no matter who it is. And that's how I'm raising my daughter. You know that if you're right, you stand up. You don't back down to anyone. . . . As she [gets] older—she's going to be the only child—so I want her to be able to spread her wings and go out. I don't want her to feel that she has to stay with me. Because it's only her and I.
>
> And I want her to be independent. I want her to pursue whatever goals in life that she has, and then at the same time, because times have changed so much, too, I don't want her to get caught up with everything that's happening in the streets . . .

and again in the third interview:

> She's imitating me all the way around. Like her godparents told me . . . she's really strong-minded. And I said, "That's the way that I'm raising her. I want her to be strong-minded." But at the same time, I want her to realize that she doesn't always have to agree with me about everything, especially when it comes to certain things, like she'll debate about the food that she likes, and I'll give in sometimes. But I want her to realize that there's a right way and a wrong way; you have to be true to yourself and honest with yourself, and I think she has developed that because if she has done something that I don't know about, she'll come and tell me before I find out.

Shawna expressed a gentle patience with her daughter's growth:

> I don't want her to grow up too fast. I still want her to be a kid, so when she falls out and has her little temper tantrums, I let

her go through the jive and the motions, and then when she's finished, "Are you done now?"

Shawna recognizes that Tasha acts differently with her than she does with her father. Her father treats her like a prima donna, reinforcing a babyish dependence, but his influence is intermittent. Tasha is more relaxed around her mother and feels free to be herself. Shawna is pleased to see that Tasha is a strong-minded individual:

> . . . she acts different around me than around her father. Around her father she acts more like daddy's little girl, the little baby, where if she got a little scratch on her she needs a Band-Aid. She needs mega-attention from him, and it could be because he's not around that much, and I have her all the time. With me she's more relaxed; she's Tasha. She's a very outgoing young lady, and I see a lot of myself in her because I was the same way. So, I find that to be real interesting because my mom's a real strong-minded person.

Two Parents Together and Apart

Tasha's father, William, has a "strong relationship" with her, one that Shawna encourages. Because Shawna bitterly resented her mother's interference with her own relationship with her father, she is especially careful to be sure that Tasha and William are given plenty of opportunity to "develop their own little special relationship." She is grateful for these visits, since it gives her time for herself:

> Whenever her father calls and he says that he wants to take her, if he goes on a picnic or he wants more than twice a week to get her, or if he comes over on the weekend, I let her go because that's more time for me to do the things that I need to do in my life. And it's quiet time with me, and that gives her an opportunity to build a stronger bond with her father. And she enjoys it because a lot of things he does with her, you know, I don't do. I let them develop their own little special relationship.

Although William is more indulgent of Tasha than Shawna would like him to be, she described their outings as quality interactions, for example, when William picks up his daughter from day care and takes her to breakfast or to the park. Even though she is only three and he often doesn't understand what she tells him, William's attentiveness to his daughter extends even to his refraining from smoking for her benefit:

> Then also I know that Tasha and her father . . . have a very, very close bond. It's . . . strange. I've never seen anything like that before. Because she has to call her dad every day. In the morning when we leave, she wants to call her dad. When we get home, she has to call her dad. And if her dad doesn't go by the day care center to see her, she tells me, and she tells me she's upset about it because she expects it. You know, she expects to see her dad every day at the day care center, and if he tells her that he's going to do something with her, he builds up her expectations—like yesterday, he came by, and he told me and her that he was going to take her to breakfast this morning. . . .
>
> These are the things he does with her, and she enjoys them because that's her time with him, that's their quality time, and she gets to talk about whatever it is she wants to talk about, when he can't understand half of the things she says anyway. It's funny [laughs] because my daughter talks fast like I do! So, he's like, "Uh huh. Uh huh. Uh huh." And then he'll catch one or two things, "Oh, sure!" [She laughs.] So they'll do that, and then she'll tell me what she had for breakfast with her dad, and she'll say, "Mommy, he didn't smoke in front of me." And so I don't have to ask because she'll tell me anyway because we have that open communication. When we go out to dinner and we're talking, I'll ask, "Well, how did your day go?" and she'll start telling, "Well, my dad came and took me to Denny's. I had pancakes, eggs, and sausage. My dad took me to the park, then he brought me back to school. And I cried when my dad left."

William's focus on thoughtful parenting and the amount of time he spends with his daughter contrast sharply with the angry man who made their home environment unhealthy, to punish Tasha's mother for leaving. His participation as a parent increased after he, Tasha, and Shawna did not live together. Shawna observed:

> And then it got better because, for him, when she was a little baby, there wasn't much that he could do with her, but then once she started walkin' and talkin', that's when he really loved taking her to the park, taking her out to eat, and stuff like that 'cause that makes it easier on them. When they are little babies, for men, they [are not] any fun.

Sometimes conflicts in their child-rearing philosophies give Shawna some anxiety, but she recognizes William's pattern of ownership and his need for control. He feels powerless as a part-time father, making him defensive when Shawna suggests changes:

> **S:** He takes her to the park. Tasha told me that her daddy lets her drive! [She laughs.] And he gives her all the junk food that she wants. I don't. I do it sparingly.

> **WP:** How do you disagree with regard to her? Do you fight about it, or are you pretty open about things?

> **S:** With her, I can't because I don't want to take that away from her, but I will discuss things with him about my dislikes, about her getting behind the wheel, even if it's in the park. But his whole thing is, that's *his* daughter. He can do the things he wants to do, and I don't want to debate with him because he's already a part-time dad. So my whole thing is, "Well, if she gets hurt that's gonna be your responsibility." And I let him know how I feel about it—I would be very angry. But I can't stop him from doin' it because he already feels as if I have all the control and I'm trying to take that away from him, something that she likes to do and he can provide, regardless of how I feel [laughs].

Shawna and William have other disagreements with regard to raising their daughter. She explained how such conflicts may be easier to resolve in the single-parent family, since children are quite perceptive about "how to play" both parents. She hinted at the differences between the "Disneyland dad's" concept of having fun and a mother's desire to have fun, but to account for education and growth at the same time (Demos, 1986; Dinnerstein, 1976):

> . . . both of your parents can be there, and they can be in a good relationship, but there's still an inconsistency when it comes to how the child should be raised and when the child should be reared and like that. And I see that a lot with my friends who have kids and they're married or they're living with the baby's father. Because the father wants to do one thing one way, and the mother wants to do something a different way, and that makes the child very confused.
>
> I had decided that it would be better off for Tasha to be raised by one of us, mainly myself, [rather] than her dad, because she [needs] structure, [not] all that inconsistency. And . . . sometimes kids play both parents. And I knew that she could play her father, from day one when she was small, because she looks just like her father, and he's so proud. So I knew that was going to be a problem. One of the things I told William when we were together is that we have to be consistent about the things that we want for our daughter and how we want her to be raised. He always thought that I was being too possessive and [he] always wanted all these things for Tasha, but what happens if Tasha don't want them?
>
> He always thought that I was making an adult out of her, and that she was just a child. And I didn't think so because I would do more of the educational things with her, and we had fun with it, but he thought that fun . . . was like going to the park, giving [her] a whole bunch of junk food, and playing games, and I do that, too, but I figure, if I'm gonna play games with her, I might as well play educational games.

Daddy's Little Princess/Daddy's Little Man

Shawna does not want her daughter to fall into the stereotypical gender role patterns that may foster dependence and threaten her identity (Dinnerstein, 1976; Llewelyn and Osborne, 1990). She tries to offset William's encouraging Tasha to be a "little priss," the way "her father wants her to be," by involving her in sports. Though she encourages the tomboy in her daughter, she allows her to be her own person, and does not push her too hard to be anything she does not want to be, recognizing that time and maturity will have a positive effect:

> So I'm trying to make her a tomboy like I was, but it's a little bit difficult because she's a little bit prissy [and] she's into things that I was never into. Like she likes to dress. She likes her hair to look a certain way. She likes nail polish, and all of that her father likes. Her father wants her to be . . . I call her the "little priss."
>
> But I'm not gonna fight her with that because I know, in time, she will change, so what I try to do to offset it [is to] get her involved in something. Like I'll go out and buy the roller skates and do the swim lessons and show her pictures where Mommy ran track, and I show her little techniques she needs to do, like pumping her arms and lifting up her feet. So then as she gets older, then she'll make the decision what she wants to be involved in. But right now, I'm making those decisions because I told her, "Well, Mommy would like for you to take dance in the fall." So, we went over to the dance school, and she saw the other little kids dance, and now she thinks she wants to do it. We'll find out in the fall whether she actually wants to do it or not. But I want to keep her involved in extracurricular activities because I really think that that helps a lot.

Shawna struggled against her daughter's enactment of socialized gender expectations, such as "dress codes," but capitulated out of respect for her daughter's choices, understanding that even if she chooses against her mother's wishes, she is developing the independence that Shawna prizes:

> Because I said I'm not gonna push her anymore. Because I was really pushing for her to be tomboy. I wouldn't buy any dresses. She could only wear dresses on Sunday. I barely bought skirts, but as she got older, she would get upset, and she would say, "I don't wanna wear that. That's for little boys. Boys wear pants like that all the time. I wanna wear a dress

like you do. You wear dresses when you go to work." So I had to say, "Okay, fine." So I started buying her all dresses and skirts . . .

Shawna agreed that regardless of her penchant for traditionally feminine dress, Tasha has her own personality, though one quite different from her mother's:

> My daughter is nothing like I was when I was younger because I was more of a tomboy, and she's more of a priss. . . . And I have to respect her for that.

William encourages learned helplessness in his daughter—an image Shawna calls the "little princess," "queen," "prima donna"—but he discourages any sign of dependence in his son. Shawna related how William's son from his first marriage, Thomas, looks to her for nurturing because he knows his father would discourage any sign of weakness, such as crying. Though she saw clearly the polarity of this treatment of the girl child versus the boy child (Baca Zinn and Eitzen, 1990; Farrell, 1972; Kaschak, 1992; Levine, 1992), it was difficult for her to show William how damaging this was for his son. Because confronting him with his inequitable parenting would threaten William's feelings of parental authority, Shawna developed her own relationship with Thomas, one that might give him a different perspective on "how to be a man":

> Thomas and I were close because Thomas couldn't talk to his mother. . . . We used to talk about things: "How do you feel about it?" and "What bothers you?" Because he was always crying, and I knew there was something wrong because I knew that my daughter . . . who is very outgoing, very verbal . . . will tell you what is wrong, but he never did. And I used to talk to his father about it.
>
> But one of the things that I realized is that sometimes it's best not to talk to a person's parent . . . because then [the parent is] on the defensive . . . "Well, you're telling me how to raise my child. And I'm not doin' this and that."
>
> And now basically what I do, to compensate for not being the parent, I won't even tell his father because he feels that his son should be telling him how he feels. But, he wants his son

to be a [man] at seven years old, and he's only a child. But then his precious daughter's a prima donna, and I'm trying to get him to see . . . how he's raising both of them. He's raising his son to be a man and be responsible, and, "You're not supposed to cry." Well, he's seven! He's supposed to cry! He's not supposed to be a man; he's a little kid! But then he's raising Tasha to be the little princess, and if she gets a little boo-boo, oh my goodness, Daddy has to kiss it, and we gotta get a treat. Thomas falls [and it's], "Get up! And take it like a man."

. . . And I feel bad for him because it's like, "No, Thomas. You can cry. It hurts. Cry." But his father is making him—his father wants him to be tough, and because he's a boy, he has to be tough. He has to learn how to deal with pain.

The power of gender socialization is such that it is difficult to break cycles which lead children to imitate even the worst of parental role models (Dinnerstein, 1976). Shawna has tried to educate William, a slow process with regard to his son, but she has been more successful in changing his behavior toward their daughter, by helping him to understand how his daughter may end up with a man who exemplifies all of William's worst qualities. After all, she told him, *he* resembled *her* father:

S: And what I'm trying to get [William] to understand is, "That's the reason why *you* have the problems that you have in your behavior, because of this whole gender thing. You want to be the man. You want to deal with pain instead of expressing yourself when something hurts. You want to internalize it all, but then it gets to a point where it just explodes. And you're gonna make your son be in that same predicament because he's gonna internalize everything. And when he gets older, he's not gonna be able to be in a healthy relationship because he thinks that a man is not supposed to communicate or show feelings about how he feels!"

WP: Are you making any progress on that?

S: We're getting there slowly but surely.

Now he can see where he had gone wrong. But now it's given him the opportunity to say, "No. I don't have to be like them." And it goes back to [his] parents, and how his father treated him. And I think that he's finally getting to the point that he realizes that he has to change and he has to break that chain, because if he doesn't, his son is going to be exactly . . . like . . . him [said slowly and deliberately].

And I talked to him last night, and I said, "You also have to realize that girls look for qualities in men that their fathers have . . . . I told you that the reason you and I were together is that you had qualities that my father had." Because I didn't realize that, and I said, "That's a part of growing up and being able to give yourself the opportunity to sit back and think about the type of relationship you were in, and what went wrong in the relationship. . . . I realize that you were a lot like my dad in many ways!" [She laughs.] And I said, "I don't want Tasha to pick the same mate when she gets older with the qualities that you had." . . . "So now it's really time for you to change. Especially as you guys spend more time together, so she won't make a bad choice in her mate when she gets older. So she won't think that it's all right for her mate to be abusive with her." And he realizes that. And he doesn't want that for his little "princess," "queen," "prima donna."

Good Guys and Bad Guys

In our discussions about the differences between Tasha's two parents, Shawna related a common complaint leveled by many single custodial mothers against the noncustodial fathers (Demos, 1986; Dinnerstein, 1976). A father's liberality and overindulgence of the children during visitation times may lead to a perception of Mom as the bad guy—the one who makes you do your homework and enforces rules of behavior—and Dad as the "Disneyland ideal"— the one for play and fun. For example, Shawna enforces good nutrition, but William allows Tasha to eat more junk food, something she mentioned several times. Before they started working together to combat his tendency to let his daughter play one parent against the other, William referred to Tasha's mom whenever he tried to enforce rules or enlist his daughter's complicity in hiding his indulgences:

Because before it was . . . "Well, your mother said, and your mother said you can't have this." Now, it's, "No, you can't have it." And if I said, "No, I don't want her to have bubble gum," he'd say, "Your mother doesn't want you to have bubble gum." And she'd get upset with me. . . . And I was always the bad guy when it came to junk food. . . . And one of the things he tells her is "Don't tell Mommy."

Now, however, because William is beginning to see that keeping her helplessly attached to him will not benefit her in the long run, he tries to parent *with*, and not *against*, Shawna:

Yes, because even with Tasha he's getting better now because if Tasha falls or she's complaining about a boo-boo that's a month old or a week old, he'll say, "No, Tasha. You're fine." [Imitating her] "No it hurts, Daddy." "Tasha, you're fine." Like yesterday, when we got home, she had to call her father. . . . Daddy had to come over because she had a tummy ache. "Daddy, my tummy is hurting me." And she was just whining. I mean, she's really good at it. And Daddy's rubbing her tummy, and I'm like, "Tasha, it's time to go to bed." Well, Daddy was like rubbing her tummy and I just looked at him, and I said, "It's time for her to go to bed," and he said, "Tasha, it's time for you to go to bed." Normally, he would say, "Your *mother* said, 'It's time to go to bed'." This time he said, "Tasha, it's time to go to bed." So then he's not putting all the burden on me.

All too familiar with two parents using their children as weapons against each other, Shawna does not force her daughter to take sides, nor does she speak negatively about her father to Tasha. Speaking from her childhood experience, she described the damage that was done to her when her mother spoke ill of her father:

I listened to my mother talk about my dad like he was a dog! And I told you I picked sides. I was on my mom's side until I had the opportunity to talk to my dad about things. And see, what I'm trying to do with my daughter is all the things I realized happened in my life. Because it made me confused about a lot of things. I thought that I had to take sides because when you're young, you're always looking for love.

She thinks that a well-adjusted single parent may have an advantage over troubled two-parent families who enlist their children in ongoing warfare (Cherlin and Furstenberg, 1989; McCord, McCord, and Thurber, 1962; Nye, 1957; Santrock, 1972). She believes that children should not be involved in a fight between two parents—apart or together:

> I never talked about my daughter's father negatively to her. Because she had nothing to do with the situation, and that's really unfair for her. I think sometimes that happens, especially when you're in a family. When you have both of your parents, and sometimes if your parents get into a fight and the kids are around, they see that and then they start taking sides about what parent they like. And we don't realize it, or, I should say, some people don't realize that when you talk negatively about that parent, the kids are gonna choose sides and develop favoritism. Well, if there's only one parent there, who can you talk about negatively? You know, you don't have that option, and I think that does a lot of kids an injustice when parents do that. And I said I would never want to do that to my child. I don't want her to get involved with a fight that has nothing to do with her. She doesn't ask for it. It wasn't her fault that she was born.

This careful child-centered parenting extends beyond the parental relationship:

> I told William, "If you're angry about something when you come over, or if you pick her up at day care, don't show your angriness around her because children are very perceptive about things." And I said, "It's unfair to her that she has to deal with your angriness or your bitterness. We need to leave things that happen at our jobs at work because when we're dealing with her, that's *her* time. She had nothing to do with whoever made us angry or what didn't go right that day. It's unfair."

Shawna believes that children learn disrespect for parents from arguments that involve them, and she is sensitive to the fact that single or married parents who do this can raise "troubled kids." She resolves to be the "bigger person" so that her daughter will not suffer this damaging influence.

> I know a lot of people that this happened to, and the kids will talk to the parent that they dislike—because they have heard so many negative things—like an adult and start disrespecting them. But that's still their father or their mother, no matter what. And it's about respect. I want my daughter to respect her father, regardless of what happened with us. And it's always being the bigger person. You know you have to be the bigger person because you don't want your child to grow up and just be totally distraught about things, and that's when they will start to "get involved with things" that people associate with coming from a single-parent household [laughs], and I don't want that for her. I think a lot of single parents . . . do a good job.

According to Shawna, dysfunction is found in all families, not just the single-parent family. Certainly, her experience has shown that the myth of the perfect relationship with the perfect kids simply does not exist (Baca Zinn and Eitzen, 1990; Rice, 1994):

> I think it's a misconception that a lot of people have about single parents, that if a child is being raised in a single [-parent] family, that's a dysfunctional family. All families are dysfunctional. There's not one family that I know of that does not have problems with the parents or the kids. So, if there's problems, they're dysfunctional. That's that Cinderella image. And it doesn't exist. You don't get married and it's [happily ever after] . . . the perfect relationship, the perfect kids. That doesn't exist—*at all!*

Instead, she believes that if single parents devote time to help their children become emotionally and mentally fit, the children can benefit from the different perspectives on life their two separate parents give them. Even though the two parents live apart, the children can have confidence that they are being cared for:

> I think that that's the advantage for kids who are being raised by single parents [who] are spending the time with them or

making sure that they are emotionally, mentally well fit. Because then they have the opportunity to look at life in a different perspective, "No. I don't have my father or I don't have my mother. Both of them don't live in the same house. But, my well-being is still being taken care of. I get to see my dad, and I get to see my mom. They're two totally different people. They're like two totally different things."

THE GOOD AUNT:
PARENTING A TEENAGE MOTHER'S
TROUBLED DAUGHTER

Shawna gave so much information about families outside of the traditional mythical ideal, that her story quilt has already been richly filled with reminiscences and observations about her childhood and her current life as a single mother. However, in the second interview, she told me about an unusual episode in her life as a parent. Shawna agreed to provide a home for her troubled niece and learned through misadventure how difficult it is to redesign the patterns of behavior and expectation that seem to be carried from one generation to the next. This story illustrates how easy it is for adolescent children, rebellious by nature, to make the same mistakes their parents did, and to operate in ways that keep them powerless to change (Demos, 1986; Dinnerstein, 1976; Llewelyn and Osborne, 1990).

That was an experience that I would not want to encounter when my daughter gets to thirteen years old. Well, I explained to you before about my background and my niece who came to live with me. Her mom was the one who had her when she was a teenager, so, of course, she was coming in with a lot of baggage. Because once she got to the age where she was at that [rebellious] stage, she really got out of control.

Her teenage sister, busy trying to grow up herself, did not have time to raise her growing family. Shawna and her brothers and sisters contributed to the parenting of their nieces and nephews, a responsibility that carried into Shawna's adulthood. Shawna's niece, Vanessa, had a difficult time identifying her mother as a nurturer, so she turned to the only "parents" she knew. Shawna's soft-hearted, save-the-child attitude persuaded her to take on a challenge that only later she would fully realize she could not win:

> As she [my sister's daughter] was growing up, my sister didn't spend a lot of time with her and her brothers because they're the oldest [of my sister's children], and we basically raised them because they were kids, and it was like a family type of thing, where they were being raised by the family. And when I was in high school, I had my nieces and nephews all the time, and when I had track meets, my nieces and nephews were there. I was the one who had a car, so I was the one who had to go pick them up in day care, bring them to track practice, and it was like they were my kids.
>
> So when I was in college, they were still my kids. I was always providing for them, buying them things for their birthday[s]. Well, my niece gets into [trouble], and she decided she's not going to listen to her mom because her mom was never there, her mom didn't raise her, so she's basically saying, "Screw you. I'm going to do what I want. You don't love me. You never raised me. You never spend time with me. My nanny, my aunts, and my uncles always did for us. You didn't do for me." So she was in a group home. She decided that she no longer wanted to be in a group home, and she wanted to go and live with her aunt, who she loved *so* much, who once provided for her and always did for her. So me being soft-hearted and "save the child," because everyone deserves an opportunity, I said, "Yes, I will take on that responsibility."

Taking a second child into her family was more difficult than she had expected. In research on "mixed families," in which adoptive or foster children are brought into already established homes, psychologists warn that the introduction of a new member to the family, especially a teenage sibling, can result in jealousy for both the adoptive child and the children of the already established home (Carter and McGoldrick, 1980). Competition for parental attention and affection is compounded in the single-parent home. In Shawna's case, her youth worked against her assuming the sole parental role. Vanessa remembered her aunt in the role she once had—a "cool" aunt—not as the mother of a toddler, and especially not as a surrogate for a mother Vanessa herself never really had:

> Well, little did I know that my niece had another motive in mind. While she was up here, she decided that she didn't like me because when I didn't have any kids, as she said, I was "cool," [and] we did more things, but now that Tasha was in the picture, it was this jealousy type of thing . . . like, "Well, Tasha has this and Tasha has that. And why can't we do this? Why can't we stay out until eleven o'clock?" "Well, because Tasha is just a baby; she's just a little girl. She's a toddler. She has to be on a schedule." . . . "Anyway, you're in school. We don't need to be hangin' out at eleven o'clock at night or with someone else."

Vanessa, a living statistic from research on children of teenage mothers, acted out her troubles in school (Hetherington, Cox, and Cox, 1977). Unable to keep track of her niece's activities and worried about crime and irresponsible sex, Shawna tried to impress her values on her niece, but Vanessa rejected her guidance:

> She was having some problems in school which I did not know about because by the time I got home from work, the mail just was not in the mailbox. I wasn't getting any parent-teacher conference letters or anything like that. And it got to the point where I used to come home from work and she wasn't at home, and I explained to her that this is not the suburbs; this is the city. "When I say that when you come home from school, I want you to call me at work, I want you to call me because I want to know that you're in that house safely and there is no one else in that house. And when you don't call me, I worry because I think that something has happened." Well, she just thought that I was bein' overconcerned and nothing would happen. What could possibly happen? To show her how naive she was, I would explain to her, "Well, you know, down the street someone got shot. And that bullet didn't have anyone's name on it."

"And because you are a big girl for thirteen, there will be a lot of guys who will want to date you, and I don't think that I'm really ready for that. And are you ready for that?" We talked about the whole sex thing. Well, she met a guy that's sixteen and she wanted a boyfriend. And I said, "No. You're too young for a sixteen-year-old." Now if he's thirteen or fourteen, I can be a little lenient and say, "Yes. You guys can be friends. Go to the movies and hang out. But as far as being girlfriend and boyfriend, I really think that you're a bit young for that, mentally, emotionally, and physically." . . . "When you have a boyfriend, what is it that you guys plan on doing? [She laughs] . . . I said, "Do you plan on having sex?" "Oh, no. We don't plan on having sex.". . . Well, we all know that we're dumb. They all know more than what *we* know [laughs]. So when I told her she couldn't have this sixteen-year-old boyfriend, she got highly upset with me and decided she was gonna go see him.

Vanessa continued to disobey her aunt's dictates and eventually precipitated a confrontation. Knowing that her mother became pregnant in her teens did not deter Vanessa, and her mother's admonition not to date an older boyfriend carried no weight. Impatient with the "games" Vanessa was playing, Shawna tried once again to help her niece end her association with "bad kids" and reminded her of promises she made to the court:

The next day she got up [to go] to school. I told her, "When I come home from work, if you're not here, wherever you are, stay there . . . because I'm not playin' no games. I don't have time to play games." I said, "You sat up in front of the court, in front of the judge in court, and you told him that you wanted to change your life. You said that if you go to live with your aunt, who provides some of the things that your mom could not provide, and she could help you with some of the things educationally, that you would be a better person, that you would not run the streets, take up with bad kids—I shouldn't say bad kids, but kids that were up to no good." I said, "But you get here and attract that same type of kid! What is the problem?"

Shawna attempted some reality therapy, reminding her niece that her grades are too low and that she could learn something from students who are positive role models, instead of hanging out with people who will help her go nowhere. She even invoked the obvious lesson of Vanessa's mother and confronted Vanessa with the possible consequences of her actions—all to no avail:

> So, she says to me, "The kids I want her to hang around with, they're all nerdy." And I said to her, "Well, what type of grades do you have? You have in the sixties. You need to be hanging around with nerdy kids! I think you need some intelligence. You need somebody that is going to be doing some positive things. And stop hanging around negative people." And I said, "If you hang around negative people, you're getting negativism, so where can you go? Nowhere. . . . Do you want to have the same life as your mom? Do you want to start having kids at an early age? Because . . . that's your reward for hanging around with these . . . kids."

Reforming her niece and being her sole provider became a strain on Shawna, and she worried about the negative influence Vanessa was having on Tasha. Still she persisted in trying to help Vanessa learn to respect herself and others:

> I said, "I do not have the time to worry in that capacity about you. . . . I don't need any more stress in my life than what I already have." And I said, "Being a single mom and working full-time and trying to provide for you and Tasha is enough. . . . Tasha is just enough, without having to worry about if you will be shot."

> It was like, "I'll change a little bit, but then, next week, I'll change something else and be bad, and the following week, I'll be good." So it was an up-and-down roller coaster, and I said to her, "You have to be a role model for Tasha" because Tasha was asking questions.

> . . . so I'm trying to teach her. "In order for you to get respect, you have to respect yourself and respect other people. When you live in this household, that means you have to respect

everyone. It's not all about me." And I said, "I'm raising Tasha that way. And when you act that way, then Tasha thinks that's all right." Because my daughter went through a whole transition when she was really getting mouthy. Oh, just talking back. I was just having a terrible time. And I'm having to control her, and say, "Oh no, don't do that." And she's like, "Oh. Neeny does it." "Well, Vanessa does it, but Mommy's gonna work with Vanessa so she won't do it anymore." So I went through a lot when my niece was up here four months.

In an altercation with another student, Vanessa, a big girl for her age, knocked a teacher to the floor. At this point, Shawna saw that Vanessa's presence in her home threatened the stability she had worked so hard to create.

Well, Wendy, I thought they were going to sue me, and I would lose the house and everything I worked so hard to get! . . . I said, "You came up here for your education. You didn't come up here to be fighting and get into an altercation over some stinky little boy that can't do nothing for you. You have to get your education first."

Still unwilling to give up on a bright, articulate young lady, however, Shawna tried to get Vanessa counseling, but she resisted:

When you talk to this young lady, she's very articulate. She likes to write. She reads. But, mentally, she's a mess. So [she sighs deeply] . . . I said, "Vanessa, you really should go for counseling." Because I knew that we were going to need some counseling, especially with her mom. . . . I said to her, "I want you to be able to function here emotionally to the fullest." [Vanessa responded,] "I don't need counseling. No. I'm all right! I don't have to deal with all that stuff I had to deal with back home. I don't know anyone here."

During the four months that Vanessa stayed with Shawna and Tasha, some new dynamics began to form, but because Shawna recognized the immense potential harm that Vanessa's influence might have on her and her daughter, she sent Vanessa home. In later correspondence with her aunt, Vanessa expressed her regrets:

She wrote me a letter. She said that she was sorry, that she hopes that Tasha doesn't pick up any of her bad ways. I [had] said to her, "It's really time for you to go because I don't want my daughter to be influenced like that. I will always love you, but I don't think that I have to take all of the things that you're dishing out . . . that it's not fair for me and Tasha. . . . Whatever it is that you want to do in life, I wish you the best. But I don't have the time to do that. I don't have the time to be running after you, worrying about what you're doing, who you're going to be in trouble with." And then, I couldn't talk with her because she lied about so many things. I [had told her], "Once you lose my trust, that's it. . . . I wanted to give you a fair shake." And I sent her back with her mother, and she's putting her mother through hell. So I said, "When I go through hell, I want to go through hell with my own daughter!"

It took awhile to heal some wounds, but with the open communication that Shawna and Tasha have always enjoyed, and the typical resilience of children, Tasha quickly recovered:

I went through a lot, and it took me awhile after she left to get my daughter back! But I talked to my daughter about it because she cried for two days because she got close to her. She was somebody for her to play with. . . . And Tasha got used to having someone else there. So it took her awhile. But it was really funny one day when her godmother said to her, "Are you happy or sad that Vanessa left?" She said, "I'm happy . . . 'cause she was bad, and now I have two bedrooms." [She laughs.]

BREAKING OUT AND BREAKING DOWN

Shawna has come a long way from that angry little girl who hated her mother because she did not understand why she was not allowed to see her absent father. She has become a mature young woman, a strong-minded leader and mentor for her daughter and for children from homes less "lucky" than hers. She broke free from an abusive and suffocating relationship, broke away from her mother's dreams for her to become a lawyer, broke down the barriers of gender socialization that inhibited both the men and women in her life, and broke out of the patterns of powerlessness she might have followed, as did some of her brothers and sisters. As a single mother, she gives purposeful attention to spending quality time with her daughter, encourages her daughter to develop a strong relationship with her father, and helps her daughter to spread her wings so she can experience the world. She is a winner, a true example of the motto passed down from mother to daughter, "If you're right, you stand your ground!"

Chapter 5

Lyn:
"Just Get On with It"

Of all the cases I studied, Lyn's story provides the fullest rendering of a woman's life over time. Her narrative begins over twenty years ago, when as a young mother of two sons, ages three and six, she decided that she wanted to get out of her marriage. Having finished her PhD while her youngest was a baby, Lyn packed up her family and relocated to a new job, a new beginning, a new life. In this, and in many of the following events, she adopted her mother's attitude about life: "Don't think about it. Just get on with it."

Her mother, widowed while Lyn was young, provided the model of a strong, independent, resourceful woman, a model that she followed from *her* mother, also widowed while a young farmer in the Midwest. Lyn is the third generation of a "tradition of strong women" in her family. Perhaps it is this self-reliant pioneer spirit that formed the basis for her child-rearing style, encouraging her sons to act on their own and to accept responsibilities so that they might learn from experiencing the consequences of their actions.

Her conviction that self-awareness is necessary for maintaining healthy relationships pervades her coping strategies. As a private person, she enjoys having time to herself, and her sons always knew that she had "a life apart from being a mother." She said that being a mother is only a "piece of me" and described herself also as a friend, professional, peer, and lover. Learning as young children to respect their mother as a multifaceted person led her sons, both self-directed individuals now in their twenties, to openly express their appreciation for their mother's supportive, but never controlling guidance, and to maintain the closeness they enjoyed throughout their lives—together and apart.

217

Her challenge as she nears retirement is to construct a new narrative for her life, one that will make hers "feel like a good life." With both sons successfully launched, she must now shift the focus away from parenting her sons and toward a life of graceful solitude, in which she can picture herself "being alone in a beautiful place."

THREE GENERATIONS OF SINGLE MOMS

It was not hard for Lyn to follow the model of her mother, who raised three children largely on her own. A strong, nonjudgmental person, Lyn's mother let her children believe in their own competence to make decisions. She also never let her children know that money might have been tight for her. She lived her life with forward momentum, thus, the motto that is the theme of Lyn's square of the quilt, "Just get on with it":

Now, my father died when I was ten, so I was raised by a single mom, for the most part. That's another reason why it didn't seem like it would be that great [a risk to live alone]. . . . She was a more traditional mother in the sense that she was— at least until my dad died—a full-time mom. After that, she went to work, but during those early years, she was there, and I never had to get my own breakfast and wash my own clothes. I mean, I wasn't doing that at the age my kids were, but the thing that I think, when I think about my mother, [is that] she's very nonjudgmental, and there was never the feeling that I wasn't competent to make decisions, and while I might make some really stupid decisions, that I would recognize them as being really stupid. She didn't need to tell me that, so it did come in large part from that influence from my mother.

She had a two-year teaching degree before she was married, and at the time my dad died, you could still teach with a two-year degree in [the Midwest]. So part of that time she taught, but what she did most of those years is worked as a medical secretary. . . . I never felt like money was a particular issue, but I knew that we didn't have as much money as some of my friends, but in my little town, nobody was rich and nobody was poor. It was all very middle class. We were probably getting close to lower class, but I certainly never thought of myself in terms of money being a problem. As I think back on it now, and as an adult, I think money must have been really tight during those years. She couldn't have been making much at all, and I don't think my dad's estate amounted to much, and money isn't something we talk about in my family.

I asked her about it when I was an adult, and she said, "Yeah, well, we did okay." And my mother's attitude toward life in general is, "Just get on with it. Don't think about it, just get on with it," so it's almost as if once it was over, it's over. It wasn't something that we talked about, and talked about the bad old days or the good old days. "Just get on with it."

Widowed very young, Lyn's mother had a life of her own and a college education, so she did not define herself solely in terms of being a wife and mother. It is interesting to note that even though she was educated to be a teacher, she worked as a secretary, another stereotypically female job, before that. Despite her experience as the sole wage earner, the desire to stay at home and her second husband's insistence that she did not need to work kept her out of the workforce for nine years, until he, too, died and she was on her own again. Strong gender role patterns such as these governed the lives of many couples in the earlier half of the twentieth century (Coontz, 1992):

> **WP:** One of the things that was a trap for women of her genera-tion anyway was that idea that women must define themselves as wives and mothers first and in other ways second. Did she have that problem or not?

> **L:** No. And I think partly because she was widowed so young. Also, she led an interesting life before she got married. I mean, she'd gone to college, which was very unusual. She was the only one of her sibs that had gone to college. And she had taught school for a few years, and I think she just felt good about herself. . . .

> . . . It was after her second husband died she went back to teaching and taught for a few years.

WP: So she stayed home at some point?

L: Yeah. She went to work when my dad died. She worked as a medical secretary and a secretary in a car dealership, but most of the time she was in the clinic as a medical secretary. She remarried when I was nineteen, so there was nine years there, and did not work when she and George were married, which was about five years, and he died.

WP: Did you ever talk about why she chose not to work?

L: No. I think, probably, . . . that George would have preferred her not to. It was sort of little town—everybody knew everybody—and he was a prominent businessman, and so my guess is, it was just kind of his assumption that she didn't need to, that she should relax. He wanted to take care of her, I'm sure.

Lyn's mother was not the first generation of women to face a life of parenting alone. She had been raised by Lyn's grandmother, whose husband died when Lyn's mother was ten years old, by strange coincidence exactly the same age Lyn was when her own father died. Unlike divorce, though, widowhood—especially around wartime—was not uncommon, since women often outlived their husbands by many years (Coontz, 1992; Farrell, 1972). Regardless of the way they came by their singleness, grandmother and mother raised families of five and three children, respectively, and taught their daughters survival skills by example:

L: [My mother] also had been raised without a father. Yeah, her father died [when she was] almost exactly the same age as me— I think she was ten—and my grandmother never remarried. And that was a family of five.

They had been homesteaders. She had gone out and homesteaded in the Midwest as a young woman. Soon as she was eighteen, she got her own homestead, and my grandfather also homesteaded, so when they got married, they had a good-sized piece of property. And she was a farm wife all of her life. She never worked anything other than that.

I don't know how long she stayed on the farm after he died. By the time I knew my grandmother, she seemed like a really *old* woman—she was probably my age [laughs]. But she didn't have her own home, and I don't think she had had [one] for quite some time. She just rotated amongst the five kids, and after my dad died, she spent a lot of time with us, primarily baby-sitting for my little brother, so that, too, really helped out, by having a second adult. But, she was never a parent to me. It was clear that she was Grandma and that Mom was the parent. So, yeah, three generations of single moms.

I mean, women are the strong ones in my family because they're the ones who live! [She laughs.] You know! But, there's a real strong tradition of strong women. I think it does go back . . . probably back to Scotland, for that matter, where you had to scratch around and make a living in the rocks, and that kind of stuff. But, taking off and homesteading . . . she never ran the farm, but clearly was out there at the time the sod was being broken. So I mean you have to have a pretty gutsy person to do that.

WP: What'd she do with those five kids after he died?

L: I don't know. They stayed together. I know my mother went into one of the small towns for high school, she and her sister. There was no high school close by the farm. It was really pretty scattered. Grandma may have had someone working the farm and paying her rent or a portion, or it may be that my mother's older brothers were old enough so that they could, but I'm not sure.

Now my grandmother's family was fairly close. They were close, both geographically and, I think, probably emotionally, but certainly geographically. And there would have been that extended family with lots of aunts and cousins and uncles that my grandmother and her kids would have grown up with.

LYN'S DIVORCE: GETTING ON WITH IT

Early in her marriage, Lyn recognized that even though married, she was "the primary parent":

For most of the time that I have been a single parent, I've really been the primary parent as well because of geographic distance, and also, even at the time we were married, I was certainly the primary parent.

Staying home with her children while finishing her dissertation magnified the uneven distribution of parenting responsibility that she felt. Though her husband often *talked* about sharing responsibilities in raising their sons, he was not extremely involved and did not devote his full attention to the boys. Turning to Lyn for approval and emotional support, he left the decision making up to her. Parenting "this adult child along with two kids" became too emotionally exhausting. She had little difficulty deciding to pack up her family and relocate where a new job and some old friends awaited her. The desire to "get out" that Lyn experienced was common among many of the women of the 1950s, who felt suffocated by the mothering role and their home-centeredness and sought other avenues to self-fulfillment (Coontz, 1992):

When Rich was born—he's the second one—I'd finished up my doctoral course work but hadn't done my dissertation, so at that point, I was just going to take a year and be a mom. So it became most apparent during that year, how much of the parenting I was doing, but even before that, we'd talk about shared parenting, and my ex-husband sort of thought of himself as a very involved parent, but it was real clear that I was the one that made decisions about the kids, and he would *help* me with the kids. And I think that both of us realized the situation. It was really during that year, when I was not doing much else besides being home with the kids, that I decided that I wanted out of the marriage.

So then I figured that I'd better get the dissertation done, so I did it in record time. . . . I was done within six months from the time I decided to do it. . . .

Being a single parent was not a major concern for me because I felt like I was in charge of these kids anyway, and I wasn't particularly pleased, comfortable, with the kind of relationship my husband had with the kids. He liked them, and he would do things with him, and they enjoyed him, but it was

almost like having another kid [because] I couldn't rely on him
to be a parent. And they never had his complete attention, no
matter what he was doing with them. I always felt that his
attention was split between them and something else. [He was]
often making sure that he had my approval to be doing whatever it was that he was doing or not doing. It felt like . . .
emotionally, it was extremely difficult for me to kind of be
parenting this adult child along with the two kids, and feeling
like he really looked to me for approval for his parenting, as
well as other things. So, like I say, it wasn't a terribly difficult
decision [to leave].

Although stigmas about divorce and single parenting were common at the time (Coontz, 1992; Schur, 1984), Lyn realized that her
boys would be better off without a poor role model, even in a
single-parent family, and that they would not be particularly damaged by the move. Caring for her own needs was important not only
to herself but to her sons, since maintaining an unfulfilling marriage
for the sake of the children would only steep her in depression and
harm them more (Kanoy and Cunningham, 1984):

What made the decision difficult was not my fear of being a
single parent because he wasn't a good role model for them
anyway. And certainly I thought, "Here I've got these two
boys, what's it going to be without a father role model?" And I
decided that it wasn't as troublesome [laughs] as it would be if
I had felt like they really had a good solid relationship with
their father. It's not that it wasn't good and solid. I guess the
only thing I can say is that I didn't think that he was a particularly good role model, and my needs took priority over the
kids' needs. It's real clear to me looking back, and I guess I
realized it at the time, and I wouldn't have made the decision if
I felt it was going to be really harmful for them, but it felt like,
"Well, I'm not going to be any good to them anyway if I stay
in this marriage," and I would get more depressed. So it felt
like it was kind of a survival move for me.

As with many men whose wives divorce them (Levine, 1992;
Rice and Rice, 1986), Lyn's husband, Jack, was stunned by her

announcement and considered it just a phase. When he realized that she was serious, his anger and desire to punish her for leaving led him to threaten a custody suit, even though he was fully aware that he was not the better parent:

> Well, he was absolutely stunned when I first suggested to him that I thought we should have a separation—he didn't realize there was anything wrong—and then he went into a kind of, "Well, I'll humor her, until she gets through this phase." And then he realized that I meant it and went through a real angry stage, when he was going to fight me for the custody of the kids, which I thought was pretty hysterical. I didn't worry about it because I knew when . . . push came to shove that he would've felt I was clearly the better parent, whether he would have said that he didn't want the kids. He probably would never say that or admit it to himself even, but I think, in terms of recognizing that I was the better parent, he would've recognized that.

Beyond his initial actions, Jack and Lyn worked out an amiable agreement. Jack paid support and did not particularly assert his custodial claim beyond regular visitation. Lyn's own advancing professional life made it necessary for her to rely on Jack for parenting the boys while she was traveling, but she finds some of these memories difficult to retrieve, since she was busy getting on with her life:

> It was for the most part amiable, and we didn't get into either a long legal battle or even a particularly heated emotional battle about property or visitation rights, or any of that stuff, because at that point, I was living in the area, and he could see the kids as much as he wanted to every couple weeks.

> A year and a half after our separation, I was interviewing for jobs. I finished my degree at that point, so I think he probably had the kids a fair amount while I was traveling, but I can't even remember that. He didn't seem like he was a very important part of *my* life at that point.

However, as is sometimes the case when women sue for divorce, Lyn allowed her own feelings of guilt and her confidence in her ability to support her family to reduce her forward vision (Kaschak, 1992). As a result, even though he fully expected that his sons should go to college, Jack was not obligated to contribute to a college fund for the boys, a fact that Lyn now regrets immensely, since both boys have had to rely on her and on student loans to finance what became protracted stays in higher education. Even as far beyond the divorce as twelve years, when their first son was ready for college, Lyn felt that Jack was not keeping up his end. In hindsight, she realizes that financial matters could have been much worse, if anything had prevented Jack from providing regular—if minimal—child support. She believes this is a warning for women currently involved in negotiating divorce settlements while under emotional pressure to break free quickly (Weitzman, 1985). Lyn's amicability and principles led to future financial constraints that might have been eased had she insisted that her ex-husband provide a more equitable financial contribution to their sons' futures:

We came to an agreement on child support pretty easily. I was being too nice, and I realized that as soon as the papers were signed. And, in fact, my lawyer tried to talk me into asking for more, but I was feeling guilty, and *I* was the one breaking up the marriage, and . . . I was gonna go off and be financially independent. But there were two things that I really made a mistake on, and my lawyer told me. One was, there was no understanding about the kids' college education, and I naively assumed he would feel some responsibility for helping the kids when they were in college. I mean, he was an educated person, and education was important to him, and it didn't seem like it was *necessary* to write in who was gonna pay college expense[s]. Well, he didn't contribute a dime to their college expense[s], as it turned out. And it was kind of on principle because it wasn't part of the agreement.

And the other thing was, I didn't insist that he had a life insurance policy with them as beneficiaries. As it turned out, now that they're essentially adults, it doesn't make much difference, but during those years when they were little kids, had he died, it would have had a financial impact on them because it would've cut out the child support.

So, it was really the college thing that was the major issue, and I tried to renegotiate that a couple of times, and he wouldn't even consider it. So it became clear to me that this was a way of expressing his anger with me because, certainly, he thought the kids should go to college, and they should go to college wherever they could get in, and it was of value to him, but he wanted to stick it to me, and [this] was an indirect way.

He was very regular about his child support payments. There was never a time that that was an issue. And, in effect, he continued paying child support for them until they reached . . . I'm not sure . . . I think he was obligated to pay until they reached sixteen, . . . but he gave that to me until they were eighteen. So it was overlapped a little bit with their college, but it didn't pay their college expenses—obviously, it came a long way from that—and it was minimal. I mean, he was making a good salary, and I could have legitimately asked him for at least twice as much as I did and we'd have gotten it, but I was being principled, and I was okay. I had a good job, and I managed.

Starting fresh in a new city might have been more traumatic had Lyn not had a solid network of support already in place. An extended family of friends and colleagues shared in their lives:

It helped a lot when I came [here] that I had good friends here. I think there would have been much more of an impact had that not been the case. But I had good friends that I had known from the [coastal] area, with kids roughly the same age as mine, and it really was like extended family, so that helped a tremendous amount. . . . We still [get together]. It's just been a wonderful support network . . . couples, for the most part, actually. Largely the reason I came to [this city] was because my closest friend in graduate school and her husband were here.

Different Boys/Different Reactions

One theme of particularly significance in Lyn's description of her two sons—both as children and as grown men—is that because the boys' personalities are so different, their responses to the divorce, their relationships with their mother and father, and their performance in school have been more the result of the interaction between their personalities and events than caused by the singular trauma of their parents' divorce. Unlike research studies that attribute causation for depressed school achievement to divorce and the single-parent home (Hetherington, Cox, and Cox, 1977; Shreeve et al., 1986; Wallerstein and Kelly, 1974, 1976, 1980; Wallerstein and Blakeslee, 1989), Lyn's many descriptions of her sons reveal that, throughout their schooling, they acted in accordance with their unique personalities, which began to form before their parents divorced. She described the ways her sons reacted to the divorce and the move. The oldest son, Paul, sought her reassurance that she would be there for him:

> Paul . . . has always been pretty much willing to go along with whatever's happening. When the train comes along, [he goes with it,] and it's always fairly hidden about what's going on with him. He's always been like that. He still is, at twenty-nine. So Paul was just kind of, "Well, okay, so we're going to move to [the city], and Dad's not gonna come with us," and he was calm, and it was really hard to sort of pull him out and get him to talk about what that might be like for him, and "It'll be okay. You're gonna be there, aren't you?"

Her more overtly emotional younger son, Rich, the one who "wears his heart on his sleeve," sought to punish his mother with angry outbursts, though he also expressed his love for her. They coped with this emotional roller coaster through communication:

> And Rich, who was less than three at that time . . . unlike his brother, he wears his heart on his sleeve. And again, he still does, so he took it out on me. He was real angry with me, and when he didn't want to go to the baby-sitter, and . . . once he got into kindergarten, we had these horrible scenes of my dragging him to the bus, . . . but it was always directed at me. He was angry at me. I'd come home at the end of the day, and he'd come running and pummel me with his fists because of something, but, on the other hand, we had an extremely close relationship because he would also let me know how much he loved me and how important I was to him, and I understood

where that was coming from, so we talked a lot.

It seemed that what Rich and I did for the first six years of his life was talk stuff through, and he was amazing by the time he was three years old. Now that's a graphic memory I have. It was after we'd moved to [the city], but not too long after, so he was probably not much over three, and I remember him shouting at me, "I hope some day you hurt as much as I do!"—from a three-year-old! But it never worried me . . .

Even though Paul's silence might have hidden an untreated wound, she feels that he "turned out fine":

I mean, I was much more worried about Paul because he had it all hidden. But maybe it wasn't hidden because he still seems fine . . .

In later years, the boys related to their parents a bit differently; Paul developed a relationship with his father on his own, and Rich turned his anger toward his father rather than his mother:

[Paul] never felt it was a particularly big deal that we left [his] dad, and we moved away, and he's actually fairly close to his dad now. Whereas Rich has kind of shifted his anger towards [his] dad. But, you know, he's an angry young man, [and] he needs someone to be angry at, I guess.

Many mothers worry that their children will idolize their absent fathers, never fully understanding what caused the disintegration of their parents' relationship. If Paul and Rich can be considered examples, however, maturity may bring recognition:

And I think that the anger is that [Jack's] not the kind of person that [Rich] wants his father to be. [Jack] wants to be a kid with his kids, and they don't like that. So he's sort of a comic figure for them almost, which is sad because he's not trying to be, but I think both of them have come to accept that, "Well, that's just the way Dad is." I know Rich at one point said, "Well, you know people ask me about my family. And I say I've got one parent, and then there's my dad." [She laughs.] I mean, it just confirms my initial impression that it wasn't going to be so terrible for them [laughs], that he wasn't going to be that kind of role model for them that I would want him to be. . . .

Well, they're older. Probably the biggest key. And I don't think until they were probably in college that it really became clear to them that their dad just didn't come through for them. Or at least it was when they could express that. Now I think that they've both really been disappointed in him for a long time but probably didn't realize it until they became more mature. . . . Paul is much more accepting of what his dad says and does, but still it always kind of . . . "Yeah. That's who he is. He always wants to give me advice and really stupid advice, but that's who he is." Rich is more likely to get angry about and is apt to react against what he sees as his [dad's] wrong values and way of life, but he's going to go down and visit him. It's not like they're alienated.

The boys' attitudes about marriage and divorce are also different, more as a function of their personalities than from the fact that their own parents divorced. True to form, Rich retains the "hurt" he feels the split caused him and vows to "never get divorced":

Now, Rich talks about how he's sure he'll never get divorced, and if he gets married, it's gonna be forever. He doesn't know that, but it's certainly a message about how hurtful that was for him, how bad it was for him. But it's no surprise because he was letting me know all the way through. . . . It would have been tough no matter what. I mean, he's just one of those kids who . . . his nerve endings are all out there, and whatever comes along rattles him, and he can get tremendous highs as well as feeling the world is dumping on him, so I frankly don't think that he would feel a whole lot different about his child-hood no matter what it had been with him. I mean, he doesn't say it in blaming ways, that I did him wrong, just that it was really tough with him. Many of his friends . . . , both of the boys, their closest friends are from single moms. I don't know how much they talked about it, and I guess not a whole lot.

On the other hand, and consistent with his personality, Paul has more of a pragmatic "wait and see" attitude:

> I'm sure Paul feels that way, that, "Oh, I'd sure hate to get divorced." On the other hand, it doesn't seem to be that *life* principle for him like it does with Rich. I can imagine Paul saying to himself, "You know, I think I'm gonna get married while I can," rather than, "Oh, this is the love of my life! And I'm gonna be with this person forever and ever." Recognizing that maybe marriage is a good thing, and maybe it'll work. That would be consistent for him.

As far as their mom is concerned, however, the boys are not shy about letting Lyn know that they value her and believe that she has "done a good job," remembering advice that she gave, or ways that she interacted with them:

> **L:** They'll tell me that they think that I'm just really great! [She laughs.] And it's almost like it's a given that they think I've done a good job. And once in awhile they'll say something . . . oh, you know, "You're just the best mom ever. I'm just really lucky to have you for my mom." It's really nice.
>
> **WP:** And they do come right out and say that?
>
> **L:** Yeah. Again, Rich particularly . . . often it will be like, "Mom, remember the time that you said da-da-da-da-da." And I often don't remember it. And they'll let me [know], "Now that was a *really* important thing" that I said or I did, or "You just didn't make me do . . . ," or whatever, so they do have these kinds of episodes that I think will sort of say to them that, yeah, I was okay.

Missing Out

Did her sons miss out because they did not have a strong father as a role model? Lyn guesses that perhaps they did, but she believes that they were better off without him, especially Rich, whose volatile emotions would have led him to an "explosive situation" with his father (Farrell, 1972; Hattley, 1959):

L: Had it been a good relationship, obviously, if their father had been somebody else, I think it would have been an enriching thing to have another adult around constantly, that really cared about them and was supportive and that they could interact with. They're bound to miss out. But given who he was, I don't feel that that was a negative to *not* have him as part of their life.

WP: How did they fill that gap?

L: I don't know if they did really. They had other adults that they know really care about them who are either my friends or family friends. I don't think there's anybody that they would feel was a substitute father.

WP: Did they need one?

L: I don't think so. In a way, it's a reaction, at least with Rich. Rich is so much more open that it's easier to see what's going on with him, but . . . with him it's a clear reaction *against* what he sees in his dad. I can see that, potentially, if his dad had stayed in the picture, it would have been . . . it could have been an *explosive* situation if Rich had developed the way he has developed, and he would do a lot of overt negative stuff, the distancing. As it is, he can talk about the stupid things he does.

As far as feeling guilty at having deprived her children of opportunities that children from two-parent families are *supposed* to have, Lyn admits that there may have been "missed opportunities" because of financial constraints. She believes, however, that her anxiety stemmed more from the weight of sole parenting responsibility than from actual examples (Schur, 1984):

And at the time, when the kids were younger, I felt that I was missing . . . actually *they* were missing opportunities because we were always strapped for money, but looking back, I'm not sure what I would have done any differently. I mean, maybe they would have taken part in more sports, or gone to camp. I don't know. I mean, it never felt like I made decisions based on not having the money to do something, but it was kind of that. And I think it was part of that experience of being single and having all this responsibility, and it was kind of the abstract,

"Oh, my god! What are my kids missing?" rather than any kind of concrete, "They can't have this, or they can't do that."

CHILD REARING:
ENCOURAGING INDEPENDENCE

From the very beginning, Paul and Rich were full participants in their own destinies. When asked to describe her parenting style, Lyn explained her own need to be independent and stated her philosophy that "the best way to learn what works and what doesn't is to experience the consequences of it." She encouraged her sons to be responsible for managing their own time, from getting up and going to school, to homework and doing their own wash. Expecting responsible behavior from her sons seemed reasonable to her, because they were not the kind of children who would take advantage of such freedom by violating the rules.

Looking back, she admits that she might have been more proactive in pushing them to reach their potential in school, but she is philosophical about the way they turned out—both of them in college pursuing careers they have chosen and seem to enjoy:

> **L:** I wanted my kids to be self-sufficient as soon as possible. So I think my style was, from the very beginning, to encourage them to do things on their own, explore things on their own, and to take on responsibilities. I think I was fairly reasonable with that. I mean, I didn't expect them to drive [or] fly a plane when they were seven years old [smiles]. But, I felt it was important. Again, I think it was my needs that took priority. It was real important for me to not feel that they were dependent on me for *every*thing forever. It was too much responsibility, so I needed to feel that they could get some of their sustenance, both emotional and everything else, kind of on their own.
>
> So they were doing things like washing their own clothes by the time they could reach the knobs on the washing machine. And we had some disasters, but I figured, well that's the tuition that you pay for learning about life. So that was sort of an underlying principle, and for the most part, I felt the best way for them to learn what works and what doesn't work is to

experience the consequences of it. So, I really didn't give them a lot of direction of what they should and shouldn't do. When they were little, obviously, I had a bedtime for them, but once they got to middle grade school, it was up to them to get themselves to bed and get up in the morning. I never took responsibility for them getting up or making sure—stuff that I felt could drive you crazy—trying to be sure that all your things are together in the morning, and that stuff. It was their job.

WP: How'd they do with that?

L: They did beautifully. I don't think either of them ever over-slept unless it was sort of intentional [laughs]. But time management became their responsibility early on, and again I think that comes from . . . I feel [it takes] all that I can do to manage *my* time, and I don't think I particularly do it well, so I sure don't want to muck them up by giving them the illusion I'm gonna manage theirs!

So they had a lot of freedom, and I think I was just awfully lucky that they didn't abuse it. Because . . . neither of them were disciplinary problems in any way. Probably the naughtiest thing they ever did was skip school. It didn't seem to be in their nature to violate the rules in a situation that way, and it didn't have to be an issue, that they were threatened or they were given sanctions of any kind for doing it. Other than getting their homework done and stuff like that, I mean, they probably were not real conscientious about it, given what their grades reflected.

WP: You didn't supervise homework?

L: Not a lot, and that's probably something I would do differently if I were to do it over. Again, it was part of this, "It's your job. It's your responsibility. And the consequences are that if you don't do it, you're gonna get bad grades, and the consequences of getting bad grades are that you're not gonna get into college." But, you know, as a third grader, that's certainly not a very compelling reason. So, at various points, both of them said to me, "You know you should have made us work harder." But on the other hand, then they'll think about kids whose parents are really on top of them to do their homework, and they never came to any good [laughs]. They hate their parents or they've dropped out, not necessarily, but it's like they, on the one hand, would like to have me take responsibility for it—"I'm not doing as well in school"—but, on the other hand, recognizing it would have been just absolutely terrible if I had tried to do that.

There's no way to do parenting in a way that they're gonna be happy with everything—I'm convinced—so I kind of had to find a style that worked for me, and fortunately, I don't think I did them too much disservice [laughs].

The Boys in School

Did such freedom and self-motivation help or hurt Lyn's boys in school? One might expect either tremendous successes, given the self-discipline they had to demonstrate, or the patterns of failure expected of children whose parents are not totally involved in their schooling (Baca Zinn and Eitzen, 1990; Hetherington, Cox, and Cox, 1977). Paul and Rich were neither. Lyn described their school performance as mediocre; neither boy distinguished himself as either stellar or substandard. Was this the result of their parents' divorce, as many early researchers have claimed? Or was their school performance consistent with their personalities, with behavioral trends apparent before and after their parents' divorce and, indeed, throughout their lives? Lyn believes that the latter is a better explanation:

They were very mediocre in school. . . . Rich, who was always acting out stuff with me as a little kid, and also during his first couple years of school, was a model child with everybody else. So he never gave *anybody* else a minute's trouble, and he's real cute and charming, and he seemed real smart. I wonder now [laughs] how he could've fooled me. So he looked like just the ideal kid, and in many ways he was. And certainly I would rather have him do his acting out with me than in another setting. . . .

Paul, all his life, has been sort of a social isolate. As a baby, as a little kid, even while we were married—so I can't attribute it to that—he would go to the day care center and sit in the

corner and watch the other kids. So it almost feels like whatever they did in school, later on, was kind of their natural
inclination versus as the result of the separation and divorce.
   But neither of them were particularly good students. They
were okay—B's and C's primarily, occasionally an A, but not
very often—and their teachers always said, all the way
through, that they had more ability, that they should apply
themselves. More so with Rich because he was much more
social and he impressed people, and . . . teachers really wanted
him to do well because he was such a nice kid. Paul—everybody always described him as, "He's such a nice boy. He's so
polite." But I think he would just disappear in class. They
really wouldn't notice him, so what he was doing probably
seemed like he was [okay].

The potential damage of low expectations for children who are
not performing in accordance with their ability and the way that
psychological testing can translate into self-fulfilling prophecy
have been documented by Schur (1984). Lyn explained how she
took Paul for treatment for what she recognized as depression (one
aspect of teenage adjustment that can be manifested in poor school
performance and is sometimes attributed to children of single parents). She was disturbed by the psychologist's focus on Paul's lack
of ability. True to his passive, accepting nature, Paul internalized
the psychologist's assessment of his abilities and lowered his expectations for the future:

When Paul was in high school, I really questioned whether he
was going to make it into a college, and, in fact, he was seeing
a psychologist for awhile. I was concerned because I knew he
was depressed. The psychologist took it as, "Well, we need to
do psychological testing. We need to find out what his ability
level is." Which is not what I was questioning at all. Well, this
guy told Paul that he probably could not make it in college,
that he was not bright enough. I went through the ceiling, as
you can imagine. Well, I think Paul believed it on some level,
but again he's, "Well, gee, I don't know. Maybe that's true, so
maybe I should do something else."

Well, it got to be his senior year, and he hadn't applied to colleges, and I was getting nervous about having the kid living in my house for the rest of his natural life [laughs], and I just knew that he was capable of doing it. So he was actually accepted at a few places, one of which was [a state university]. And, at that point, [the state university] was really being threatened with big budget cuts because of their enrollment drop, so I think they may have been scraping the bottom of the barrel. I was a little surprised he got in. It turned out to be just the most wonderful experience for him that I could have asked for. He got there and he felt smart, and he just hasn't stopped. He had a dual major in Psychology and Art History. He did a year abroad, and he ended up on the dean's list every semester. [He had just found his niche.] And now he's in a physician's assistant program which is extremely challenging, and he's struggling, but he knows he's competent. He knows he's capable. So he just didn't get . . . it didn't click for him until college.

Lyn explained Paul's delayed renaissance as a combination of influences from both his own personality and her example. In addition to his tendency to be passive and to avoid taking on responsibility for his own learning, he likely adopted her own ambivalence about whether she should push him forward or allow him to find his own way—even if it meant not attending college. She speculated that, watching her, a highly educated woman, work so hard, turned him off to the idea of higher education:

I think a lot of it was him feeling such an outsider socially in high school. Plus his passivity of, "Well, whatever people tell me I should do, well, I'll do it," but not really take any kind of responsibility for his own learning, which is not uncommon for a kid, but it seemed extreme in his case. And they were tough years because I was on his back, trying to balance my conviction that hollering at him certainly isn't going to make him do any better, and so what if he doesn't go to college. Just because it's my values, doesn't mean it's important for everybody in the world, which I could never *really* believe, but I was working hard at it. And he obviously had picked up on that ambivalence that, "Yeah, I want you to do well, but if you don't it's gonna be okay," and, of course, feeling like . . . part of all this is watching what my life has been like. And I was really *working*. You know how the first two years on a job was really intense. I was working all the time, and I'm sure on some level he felt, "I'd never be able to do that anyway, so I'd be better off just not giving it a shot." I think there was that feeling of, "I can't really do what Mom wants". . . . what he thought I wanted him to do, which was go get a PhD and teach in college, and so "I just won't try."

The reasons for Rich's slow progress toward his goals were different from his brother's, with Rich also acting in ways consistent with his personality. Rich had to "try on" different lives, to experiment, to move toward his goals only when they presented themselves to him, and to learn the hard way. Perceptive mentors encouraged Rich, and Lyn, working in the background, facilitated his eventual move toward finishing his college education and starting a career that would use his talents and satisfy him:

[Rich's] grades were a little bit stronger all the way through, but still he was coasting. He started college at [the university], and I think just partied real hard for two years and didn't flunk out. He could have stayed, but . . . his good friends were leaving, so what's the point in being there if your party animal friends aren't going to be? So he decided to come to our college, moved home, and halfway through the semester, I just about killed him! [She laughs.] He didn't know what he wanted. For a year and a half, he did menial labor and shared an apartment with friends. That made me nervous, fearing he would never finish, but that ambivalence, that's just him.

He decided he wanted to be an English major at the local university, and he did very well. He was a hard worker. So he finished. He did well, and he had a couple of instructors who were just wonderful with him and who really made him feel like was a talented writer. . . . So through this, even though at the time he decided he wanted to be an English major, he'd been talking about teaching, and as a kid, he talked about wanting to be a teacher . . . so he finished his degree, and it was, "So I think I want to be a teacher."

Well, naturally a Bachelor of Arts can't be a teacher; you need to do certification. "Oh, okay." The university program in teacher education is through the night college, or one of those; anyway . . . it's really tough to get in, and it sounds like it's kind of a scattered program. So he applied for teacher certification, and they said they weren't taking any certification-only students. They said, "If you want to earn your master's degree, you can apply, but we're not doing teacher certification." So he finished his degree in December.

So that spring he went out to the West to work with my brother, who's an archaeologist. He had worked with him one summer previous to that and explored the [university out there] to see if he could get into teacher certification there, and he couldn't. They weren't doing teacher certification. Well, then I started getting a little nervous because my assumption was [that] he would be able to go someplace and do a semester and get teacher certification and be okay. Well, in the meantime, I found out that the department here was again accepting certification-only [students], so he got his application in and was accepted, and that's what he's doing now.

The long road to self-definition for Rich finally ended, and similar to his brother, he finally proved to himself that he is a capable person. Lyn stated, "I think now he really feels like he knows something. I think before it was kind of like a cover."

Getting Launched

In several interviews, Lyn referred to her sons as successfully launched. She is in close contact with both of her sons and interacts with them as peers:

So, at this point, I feel like they're both "launched." Paul will be done with his program in another year. . . . He'll finish and he'll be fine. Rich probably won't get a job teaching [right away because jobs here are scarce], but he'll do something [in the meantime].

In terms of where we are right now, I guess the way I can describe the family is, both of the boys are still in really close touch with me.

Although Rich is living with his mother again, Lyn explained that they perceive this arrangement as being different from the familial obligation of the past. Interacting as peers, she enjoys his perceptive input in their discussions about teaching, a professional interest they share. Although sometimes tempted to offer advice, she recognizes that Rich is an expert in his own right, marking a shift away from the mother-son relationship toward a more balanced one:

Rich is living with me, and so there's that physical closeness, plus we share a lot of interests and concerns and things. So he comes home and tells me about his day, and I tell him about what my class has been like and what issues came up, and he talks about what a student has written that was interesting and how do we respond. And it's almost on a peer level at this point, which is really nice. And I still for the most part feel like that I want to give him advice, and I have to stifle it because . . . I realize that he knows more about what he's doing than I know about what he's doing.

And that's been kind of an interesting shift—that I always assumed that I really knew more about whatever, than he did, and that's not true. And he'll give me advice, and I'll solicit his input on a very genuine level; whereas in the past it might just have been more to engage him in a process of discussing something, now it's genuine when I say, "What do you think? How do you think a class will take to this? If I try this do you think it will work?" Or "This is how I handled that and I'm not really comfortable with it. What do you think?" That's very nice, and it's creating much more of a balanced relationship. On the other hand, it's clearly, "I'm Mom and I pay the bills," and I'm responsible for things, stuff, life, in terms of pretty much just make sure there's food there and that kind of thing.

Yesterday he went out and washed and waxed my car and really did a nice job, cleaned it all up. And I thanked him for it and how nice it made it look, and he said, "Well, thanks for letting me live here, and for paying for school. I really appreciate that." . . . We're both kind of recognizing that he is at that point where, all else being equal, most people his age are off on their own, and they're independent, and they don't live with Mom, [and they have] a job. And so, acknowledging both that it's fine and it's working, but we need to mark it, instead of just life as it used to be five years ago.

Different in their reactions to the divorce, their attitudes in school, and their pursuit of careers, each boy also relies on his mother in different ways. Unlike Rich, who shares his mother's residence and receives continued support as he finishes his degree, Paul looks to his mother only when he needs to communicate or someone to listen as he vents frustrations and works through problems:

> Paul is in close touch because he . . . I think primarily because he's in a transition stage. . . . I am likely to hear from Paul once or twice a week, but right now, he's finished his first year in the physician's assistant program, and he had about a two-week break, and he's gonna come home—the only time he's been home this year—but has had to find a new apartment, figure out what he's going to be doing as far as a car for next year. . . . So I think Paul's way of dealing with transitions and stress in general is he needs to talk about it. And he isn't necessarily asking for advice, although I'll give him some, and he can either take it or not take it and that's okay with both of us. But it's important for him to tell me what he's . . . if things are real stressful . . . "I'm just working so hard; I don't know how I'm gonna get through this," or he'll tell me how many phone calls he's made to try to locate apartments and why this didn't work out or that didn't work out, and a lot of just kind of getting it out there.
>
> I see it as his way of using me as a support system, which is very different than the way Rich would use me as a support system. So, in that sense, I'll know what's going on in Paul's life even though I don't see him, and then I won't hear from him for awhile, and so I assume then that things are going okay. We'll talk once a week, or every ten days or so, but during these transition times, he'll call every couple of days, or he'll call,

and I know that today is going to be a decision-making day or something.

Even though by the material criteria of independence—jobs, income, spouses—Lyn's sons are still connected to her, she considers them independent adults who are willing to solicit her support:

So . . . we're all still real close, but at the same time, with both of them, it's clear that they're launched, in the sense of they look to me for support, but there's no question in my mind that if I weren't there, they'd be fine, and it's more like—they're adults—they're doing it. They know how to do it. But . . . they're not out, they're not independent, they don't have jobs, they don't have incomes, they don't have spouses, and so there's still the kinds of stuff you get from all of that, that kind of still connects them to me. And much of it is much like a peer, you know, the kind of thing that a friend might call up and say, "Oh God, this is driving me crazy. . . ." They're not expecting me to do anything about it.

Unfortunately, her sons' financial dependence while they finish college reawakens memories of how their father did not provide for aiding the boys' transition to independence. This residual negative effect of the divorce and Jack's current differential treatment of his sons rekindle Lyn's anger: "There's that bastard doing it to me again!" Because the boys have nowhere else to go for financial support, they must ask their mother, a situation that Lyn described as unhealthy, but unavoidable (Weitzman, 1985):

Now . . . both of them need financial support from me in different ways. Paul, this past school year, has had loans to carry him through almost completely, but he's without an income this summer and hasn't determined yet whether he's going to get his full loans for the fall. Will he need to come up with a couple thousand dollars to get into a new apartment? And he's gonna have to get a new car, so there's big money that he needed for summer, and so I suggested he ask his dad, and he was obviously hesitant to do that, and he had reasons why: "Well, this wasn't a good time." So finally he did ask his dad about a car, and his dad told him that he didn't have any money right now. He'd had to go on a trip, and he didn't get reimbursed for all of it, so he was really strapped.

And, what it brought up for me was, "There's that bastard doing it to me again!" He's making me feel like Paul just is not a priority. What it does is then turn it around so that he's going to have to get the money from me. So it feels more like an attack against me, except Paul's the one who's left feeling like, "Gee, my dad doesn't come through for me." I can just get angry and call him a son of a bitch and a cheap bastard.

What makes it particularly irritating is that he'll always come through for Rich. He bought Rich a car last summer. And Rich went down there sort of with the understanding that he would help him find a car and help him finance it, and he would be making payments to his dad. . . . I think that's what the understanding was. Well, his dad never said anything about Rich paying it back. Well, Paul knows that, and I can't blame Rich for not insisting that he [repay his dad]—well, I wouldn't either [laughs].

So it really irritates me that . . . he's so unbalanced in his [treatment of the boys], and I don't think he knows it. He's just so unaware. I don't think Jack knows . . . how it sounds to Paul. Paul really doesn't like borrowing money from me or having me pay for things for him, but he's in a situation where he doesn't have an alternative, and I don't think that's a very healthy situation for him—certainly isn't for me! So that, too, is a kind of connection. It feels like it's not natural for somebody who's almost thirty years old to have to go to their mother and say, "Can I borrow some money to live on?"

However, despite the emotional and financial "ties that bind," Lyn asserted that she makes her decisions independently of their impact on the boys. With the launching phase largely completed, she is ready for a new phase in her life, one that will focus on her:

I mean, the kids haven't been . . . in a sense they haven't been central to my life in recent years, the way they were all through high school and even when they were getting their undergraduate degrees. It still felt like I kinda need[ed] to stay put and make sure that I had enough money to cover their tuition and that kind of thing. It was pretty central. Well, they're both still in school, but the end is in sight and [laughs]—knock on wood. So it feels like it's a different phase, and I'm moving into it—I'm in it but I'm just kind of aware of being in it.

MYSELF ALONE

Coming Along

Lyn mused that sometimes having one parent allows that parent to maintain consistent child-rearing practices, which is "easier," but she has a healthy respect for the benefits of having two adults to balance any possible extremes (Dinnerstein, 1976; Farrell, 1972):

> I think that in many ways it's much easier raising a child by yourself because you don't have to negotiate that stuff. You just do it the way . . . I'm not sure that's *necessarily* to the advantage of the kids, but it's certainly easier. I think that having two parents that don't agree on everything can create a healthy skepticism and balance, but in terms of it being easier, I think, in many important ways, it's easier to be a single parent.

Looking back over more than twenty years of single parenting, Lyn reflected that although her sons were a primary focus during their early years alone with her, they were not her entire existence. Fulfiling her children's needs did not necessarily mean sacrificing her autonomy, and she believes her boys have benefited from her own self-actualization. She thinks that it is wrong for a single mother to assume that she must give up her life simply because she has sole responsibility for parenting (Gilligan, 1982; Kaschak, 1992). As a professional working with families in therapy, she considers such an attitude unhealthy because it fosters dependencies and resentment:

> I think I've got a great life, and I think I have had. I don't have regrets. And I feel like that I've really done what I wanted to

do, and I feel that my kids have kind of come along, rather than be central. I don't feel that I've given things up because I had kids, or given things up because of being a single parent, and it's really gratifying to see that they've grown up to be these great young men, but I'm not sure that if they turned out to be bums, I don't know what I could do. I don't know if I could look back and say, "Well, these are the mistakes I made. I should have done this differently."

It's like, I did what I needed to do, and the kids seemed to have not only been okay but been strengthened by that. I think probably the biggest mistake I would have made was to feel that, "Oh my God, now I've got total responsibility for these kids, and I have to devote my life to them."

I'm teaching a course right now on working with families . . . and we had someone come in last Friday to talk about her role as a professional, working with families and empowering them so that they can make [therapists] unnecessary in the long run. . . . And she made the point that when you start off going out of your way to do things for families, eventually you're going to start resenting them. And you're gonna feel like it's a drain on you, and that doesn't do them any good in the long run.

And I think it's much the same having kids. I mean, obviously you have to go out of your way if you've got children, but I think you have to minimize that. They have to feel important. They have to feel loved. They have to feel secure. But, if parents give up their own life for those kids—and I think as a single parent you're almost more likely to do what you have to do to—you can't help but resent that in the long run, that you look back and say, "Oh my God, if I didn't have this life, I could have had this other life, and I would be so much happier and richer, and better educated, [etc.]."

I feel like that kind of "selfishness" is important, and not to feel guilty about it. You've got to meet your own needs if you're going to be able to meet the kids' needs. And again, that's kind of my professional orientation as well, that you've got to take care of the caregiver, and it's probably easier to identify that in myself because of my professional education.

Knowing and acknowledging herself as a multifaceted person has helped Lyn to maintain her self-esteem and to get on with her own life, while she was a parent and after her sons had grown. She explained how her sons understood her as a person, not just a parent:

> Well, I don't really know how it happened. It feels like it's just who I am, and I guess my sense of myself; you know, a piece of me is Mom, but there's other pieces, and so that's always been the case. . . . They know my friends, and they care about my friends almost again like peers. . . . It's clear to them, and always has been, that I've got a life apart from being a mother. There's the work me, and there's also the me with a circle of friends, and the me that travels, and the me that wants to be left alone so I can read, and they've respected that.

I asked her if she thought that the ability to understand a mother as more than a mother might be a phenomenon more common with the children of single mothers. Although recognizing that she could not speak for all single mothers, a group that includes many of her friends, she hypothesized that this ability may be a function of a single mother's need to assert her independence or of children's tendency to consider two parents as a unit, not as individuals (Llewelyn and Osborne, 1990):

> Most of my friends are single mothers. . . . They all deal with things differently. I don't know. I think it may be more typical of single mothers because you have to be more aggressive or more assertive about it to make that happen, than when you're part of a couple, you go off and do your thing and Dad's there. Whereas you're more likely perhaps to be part of a couple versus an individual in the minds of the kids. You talk about your parents. "My parents did this, and my parents did that, and my parents instilled that in me," which makes each individual less of a person. So I think it probably is different for single parents.

Lyn does not believe she sacrificed career opportunities for the sake of her children. Her career has been a combination of circumstances and conscious decisions. Though she admits she could have focused more on certain aspects of parenting, she certainly has no regrets and believes that even if she had decided to be more aggressive in her career, her children would not have suffered (Milne et al., 1986; Mischel and Fuhr, 1988; Coontz, 1992):

> I've been aware that it seems like things just happen rather than my deciding this is what I want to go after. And that has worked. At times, I guess I feel like, well, maybe if I *had* been more goal oriented and more visionary, somehow, about what I wanted, it would have been different, but I can't say I would want it to be different in those ways. I don't have any regrets. I think I can say that pretty much categorically, except some parenting things . . . looking back to when the kids were little. I remember when we talked about some of those things, things that I wish I would have paid more attention to, but in terms of how I've done my life, I don't have any regrets.
>
> I decided pretty much early on in my professional life that being famous wasn't important to me, and that I wanted some degree of recognition, but I didn't have to be famous in my field, and that's one of the few deliberate decisions that I made, and I certainly don't regret that. It felt like that was a decision I needed to make because there [were] pressures that if I were going to do that, I would need to be at a different institution, I would need to do my profession differently in terms of more publishing, research, and that's not what I like to do. So I had to get comfortable with that, that it was going to be okay not to have . . . I didn't want to do those things, so it had to be okay not [to] get the end result that those things would get me. And I'm sure that it was easier to make that decision by saying, "Well, I've got these kids that I'm responsible for; they need a big part of my life," but I think . . . that's sort of an excuse, that if that's the kind of professional life I wanted, I could have done it even with the kids, and I'm not sure they would have suffered a whole lot for it.

Lyn's ability to make and stand by decisions that fulfilled her needs kept her from succumbing to the "superwoman complex," a phenomenon she believes may simply be a temptation for all adult females because they have been socialized to be other-oriented (Coontz, 1992; Gilligan, 1982; Llewelyn and Osborne, 1990):

L: But in terms of my jobs, my multiple jobs [laughs], I like what I'm doing, and I've been very content doing it and feeling like I've pretty much carved out what I want to do. And I think there would be the kinds of frustrations that would go with a job anywhere, and it's never gotten bad enough—"It's a terrible place to be"—there's always enough positives.

WP: I think women are particularly vulnerable to that feeling that they *must* be all things to all people, the superwoman complex, I guess. How do you negotiate those feelings?

L: I don't think that's been an issue with me. It may be, more than I'm aware of, because I think that you're right. It may be something that's just part of being an adult female, but I think I've always been fairly clear about what I didn't want to do and what I didn't want to take on. One of my friends has commented how she'll say, "I know what you'd say in this situation. You'd just say, 'Well, that's not something I *choose* to do.'" And I guess I do say that a lot, whether it's something that's supposed to be fun or something that's an obligation, whatever. I'm comfortable saying, "Well, no, I don't choose to do that." And I think that being clear about that has really helped. You know, "I don't choose to participate in PTA. It's not something I want to do," whatever.

She talked about being comfortable with a degree of "selfishness," although perhaps she considers it self-fulfillment, finding solace in taking care of herself. She described how she avoids feeling guilty about not focusing too much on fulfilling the needs of others (Bequaert, 1976; Falicov, 1988; Levine, 1992; Kaschak, 1992; Rice and Rice, 1986):

I think that it's just recognizing that there's such peacefulness that comes from stepping back and having my own space and my own issues. It comes from recognizing that we can't fix other people's lives. So it kind of takes the pressure off of, "Oh my God, you have to do this for those other people." You *can't* do it for other people. So I think that by being more in the background and giving people support to do things themselves and to make those decisions, and whatever, is more my style than to say, "So-in-so's depressed" or "So-in-so is under all this pressure to make these decisions, so I'd better call her up and make her talk about it," or whatever. I'm just not comfortable doing that, and it feels like it's too great an expense to me. So it goes back, I guess, again to that selfishness and being comfortable with being selfish and feeling like I've got to take care of myself because nobody else is going to, and really feeling comfortable with that.

An Antidote to Guilt

Lyn described selfishness as her "antidote to guilt." Though she maintains some residual guilt from "being the bitch" by breaking away from her marriage, a feeling that is common for women who leave (Kaschak, 1992; Schur, 1984), Lyn explained that when one understands how difficult it is for any person to change or affect the behavior of another person, one cannot feel guilty about not being able to "make someone's life right." This is not a welcome concept in American society, where the Judeo-Christian ethic of *selflessness* is celebrated and the word *selfishness* has only negative connotations (Ehrenreich, 1983; Gilligan, 1982; Kaschak, 1992):

WP: Where does guilt come from?

L: I felt it when I was married, being such a bitch to leave, ruining everyone's life, but other than that, I don't feel guilty. My mother would never use guilt. Of course, she and my sister have had trouble, and she could say that she felt bad about it, but she didn't feel guilt. My mom and I would talk about it, and she'd say, "Was I really a bad mom? No. I wasn't." I guess being selfish is an antidote to guilt. When you realize how little you can do *for* or do *to* other people [to change them], you realize that people are self-contained. Look at how hard it is to make someone's life right *or* miserable. What happens to others is of their own making. In our society, being selfless is okay, and being selfish isn't.

Perhaps, she mused, her orientation toward self-actualization is consistent with her introverted personality, a characterization that surprised me because Lyn's professional persona is entirely the opposite. She is active in just about every aspect of campus life, a willing mentor for new faculty, and a prominent leader in the campus community. She accepts this dichotomy:

> **L:** I'm a very private person, and I *really* look forward to being alone [laughs]. . . .
>
> I really do think it's a very old kind of orientation for me. I think probably even when I was a young person, I was always comfortable being by myself. I never felt like I needed to have friends around to be okay. I liked to read and do [my own] stuff even as a young kid.
>
> **WP:** Do you think you're introverted?
>
> **L:** Yes, I do, very much so.
>
> **WP:** That's interesting because your public image is so different.
>
> **L:** [laughs] Yeah, I know. No, I'm very much an introvert. My inner life is much more real to me. I think my life would be *very* unsatisfactory for many people because there's a minimum of social contact from my perspective. I mean, looking at other people's lives, I just don't spend near as much time with people as others, but it fits.

Lyn worries that this may not have been a good model for her sons because the isolation might be difficult for others. However, she explained that her sons have found "their own way," once again very much in keeping with their different personalities:

> I think that it's not a particularly good model to give my kids because, like I said, that kind of introversion is not . . . that kind of isolation is not what most people would be comfortable with, and yet that's kind of the model that they have from me, and I'm not sure, [but] I don't think it fits *them* as well as it fits me. But . . . they'll find their own way.

They're both more on the introverted side than extroverted. And it shows up in different ways. . . . Rich, when he's with people, is very expressive, and he is really *with* the group and fairly central to the group—I think—although he doesn't necessarily describe himself that way. But it seems like he makes conversation easily and he tells jokes and seems to be very comfortable with whoever he's with.

Paul, on the other hand, is much more likely to be in the background, but of the three of us, he's the most assertive about finding people to do things with and cultivating friendships. So both of them play out this conflict between my inner world and my need for the outer world in different ways.

When I was overseas for seven months and Rich was living alone, part of that time he wasn't working, he wasn't going to school . . . but he would go for weeks without seeing anybody, and I really worried about him. And some of my friends let me know they were worried about him because he had his days and nights turned around—sleeping all day and get up at night and write—very hermity. I think he thinks of it as being a sort of odd phase in his life, but periodically he'll do that. So I guess that's a long way of [saying I] realize that I'm somewhat troubled by that model I've given them, and maybe if I'd been a more social person . . . I might have worked to try to do it differently.

The Self in Relationship

Her ability to integrate her motherhood into her personhood was evident in our discussions about her relationships with men. While her sons were young, she kept a long-term relationship with a man separate from her relationship with her sons because they were not as important to her companion as they were to her. She understood how this man did not fit into her family and she would not "divorce her kids" for the sake of a new marriage:

Again, I was not too hesitant to put my needs before my kids at times. They never really liked any—well, that's not true—for the most part, they didn't like the men that I was seeing, which is not surprising, particularly the person who was the most long term. We were together probably for about five years. It was shortly after I came to [the city], so it was at that really—for Rich particularly—that really tumultuous time. And this fella was very nice to them, but I think it was pretty clear that they were not important to him. And so we really had to keep our relationship separate from my relationship with them, and then occasionally we would do things that was all of us, but it was never . . . it wasn't as good as either of the other choices. I knew from the very beginning in that relationship that I'm not gonna marry this guy and I don't want to live with him. We would travel together, and we would get along beautifully when the kids weren't there. I mean, we always got along together, quite comfortably, outside of the country or when we were traveling. It worked out just fine. If it had been just the two of us, we probably would have married, but in my mind, it was never going to work because I knew that I would have to . . . divorce my kids [laughs] . . . for that to work.

Though several relationships were satisfactory for her and some men were agreeable to the boys, she was careful of herself and of her son's lives:

On some level, it was real clear where my priorities were. The woman he married actually left her children. The other fella who was probably the most significant relationship they really liked, and I think would have been quite happy if we had gotten married, but he was *nuts!* [She laughs.] I mean, I was that much in love with him. I was just so taken with him, but again, I knew at the outset, "God, I'd have to be crazy to get into a marriage with this guy." You know, we had great times together, and he's fun to play with, and again, we had so much fun, we'd travel together, but I never knew who he was gonna be. So it really was only with this first one that it became an issue, where I felt like I'd have to make a choice between a relationship and my kids. And they for the most part didn't seem particularly bothered when I was just going out with people. I mean, they'd want to know, "Who is that?" And I would try not to have anybody kind of imposed on their life unless I knew they were gonna be around for awhile.

We talked about the extra dimension that having a relationship brings to the experience of being a woman. Lyn feels that getting in touch with one's womanhood does not depend on being involved with a man (Bequaert, 1976):

> There's ways to do it that doesn't have to involve a man. Obviously having women friends is very important. And . . . having a man in my life clearly highlights that woman-ness. But I haven't had a man in my life for quite some time and it feels like it's . . . established that I am a woman, and I've got interests and things that revolve around that.

In fact, becoming part of a couple again is a somewhat intimidating prospect for Lyn. As with some of the other women in this study, she fears the loss of autonomy and self-identity that comes from feeling needy (Dinnerstein, 1976; Levine, 1992). She reiterated that losing yourself in a relationship—whether with a spouse or children—is not healthy for women:

> I think that's a very real issue, and that when I have been with someone, it feels like a balancing act, that it still is really easy to fall back into being part of a couple. It's scary to me how easily and quickly that can happen. Not that there's anything wrong with being part of a couple, but you know what I mean, losing your autonomy and selfness in that. And it's not something that I'm able to handle easily. I don't think I've ever been really successful at being in a relationship and still feeling like I was okay by myself. I get needy.
>
> It pisses me off! [She laughs.] Really does. That person becomes—clearly they should be important—but they shouldn't be . . . *too* important! Any more than your kids are important, but they shouldn't be *too* important. There's a line that you cross, and you do lose chunks of yourself that's hard to get back.

Does she feel she has missed something by not being part of a couple? Yes and no:

I think I have missed creating a history with somebody that is a contemporary, rather than one of the kids, because their history with me is always gonna be from the perspective of being my kids, and I think there's something lost by not having that other adult who you can talk about, "Well, remember that time that . . ." [or] whatever, and remember things together, and remind each other about what happened and how things have changed. I mean, it's really hard to do that as objectively and with as much pleasure by yourself.

My assumption is that my life would be less peaceful, in a sense not necessarily negative, but that I have always experienced relationship as being tumultuous in some way. Again, not on the outside. I never fight with people, and there's not that kind of overt stress or disagreement. Even in my marriage it was sort of, "Well, I think I have to end this, so good-bye!" [She laughs.] But emotionally, it feels like I invest an undue amount of emotional energy and worry. I'm either ecstatically in love, you know, and it's just that's so pervasive and . . . that's what my life's about, and . . . you get over that after awhile. And then it becomes worry about maintaining it or changing it, or I don't know—I don't know what happens. But it seems like it's so central! I think that's the nature of being part of a couple, and I think that's a good thing. There's also the downside of it, and it's hard for me, I guess, because I almost focus on the downside.

When I shared with Lyn my own concern about being afraid to disrupt my peaceful, solitary existence, she described this as common among women. And although she searches for model relationships among other couples, Lyn has difficulty finding any that fit a model she would adopt. She thinks a marriage between friends is best, but even that has drawbacks (Dinnerstein, 1976):

> One of my friends who has voluntarily not had children [is] very involved with her career, and I think that that's the most important thing for her, but she's also got lots of friends, and she and her husband do a lot of things together and some things separately. And it's almost like living with your best friend. And I guess that's the model I would really like.

But boy it gets tough when it becomes sexual! You know! [She laughs.] I think . . . really what I would like is a relationship where I was living with my best friend, and if it could also be sexual, that would be great, but I don't see where that could really happen [because sex really messes up a good friendship]! And I don't know why. I mean, there's books written about what happens in sexual relationships, but intellectually, or emotionally, I can't figure out, "Why is that so damn hard!" Once you get your genitals involved, everything else just gets harder! [She laughs.]

Women and Children

Having close women friends who did not have children helped Lyn maintain a balanced perspective. She believes that both she and her children benefited from being around adults whose lives did not revolve around their children:

One thing, now that I think about it, that has helped me is that my closest friend does not have children, that's the woman that I often travel with and see fairly regularly, and so when we're together, it clearly doesn't revolve around children. And even when the kids were small, and she would be with us, she would treat them more like peers or adults, which I think kind of modeled that for me as well. And I think if she had had children, there would have been less of that happening because then there would be adults and then the children, whereas this was more [a] group of *people* together . . . doing things or talking about things. And I think that has played a role.

Women are socialized to believe that they must become mothers, that they need to have children to be complete. Women's self-image becomes so inextricably linked to their biological functions (Blake, 1974; Gimenez, 1984; Kaschak, 1992; Schur, 1984; Veevers, 1974) that inability to assume the mother role can be traumatic, even for those who do not want children:

She never wanted children—she comes from a really screwed-up family—but she had a hysterectomy about six years ago and was not prepared for it. I mean, she went into surgery thinking they were going to just do a biopsy and woke up and everything was gone, so she [had] lots of anger. And I think she's still trying to sort out how much of that is . . . because she was still very much childbearing age at that time—she's quite a bit younger than I—but I think has come to the conclusion that, no, she really didn't want to have children, and that she wouldn't have children even without the hysterectomy. But it's taken a long time to have peace with that. . . .

Lyn's friend rationalized her loss by saying she would have been a lousy mother anyway, but Lyn believes that no woman can predict the type of mother she would be because motherhood changes one's self-definition (Chodorow, 1978):

> [She] will frequently say things like, "Oh, I would have been a terrible mother when I see how you do that." And she also was very reinforcing to me as feeling like I do a good job of parenting, and has known us for many years. [She] sees herself as much too selfish ever to be a good mother and too flighty, and she's probably right, although you can't look at somebody when they're forty years old and say, "This is the kind of mother you would have been," because she obviously would have been a different person if she'd had children.

Childlessness for women carries a social stigma, as does single-ness (Bequaert, 1976). Lyn has many friends who affectionately call themselves the "VC," for "voluntarily childless" (Veevers, 1974). These women are happy with their life choices, but others claim that they will regret their decision as they age (Farrell, 1972).

> I mean that's what worried me, is, "Oh yeah, it's easy to say when you're twenty-five or thirty-five years old that you don't want kids, but my God, what's gonna happen when you're fifty? . . . Are you going to regret it? And they don't seem to. But, boy, talk about being a discriminated-against minority. People treat you as if you're an oddity if you don't have kids. . . .

One reason why so many aging single women experience "baby hunger" to the point of obsession is the mistaken belief that if they do not have children, they will be lonely "old maids" with no one to care for them. Lyn, however, pointed out that procreation does not necessarily come with a guaranteed family for life:

> And there's certainly no assurance when you have a baby that thirty years later they're gonna be around to take care of you. I mean, they might still be in your life and be a pain in the ass, or they might go off and join a cult [laughs], but you can't assume that you'll have children so you'll have somebody to take care of you.

COPING WITH DEPRESSION

Lyn's admission that she is chronically depressed, and has been for years, was somewhat surprising given the number and magnitude of the life actions she has taken and the active life she currently leads. She explained what her depression feels like, suggesting that it is exacerbated by the dull winter weather of her region:

> But it's sort of this chronic feeling like . . . I really want to be someplace where I feel good about the environment, someplace beautiful, someplace where I want to be outside, someplace where . . . and summers [here] are great, but most of the time here I'm depressed. Literally, there's not enough sunlight. Winters are awful for me. I really feel oppressed by it. So there's this, "Well, if it's really that important, why don't you get up and go?" And that's probably the most chronic debate I have with myself. . . .

> I've never gotten frozen with the depression. It's never been that extreme. It's been more everything was just such an effort. It felt like for years that everything was—I don't know—the way I describe it is like wading upstream, and you don't even know the steam is there until you can somehow step out of it. Or like moving through molasses, and you do it because that's just what you need to do. So the depression was never debilitating, and it probably didn't keep me from doing things, but it was just being exhausted all the time, and feeling like every-

thing, all decisions and all actions were really hard. And in the last few years I've pretty much got it under control. I don't think anybody would be aware of it because I don't function any differently.

She has successfully coped with her depression by participating in therapy, and finally taking medication to control it. She believes that depression is a physiologic condition stemming from a genetic predisposition in her family. This view is certainly consistent with those of Kaschak (1992) and Schur (1984), who assert that because women are taught to derive their self-images from their bodies, they are somehow responsible for controlling them, a concept antithetical to the use of medication for treatment, even though medication can help a person live a normal life:

I've had therapy for years, but it's being on medication that's really made the difference.

I'm convinced that it's a physiological condition. I think I've been depressed since childhood, and there's depression on both sides of my family, and going back a generation, so it's just almost inevitable, I think, that my siblings are depressed too, but they won't acknowledge it [laughs]. If I were diabetic, I would control it with diet and insulin or whatever was needed so that I could live normally, and that's what it feels like to me. It feels like it's just the reasonable thing to do to be normal. It's like I'm taking estrogen to sort of maintain a normal state—whether it's normal or not, I don't know. I have some real questions about that—but you know what I'm saying. It doesn't feel like it's taking care of an illness so much as it's just maintaining some normalcy.

OLD AND NEW MYTHS

Cinderella and Georgia O'Keeffe

In our final interview, Lyn talked about aging and recreating her life, dispensing with the old family myth of grow up, get married, have kids, and live the perfect life. Somehow her life never quite measured up to that image (Chodorow and Contratto, 1976). Her new image of herself is unlike the "Cinderella myth" because it is actually attainable:

> Oh, yeah, the mythology that there's going to be a happily ever after, if we could just do it right. . . . I think that you can't help but have that as part of your mythology. I still at times will say, and I'm joking, but it's not really a joke, "This isn't the way my life was supposed to be. This isn't in the script." And somehow it's there, this image of you grow up and you get married and you have kids and they're healthy and they're smart and they're attractive, and you live in a beautiful house, and all this. You know, the ease with which I can create that says that it's there. . . .
>
> . . . I'm working on my new narrative. I think that what I'm working on is creating a new myth, even recognizing it's a myth, but it's different. And it has to do with me being alone in a beautiful place and having my dogs and cats and my herb garden, and it's the Georgia O'Keeffe image. I'm standing there with my long flowing gray hair and my flowing skirts, and the sun is shining off my wrinkled brown skin, you know? But it's a new myth. And I like that. I like that sense of having something else that seems like we can live happily ever after. But it's still a myth. I realize that, but it feels like a more attainable image.
>
> It's much more attainable, or at least it feels like I can live with pieces of that. That any piece of that could be very satisfying. It doesn't have to be the whole picture. It's hard with the Cinderella myth to pick out pieces of it. That doesn't do it. That's not it.

We discussed the way that myths and images help or hurt women. Lyn observed that not all myths are damaging, but that an appropriate life myth helps one to define one's life and to set goals. A myth of dependence, on the other hand, as for many women who expect their children to care for them, which is only an extension of the Cinderella myth, can lead women away from self-sufficiency (Davies, 1993; Schur, 1984). To fight against such tenuous future dependencies, Lyn believes that women need to chart a different course:

> I think you almost have to start creating a new myth for your-self, and new narrative about what's gonna make this feel like a good life. What's gonna be the right goals, or something to be striving for, because once you give that up . . . I mean, I don't think you can really give it up, that image of somebody being there to take care of me. I think that [for] most single women, one of the real underlying chronic worries is, "What's gonna happen when I get old?" Well, most women are alone when they get old anyway, even if they've been married for most of their lives, because we outlive husbands. But still there's that, "Well, I'll have his estate. I'll have to live close to the children," or whatever. It's sort of the extension of this Cinderella myth, but it's not a very good outcome, I don't think. So I think in order to get comfortable with giving that up, you almost need something else to replace it.

The Myth of Motherly Infallibility

As we discussed myths and images for women and mothers, I was reminded of Bronwyn Davies' research, described in her books *Frogs and Snails and Feminist Tales* (1989) and *Shards of Glass* (1993). Folklore is loaded with unhealthy images for women, from the wicked mothers to the sweet helpless princesses who are contin-ually being rescued. Alongside the "bad mother" image, however, is an equally strong "good mother" (Dinnerstein, 1976; Farrell, 1972; Kaschak, 1992; Levine, 1992; Llewelyn and Osborne 1990). Lyn saw her own mother as the embodiment of the good mother, and despite recognizing that this was a child's naive interpretation of a mother's life (Coontz, 1992), having such a strong image of pa-tience and perfection led her to feel inadequate in comparison to her mother:

> In terms of true mythology or folklore, the mothers are more often bad. I guess I think I've been pretty clear about my mother being a role model, and probably not realizing how there's a mythology that goes with *that*, even if it's that direct a

model, because clearly I don't know what it felt like being her. I knew what it felt like being her kid, but you can't really know what's going on with somebody else, so I think probably my image was that she always seemed to know the right answer, always seemed to be responding in ways that were supportive but not controlling. I had this image that to be a good mother is to do it like my mother. And so when I would really lose it and shout at the kids and scare them, I would think, "Oh my God! I'm not a good mother. My mother would never do that!"

She described another example of the infallible, independent, perfect mother, Marmee of *Little Women* (Alcott, 1924), as one mother myth she would like to follow, but obviously existing only in fiction (Davies, 1993):

I was trying to think about the culture and the literature and the myths, and the mother that I think of is the mother in *Little Women*. They're all sitting there before the fire, and they're all close, and they're having a good time, and they're laughing, and she's a strong person, and she's her own person and very supportive and very nurturing for all of the girls. That's kind of my image of what a good mother should be. Now, she didn't go off to work every day. . . . I don't try to fit that together with what it would mean for my life. But somehow that sense of being very strong, and your own person, and yet very loving and giving and nurturing—whether or not that's ever attainable—probably not. There's a reason why we call that fiction.

The March Hare: Myths About Time

Each of the women in all five cases studies has discussed the constraints of time and the stereotypical assumption that single, working mothers have less time with their children, who therefore suffer more than children from two-parent homes with stay-at-home mothers (Baca Zinn and Eitzen, 1990; Krantz, 1988). Lyn added a new dimension to the discussion:

I think . . . there's good evidence—and I don't think that anybody's looked at this is terms of parent-child literature—

but spending more time with somebody . . . I'm thinking of Hunt's work, where you spend ten minutes with somebody and you just flip into a different kind of interaction with them, and then the longer time it gets into, even if you start out being strangers, it's like this space thing, if you're standing close to somebody, eventually you have to start talking to them. I think the same thing is true of anybody. Just having blocks of time together changes the nature of the relationship, but I'm not sure that doing that real often is necessarily a factor. So I think that as a single parent you do have big blocks of time with your kids—you go on trips together and you're in the car—so you do have those times to develop the kind of intimacy that you need time to develop, even though it probably doesn't happen as often as . . . with a stay-at-home mom.

Lyn values her time alone, and she does not believe that having more time with her sons would necessarily have improved either her or their lives:

Well, from the time my kids were little, even when we were home together, it was important to me that I have some time to myself and not be with them. So I can't imagine that I would have been that much more responsible or accessible to them if we had more time together.

On the other hand, I think, "Oh my God. Thank God [my job] protected my kids from being around me more!" [She laughs.] Really! Because I don't think I'm suited for full-time motherhood. I just don't think I would have made their lives very pleasant if I felt like they needed me for long periods of time or that I had to entertain them. I mean, it just gives me goose bumps to think about doing that!

Lyn views time shortage, not as gender based, but as a phenomenon of the American culture, a natural inclination to describe oneself as busy (Coontz, 1992):

L: When you run into somebody you haven't seen for awhile, whether they're a man or a woman, they're gonna tell you how busy they are—a professional person, or probably it doesn't even have to be a professional person. You know, "What have you been doing?" "Oh, God, I've just got so much going on! I just haven't have time to. . . . " It's our expectation for ourselves, that we're real busy.

WP: It's kind of an American thing?

L: I think so.

WP: You've traveled a lot. Do you find that in other countries?

L: Not as much. No. And people comment about how fast Americans talk. We sure *talk* about how busy we are.

RETIREMENT: NO PLACE FOR WOMEN

In our discussions about herself, her friends, and the Cinderella myth, Lyn analyzed the aging single woman's fear of growing old. Facing retirement, she noted, is also different for women and men in American culture. A woman's concept of retirement as "her husband's" is a logical extension of the expectation that women's work is not supposed to be important to them (Llewelyn and Osborne, 1990):

But I think that often when you ask a man, "What are you going to do when you retire?" there's the people who have been the workaholics, and they're gonna have a terrible time. Probably most men will have more trouble. But they have this, "Oh, I'm gonna play golf every day. I'm going to go fishing. I'm gonna do my garden. I'm gonna. . . . " There's sort of this senior citizen role that's very easy to tap into for men—"Now I'm not working, so now I can do X"—but with women, working is not really supposed to be that important to them, so there's not that kind of, "When I finish this then I'm gonna move into a different phase of my life." It's more like, I bet more women are asked, "What are you gonna do when your *husband* retires?" than they're asked, "What are you gonna do when *you* retire?" Because then, that's a significant thing in your life when your husband retires. Then you can travel. But to ask a woman, "What are you gonna do when you retire?"

You're gonna continue doing what you've always done. "Well, I'm gonna clean the house and [etc.]."

As an independent professional with a successful career, Lyn will be able to retire relatively soon. She faces retirement with her characteristic determined self-awareness:

I have realized that I'm going to be able to retire in not so many years . . . and who knows about the future, of course, but it feels like for the most part I'm through that launching phase and have shifted the focus more onto, "So what am *I* gonna do when I grow up?" [She laughs.]

CONCLUSION

Lyn's story has told much about a woman's struggles to be independent, to maintain a self-*full*ness that some would call self*ish*, but which has clearly benefited both her and her sons, who are successful, pleasant adults. Her unusual heritage of strong single mothers is evident in her own easy assumption of the many challenges of single parenting, and in the awareness that happiness for her does not depend on any man.

Chapter 6

Sarah:
"Reparenting the Child in Me"

It was Sarah's final interview that encouraged me to use the quilt metaphor to tie all of the cases together. In our third interview, she shared with me a number of pictures she had cut from magazines to represent the many facets of her life as a culminating part of her art therapy. Earlier in her therapy she had created a collage to help her get in touch with her feelings about herself. She told me it was full of dark images, especially ones of her mother. It was, she said, "very depressing." However, the many positive images of womanhood composing her final collage were evidence that she has rewoven the fabric of her life.

Sarah's story resembles a play, with a cast of characters, several critical settings, and a number of plots and subplots. I have chosen to construct her narrative in this form, weaving the different elements together as warp and woof of Sarah's square of the quilt. It is not my intention to romanticize Sarah's life or to present the people in it as caricatures, but Sarah herself had a straightforward, yet poetic way of describing the events, places, and people in her life, so her portrait developed quite naturally as an extraordinary drama.

THE CHARACTERS

Sarah

An abused woman who was once an abused child, Sarah is "reparenting herself" as the mother of two daughters and grandmother

265

of Joshua; happiest as a student, she is still learning to face the past, present, and future with the same confidence she, as a teacher, helps others find.

Julia

Sarah's oldest daughter once attempted suicide during the worst of her adolescent hormonal mood swings—an unfortunate characteristic of females in Sarah's family; a teenage mother, Julia manages to cope with the problems of a thirty-year-old at age nineteen.

Annie

Sarah's youngest daughter was "born bringing peace," somehow able to negotiate a drunken father's moods to curry his affection; now in the throws of adolescent rebellion, Annie was described by Sarah as "a lovely person, just not to me."

Garry

Sarah's second husband, and father of her two girls, was an alcoholic whose disparagement and humiliation of Sarah was far more damaging than physical abuse.

Sarah's Mother

Once the matriarch of the family, she preserved her marriage at great cost to her daughters; steeped in a tradition of Christian martyrdom, she enabled an amoral husband to lead a life that terrorized his daughters and tried to pretend that it was normal.

Sarah's Father

A schizophrenic who alternated between roles as a "playboy" and a "pillar of the church," he was "self-centered and undependable," scarring his daughters in ways they could not fully articulate and leaving a trail of mistresses and shattered lives.

THE SETTINGS

China

The place where Sarah was raised. Located there on military assignment, her father took her to geisha houses and used her as a black-market courier until he was caught.

Sarah's Home

Sarah was once thrilled with her "wonderful house," but it has become "a mortuary of lost dreams." She believes it represents herself and is currently reconstructing it to make it worth selling. From the profits, she will move to a different place and begin her life anew.

School

Sarah has experienced three kinds of schools in her life: ones attended by her daughters, where she participated in their educational experiences as much as possible; ones she attended, proud of her intelligence and Ivy League training but amazed at how that shining image paled in the face of her life experiences; and ones in which she taught, where she encountered both great triumphs and bitter disappointments.

LIVING IN A DYSFUNCTIONAL MARRIAGE

Sarah had been married once before her marriage to Garry, but both she and her first husband still had some growing up to do, so she left. She explained how she married Garry "on the rebound":

I had been married [the first time] right out of college, and in retrospect I think if I'd given it a few years and let him grow up, it might have worked, but I wasn't terribly committed and thought I deserved better, and he didn't want to have children and I did, you know. So I kind of walked away from that one.

We're still friends. Then I married Garry, really on the rebound from a very passionate relationship that didn't work out, and I wanted the stability. I wanted the children very much. I wanted a stable home. Meanwhile I was bouncing around like a ping-pong ball.

Her quest for stability proved ill-fated, since Garry soon showed a penchant for drinking, something Sarah thought would lessen as he became more settled in their family life. This misconception faded quickly, but when her daughters were born only sixteen months apart, circumstances changed her life plans, and she was prevented from taking action. She explained that because hormone-related depression is characteristic of females in her family, becoming pregnant was not just a psychological boost but a physical and chemical antidote for depression (Markson, 1993). Because of conditions at work and her total involvement with her babies, Sarah realized that parenting was her calling:

From the beginning, I was disturbed, I think, about his drinking, but having never had any experience with drinking, . . . I assumed that as he got happier and more settled, whatever, that it would taper off. And it didn't. And I assumed that I would grow more attached too. And I certainly was grateful and happy for the home. I was a teacher and . . . oh, golly, I must have been thirty-five.

Then I got pregnant with Julia, and I really loved that. That was *really* what I wanted, plus biologically I'm a lot less depressed during pregnancy than normal, which seems to have happened to Julia too—it certainly got her out of her manic-depressive swings. And that was really exciting, but he wasn't very involved or very supportive. He wasn't negative about it at all, but I began to realize how little emotional competence he had.

And then I had expected to take a two-year leave of absence and then go back to teaching. Very quickly I began to realize that parenting was more of a calling for me. It was way better for me to do that, but I wasn't exactly sure that I was willing to give up my tenure, and then right away I was pregnant with Annie. They're sixteen months apart. And I wasn't sure that . . .

I thought that wasn't a good idea because by then I already knew that I wasn't very happy with Garry, and I knew in the back of my mind that once I could go back to work and get myself on my feet, that Julia and I would be better off without him, so another baby wasn't my first choice.

Sarah, unable to extend her pregnancy leave, decided to stay home, work part-time as a substitute teacher and test proctor, and devote time to her daughters:

I asked for an extension of my leave because of the second baby, and they wouldn't give it to me. They would only give me the two years, which meant really only eight more months, and I knew from my experience with Julia that I was not going to return to teaching with an eight-month-old baby. And one of the neat things about being married to Garry was that we could afford for me to stay home. Whatever he did, one of the ways he convinced himself that he wasn't an alcoholic was by getting himself to work every morning at eight o'clock.

And so I at that point resigned my teaching position and started doing a combination of subbing, because then I could tell in the morning if things were gonna be a nice steady day, when the kids were gonna be fine with somebody else, or whether they're gonna [need me] . . . and occasionally I would slip, and one of them would throw up when I was getting ready to sub, and I would say, "Why am I doing this for forty-five dollars?" Also I started working for ETS [Educational Testing Service] preparing people for licensing tests, which is really good pay part-time.

And I really loved getting this house—I think this house is wonderful—and [I] got very busy with things with the kids. I was with a campfire group with them for awhile and was involved with Sunday school, homeroom mother, and that kind of thing.

The Intervention

It became apparent, however, that Garry's drinking would soon reach a crisis point. Perhaps because of her mother's urging, perhaps because she loved her daughters so much, and perhaps because she was not financially self-sufficient, Sarah tried to get her husband into treatment:

> But I really knew, more and more, that I had to get back to teaching because I was going to have to support myself one way or another. Either I was going to have to be single or he was going to have some kind of crisis where he was no longer able to function. Eventually I decided that I wanted the family whole enough to really make an all-out effort to do an intervention and try to get him to go get treatment and see if, sober, he was the kind of person I could be married to or not. I really didn't know whether he had it in him. But he was very angry about it—agreed to go, and then backed out on it.

An unfortunate pattern for alcoholics is a persistent belief that simple personal determination can break the habit, but as this fails each time, alcoholics begin to project their own self-blame onto their families (Falicov, 1988). Sarah endured this cycle many times, but she courageously chose to use an intervention strategy suggested by counselors at the alcoholism center where she and her daughters were already getting help, but this was no easy task:

> It was professionals who had been counseling the girls and me from the alcoholism center. A guy Upstate . . . is considered the best at doing these things, although he said it's like throwing a live hand grenade in your living room. There's going to be shrapnel; there's going to be fallout, even if it works, because men don't like being confronted like that. The girls were prepared and had the counselor who had been working in group with them here, sitting with them. I was here. His mom was here, and one of his son's wives because that son also had a problem with alcohol, and she had had an alcoholic mother, and she had things she wanted to say to him about it.

> And the girls and I each told him how we were experiencing him.

Garry had been married before but divorced his wife because she drank, a somewhat typical manifestation of the alcoholic's tendencies toward denial and projection (Carter and McGoldrick, 1980). Sarah's explanation of who came to this confrontation and who did not was revealing. Those who worked with Garry and knew his drinking habits were reluctant to come. The "company" chose to ignore the drinking since they felt he was still productive (Coontz, 1992; Farrell, 1972):

> A lot of people who could have been helpful didn't. People don't like to show up for things like that. And the woman from work who had—his liver had shown up a couple of times in his yearly checkup—and she had tried to get him to get counseling and to deal with it, and he had refused. And because his bosses said it was not causing a problem, which I don't understand because I know that he drank at lunch and slept the afternoons away. But I guess he got his work done enough in the morning. He was good at what he did, so they didn't come. But anyway, I had hoped that she would represent the company, but she said that, no, unless his bosses had a complaint, there was no way she would touch it.

Living with a Drunk

Steadfastly unrepentant, Garry agreed to go for treatment but really had no intention of doing so, and he continued to disrupt and manipulate his family. Sarah's self-esteem suffered from his constant verbal punishment, causing her to become depressed (Farrell, 1972; Gornick and Moran, 1972; Kaschak, 1992; Levine, 1992; Markson, 1993). Her daughters reacted to his behavior in different ways.

> But anyway, he was really resistant, but he finally ended up— just to get us off his back—agreeing to go for treatment, but then he backed out of it and was going to take care of it himself. I mean, he never went to an AA meeting.
>
> And it was terrible stuff because Annie used to watch out the kitchen window when he arrived home from work. And if he was stumbling around and swearing in the garage or whatever, then she would just disappear, and if he was in a better space, she would go and crawl in his lap, and she was pretty good at getting [positive] strokes from him, and that gave *him* some.

Julia was just more of a head-on person and just became more frustrated with him. And one of the things that really bothered me was his blatant preference for Annie. I mean, I just don't think that's right, but I was miserable, and he was more successful than I realized at the time at just dragging down my self-esteem. I was getting more and more depressed and more and more immobilized. And didn't even really know.

"Paper Bag Issues"

Garry's abuse of Sarah did not take the form of physical violence, though he once came close, and he would lash out at her for simple issues, episodes she called "paper bag issues," or being angry just for the sake of being angry (Levine, 1992):

There was only once, when I had taken a thermos that he had taken to the football game, actually believing—although I don't know why, if I'd thought about it I would have known better—that it was coffee and dumped it out, and it was gin, and when he found out that I had dumped it down the drain, he was really, really pissed, and so at that point he started towards me and he had his hand up, but he thought better of it and walked away. And that was the only time I ever thought he might hit me.

But it was verbal abuse, and it was what I came to call paper bag issues, and I called them paper bag issues because he would take a paper grocery sack and turn down the top of it and put it in the car for garbage and beer cans and stuff, and instead of emptying it, I had thrown it out one day, meaning to replace it with another one, and something else had come up. And when he found out I had thrown it out, he started ranting and raving about how awful a housekeeper I was. And that one time I could really see the absurdity of how upset he was getting about a paper grocery bag that obviously could be replaced easily, and after that it became like a totem for him. When he would start yelling at me, I would detach and start thinking, "Now, is this a paper bag issue?" And I could see that it was, and he was just yelling for the sake of venting, not because it had anything to do with me or reality of any sort that was significant, and that kind of allowed me to begin to see just how absurd what I was putting up with was.

It was not his humiliation of her, however, that caused her to galvanize into action; it was her feelings of responsibility to her daughters. Drawing strength from her desire to protect her daughters against what she viewed as a bad example of a relationship between a man and a woman, disliking also his pattern of emotional nonsupport, she proceeded to divorce him:

> What really gave me the strength to do the intervention and then to carry out the divorce when he didn't do anything about the drinking was that, as the girls got older, I did not want them to see that marriage. I did not . . . I didn't have the strength to say, "I will not be treated like this!" But I *did* have the strength and wisdom to say, this cannot be the way my daughters see a man treat a woman. I don't want them to go into whatever relationship they have thinking that this is the norm, that this is okay.
>
> And he really wasn't there for me when my father died, and I knew that it was going to be much more difficult for me when my mother died. And I thought, "This is crazy!" If anything were to happen with the kids, if anything were to happen at all, when one might want to have a spouse that would back you up, that he would make it worse rather than better. And I thought, "This is crazy! Why am I putting up with being miserable for this?" And so I started the divorce, and I don't think he really believed it because I hadn't stood up to him in a long time, until I did the intervention and divorce.

It was then that her financial dependence on him became a battle over property. Her contributions to their home as wife and mother had no exchange value, so they were easily discounted. Garry exerted his ownership rights by staying in their home, a move enforced by his lawyer, a common occurrence in divorces where desertion of the spouse is not the mitigating factor and suit is brought by the female (Weitzman, 1985). For one-and-a-half more years, Garry defended his "squatter's rights" and made their lives a nightmare:

> And he also refused to move out of the house, I think, partly on his lawyer's advice, but it meant that for a year and a half we lived in this house with the corpse of a marriage. Walking around it, living in separate rooms, doing his own laundry, living separately, but he was here. And it was pretty bad because towards the end he passed out and he got really bitter, and after the kids went to bed and were asleep, he would sit down here and drink beer and put porno videos in the VCR. But because he was so far along with his drinking, he would pass out, and it would just keep playing and rewinding. And I said to him, "You can't just do that. You do not know if one of the girls is going to wake up and come downstairs." But as far as he was concerned, they were asleep and that was his time, and I wasn't going to do anything about it. And so that was just a really tense time.

A HISTORY OF ABUSE

Getting out of the dysfunctional marriage should have been a relief, but Sarah's self-esteem had suffered tremendously. Only after she returned to teaching did she realize that she had internalized all of Garry's insults. When her students treated her badly and her classes soon became "out of control," she understood that she had become accustomed to being abused and ignored. This eventually cost her that job and dealt a further blow to her self-esteem. Unfortunately, women who are abused often absorb the abuse as part of their self-concept (Gornick and Moran, 1972; Levine, 1992; Schur, 1984).

This "surrender" behavior had deeper roots, however, ones from her own childhood, that she only remembered through counseling. She voiced the dilemma of abused women and children who live in dangerous relationships when she described such a situation as living in "a disaster zone" (Daly, 1974):

> So eventually he moved out, and I took a teaching job thinking I could bounce right back and I was going to be fine once he

was out of my life, and I didn't realize how depressed I was. I didn't realize how low my self-esteem had gone, and I don't think I realized how much bad stuff I had learned to just ignore. And as a teacher, that was disastrous because classes, especially lower-track classes, get beyond your control before you realize it. It was almost as if I'd gotten so used to being abused and ignored that I just took too much from students. And it was an awful year. I had one wonderful class and two classes that were really out of control. But I was not invited to return, and [I was] kind of devastated, and I was in counseling then because I began to realize that the fallout from all of this was greater than I thought it was, and that it had all been possible because I carried in me much more of a history of abuse than I realized. Because my family of origin had pretended everything was fine and rosy, and I didn't realize that I had been kind of hunkered down in a disaster zone.

An Amoral Father

Linguists and psychologists alike would be puzzled by Sarah's assertion that since her earliest childhood memories were laid down "in another language," she lost touch with those memories after she "forgot" the language. As we talked, her memories surfaced but were jumbled and indistinct. What she described, however, was clearly a traumatic and dark time for her, when both her parents used her to further their own purposes:

My father, I think, was schizophrenic, but he certainly was constantly running around with other women, and losing jobs over it because he taught in private church-run schools.

Eventually, when I finally was able to really look at it and put my memories back together, I realized it was a whole lot worse than I had remembered. A lot of the worst of it for me happened when we were in [China] and happened in that language, and so when we came back to the States, I kind of forgot the language and forgot the whole experience. So, anyway, while we were there, he had a mistress that was a house servant with us until she became pregnant, but he would take me with him to the city, and I guess essentially my mom was sending me along as a three-year-old to keep him out of trouble—that he wouldn't do anything if I were there. But he did see the woman, and she at one point was living in a house of prostitution, and she had the baby and got him involved in black marketeering.

He was trading army rations and nylons for artifacts, mostly small ivory carvings, and essentially he needed me to transport them because who was going to check a three-year-old little girl? So when he got caught and shipped back to be court martialed, I felt somehow responsible that he had . . . he ended up not standing court-martial because they thought he was crazy and put him in an army hospital instead. And they wanted to keep him. They didn't feel that he should be . . . that he was simply too—what's the word when you've got no social conscience? Anyway, but my mom insisted that she wanted him discharged and basically spent her life baby-sitting him.

The story she told me needs no elaboration. Its shocking quality is graphically represented by a scene she only recently remembered, as if in a dream. Because of technical problems, I did not get her exact description on tape, but the vignette is worth mentioning because it may explain why it took her so long to remember the terrors she experienced at her father's hands. Sarah remembered that when the authorities came to take her father to jail, he threatened her with a symbolic act. He broke the neck of a "kitchen dog" as he shouted at her in a foreign language. Today, she is not certain if this action represented what he would do to her if she "told on him," or if he threatened her own cherished pet, or—even more devastating—if he was showing her what he had done with the illegitimate baby of his mistress, a child who literally "disappeared" from Sarah's memories.

As an interesting sidebar to her story about her father, Sarah explained that the substantial trust fund she had inherited upon her mother's death was actually bequeathed by her father's long-term mistress, a wealthy woman, who—knowing the father would squander the money—gave an inheritance to Sarah's mother, who in turn kept it in trust for her daughters.

Sarah's Mother: A "Christian Martyr"

Although she knew her husband's proclivities, Sarah's mother stoically maintained that life was better with a man and pretended that all was as it should be (Chodorow, 1978; Falicov, 1988), a front that had damaging consequences for Sarah and her sister:

> **S:** She felt that, no matter what, you were better off with a man and to have the ability to pretend to the world that everything was normal.
>
> That was definitely what she did, and I think that it cost my sister her sanity. I really do. [Long pause.]
>
> **WP:** When did you get out of the family?
>
> **S:** When I finished college and married my first husband.
>
> **WP:** So you weren't in a hurry to get out?
>
> **S:** I don't think I realized that the myth wasn't true. And I didn't realize how unhappy or emotionally shut down I was because . . . here I was this really bright student, and just successful at just about everything I tried and looking forward to the future, and I just . . . it took the fact that I didn't get back on my feet after the divorce for me to realize that I was more accustomed to abuse than I realized, that I had more problems than I realized.
>
> . . . and my sister was so bitter and negative about it that she hated life, and she couldn't stand that I was somehow happy and reasonably successful in the midst of all this, and so she really tried to tear me down anytime that she could. She was just a crazy lady.

Sarah's successes in school were downplayed by her mother since her sister was not an achiever, and Sarah's mother attempted to protect her sister with illusion as well:

> I mean, if I had gotten something like this [pointing to her daughter's many prize ribbons], because my sister was not an achiever, anything I achieved was kept very low-key. For in-

stance, they never celebrated my graduation other than just—
they took me to a little restaurant afterwards. My wedding was
almost pathetically tiny because I was getting married before
my sister who was five years older than I and never had any
real hope of getting married. I would come home with report
cards and my mom would look at it and say, "Well, that's very
nice, but be careful because your sister didn't do so good, so
don't mention it."

Such actions seem cruel and unjust, but Sarah revealed that her
mother was steeped in a philosophy of martyrdom, believing that
the strong should protect the weak. This Christian ethic typifies
what Coontz (1992) calls "Irrational Altruism" (p. 52). In a chapter
appropriately titled, "My Mother Was a Saint," Coontz asserts that
the self-sacrifice of women was in part a cover-up that freed husbands for all kinds of self-serving actions by keeping women tied to
the home through moral obligations and personal dependencies.
Her mother's downplaying of Sarah's intelligence was part of
women's socialization to keep the division of labor crisp and discrete—the affairs of men were not the affairs of women. According
to Coontz, this myth has been a tenacious argument for those who
desire to "return to traditional gender roles," but, she notes, this is a
"flawed analysis." At best, men and women "hid their resentment or
pain well enough to stay married" (p. 65). Her expectations that her
own daughter would *wish* to internalize these values also led Sarah's
mother to encourage her to stay with her abusive husband, to be the
kind of woman her mother was. Society so strongly reinforces
mother modeling that a daughter can become so caught up in her
mother's image that she literally becomes what her mother wants
her to be—a reproduction of herself (Chodorow and Contratto,
1976; Dinnerstein, 1976; Levine, 1992). Sarah fought against this
and declared her independence:

S: It's amazing for somebody who was a feminist and had run
consciousness-raising groups in the seventies that I was as dependent for my identity as I was. I suppose it's not surprising
when I looked at how my mom campaigned for me to stay with
or go back to Garry. In her quiet way, without ever yelling or
practicing any coercion that I understood as coercion, she was

very committed to making sure that I was the kind of person, the kind of woman *she* was and valued. It was very, very upsetting to her when I really started deviating. It was upsetting to her when I went to [college] because she thought I was too threatening of a spouse. I don't think of myself as a high-powered person now. [She thought that] brightness was something to enjoy and utilize in a refined way, but it will lose you more in the long run.

WP: Where did she get those values?

S: Almost out of the air she breathed. I don't think they were unique to her. I mean she had a very clear Christian ethic that said those of us who are strong and well—which is the way she defined me—have an obligation to absorb all the trouble.

She was surely an enabler. And I can remember when my first husband got really frustrated with it, he said, "Who do you think you are, Jesus Christ?" She said, "You couldn't have paid me a better compliment." She always felt you needed to sacrifice yourself. At one point I argued with her [that] that was not the point; the point was that He had done it *once* for our sake. I wrote a letter and said, "I feel like Isaac writing to Abraham," and I told her I chose not to be the goat.

She never forgave me for divorcing Garry and making the change. She never forgave me for making the opposite choice than she did.

SARAH: REPARENTING HERSELF

As Sarah started to get in touch with the suffering she had learned to accept as "part of her life," she also began to find ways to engage in the re-formation of her identity and the celebration of herself and her daughters (Falicov, 1988). As a child she had been happiest as a student, and her therapist suggested that she return to being a student because it was there she had the strongest identity:

My counselor, after getting to know me, was the person who suggested I return to school because she felt that as a student I had a strong identity, and it would allow me to experience the best part of what I liked about teaching, without the disciplinary aspects that I clearly wasn't [suited for]. She felt that I didn't have the inner resources to deal with it, and I think she was right, because I really loved the courses that I taught at the college level, especially for returning adults. It was a lot of fun getting people to see that they really weren't mute, they did have a voice, they did have things to say, and that they could read and relate to literature and get involved with other people in talking about what it meant in the context of their lives and their experience. And these were people that, by and large, had awful public school experiences and had left and now were returning . . . and it was just wonderful to watch people blossom and begin to say, "Hey! I'm really not so dumb!" And it's been great.

Returning to school was even more difficult because her daughters resisted both the financial strains it would entail and the time she would devote to herself rather than to them. With typical teenaged self-absorption, her daughter Julia indignantly declared, "This is *our* time. You should be earning money!" Sarah, however, asserted her right to "take care of herself" before it was too late. Learning had always excited her, and she recognized her talent for empowering others. Being able to use this talent helped her to empower herself:

> . . . but then for about two years after I lost that job, I was really tight for money, and Julia really resented and gave me hell for going to graduate school for my master's rather than earning something. I mean she outright said, "These are supposed to be our years!" And I said to her, "Look, I'm too old not to do something to take care of myself right now. I have got to have the master's by the time I'm fifty or it's gonna be useless."

> I like learning new things. I get really excited about what I'm learning. I enjoy working with new teachers. I think I have a talent for expressing how things could go more smoothly, for recognizing what's going well, and for affirming it. In just

being able to recognize people's strengths and help them to build on them, it's a delight to be doing this. It empowers me.

When I asked whether, as the result of her own experiences, she would advise her daughters to work so that they would not fall into the financial dependence trap in which she found herself after divorce, she replied:

> I wouldn't say either thing. I would listen to what they were . . . what their thoughts on both sides of the issue [were], share my experience, and the pluses and minuses of the way I did it. . . .
>
> I don't think there is a right or a wrong way of doing it. You do what you do on a year-by-year or minute-by-minute basis, and it has some benefits. And I guess what I've had to struggle with is . . . I mean, I even feel the same way about the divorce—and it's not a question of whether it's the right or the wrong thing to do. It wasn't either. It became what I had to do, and going back to school became what I chose to do, even at financial sacrifice.

In referring to her daughter Julia's parenting choices, she reflected that people "exist in relationship," and that this may involve sacrifice and costs (Gilligan, 1982). Sarah believes that no one but God can be a perfect parent, and we turn to God to help understand the trials we endure as a result of our choices. Then Sarah explained that the model for parenting she received from her parents was so harmful to her that her own parenting was a "reaction against it," an attempt to heal for her children and for herself, a process of reparenting herself (Chodorow, 1978; Llewelyn and Osborne, 1990):

> I think that both facts are so, that we are individuals and really have to do the best for ourselves, and that we exist in relationship, and we have to make sacrifices to support and maintain that relationship, and in the case of our kids, they really are dependent on us at some point, and we really do have to factor that heavily into the equation. And I don't think that there is an answer. I don't think that there is a right way. I think that there are going to be costs to whatever choice you make.
>
> And I don't think we *can* do perfect parenting. And I guess, or it's more than I guess, I *know,* that for me, that would be

very very hard to deal with, if I didn't believe that, ultimately, God was our parent. And that almost we have to be inadequate as parents in order for us to turn to God and grow to understand. My mom was a good mom for young children. I have a real awareness of what I didn't get as a kid, what harmed me, what I hurt from, so in the passage of parenting, basically, I was reparenting myself, reworking that. . . . In other words, by doing for them what I lacked, I was somehow doing it for myself. I was somehow reparenting the child in me.

When asked to elaborate on the kinds of activities she saw as "reparenting," Sarah explained that her decision to divorce and her determination to finish her education and assert her self-worth while protecting her daughters' feelings of importance were primary. The "little things," too, were significant. On the wall behind us were displayed many ribbons Annie won at 4-H dog shows, and the room was full of pictures of her girls engaged in the activities of which she felt they should be proud. She elaborately celebrated birthdays and special events as a way of honoring her daughters as persons, something her mother minimized in Sarah's childhood. She is reserved in judging the results, however, since her parenting style did not necessarily protect her daughters from life's struggles:

> Well, on a big basis, things like the divorce, things like standing up and saying, "I am going to finish my education. I am worth something in this and you are too, and I will do what I can to balance those needs, but. . . . " On a little basis, things like really make a big deal of their achievements. . . .

> And, you know, so I was really careful to maximize theirs. In fact, I overdid birthdays and things to just celebrate their existence. I really loved it, and it paid off. I mean, we've still got Annie's horse collection sitting up there. I don't know how long she played with it. She's outgrown it, but it's hers, and it's part of our heritage we built up with the family, and after about the third horse, my mother said, "But she's got horses. Why are you buying her another one?" It just was that sort of thing I redid because I just didn't feel celebrated or honored as a person. And I think an awful lot of what I struggle with you can see the

results of that. On the other hand, I did celebrate my kids, and they're struggling, too, so [laughs] who knows?

Several times in separate interviews, Sarah expressed her amazement at not being the Ivy League woman of the sixties with a strong tendency toward self-advancement; instead, she lived for and through her children (Chodorow, 1978; Coontz, 1992):

> I have been limited in my own life because I have lived too much through the achievements of my children. This is really weird stuff for a person who's from an Ivy League school and a liberated woman! It's actually taken a good deal of pride, courage, and affirmation to go back to school.

Sarah's own self-esteem is in flux. She described her "self-talk" as paradoxical, swinging from pride in herself and her achievements to guilt about her children's lives (Schur, 1984). However, mostly, she described herself as "*more* than a survivor":

> Sometimes I think, "Wow! You are a strong, bright, competent person. You've really managed and are going places and doing things. It's amazing what you've achieved." And then there are moments where I feel lazy and I know that somehow I've failed and caused all my own and all my children's grief [laughs]. And anyplace between those two extremes, and probably neither of the extremes is quite true. See, I see life as very paradoxical, and I think we are living paradoxes. . . .
> When I think about it, I sure wouldn't want to be back in what I had. . . . How awful to have a relationship make the ordinary traumas of living and dying worse, rather than better. And so I guess I alternate between self-pity because I've got to face it all alone and pride that, in fact, I find ways of doing that. I really do put together whatever network and whatever— I'm *more* than a survivor.

Sarah talked about how she sought—and provided—support:

> Because housekeeping is one of the weakest of my links, and one that I feel least willing to tackle, I have somebody, who's

actually quite a good friend, who comes in and does some of
this for me once or twice a week. But I've had a lot of counseling and a lot of therapy, and the church is a real support
network, socially and morally and in terms of providing social
events and outlets for my sense of competence as a student.
I'm a member of the Order of St. Luke and really good in the
healing ministry and in helping other people with problems.
And I have friends. Most of my friends have grown out of
support group situations, friendships with both men and
women from therapy groups, friendships from healing with
my eating disorder.

Sarah explained that she was a compulsive overeater who drew
"comfort from food that I should get from other people." She added
that she was doing well with medication and therapy, but that stressful events sometimes triggered binges (Kaschak, 1992; Schur, 1984).
Sarah experienced several such stressful events in just a single year
of her life:

I was just getting into my master's program when my sister
died suddenly. She hated life and wanted to make others miserable, too, so even for her it was a blessing. Because my
mother was older and frailer, I worried about my sister looking
after her. I worried about her being abused, so when she died,
it was a blessing. I didn't want to go back home for that, but
that was only my first semester, and I dealt with it. The second
semester, I was flying and getting lots of positive strokes.
Then my mother became critically ill and required placement
in a hospice. I had to manage it all from here, with lots of
commuting and responsibilities. I was still quite attached to
her, and I needed reconciliation. I had moved away from her to
defend my own choices, or *not* to have to defend them. When
she was dying, I was the only adult left in my family, and it
was very stressful traveling back and forth and dealing with
emotional stress, trying to help her not feel guilty about her
life and not feel guilty about her dependence. It really inter-
fered with my schoolwork. I guess that's part of being a mom
and a student—life interferes. Well, here I was, the single
functioning adult in the whole family with a dying parent. I

had no extended family to fall back on. In a way, now I'm not just a single mother, but now I am the matriarch of the family.

As if this was not enough, she returned from settling her mother's affairs to find that her daughter, Julia, was pregnant:

> I really faltered for awhile when my mom died, but it was a difficult year. I had come out of the divorce a couple of years before and was really depressed. My sister died and then eleven months later my mom died. . . . I got back here and said, "Finally, that's taken care of," because I had disposed of the estate, and I said, "I can finally just relax and get back to my studies and be okay," and Julia said, "Mom. I'm pregnant"—at sixteen, and so I was back on the roller coaster.

The depression she described earlier that immobilized her during marriage returned in full force after these multiple losses (Gornick and Moran, 1972). Feeling as if she had "lost control" of herself and those she loved, she experienced a crisis:

> I went into a real depression, when I was biologically, emotionally, and spiritually depressed, so that I finally had to get Prozac and spend some time in the hospital. I had one bout soon after the divorce and another after I learned Julia was pregnant. I had just taken an exam that I was truly worried about, and when I went out of the exam and went to where I thought I had left my car, it wasn't there, so I sat down right where I was and wept. A really nice woman came along and realized my extremity, and she was very reassuring and called security and stayed with me. They came and got me and we found my car, but I was trembling and out of control. They took me to the hospital and I called my therapist. I guess it was just that I was feeling so out of control, knowing that I was now the matriarch of the family and the only adult, and now with a pregnant daughter. The hospital kept me for five or six days and helped me to see my strengths again. I felt like I had no control over my life. They spent days showing me all that I've accomplished.

SARAH'S DAUGHTERS: ADOLESCENT STORMS

Julia: Hard Lessons, Only Younger

Before she became pregnant, Julia experienced what Sarah explained as "something in our family about adult female hormones kicking in that throws you into a very, very difficult space emotionally." Unable to cope with this unseen, but certainly powerful force, Julia had been "absolutely off the wall for a year or so." She became depressed and attempted suicide (Carter and McGoldrick, 1980; Demos, 1986; Levine, 1992):

> It manifests as real depression and real uncertainty about who you are, but the first thing that happened was a call from the school that she had been taken by ambulance to the hospital because she had swallowed a whole bottle of sleeping pills. . . . About a year, maybe a year and a half, before she got pregnant. I think she had just turned fifteen, and that was hard. That was just a call that I'd never expected to get because she had been such a secure ebullient child.

Some research links single parents to teenage suicide (Hirsch and Ellis, 1995) and eventually also to teenage pregnancy (Cooper and Moore, 1995). Julia's participation in both forms of "deviance" followed her parents' divorce by three years. Because of reported connections between these phenomena, I asked Sarah about Julia's reaction to the divorce:

> She was in sixth grade, so she would have been twelve. She was very glad that I was doing this, and in fact, when he was explaining why he wasn't going to go for treatment right after the intervention and telling me how wrong I was, afterwards she said to me, "Mom, why do you let him talk to you like that?" So both girls were very, very supportive, and she really wanted the divorce.

Though it is really impossible to determine what led to Julia's troubles, and not entirely illogical to connect their occurrence with her family's troubles, Sarah added further context. She described a genetic tendency in their family for females to experience depression and mood swings during periods of hormonal fluctuations in their lives.

One additional factor that might have contributed to Julia's early rebellion could have been the internalization of her father's disparagement of her mother (Levine, 1992). Sarah said, "She resented school because she bought into her dad's idea that I was the perpetual student who stayed in school because I couldn't face the real world." It was Julia, after all, who resisted her mother's decision not to work but to return to school, claiming that she "owed" her daughters *their* time. Perhaps she has since had a change of heart.

As it did for Sarah, pregnancy made Julia a different person. It was when she became a young single mother that she truly matured and found the strength to work, go to school, and raise her son, but she has a realistic assessment of her situation and makes intelligent choices, reconciling her dream of one day going to medical school with her current reality of motherhood. Sarah is saddened that Julia must face the same problems Sarah did at thirty-five when she is only nineteen (Kissman and Allen, 1993). Her "high-powered" determination to make a good life for herself and her son stands in stark contrast to the baby's father, still by all standards a *boy*friend whose irresponsible behavior may eventually lead Julia to leave— as her mother did. Sarah suggested, however, that maybe children must improve upon their parents' example:

WP: How is Julia coping with single parenting?

S: She often talks to me about herself and her responsibility to her son. She feels that really without him she wouldn't have the maturity and self-respect to go to school to be a physician. She cannot possibly commit herself to that much schooling right now, though. She's essentially a single parent because even though her boyfriend's around, he didn't finish high school, and he used his new family as an opportunity to not have parents and to do as he pleased. She's painfully aware of the fact that because of the baby she knows things she would not yet have realized, but also because of him she can't move forward. She's finished training as a phlebotomist. The woman who taught the course mentored and encouraged her to train as a medical tech-

nician, but she can't support nine hours of course work a semester, plus working, plus raising a baby. She's high powered,
but she is struggling with outgrowing her boyfriend, but she
doesn't want to take the baby away from his father.

He seems to stay dependent. He doesn't even have his driver's license, so she has to drive him everywhere. He's bright,
too, but he's irresponsible. You've gotta give him credit for not
leaving the way most teenage fathers do.

It's funny for me to see her struggling with the same problems we struggle with. It's strange and sad to see her handling
the same situations I did and doing it so young, facing at nineteen what I was facing at thirty-five. Maybe that's progress.
Maybe we do have to redo what our parents stumbled over.

Annie: The Peacemaker Turns Troublemaker

Annie, Sarah's younger daughter, had been the one who could
find a way to gain her father's affection by carefully assessing his
state of sobriety or drunkenness. She was the one "born bringing
peace," a joy to Sarah throughout her childhood. She had also
helped to support her mother during the divorce, though she was
more ambivalent than Julia, having found ways to remain close to
her father (Kaschak, 1992; Levine, 1992). However, as time passed,
Annie learned that her father just did not care about her on a day-to-
day basis, and she became more embarrassed about his maudlin
displays of affection:

Since then, Annie gets really upset because every year there's a
Christmas concert, and at the end of the concert, they do the
Hallelujah chorus, and anybody in the audience who's ever
sung the Hallelujah chorus is invited to join. And he'll always
go up on stage, and . . . by that time in the evening, he's visibly
drunk, and . . . he would be really maudlin about it and sing out
and want to put his arm around her and he would smell, and she
would get really embarrassed and upset. It got to the point
where she tried to not let him know when the concert was, but it
was always posted outside the school, so he would show. [She
laughs.]

He came up here in the summer. He went down to a nudist camp in Florida, and he would have them down once a year and take them to Disney World, and . . . they were his little princesses for that week, and the rest of the time he'd just kind of forget about them. But she could pretend it was the distance. This year just past, he had to have surgery, so he stayed up here all winter and didn't have any more contact with her than he did down in Florida, and she really hurt from beginning to understand that she really wasn't part of what he cared about on a day-to-day basis.

While her older sister Julia was struggling with adolescence and her pregnancy, Annie supported her mother, but almost as soon as Julia went off on her own, Annie became the "handful":

Annie was very, very supportive of me during all the time that Julia was off the wall, and during her pregnancy, and whatever, and then almost as soon as Julia moved out, it was like, "It's my turn!" And she started getting . . . she's been a handful this year, just really blowing her academic talents. I got her the car really because I had gotten a place for Julia and the baby to live in, and so much of my focus was on helping her get set up so that she could handle that, that I felt Annie should have something to reward being a regular teenager. And once she got the car, she was off and running and very quickly began to act as if my authority was irrelevant. So we struggle over that a lot.

Active in cheerleading and 4-H club, Annie was, as Sarah described her, "a lovely person, just not to me." She barely survived her last year in high school. Handing in an English paper late kept her from graduating with her class and required her to attend summer school, where she finished with her mother's help. Annie, however, also sent a public message to her mother that she disregarded her authority and wished to assert her own (Carter and McGoldrick, 1980; Kissman and Allen, 1993). Sarah described another phone call she never expected:

And I got a call from her a few weeks ago, "Mom. Come get me. I'm at the police station." She'd been caught shoplifting. And that was another call I never thought I'd get.

I asked Sarah if she thought Annie was going through the same hormonal storms that both she and her oldest daughter had experienced. She said that it was possible but that she is troubled by the fact that Annie aims her misbehavior directly at her, punishing her when she attempts to enforce rules. This is certainly not an atypical manifestation of teenage rebellion. Sarah's motherly guilt, however, is intensified by worries that her single parenting is somehow the "cause" of Annie's misbehavior (Levine, 1992). Sarah described the events leading to the shoplifting incident:

WP: Do you think she's going through this same thing?

S: Yeah. So I can only hope. I look at Julia and I can say, "All right. She will. . . . " But Annie basically did that because she was angry at me, because about four or five days before that, on the weekend, she'd come in about two a.m., and I was lying on the couch, and I woke up and said, "Good night," to her and "You're late," you know, the normal stuff. And then the dogs woke me up about four-thirty in the morning, and when I went out to take them out, her boyfriend's car was in the driveway. And so I went upstairs, and they were both sound asleep, and I said, "It's not all right for him to be here." And she said, "We were just exhausted and crashed." And I said, "I don't care. You don't let yourself get so exhausted you can't drive. And this is my home." And she said, "Well, what do you think we were doing?" And I said, "Well, obviously, you're getting my imagination going on that issue, but you have told me that you two have decided not to do that, and I believe you, but you're certainly not making it easy on yourself by having him here overnight, and it's not acceptable to me in my home." And she said, "Okay. We won't do it again. Can we go back to sleep?" And I said, "No! He has to leave!" and she was *so* angry at me that I made him leave at four-thirty in the morning that when I asked her about the shoplifting, she said, "I was mad at you.

And I knew you were mad at me, and I didn't think you were going to give me any extra money for shopping."

Sarah refused to pay her daughter's debt so Annie had to face the court's decision. Trying to be fair, and perhaps wishing to share the burden a little, Sarah told Garry about the court date, but he only made matters worse. Annie was angry at her father's interference because she and her mother had already decided to accept the court's sentence of community service:

Her father wasn't much use. She was really angry that I told her father because her father showed up in court. And when he showed up, she was really mad and said, "You don't think that he will be any help, do you?" I said, "I don't have any idea, but he is your father and he should be involved." And [then] his lawyer show[ed] up, and he went and talked to him about it, whereas Annie and I had already made the choice, based [on] what the judge had said at the arraignment, not to get a lawyer. We knew it wasn't going to [be] any use. The judge gave us the opportunity to get one, but we felt that the sentence was appropriate. I wouldn't pay the fine. . . . She's ending up doing thirty hours of community service and three sessions of anti-shoplifting training that ends with a trip to the prison, which is good.

Once again, Sarah was alone in having to cope with her feelings of guilt over this dramatic episode (Skolnick, 1978). Still struggling with her mother's pressure to stay in the marriage, this event triggered grave self-doubt. Sarah's anxiety that her daughter's bad behavior is a direct result of divorce and single parenting is reinforced by research reports connecting all sorts of deviant acts to single mothering (see Defining Family, subsection Deviance and Defiance, in Chapter 1) and by popular acceptance of the notion that single parenting—no matter how educated and well-off the mother may be—automatically causes damage to the children (Carlson, 1992). Thanks to the support of her pastor and his wife, however, Sarah at least was able to engage in more positive self-talk:

I still struggle with it, even though I know better and even though I've resolved that, intellectually and to some degree emotionally, there are times when something happens, like Annie shoplifting, when I wonder if [my mother] was right. It was funny because one evening I was praying with my pastor's wife . . . and [the pastor] came in the room and said to me, "You are not to blame." It was so interesting because he must have sensed my struggle with Annie's shoplifting. He was so strong. He said, "God really wants you to understand that you are not to blame." And I think that mothers in general do this, especially single mothers. I know better, but it takes a lot of self-talk.

The pastor was helpful again when Annie and her mother needed to resolve another conflict over Annie's inappropriate use of Sarah's ATM (automatic teller machine) card. For Sarah, who does not see herself as a stern disciplinarian, enforcing rules is difficult and causes emotional stress. Instead of trying to deal with this event alone, she sought the support of someone whose opinion Annie would value, and against whom she did not need to rebel:

I've turned to [the pastor] some because while he's a much stricter parent than I would be—I mean, he and I would be at loggerheads if we were married, about some things—but nonetheless it's been really useful to me. Like when Annie this last Christmas borrowed, but without permission, my ATM [card] and took money out of the account in order to buy Christmas presents, meaning to put it back, but then of course she didn't have it, and she was stuck in the position—which is a normal human position of not being able to put it back before she gets caught—and I was really upset about that, and needed to deal with it, and she was not communicating with me very clearly about it at all. And I took that to him, and the two of us had three sessions together, and it really was very useful, and I thought it was helpful at that point to have another authority figure in her life helping us deal with it.

Annie's actions would not surprise anyone who studies adolescents. In fact, developmental psychologists have many names for this stage of rebelliousness and assertiveness that translates into teen-agers' overt actions against parents (Carter and McGoldrick, 1980). Challenges to parental authority are commonly reported, regardless of the parentage of the teenager, with the phenomenon exacerbated between same-sex children and parents (Dinnerstein, 1976). Given this widespread occurrence of child-parent conflict in adolescence, it would not be difficult to make a connection between single-parent families and episodes of teenage deviant behavior. However, such a correlation also holds for teenage children from otherwise happy, normal two-parent homes (Krantz, 1988). Annie shows herself to be a typical teenage girl through her material orientation and jealou-sy of her mother's attention toward her sister:

> Annie, right now, really believes that she's a deprived child, and if you look around this room, you know that Annie is *not* a deprived child. [The room is filled with pictures of the girls, especially Annie in her cheerleading uniform, ribbons on the wall, collections, books, games, etc.] I don't know.

> Recently, Julia has my mom's car, but it finally totally broke down. Now I had gotten Annie the MG sort of to celebrate, and that's when I realized it was not a safe car. I got her a jeep, a neat little car for a teenager to have, but I was hoping that if she could drive herself places, it [would take] one more stress off me, when I was trying to juggle my schedule and hers, and I was perfectly happy for her to have that. Well, now I'm helping Julia buy a new car, and Annie is jealous and wants to know, "Well, are you buying me a car, too?" "I already bought you a car. What are you talking about?" "Well, that's not a car; it's a jeep." Well, give me a break, here! I think she would be happy if I bought her the car I drive! I mean, "Grow up, kid! You're not deprived!"

> . . . but it really annoys me because she has *so* much more than I ever had. More than I *needed* to provide her, given the strapped circumstances that we were in for a time.

Sometimes, however, Annie put aside her antagonism for her mother and allowed her to help. Following the morning described next, Sarah received a card from her daughter with a personal message implying that she acknowledged her mother's exasperation with her behavior but wanted her to know that she still appreciated her mother's support:

> Annie right now wouldn't give you two cents for me as a mother or a woman or a role model. She's seventeen. On the other hand, this morning she was caught short having read only one of three stories that she had to read and had me read and encapsulate one of them, and that's the kind of compromise thing. I mean, there was a point at which I believed that either somehow I could have talked her into doing it right and giving herself enough time to do the task or left her entirely to face the music because, after all, it was her own [fault]. Whereas now if there's something I can do to help her some, then I do it, sort of with her, and I don't really even consider it cheating terribly because it's modeling for her *how to* think about the story, *how to* extract in a quick reading what you need in order to be . . . because she had to be able to write about it.

FAMILY: WHEN IT WORKS

In the second interview, while we were discussing Julia's newly created family, Sarah's loss of her entire birth family, and Annie's troubles in school, Sarah commented that "it's wonderful when family does function the way it should." She would have been grateful for extended family to help with raising the children. She can also see definite benefits to having a second adult to help share the responsibility, a good role model for her girls who would show them an example other than the abusive relationship they saw between their own parents:

> I don't have anybody to be a good male role model for my girls. I think it hurts them. Julia just loves her boyfriend's family—the family picnics, having a "mother-in-law" to go to and help with the baby. I really think it's easier to be a single mom with an extended family to go to. . . . I think it's wonderful when family does function the way it should. I mean, I

really think it makes sense to have two adults to share the responsibility. And I really think it makes sense for there to be a model around of a person of the opposite gender, for boys in terms of how to be, and for girls in terms of what to expect and demand from a man . . . so that we don't let ourselves get abused. But I, for instance, *had* a father and I would have been better off without one! [She laughs.]

She was careful to note that having a father present in the family is not necessarily a guarantee of having a helpmate, her own childhood being testament to the damage that can be done by a present, but destructive father. Instead, she would seek a sort of "wife" to help with the mundane chores, to give her emotional support, and to share life's stresses (Baca Zinn and Eitzen, 1990; Rice and Rice, 1986). Though this description might fit a male companion, her experience has taught that this kind of role is more expected of women than men, thus her choice of *wife* to describe the nurturer, rather than *husband* (Farrell, 1972):

What I would really love is to have a wife, and I don't mean that in the sense of lesbians. I just mean I think it would be neat to have somebody do my cooking and cleaning for me and feel emotionally responsible to check up on how I was doing and give me lots of [positive] strokes, and take care of my kids in difficult situations. But, on the other hand, I would never put another human being in that bind because it really does mean living for and through other people, and there's got to be some kind of happy medium where both people can do that for each other, and there are two people to take the stresses. It seems to me—time management, money management, disciplinary things—to have another adult to talk over with, what the kids are doing and whether it's normal growing stuff or whether it's out of line and requires special attention, would be magnificent! But, my experience is that, for the most part, women are better socialized to do it than men.

A common wish for single moms is a desire for adult companionship and support, but they are quick to remind themselves that their own situations were far from supportive (Bequaert, 1976). Sarah envisions an ideal situation in which a male companion is present to help her, she realizes that her reality is far from that ideal:

> So, yeah, I would love to have another adult to help shoulder the burden. I'd love to have somebody here who I could bounce my thoughts off of and who would see when I was feeling too guilty and say, "That's not your [fault]." But the reality, at least for me, of my marriage was that instead of that happening, he simply fed into the guilt and the responsibility and defense that I was somehow lazy and irresponsible, and so that instead of being a helpmate, he dragged me further into the pit.

Reminders of that ideal abound. Similar to Judith, who was disappointed with her less-than-perfect family, Sarah described how she and her daughters envied families that appeared to fit that model. Sarah's voice was quietly emotional as she explained how this longing can be stimulated:

> Just like yesterday, [her father] had asked Annie when she would be showing at the Farm Festival because one year I had let him know and he had really enjoyed seeing her. But when it came right down to it, he wasn't there—he probably forgot; he was probably off drinking somewhere. . . . Then it causes more pain and more harm than it is worth. Now she actually didn't want to have him around because even if he's in a stage where he doesn't believe he's drunk, it's visible enough to other people so that she's embarrassed by it. But [long pause] she sees, and I see, families that are there where the father is proud and supportive, but in an appropriate way, and because he himself is a successful independent person. . . .
> That makes me very sad for my girls, and very sad for myself. I experienced it one night; we were raising money for the cheerleading squad because they were going to nationals, and we were having a fifties jam to raise money for them, and some of the families were there and really enjoying it together—and a dance is a difficult situation to be at anyway without a male partner, but I was doing fine. But there came a number when the fathers were dancing with their daughters and I just

really broke down in tears because that wasn't. . . . [This was difficult for her to relate.]

Every once in awhile you do see a family that clearly functions the way families should, but I'll agree, it's rare! But when you see it, you say, "That's what *I* wanted."

The strength of the ideal was present in her parenting expectations as well, although now, having redefined her family, she is able to accept her daughters for who they are, without feeling guilty:

WP: You've said in talking about your girls, you've redefined your family. What was it before? What is it now? What changes?

S: You know, I don't know how much of that has to do with the sense of being a single mom and how much to do with their getting older. I really believed that I was somehow going to be able to produce perfect kids. A *long time* I was able to maintain that! Whereas now I'm much more willing to go with the flow, accept them for who they are and not feel too terribly guilty about it, and try to share with them what my experience and ideas are on the subject . . .

SCHOOL AND THE SINGLE PARENT

Because Sarah is a teacher *and* a mother, she believes schools often act as if the home is simply an extension of the school. Sarah asserted that, despite their rebellious teenage behavior, her daughters were quite successful in school. She believes this was due to the way she had encouraged curiosity and an interest in learning from their earliest years. Similar to Kathleen, whose few hours with her daughters were often spent doing homework, Sarah views much homework as an imposition on her time with her children. This discussion led to her affirmation that learning is not the exclusive purview of the school:

WP: Up until these last couple of years, would you say that your daughters have had a fairly successful time in school?

S: Oh yes, very.

WP: And what contributes to that, do you think?

S: Some of it definitely was my reading with them and taking an interest in what they were doing. Even before, when they were preschoolers, if we went someplace interesting, or would have an interesting experience, we would come home and draw pictures about it together. And they would tell me things and I would turn it into a little story, and either they would do the pictures and they would do the story or I'd ask them questions, interview them the way you're doing, and from that put together a story. And I might outline some pictures for them, and they would color them and add detail, but getting to know about things, getting to learn about things is always interwoven pretty easily and naturally with our lives, so that learning and finding out was pretty natural.

WP: So they learned to learn from you? They learned to be curious and how to relate their experiences?

S: Yeah. And they understand, I think, better than many kids did how the different disciplines that we learn kind of inter-relate and interweave, and they see how it's used. . . . But I'm also part of their problem with school because I have always felt that home life and family experience was more important than homework. And so, I really *resent* some forms of home-work. Some things have to be done at home. There's no way around it. But a lot of forms of homework to me are just an imposition. And I'm sorry, but if my kid wants to talk to me about something important, or even if they want to play Scrabble or Mah-Jongg with me, that's more important to me than writing a spelling list . . . and if we're going to go some-place interesting, I think that's much more educationally valu-able.

And I really think when the school has kids six hours a day, that they ought to be able to accomplish in that six hours what they have to accomplish. And leave you *your* six hours to accomplish what *you* have to accomplish. I resent it—which is an odd point of view for a teacher—so that some of their putting other things first . . . and Annie will get very busily involved in organizing her dog show things, or whatever, instead of doing what she's supposed to.

I find [homework] very intrusive. And I would sometimes write notes to the teacher and say, "I'm sorry, but I consider such and such more important."

As a teacher, Sarah understands why schools feel that they alone are responsible for education, but as a mother, she believes that they should not attempt to control parent-child interactions during after-school hours. She fears that her daughters have internalized her attitudes about school and home, but she makes an important distinction between having respect for learning and resisting the school's "ownership" of time:

I tended to [have time to read to them only] during the summer or Christmas vacation, and that's lousy! That is really lousy! Of course I understand why schools feel they have the whole responsibility for their education, but it's an affront to women as mothers, to their adulthood, to their responsibility towards their children. I'm sure that Julia, for instance, is going to experience the same thing when her son starts going to school. Those first couple of years it's not so bad, but along about fifth grade it starts getting, and it just keeps on getting worse until senior year. But I really believe that Annie is learning as much that she's going to use in her adult career, and certainly in her adult personal and family life, from her cheerleading and her dog showing and even her relationship to her boyfriend than she is from [homework] and I think she's picked up that essential disrespect from me. And you know very well that it's not that I think there's something wrong with learning! I mean, I love to learn. I love to study. I love to be in classes—both as a teacher and as a student. But I don't think it owns your life. And when it starts trying to own the evening hours when you have something, it's just too much.

THE FINAL ACT: PICKING UP THE PIECES

At the conclusion of our last interview, Sarah took me on a tour of her house, which she said represented her:

The house was a mortuary of lost dreams and awful abusive memories, and yet I really wanted to provide the continuity for my girls, with so much being disrupted, and let's face it, it's beautiful! It's a wonderful place. But I was so broke that there was very little I could do about it, so when I did finally inherit some money, I did have one room, to make it kind of a sanctuary of *me,* make it mine. And then for awhile I was getting five hundred dollars a month from the trust, which is how I did all the other repapering and air-conditioning.

And then my investment person got together with my trustee and said, "Look. She cannot continue withdrawing at this rate and also build for any kind of retirement." And all of them had judgments about my not working during these years and whatever. And in some ways the trust is a wonderful thing, and I really do need it because I would spend irrationally. I mean, if it's there, I feel it's there to be used, but now I really have to think that out and assert it. I have to say assertively, "I *am* going to withdraw four thousand dollars to help Julia buy a used car." That *now* is just as important as whatever it earns for the future, and I've had to in my own mind and in my own therapy really sort out what in the present *is* a really valid way of spending resources, but for instance, rather than drawing from the trust, I'm remortgaging the house to finish up the work on the house. I mean, it will be less when the house is sold for me to put into resources, but it also means there will be more because the house will be worth more.

Then when I get a job somewhere, I'll sell this house. The house represents myself. I haven't eradicated really truly bad and self-disrespectful housekeeping habits. I developed a real resentment of keeping house because [Garry] monitored and judged and declared acceptable or unacceptable everything I did around here. He was so abusive I always had his voice in my head. I get passive-aggressive about it and make a mess.

CONCLUSION:
A DISASTER AND AN IRISH BLESSING

As I was preparing to leave her home after our final interview, we were shocked to discover that an ancient wooden carving her grandfather brought home from China—a beautiful painted screen carved from a single piece of wood—had fallen while her cleaners were vacuuming. The screen was not entirely destroyed, but pieces of it were lying on the floor and a hole gaped where the intricate lace-work was missing. I was horrified, but Sarah maintained her quiet composure and explained that this was a symbol of what had happened in her life. What was once whole was now in pieces, but she felt confident that, similar to her life, although broken, it was not irreparable.

She then read me a poem, an old Irish blessing for mothers, that she said once gave her comfort when she was sad and in need of inspiration:

God keep my jewel this day from danger
From tinker and pooka and black-hearted stranger
From harm of the water and hurt of the fire
From the horns of the cows going home to the byre
From teasing the ass when he's tied to the manger
From stones that would bruise and from thorns of the briar
From evil red berries that awaken desire
From hunting the gander and vexing the goat
From the depths of sea water by Danny's old boat
From cut and from tumble from sickness and weeping
May God have my jewel this day in His keeping.

Chapter 7

Viewing the Quilt:
Patterns and Themes

INTRODUCTION

Many research studies and texts claim to document the dissolution of the American family and thus participate in mother blaming,
especially with regard to single mothers. However, feminists, such
as sociologist Judith Stacey, clinical psychologist and family theorist Joy Rice, historian Stephanie Coontz, and critical theorists, such
as Dorothy Dinnerstein, Judith Levine, and Warren Farrell, have
reanalyzed the data on women, men, and families and drawn different conclusions.

Even members of the same interpretive community do not always agree. Joy Rice points out that many family researchers base
their interpretations of women in family life on tried-and-true theories, such as the family life cycle theory, first postulated by Emily
Duvall and Ruben Hill in 1957, a time historians have called an
aberration in the history of the American family. Any interpretations based on such theories are indelibly etched with the cultural,
economic, political, and social realities of the time period from
which their data are drawn.

My analysis of the results of these five case studies is no different. From the literature choices I have made, to my presentation of
the cases, the results reflect my own conviction that individual
women are human agents actively engaged in the construction of
their own destinies, but they do so within the historical, social,
economic, political, and cultural contexts of their lives. Readers will
bring to these chapters their own ideologies, values, and scholarship. Some will have insights I have not revealed or dispute the

interpretations I offer. This analysis may be considered optimistic and liberatory by some, overzealous by others, but I must necessarily see these data through the eyes of the participants and again through my own eyes. In discussing the inherent uncertainties of phenomenological in-depth interviewing, Seidman (1991) notes:

> The narratives we shape of the participants we have interviewed are necessarily limited. Their lives go on; our narratives of them are framed and reified. . . . So, as illuminating as in-depth interviews can be, as compelling as the stories are that they can tell and the themes they can highlight, we still have to bear in mind that Heisenberg's principle of indeterminacy pervades our work. . . . We have to allow considerable tolerance for uncertainty. (p. 103)

I acknowledge this "uncertainty" and trust that others may see different stories—perhaps their own—in this chapter.

Many cross-sectional themes might be discovered in the rich data of these case studies. To help readers follow the multiple connections among the women in Chapters 2 through 6 and the women represented by the research discussed in Chapter 1, this chapter first summarizes pertinent observations from each of the five narratives, then synthesizes the themes by following the same conceptual divisions used in Chapter 1.

FAMILIES AND PARENTING

Since I intentionally constructed the literature review *after* I had crafted each woman's narrative from her interviews, I was impressed by how many aspects of these women's life stories were also represented in many different texts. In this section, I summarize how Judith, Kathleen, Shawna, Lyn, and Sarah enact parenting and experience family life, both during marriage and beyond divorce, and discuss the connections between their lived experiences and those of other women, as outlined in the literature cited in Chapter 1, that is pertinent or parallel to those experiences.

Judith: Controlling and Intergenerational Patterns

Judith blames herself for adopting what she described as a controlling or overresponsible attitude toward parenting. In her many references to her controlling nature or being codependent with her son, she suggested that she may be too involved in decision making and that she and her son depend on each other for nurturance. Perhaps further observation of her interactions with her son may support the idea that her behavioral patterns demonstrate control of her family, but I believe that in making these assertions, Judith has internalized some of the labels attributed to mothers in much of the self-help literature she reads. Perhaps she participates in mother blaming, worrying that she is what psychologists call "enmeshing, domineering, or smothering" (Boss and Weiner, 1988, p. 238). Van Wormer (1989) attributes mothers' attempts to control to their feelings of responsibility for the mental health of their families when they have little actual control. Feminist psychologist Kaschak (1992) is critical of habitually blaming mothers for "doing just what is required of them" (p. 57), which in Judith's case was encouraged by her husband's behavior.

Judith attributed her parenting style to her family history. Her mother was overprotective and her father was virtually absent. Because she never enjoyed the mythical Ozzie and Harriet family when she was growing up, her persistent quest for the perfect nuclear family made her work ever harder to maintain the illusion that she had found it. When she finally recognized that her own situation did not measure up and her husband announced his desire to divorce, her dreams were shattered, as with many American women who buy into the mythologies surrounding images of the family (Baca Zinn and Eitzen, 1990).

The five family myths (see Chapter 1) proved to have destructive power in Judith's life, as she learned that the life she thought she was living was an illusion. It is interesting to note that in her narrative she described her current situation as her new ideal: "You have two parents who are very conscious of being supportive of each other [for the sake of their son's successful adjustment to divorce], so it seems to be an ideal situation."

She contrasted her parenting with her husband's under-responsible parenting. His total absorption with work and emotional absence made what Dinnerstein (1976) refers to as a critical asymmetry in child care responsibility (p. 40). Farrell (1972) hypothesizes that men can see themselves as less responsible for child care because of generationally transmitted parenting myths that teach women how to be nurturers and discourage men from assuming that role (p. 109).

With single parenthood came a surprising change in both Judith's and Mike's parenting, so that "the whole dynamic is better." Not much has changed about her own routines, since the amount of role juggling she had before and after the divorce stayed about the same. However, less emotional space is taken up by resentment of her husband for not participating. Though it is hard to let go, Judith is beginning to encourage her son's independence from her. Feeling somewhat anxious about Mike's lax parenting style, she is encouraged by what she sees as his increasing attentiveness to his son while he is the sole caregiver. This improved parenting for both of them is a benefit of divorce also observed by Hetherington, Cox, and Cox (1977), who found in their study that two years after divorce, one-fourth of fathers and one-half of mothers reported better relationships with their children.

Judith's son still sees her as the "comfort person" and his father as the "play" person, a gendered division of parenting roles that has evolved over the historical development of families (Coontz, 1992; Demos, 1986; Dinnerstein, 1976; Farrell, 1972). However, with the artificially imposed time constraints on Mike's joint custodial responsibilities, Judith feels that he is spending more quality time with their son, and she is happier with the open communication and the warm and supportive times she enjoys with Ian during every part of the day they spend together, whether on a morning drive to school or in the evening when they discuss the details of their days.

Kathleen: Guilt and Overcompensation

Kathleen's sensitivity to the social stigma attributed to single parents was exacerbated by her brother's comment that their mother and father were actually raising her children because they provided day care while Kathleen worked several jobs. This was reinforced by her mother, who tried to make Kathleen regret her decision to divorce. To compensate for possible single-parent inadequacies, as perceived by others, Kathleen did everything: switching from three jobs to a more manageable *one,* skillfully managing scant financial resources, working with her daughters on hours of homework even when she was fatigued, sending her daughters on expensive field trips, and making her presence felt in their schools.

Partly because of the rapidly changing political and social forces shaping her life as a young woman in the 1960s and 1970s, she rejected her mother's choice to marry, stay home, and raise the kids. She considered her mother "spoiled" by those who kept her dependent, although she followed the strict gendered division of labor and moral codes her generation was socialized to respect (Coontz, 1992). Kathleen is the "do-both" woman researchers call the "supermom" (Baca Zinn and Eitzen, 1990; Coontz, 1992; Llewelyn and Osborne, 1990). Because Kathleen chooses to pursue a career and maintain the traditional jobs of motherhood, she is often caught between the stressors of the working world—such as late hours, low pay, and worries over doing everything right—and the frenetic activities in her home, which begin with morning "send-offs" and end with dinner preparation and cleanup, homework, chauffeuring, and exhausted sleep (Blake, 1974; Gimenez, 1984; Llewelyn and Osborne, 1990). Far from being peaceful, Kathleen's home hours were sometimes the "most stressful part of the day."

Despite the multiple role juggling she faces as a single parent, Kathleen is comfortable with her self-concept as a worker and a mother. She has alternated between guilt about not being able to spend more time with her growing daughters and confidence that their day care experiences benefited them. Rutter's (1977) and Kagan's (1984) studies of working mothers and the effects of day care on their children would support Kathleen's assertions about the many benefits her daughters enjoyed from their Montessori day care. Her pride in her daughters' accomplishments in school and her neighborhood designation as "the ultimate Ma" are evidence of her own success at ensuring the quality of her parenting while she seeks self-fulfillment in work. This self-assurance and confidence in their abilities to "do both" is reported often in case studies of single mothers (Kaschak, 1992; Kissman and Allen, 1993; Llewelyn and

Osborne, 1990; Stacey, 1990). Kathleen observed that as her daughters become more independent, she has more time for herself.

Kathleen's ex-husband virtually disappeared from her narrative after she described her divorce. His peculiar affinity for pornography and her suspicions that he might molest their daughters make him the embodiment of what Levine (1992) calls "The Brute" (pp. 136-152). Aside from occasional contact, he is truly absent from their lives, which Kathleen encourages by failing to enforce the support agreement her ex-husband soon abandoned along with his family. Her choice not to encourage the involvement of the girls' father in their lives for their own protection is a factor rarely mentioned in family therapy literature (Carter and McGoldrick, 1980; Kissman and Allen, 1993). Perhaps this is also a significant reason why many mothers do not seek enforcement of child support. Similar to Kathleen, single mothers interviewed by Bequaert in 1976 "considered the fathers to be inadequate or downright unfit, and [referring to life without the father's presence] none of them would have had things arranged any other way" (p. 29).

Shawna: A Legacy and a Future

When I read Baca Zinn and Eitzen's (1990) hypothesis that "for black women, the birth of a first child and the beginning of marriage have become two separate events" (p. 120), I immediately thought of Shawna. A young woman in a serious relationship with an older man, she unexpectedly became pregnant. This was a blow to her because she felt that she had disappointed her family. Shawna believed that she was expected to live out her mother's dreams for her to become a lawyer, but she, too, hoped that she would not simply repeat the misery of her mother and her sisters. Shawna did not rush to marry her daughter's father. Though they became engaged and agreed to live together, Shawna stated, "I did not want him to feel that it was just that was the right thing to do because we had a child together."

This proved a wise decision. William was extremely possessive and tried to control everything from her clothing to her hairstyle; his "hold on her" eventually became more than symbolic. Shawna was enchanted with her new baby, and William was jealous of the time she devoted to her and the effect it had on their relationship (Llewelyn and Osborne, 1990). Shawna returned to work and reasserted her independence. William started to drink heavily and to become ever more suspicious about Shawna's fidelity, which Shawna found curiously humorous, since she did not understand how men could think "that a woman can do something when she's working full-time and has a child."

William picked a fight with Shawna perhaps because of his insecurity about her love (Farrell, 1972) or because he felt increasingly powerless to control her every move (Coontz, 1992). In a critical confrontation that ended in physical violence, Shawna realized that this was definitely not the relationship she wanted her daughter to see as she grows up. Part of Shawna's heritage from her own parents' stormy thirty-year marriage and eventual divorce was the memory of their open confrontations in front of their children, conflicts that various researchers have shown are far more damaging to children than divorce (Herzog and Sudia, 1968; McCord, McCord, and Thurber, 1962; Nye, 1957; Santrock, 1972). Wishing to prevent this from happening to her daughter, and rearming herself with the strong determination she learned from her mother, she stood up to William, and they ended their common living arrangements.

Parenting apart gave Shawna the opportunity to raise her daughter to be strong, and for both mother and daughter to "provide happiness in our lives." Shawna, who enjoys parenting Tasha, described their many daily activities involving communication and interaction that are rich and loving, enabling them to build a stronger bond with each other. She explained how Tasha's periodic bouts with asthma put a strain on her role juggling because work "doesn't really care if you are a single parent." The choice to use her sick time when her daughter is ill is not difficult for her because "my daughter adds something to my life that my job doesn't offer. . . . My child loves unconditionally." It is no wonder, then, that Tasha is proud when her day care friends call Shawna "the best mom."

Similar to Judith, Shawna believes that the quality of her daughter's relationship with her father has improved immensely with the separation of mother and father. She has learned from her angry rebellion against her own mother for keeping her away from her father that girls are perhaps most harmed by paternal neglect, and that it is important to promote the special relationship Tasha has with her father—even if Tasha idealizes her father, as many daughters do (Levine, 1992; Dinnerstein, 1976).

During the times when William is alone with his daughter, he focuses on her, listens to her, and develops his emotional connection to her. Unfortunately, that also includes being the overindulgent "Disneyland dad," something he shares with Judith's husband, Mike, and many other fathers, both single and married (Kotelchuck, 1976; Lamb, 1976, 1977). She is philosophical about that and allows William to do what she considers only part-time parenting, but together they are making progress in a conscious effort to lay aside their differences as a couple, working together for the benefit of their child. Shawna believes that children should have confidence that their "well-being is being taken care of," and that they should never have to feel that they have to side with either parent to earn his or her love.

Lyn: Promoting Independence

Lyn's parenting philosophy contrasts with Judith's and Kathleen's. As a woman who has already "successfully launched" her two sons, Lyn reflected that her parenting follows the models laid down by her mother and grandmother, who became single parents through widowhood. Lyn's mother's motto—"Just get on with it!"—is an apt descriptor of Lyn's family life after her divorce twenty years ago.

Consistent with the general evolution of the mother as the primary parent in twentieth-century parenting (Demos, 1986), Lyn claimed that she was the primary parent in her marriage, and that she did not choose to parent three children—her two sons and a childlike husband. She gave no specific evidence of her ex-husband's behavior to support her reference to him as childish, but this exemplifies Dinnerstein's (1976) hypothesis that "female dominated childrearing" encourages men and women "to regard each other respectively as silly overgrown children" (p. 36). Similar to Judith's husband, Mike, Lyn's husband talked about being more involved, but Lyn felt that he never actually was. Farrell (1972) notes that this is one result of a strong social history of absentee fatherhood, allowing even somewhat role-conscious fathers to "get away with giving lip service to a desire to spend more time with their children" (p. 32), whereas women are still made to feel guilty if they divide their time between children and work.

Lyn, with two generations of single mothers in her history and a promising career, believed that her boys would be more damaged by an unfulfilled, depressed mother than they would by leaving a "poor role model" father. She decided to leave, and get on with her life. She did, however, admit that "it would have been an enriching thing to have another adult around," and that her sons were "bound to miss out."

Lyn's boys were expected to be responsible for their own time management and to become equal partners in the chores of family life, an attitude that she believed would help them to learn from experience "what worked and what doesn't," with little fiascoes being "the tuition [paid] for learning about life." Promoting this type of independence was a "safe bet" because her sons' personalities did not lend themselves to breaking rules. With children studied in other research, however, such early independence is not always considered a strength. In fact, single parents are often criticized for expecting adultlike responsibility too early (Carter and McGoldrick, 1980). Such research conclusions were critiqued by Rice (1994), who added that other research praises the children of single-parent homes for such behavior (Kurdek and Siesky, 1980; Richards and Schmiege, 1993).

Since her two sons are doing well as adults, she feels no regret about her parenting, but ponders whether she should have intervened more actively in the boys' schoolwork. Had she done so, they might not have ended up with grades that left them struggling to get into college. With her policy of noninterference, Lyn may seem to be the kind of single mother researchers criticize, having insufficient time to support her children's schoolwork. She is in stark contrast to Kathleen, who "worked twice as hard" to be supportive of her daughters. Perhaps this inconsistency is a reflection of their differing opinions about mothering and child rearing, rather than their status as single parents. This is supported somewhat by her comment that although her sons wished she had pushed them harder, they also admitted that some of their friends resented their parents for too *much* interference.

She reflected that in the long run—a time frame few research studies assess—her sons have made their own way, found happiness and career satisfaction, and turned out just fine. Although she admits that the early evidence of her sons' success is somewhat contradictory, at the time of publication of this book, both young men had completed school and were gainfully employed. When asked if her sons ever revealed their feelings about their childhood, she explained that they have openly expressed their admiration for their mother, telling her she has been "a great mom."

Lyn's ex-husband maintained his support regularly throughout his sons' minority, something she is grateful for since finances were tight. Wanting to get out of the marriage as soon as possible, however, Lyn failed to make provisions for the extra expenses of college, which came back to haunt her as the boys entered adulthood with the concomitant expenses, a phenomenon common to divorced couples (Weitzman, 1985; Rice and Rice, 1986).

Now that her sons are adults, Lyn relates to them as peers. She attributes their ability to see her as a person partly to their early interactions with her friends who had no children, but mostly as a result of their seeing her function as more than just a mom. Lyn is reluctant to attribute this to being a single parent, but she thinks that single mothers, especially, "have to be more aggressive or more assertive" about their individual identities.

Lyn believes that maintaining separate identities is important for single parents because they are susceptible to resenting what they give up for their children. Single parents should not succumb to the temptation to overcompensate for their "oneness" by sacrificing their own needs to live life for or through their children. This is the criticism Kaschak (1992) levels at Gilligan (1982) for forwarding the notion that the highest level of women's moral development involves self-sacrifice for others through relationship.

Lyn did admit to having a certain residual guilt about "being the bitch," the one who left, but she asserted that "selfishness is an antidote to guilt" and explained how she did not participate in the "superwoman complex," nor did she blame lack of career advancement on her motherhood. She was comfortable about asserting her own needs from the time her sons were young to their adulthood.

Sarah: Reparenting Herself
and Surviving Adolescent Daughters

Sarah's experiences in her family of origin and in her married life typify the dysfunctionality Sarah came to recognize as being "hunkered down in a disaster zone." With vague, but distressing memories of being used by both parents—by her mother to keep track of her father, and by her father as a cover for an illegal business—Sarah mused about the models her parents posed, ones she actively sought to repattern for herself and her daughters.

Despite her pride in an Ivy League education and her association with the 1970s Women's Liberation Movement, Sarah stayed in an abusive marriage with an alcoholic husband who systematically destroyed her self-image until she had little self-pride left. Sarah's joy in motherhood, however, survived even the specter of her husband's alcoholic abuse, and she discovered parenting as her calling. Convinced that she could raise "the perfect children," she welcomed her daughters' births, even though they came close together. When her pregnancy leave ended and she had to choose between staying at home with her two small children or returning to work, similar to Judith and Kathleen, she tried to maintain "the best of both worlds" by working part-time at jobs that allowed her to arrange her schedule as she felt necessary. The price for this, however, was financial dependence on her husband and living in an abusive home.

Sarah believed that if she could "fix her family," she could "fix the world" (Lerner, 1988), and for the sake of saving the relationship, she tried to change her husband. Sarah typifies a relational sense of morality that Gilligan (1982) identifies as the "natural" inclination of women, but Kaschak (1992) describes it as a remnant of women's socialization to be nurturers of men. Eventually, however, to protect her daughters from harm, Sarah confronted her husband directly with his destructive power in their family.

Failing to change his behavior, which was not truly unexpected, given the lack of *real* control women have over the behavior of their family members (Kaschak, 1992), Sarah finally ended her passive acceptance of abuse and divorced her husband. She did not want her daughters to grow up thinking their father's behavior was the norm, and she was determined to minimize the damage already caused by life with an alcoholic, described by family psychopathologists as "distinctive for its pervasive and destructive consequences" (Falicov, 1988, p. 225).

True to his only connection with reality—money—Garry maintained his child support financially, but Sarah described some painfully embarrassing times when he literally "stumbled" back into his daughters' lives, only to create confusion and encourage their attempts to prevent him from knowing the details of their lives.

Sarah made a conscious effort to be involved in her children's lives, to participate in school activities, to celebrate all special occasions lavishly, and to delight in her daughters' many accomplishments, attention that she never enjoyed during her own childhood. She called this "reparenting myself," an attempt to be the kind of mother she wishes she had had. This is exactly what has been communicated by other women who considered their mothers cold and unaccepting, an observation that emerged in a therapy support group with the theme "Our Mothers/Ourselves" conducted by psychologists Llewelyn and Osborne (1990, p. 157).

Beyond the divorce, as a single mother, Sarah faced her adolescent daughters' turmoil. Research on adolescents presents significant evidence of higher rates of depression, eating disorders, phobias, neuroses, depersonalization (loss of the sense of self), and attempted suicide among girls to support the notion that adolescence is more problematic for girls than for boys (Llewelyn and Osborne, 1990). It is interesting to note that such behaviors have also been attributed to both boys and girls of single parents (Coffman and Roark, 1992; Hirsch and Ellis, 1995).

Mothers, particularly, are the targets of teenage daughters who struggle to individuate from their mothers (Dinnerstein, 1976; Levine, 1992). Llewelyn and Osborne (1990) suggest that a girl's strong identification with her mother causes an internal conflict: "Hence rebellion against this tie is often fraught and highly 'irrational' in nature. Alternately, the anger may be denied and expressed instead through a variety of self-destructive actions and depression" (p. 29). Sarah noted that women in her family seem to experience depression when hormonal levels are changing, and she hypothesized that this affected both of her daughters.

In addition, as Chodorow (1978) describes, mothers identify closely with their daughters, and because of their knowledge about the abundant dangers faced by young women in a violent society, they are careful to protect their daughters, thus discouraging independence. Though Sarah did not seem particularly protective, she was more anxious about her second daughter Annie's rebellion, since she had observed the difficult consequences of Julia's adolescence and had always enjoyed a close relationship with Annie.

As a single mother, Sarah has bouts with guilt, not unlike Kathleen and Judith. She is sensitive to the single-mother stigma imposed by society (Schur, 1984) and blames herself for her children's problems. She is fearful that the problems her daughters have experienced may be at least partially attributable to their "inadequate family structure." Kissman and Allen (1993) remark that this is a common confusion of single mothers of adolescent daughters, despite the fact that Marsh (1990) who studied the effects of family structure on academic achievement, attitudes, and behaviors, concluded that "children's growth—at least in the last two years of high school—is surprisingly unaffected by different family configurations" (p. 339).

Sarah sought assistance from her church, particularly her pastor, who helped her understand that she was not to blame for Annie's acting-out behaviors. Kissman and Allen (1993) suggest that single parents need to mobilize their support networks, and that single mothers, particularly, should be "encouraged to name their experiences rather than attribute such problems to personal inadequacies" (p. vi).

Although Sarah sometimes compares her family to families she sees in public who seem to "have it all," she recognizes this as nostalgia for what she always wanted. These moments of comparison, however, are giving way to maturing self-knowledge that she is currently "redefining her family" and learning to accept her daughters "for who they are," without feeling guilty.

Synthesis of Common Themes Concerning Parenting and Families

Changes in Parenting

All five women discussed the ways their parenting changed from earlier notions, mostly passed down from mother to daughter and found in idealized images offered by media and politics, to real and often beneficial adjustments made as single parents. Their parenting styles differ: Judith, Kathleen, and Sarah are involved in their children's lives; Lyn and Shawna prize and encourage independence. Improvements in parenting followed divorce for all of the women. All have gained confidence in themselves as effective parents and assert that their children are developing—or have developed—successfully. With the exception of Sarah, who is currently coping with her daughters' rebellious behavior, the mothers' assessments of their children are positive, and there is evidence of the mothers' success: for example, two of the women—Kathleen and Shawna— enjoy the designations "ultimate Ma" and "the best Mom," respectively, terms applied by their daughters' admiring friends.

Readers may question whether Lyn's sons were truly "launched," whether Judith's son's "stay-at-home" preference is evidence of overdependence on his mother, and whether Sarah's two daughters typify the deviant behaviors often connected with children from families disrupted by divorce and subsequently headed by single mothers. When considering these examples from a "deficit comparison model," they may seem problematic, but it is important to acknowledge that the behaviors of children and mothers who seem to fit the "deviance profile" may be analyzed differently from within the context of their own construction of meaning, rather than in comparison to some external standard of normalcy. Sarah, for example, has consciously set aside the models of perfection she once wanted to emulate so that she could redefine her family. This supports the theories of family researchers Rice (1994) and Stacey (1990) who call for further studies that allow persons *themselves* to reveal and inspect the many ways they construct their families, without the burden of comparison with a singular ideal.

All of these women have sought effective support networks when they needed them, and all spoke highly of the successes of their children, who often assumed responsible roles in their families.

Juggling Multiple Roles

All of the women are confident in their ability to parent their children effectively. Some expressed exhaustion and exasperation about juggling parenting, work, and school, but this is typical of working parents, in general, and working mothers, especially. Judith voiced an important observation that may be assumed represents all of the women, though only she and Lyn commented on it. She related that the number of roles she now juggles has not changed much from when she was married. Researchers who remark on the single mother's task overload (Hetherington, Cox, and Cox, 1977) do not account for the gender role socialization of women and men that encourages an inequitable division of labor. Working married *and* single mothers are similarly burdened with an asymmetrical responsibility for family life.

Single mothering also has additional strains, which two parents may or may not contend with equally, because single mothers often lack backup systems. For example, Shawna described conflict between work and family obligations in needing to use her personal sick time to care for her ill daughter. Still, even if she were married, it is more likely that she, rather than her husband, would stay home with the ill child because society expects a mother to fulfill the role of primary caregiver, viewing her income as secondary to the husband's in regard to family welfare (Farrell, 1972; Kaschak, 1992). The difficulties of overturning this inequitable societal prejudice are exacerbated by the continuing inequities in male and female salaries and in the many ways that "gendered" jobs are equated with the value of particular services.

Absent Fathers/Husbands

Absent fathers and husbands characterize all five stories. Judith's husband was emotionally absent during marriage but improved his interactions with his son after the divorce. Kathleen's husband was suspiciously "brutish" (see Levine, 1992, "The Brute," pp. 136-152) and virtually disappeared from his daughters' lives after the divorce, which Kathleen encouraged by failing to enforce support. Shawna's experience with absence came primarily from her father's desertion and her mother's preventing her from visiting him. This is not something she wants for her own daughter, so she encourages her daughter's father to be an active parent, if part-time, and respects her daughter's relationship with him. Lyn preferred raising her sons alone to staying married to a husband whom she felt was a poor role model. He maintained his support payments but refused to help the boys with expenses as they entered college. Sarah's alcoholic husband was destructive to himself, to her, and to his daughters. His inability to face his alcoholism motivated Sarah to free her daughters from the abnormal family model they were learning in their lives together. He provides only financial support, occasionally reappearing to embarrass his daughters with drunken, maudlin affection.

Confusion exists about the degree to which single mothering actually involves a father's participation. The single-parent family often is not one woman alone raising her child entirely without support or help from the father. In this study, not all of the women have the need to maintain their lives totally separate from the fathers of their children. Though they would prefer to be totally free from the painful past represented by their ex-partners, Judith and Shawna are wrestling with new approaches to custody; they are, similar to the women in Bequaert's (1976) case studies, "devising new ways to share parenting, recognizing that divorce need not deprive their children of healthy, close, and loving relationships with a father who is also an ex-husband" (p. 34). All mothers except Kathleen received regular support from the fathers of their children, though the fathers' contact with their children varied according to the circumstances of the divorce.

Comparing Themselves and Their Families
to a Mythical Ideal

Idealized images and internalized stigma are present in all five narratives. Mother blaming seems to be an experience all of the women have faced, either from others or within themselves. Comparing themselves unfavorably to mythical notions of family and mothering, some worry about being measured by others according to pervasive beliefs about single parents. All, however, are strong enough to see that the realities of their lives belie such stereotypical images of instability and disaster.

Judith seemed most disappointed by failing to attain the ideal family, but she recognized the mythology in this aspiration and realigned her family image by acknowledging its strengths for her and her son. Kathleen suffered from felt single-mother stigma that was reinforced by her brother, who questioned her ability to parent alone, and her mother, who made her feel guilty. To protect her family against "becoming a statistic," Kathleen exerts "supermom" effort to live her "several lives" efficiently. Shawna was most hurt by feeling that she had failed her mother and her family by becoming pregnant, thereby losing her opportunity to pursue a law career, as her mother had wished. She decided not to marry her baby's father simply because "they have a child together," going against societal expectations. Sarah, convinced that she could "produce the perfect kids," found herself instead in an abusive marriage that recalled the abuse of her childhood. Although she once looked longingly at families who seemed to be enjoying the life she wanted, with maturity—hers and her daughters'—she is better able to acknowledge the value of what she has.

Lyn is perhaps the one most resistant to the mythologies that surround mothering and families, but she is the third generation of mothers who have made it alone. Possibly because of the many childless friends she includes in her support network and the enjoyment of watching her sons thrive on their own, she can talk about the "Cinderella complex" in others but finds little of the "handsome prince rescuing the beautiful girl" appealing in her own life narrative.

GENDER WARS REVISITED

Given the massive historical evidence that gender roles are culturally, socially, economically, and politically derived rather than sexually natural, the tenacious maintenance of gender-associated divisions of labor and socialized gender role expectations seems to transcend historical context (Demos, 1986; Coontz, 1992). The importance of considering sex roles and gender roles separately is explained by Baca Zinn and Eitzen (1990):

> The sex-gender system combines biologically based sex roles with socially created gender roles. In everyday life, the terms "sex role" and "gender role" are used interchangeably. This obscures important differences and underlying issues in the study of women's and men's experiences. (p. 126)

Sex roles involve behaviors entirely determined by an individual's biological sex, such as reproductive functions. Gender roles, though they may be assumed to arise somewhat out of sexual functions, are actually social constructions containing self-concepts, psychological traits, and family, occupational, and political roles *assigned to,* rather than *arising from,* each sex. The difference between them, albeit far from distinct and discrete, and the results of inaccurately interchanging them are important as we consider the many ways that gender role enactments are played out in these women's lives.

Judith: "Different Types of Men and Different Types of Women"

Judith replayed the gender roles of her parents in her marriage. Though she did not want to be like her mother, trapped in a loveless marriage by financial dependency, she sees now that the unequal distribution of labor she disliked in her parents was not unlike the division of responsibility she shared with her husband. Similar to the "perfect mother" described by Chodorow and Contratto (1976), she assumed control of the daily details of family life, smoothing the way for Mike so that he could "focus" on his career and perhaps find time to be with her and their son, Ian. She did not realize that she was emphasizing Mike's irresponsibility.

He came to resent what he perceived as her control over him, perhaps echoing what has been described as male fear of the mythical power of motherhood (Llewelyn and Osborne, 1990). It is interesting to note, however, that, as Van Wormer (1989) suggested, Judith's control was relegated to responsibility for the well-being of the members of her family; it was Mike who *actually* controlled the family's schedule, expecting Judith and Ian to live their lives around his daily rhythms. Internalizing gender role expectations, Judith based her self-esteem on the smooth functioning of her relationships and expended most of her efforts toward maintaining them to the benefit of everyone but herself. Mike, on the other hand, based his self-worth almost entirely on his work, *in* but not *of* the world of his family (Gilligan, 1982).

Mike's fathering behavior, claimed Judith, originated with the model *his* father provided, a man who was first absent because he was absorbed in business, and then absent because he died when Mike was young. Mike actually became the father by whom he felt abandoned, a second generation of "The Abandoner," described by Levine (1992) as "engaged in another world, focused on his job outside the family, and only an occasional visitor at home" (p. 115). Judith was a victim of the Cinderella myth. She knew this was unrealistic, but when she discovered that the image of family harmony she had learned to prize was no longer viable in her life, she was so unnerved that she experienced depression in the form of crippling anxiety attacks.

Considering the transmission of gender role expectations across generations, Judith believes she is deliberately not reenacting her own mother's life, and she expects that her son will break free from gender role stereotypes as well: "Obviously he'll think that women can do anything. . . . He's just gonna have a very different attitude toward women." If she had a daughter, she said, she would certainly encourage her to recognize her self-importance, to "make it in the world," without expecting to have a partner to care for her.

Judith believes that single-parent families are "breaking a lot of the traditional roles," and she observed that Ian is already asserting a more active role in their new family, social role training that she thinks will make 'him a wonderful partner someday. She does not think Ian believes that "he's gonna marry someone and take care of her." Perhaps as one of the generation that Levine (1992) describes as having grown up "without the hegemony of the two-parent, split-role family" (p. 194), Ian will be one of many sensitive individuals who are not "the little men of big men," as Judith described them. She thinks "that's really starting to change what happens to relationships."

When asked about the importance of male role models, Judith answered that boys need *many* role models—"different types of men and different types of women." In one of Levine's (1992) case studies, a young black mother echoed this assertion when discussing the "lack of male role models" for her son:

Where I come from it doesn't seem that unusual. There are plenty of boys out there who were raised by their mothers, their grandmothers, and households of women. I feel like [my son] gets a large variety of women who have different personalities who bring different things to his life. (p. 193)

Ian has benefited from seeing his mother engaged in a multiplicity of roles, and from having his father's increased, rather than decreased, attention.

Kathleen: "I Am Not My Mother!"

Deviating somewhat from what Chodorow (1978) calls "the reproduction of mothering," Kathleen perceives many differences between her mother's ways of thinking and acting and her own. She joked about looking into the mirror and seeing her mother, but she asserted that she does not use guilt to manipulate her loved ones, as she feels her mother and her aunt did. She described her attitudes toward sex, open communication, religion, morality, maternal expectations, marriage, divorce, and child rearing as significantly different from her mother's. Kathleen, angered by her mother's "I told you so" disapprobation of her failure in marriage, has tried not to internalize that negative opinion, but she admits that she works ever harder to show her mother that she is "a good person."

She chooses to enact a somewhat traditional division of labor in her home; she does the ironing, cleaning, and other domestic chores, which she laughingly attributes to an "inbred Polish heritage." Not unlike many women whose work at home focuses on maintaining the harmonic flow of life for their families—what Gilligan (1982) calls women's relational orientation to moral goodness—Kathleen stated that she *chooses* to take on the roles with which she is comfortable. She remarked that the way she and her companion, Michael, have divided the tasks of their family works well for them. This may be what Levine (1992) calls "a comfortable discomfort" inherent in practiced gender roles (p. 386), but Kathleen asserted that as their relationship matured, labor division "just evened out." She maintains that the central connection between them is "mutual respect," something she did not enjoy with her first husband, who exerted his authority over her, even as far as dictating the amount of space she was allowed in their closet.

Kathleen contrasted Michael's sensitivity to her needs and active bolstering of her self-confidence with the destructive ego-centered carelessness of her ex-husband, David. In Kathleen's story about her divorce, David is portrayed as a "Brute," but he also fits Levine's (1992) description of the "Beast." Truculent, self-centered, posturing, and dangerous, the beast asserts his power over women in his sexual habits, his fierce defense of his rights to control her, and his conviction that the world exists for his pleasure (pp. 135-182). David enjoyed pornography, drank, commented on wanting to "watch his daughters undress," spent money lavishly on himself, but jealously guarded Kathleen's expenditures, left literally all domestic chores to Kathleen, and committed adultery with a young college co-ed—the act that ultimately brought Kathleen to her senses. As we discussed a man's ability to parent alone, Kathleen complimented Michael, saying that, with his energy and commitment, he could be a good single father.

Kathleen's perception of her dual roles as wife and girlfriend to Michael highlights the way gender role expectations change as men and women exchange premarriage courtship interactions for marital obligations. She described feeling like a girlfriend during their good times together, and feeling more like a wife in times of stress, when they need each other for support and closeness. In a way, the unusual nature of their noncohabiting relationship has become comfortable for both of them, keeping the courtship alive, but providing the security of an available partner for emotional and ego support.

Kathleen joins Judith in her optimism for the next generation. Her two teenage daughters have never talked about "wanting to get married and have a family." Instead, they talk about careers, especially those which only a generation ago were unusual for women to hold, let alone to which they might aspire.

Shawna: Breaking Free

Shawna is the woman who, "though proud and adventurous," is "guided by some sense that there is mutual justice, protection and comfort [in a] balance of power . . . [but] loses [her] identity to the traditional set up" (Dinnerstein, 1976, p. 158). She indicated her contempt for this position, however, when she said, "I had to sit in the house and take his treats, and be this submissive woman. But prior to that time . . . I wasn't submissive." William's possessiveness is an example of what Dinnerstein (1976) calls men's "double standard for sexual behavior" that "includes the assumption that [the woman] is a natural resource, as an asset to be owned and harnessed, harvested and mined, with no fellow-feeling for her depletion and no responsibility for her conservation or replenishment" (p. 36).

In addition to losing her independence and identity in her relationship, Shawna faced the disappointment of having to choose motherhood over career aspirations. Her choice to have and raise her child was affected by her assumption that she might medically be unable to have another one, something Blake (1974) and Gimenez (1984) claim results from the pressures of a pronatalist society that places becoming a mother above all other functions of a woman's life. Her decision, too, was based on her moral convictions, passed on from her grandmother, the minister, and perhaps also on already having been a participant in the rearing of her sister's children. This willingness of extended family to raise the children, suggests Coontz (1992), is a strength of the black community's "celebration" of children (p. 252). Shawna does not believe her choice has affected her life adversely. She has redirected her career. If she eventually decides to return to law school, she wants to be sure it is *her* goal and not merely the translation of her mother's aspirations for her.

Shawna has learned much from the lessons of gender division she saw enacted by her father and brothers, the ways they exerted their sexual dominance over women, cheated, and acted—as she said—like "dogs." Farrell (1972) comments that males objectify women not only to satisfy their sex drives but to prove the strength of their "manhood" to other men (p. 47). By choosing William, a man who tried to exert his ownership of her, "like in slave days," and whose chronic drinking led to their eventual breakup, Shawna chose a partner who resembled her father in many ways. Though her father was a hazy figure in her youth because her mother protected her from him, Shawna resented her mother and idealized her father. As Levine (1992) explains, the images of mother and father are "entrenched symbols" in our society. "Even a father a child has never met is present in that child's wishes, desires, and fears" (p. 194).

Shawna is determined to give Tasha a more balanced exposure to male and female roles. She dislikes the ways that William encourages his daughter's helplessness and "prissiness" and tries to offset this influence without confusing her daughter. She works carefully to encourage Tasha to participate in athletics, to which Shawna attributes her own tenacity and winning spirit. Consistent with her belief that "you have to be true to yourself," Shawna at first dressed her daughter in gender-neutral clothes, but she soon discovered that her daughter had other ideas. Although allowing her daughter to make her own choices, Shawna carefully provides opportunities for Tasha to "pick" the activities she would like her to try.

In describing the values she modeled for her daughter, Shawna stated, "I want her to be strong-minded." Apparently, at three years old, Tasha already is: "My daughter is very independent. She expresses herself well." Not wanting her to feel responsible for keeping her mother company, Shawna encourages Tasha to "spread her wings," to move away from dependence on her mother. For this, Shawna would certainly be lauded by family therapists because she obviously does not expect her child to assume an unchildlike parental comfort role (Kissman and Allen, 1993). Encouraging her daughter's separation from her is considered a healthy attitude by psychologists who see the girl child as potentially having more difficulty individuating from her mother (Dinnerstein, 1976; Llewelyn and Osborne, 1990; Kaschak, 1992).

Shawna tries to help William see how damaging his gender-locked expectations can be for their daughter, and for William's son, Thomas, who at seven is expected to act like a "little man." Shawna provides an alternative viewpoint for Thomas. She tells him that he is certainly allowed to cry if he is hurt. Such differential enforcement of gender roles is difficult to break, as it is socially reaffirmed and carries the weight of generational transmission (Dinnerstein, 1976; Farrell, 1972). Researchers have found that fathers, particularly, are anxious that their children exhibit proper sex role behaviors (Farrell, 1972; Levine, 1992).

Shawna, however, is optimistic that she and William can break away from these patterns for the sake of the healthy development of their daughter. She points out to him that neither of them wants Tasha to end up with a man who exemplifies all the worst qualities that even William dislikes in himself. She explained, "That's part of growing up and being able to give yourself the opportunity to sit back and think about the type of relationship you were in and what went wrong in the relationship."

Speaking up, or "standing up," as Shawna's mother taught her, is difficult for women who are punished for their rebellion against the social order (Faludi, 1991), but Shawna was not afraid to fight back when William physically restrained her, nor does she hesitate to choose her parenting responsibility to Tasha over obligations at work. She works to mentor other children whose families may not be as "lucky" as hers. She took that responsibility quite personally when she attempted to help the troubled daughter of her sister, but, in that case, fighting against peer group loyalty and adolescence proved to be a task even her strength could not accomplish.

Lyn: A Tradition of Strong Women

Lyn made a conscious decision to parent on her own when divorce and single parenting were still highly stigmatized. However, she had no fears about going off on her own, being the third generation of strong women in her family, a tradition that went perhaps even as far back as earlier Scottish ancestors who had to "scratch around and make a living from the rocks."

She modeled her mothering style after her own mother, a nonjudgmental person who let her children believe in their own competence to make decisions. She gave a candid—and unfavorable—comparison between her own mothering and her mother's. Her image of a good mother was that of her own mother, and when she acted in ways that she felt were untrue to that image, such as yelling at her children or losing her temper, she would think, "Oh my God! I'm not a good mother!"

Her mother, who had a college degree in teaching and worked for many years to support her family on her own, stopped working after she remarried. Lyn explained that her stepfather felt his wife should "relax" and that he was afraid, as a prominent businessman in a small town, a working wife would make him "look bad." This was typical of their generation. Men made the decisions about whether or not a wife should work, taking the breadwinning role seriously, and considering female employment a threat to the natural order, which generally meant the postindustrial division between household and paid labor (Coontz, 1992; Demos, 1986).

Lyn preferred raising her sons on her own, but she added that "it would have been an enriching thing to have another adult around . . .

[someone who] cared about them, was supportive, and that they could interact with." Lyn believed her husband did not contribute to her family in that way, describing him as a negative influence on their lives. Even though he provided regular support payments, he did not help pay for his sons' college education and treated them differently with regard to other financial support. In their adulthood, the boys have learned to accept their father's uneven treatment because "that's just how Dad is." It should be pointed out that a mother's opinion of her ex-husband certainly influences her children's view of him. In Lyn's case, however, her sons had many opportunities to interact with their father as adults and to form their own opinions from his interactions with them.

Anxiety over lack of "good male role models" and the belief that a strong dominant female would damage a boy child's healthy sex identification are based on the assumption that rigidly defined boundaries for sex roles help male and female children develop healthy personalities (Boss and Weiner, 1988, p. 238). This concept is perhaps a vestige of Freudian psychoanalytic theory. Schur (1984) and Dinnerstein (1976) critique this viewpoint and discuss the psychoanalytic origins of the commonly accepted fear that mothers exert some type of superhuman power over their sons, claiming that men are psychologically threatened by women because they are both awed by and fearful of women's ability to give birth. Such a great power in motherhood "evokes the terror of sinking back wholly into the helplessness of infancy," a fear that inhibits both women and children from fully experiencing their natural connections (Dinnerstein, 1976, p. 161).

In fact, when asked whether she thought the boys *needed* a father figure, she replied that she did not believe they did. She was confident that the boys enjoyed their many relationships with other adults, either family or friends, and benefited from the career guidance and confidence in their abilities gained from male and female mentors they met in college.

The boys, who have grown into young men, have different views of marriage, family, and male-female roles within the family, as they have about many things. Lyn believes that Paul's quieter, more ambivalent personality might make him accept a traditional type of marriage, believing that "maybe marriage is a good thing and maybe it'll work," whereas heart-on-his-sleeve Rich has a firm conviction that he will be an equal partner in any relationship he has with a woman, and he will "never get divorced." The effect that the many differing personalities of children may have on gender role identification and adjustment to divorce cannot be underestimated, and yet it often is. Psychologist Arlene Skolnick (1978) believes that "the myth of the vulnerable child" is exaggerated, and that children have much greater agency than that for which they are credited.

Lyn's self-confidence in her abilities and acknowledgment of her limitations extend to her gender identification as well. She discussed her relationships with men and expressed her feeling that getting in touch with one's womanhood does not depend on being "involved with a man." This sense of herself, she remarked, was apparent to her sons, who acknowledged her many roles: in relationships with men, as a peer in many friendships that did not necessarily involve children, as a professional, and as an individual: "It's clear to them, and always has been, that I've got a life apart from being a mother."

Lyn provided one final outstanding example of stigma associated with gender role expectations in her discussion of her voluntarily childless friends. Veevers' (1974) study of women who choose not to have children, Schur's (1984) *Labeling Women Deviant,* and Llewelyn and Osborne's (1990) case studies discuss the stigmatization of childless women. The cultural valuing of pronatalism is described by Blake (1974) and Gimenez (1984). Lyn's story about one voluntarily childless friend illustrates the power of the female sex role of mothering. This friend, who had chosen not to have children, was extremely angry with the medical profession's callous disregard for the symbolism of losing her childbearing capability when she woke following biopsy surgery to learn her uterus had been removed. Llewelyn and Osborne (1990) remark that women who are infertile face such tremendous challenges in their sense of identity that even previously fulfilled interests and achievements pale in the face of an inability to conceive (pp. 133-134). Kaschak (1992) reminds us that it is not necessary to connect womanhood with mothering: "Not all women grow up to mother or want to. Not all those who *do,* want to" (p. 119).

Sarah: Violent Men, Sacrificial Women

Sarah's experiences with gender have been primarily negative. Her mother was almost a textbook study of the idealized woman of the 1950s, loyal to her husband in all things, faithful to her role, the "perfect Christian martyr." As the unrealistic demands of self-sacrifice and misery drove many of the women in her generation to alcohol and tranquilizers (Coontz, 1992), Sarah's mother "kept up appearances" that hid an amoral husband, a schizophrenic older daughter, and a host of indignities leveled against her by her husband, a tendency mimicked by Sarah in her relationship with Garry. Sarah's father was schizophrenic, according to her estimation, as well as that of armed forces medical personnel who dismissed his court-martial in favor of institutional care. Her mother took over the care of her "sick, weak" husband, as she expected her daughter would do with her own alcoholic husband.

Sarah tolerated and internalized her husband's insults, lowering her self-esteem (Gornick and Moran, 1972), and immersed herself in the joy of being a mother. It is impossible to separate their male-female gender role conflicts from those conflicts brought on by Garry's alcoholism, but Sarah commented that one way he kept convincing himself that he did not have a problem was his ability to go to work everyday and to provide financially for his family. Thus, his breadwinning function became an icon of his masculine pride that eclipsed all of the other devastation he brought to his family.

In fact, until very recently, the courts have traditionally enforced the male right over his wife and children earned along with his salary (Coontz, 1992; Demos, 1986; Farrell, 1972). This rightful "ownership" of property was exerted in Sarah's case when the courts allowed Garry to remain in his residence and Sarah was forced to live for a full year with the "corpse of a marriage." Weitzman (1985) points out that male earning superiority, especially in couples where the wife has assumed a traditional domestic role, is indeed rewarded by the courts when they force women to sell their homes so that the property may be divided "equally." This illusion of economic parity often leaves women at a decided disadvantage.

Sarah attributes the tremendous force that shook her from the inertia of a deteriorating marriage to her desire to protect her daughters from continued exposure to a distorted view of relations between men and women. Julia, herself, expressed her angry indignation: "How can you let him treat you like that?" Levine (1992) comments on the anger and confusion girls, especially, may suffer when they observe the harm their fathers do to their mothers and adds that girls suffer most when they do not have opportunities to construct meanings of masculinity and femininity by watching healthy interactions between adults. In fact, Annie learned to gauge her father's behavior and gained his affection by approaching him when he was not violently drunk. Kaschak (1992) describes female clients raised by their fathers who become "hypersensitive" to their needs. Levine (1992) describes cases she has studied in which a daughter's interactions with her father, even if he does not spend much time with her, can become romanticized. The absent father is seen as a precious commodity, an exciting visitor (p. 198).

Although drawing her conclusions from interviews with many other women, Levine (1992) seems to be writing about Sarah and her daughters. She describes the way that girls who "experience their father's absence" may initially turn all of their resentments on their mothers but eventually identify their own "disappointment" with their "mother's disillusionment," and "together they steel like terrorists to explode the ideal of the perfect father" (p. 213).

The "paper bag issues" Sarah constructed as a "totem" for Garry's vicious verbal attacks on her illustrate the inequities of male domination over the women who run their homes. Coontz (1992) and Baca Zinn and Eitzen (1990) both comment on the ways that financial dependence of the domestic spouse leaves her powerless in the economic world, and thus of lower status in her family. Resentment for the resultant inequities flows both ways. In Sarah's case, Garry's attack on her housekeeping skills may have resulted from his expectation that his breadwinning role automatically made Sarah's domestic role obligatory. Though she gives no assessment of her housekeeping abilities or interest before marriage, now beyond the divorce, Sarah sees her disinterest in housekeeping as passive-aggressive resistance to his "voice in her head":

The house represents myself. I haven't eradicated really truly bad and self-disrespectful housekeeping habits. I developed a real resentment of keeping house because he monitored and judged and declared acceptable or unacceptable everything I did around here. He was so abusive, I always had his voice in my head. I get passive-aggressive about it and make a mess!

Although Sarah's youngest daughter, Annie, is in the throws of adolescent rebellion, her oldest daughter survived them and is doing very well as a young single mother. In addition to the various responsibilities she has had to assume as a young mother, she is working toward a career, inspired by a mentor at her college. However, Julia is painfully aware that because of her young child, the devotion to schooling represented by her aspiration to be a doctor must wait. She has moved forward by inches, entering medicine as a phlebotomist, working toward a two-year degree in medical technology. Sarah described her as "high-powered" and quickly "outgrowing" her baby's father, who lives with them. Unlike most teenage fathers, he is at least a "present father" for his baby, though Sarah believes he views his new family as an opportunity to break free of his parents and do as he pleases. Sarah described him as "bright, but irresponsible" and points out that though he is old enough, he has not even aspired to obtain the icon of all teenagers' ascendancy to adulthood—his driver's license.

Synthesis of Common Themes Concerning Gender Roles

Intergenerational Role Transmission: Breaking New Ground

All of the women discussed the ways they differed from their mothers, and the hopes they have for their children in breaking free from the oppression of gender-locked behaviors expected of their mothers. Judith did not want to be like her mother, trapped in a loveless marriage "for the sake of the kids." When other women assure her that she will marry again, she rejects that image, but she understands that the women of her mother's generation have internalized the expectations of women's dependence on men for wholeness and "want everybody to be in that same mold, too." She has arrived at a different conclusion. Kathleen resented her mother's strong pressure to hold her to the standards her mother's generation perceived as ideal. She declared her independence with the assertion, "I am *not* my mother!" She does not believe that she uses the same kind of guilt her mother used on her to manipulate her own daughters. Shawna did not want to simply follow the path her mother expected her to, but to make her own choices, led by her heart *and* her head.

In addition to criticism, these daughters offered praise for their mothers. Shawna reenacted her mother's strength of character in standing up to the man who abused her. Lyn carried on a tradition of independence passed along by the strong women in her heritage, though Lyn found some of her own mothering behaviors to compare poorly to her mother's.

Sarah experienced the most difficulty with the gender roles she saw enacted by her mother and father. However, even though Sarah's mother's voice remained strong and gave Sarah second thoughts about divorcing her abusive husband, she made a concerted effort to mother her daughters in all the ways she felt were lacking from her childhood.

Hope for the next generation resonates in these women's stories. Judith believes that her son's greater emotional and active involvement in their family life is evidence of a breakdown of traditional roles, an experience that is likely common to other children of single parents. Kathleen's daughters talk about their futures in terms of careers and college, rather than marriage and families. Shawna hopes that her young daughter will see different roles for men and women than she did as a child, and she perseveres at helping Tasha's father to see the importance of breaking out of his patterns of gender role enforcement. Though neither of Lyn's sons is currently moving toward marriage, she believes, since they did not see their mother sacrifice her life for their sake, they can appreciate the personhood of the women they may have as companions, although their enactment of their masculine roles may differ in accordance with their personalities. Sarah's daughter, though a young single mother, is moving forward in her life, independent of her baby's father.

Men versus Women: "Me Tarzan! You Jane!"

Though the title I have chosen for this theme is somewhat tongue-in-cheek, the subject is not really very funny. The women described the men associated with them as typifying the dominant possessiveness and posturing of socialized masculine gender roles. Judith's husband resented her for controlling him, when it was he who actually dictated the rhythms of the family. Kathleen's husband was a "beast" who enacted what Farrell (1972) lists as "The Ten Commandments of Masculinity," a caustic list of the major tenets of male socialization that describes activities to retain domination over women and hold oneself as the center of the world (p. 30). Shawna's companion had real problems with jealousy and possessiveness over her. She acquiesced for awhile but ultimately rebelled against his physical and psychological hold on her. Sarah's husband, the alcoholic, was intent on denying his problem, destroying Sarah's ego in the process. Her father's legacy of schizophrenia and amorality rained destruction on all of the women in his scope—his wife, his mistresses, his two daughters. Sarah hoped that divorcing her husband would prevent her girls from being further damaged by seeing daily enactments of the destructive power men have over women.

The males of the next generation provide some evidence for an argument that generational reenactment of masculine power is not inevitable. Since only four male children are represented in this study—Judith's young son, William's son from his first marriage, and Lyn's two young men—it is impossible to generalize, but all five of the women have observed that the young males in their families are "breaking new ground." Though some of the women speculated about the positive influence of strong father role models, they also asserted that role models come in all forms—male and female, friends and relatives. The boys and young men expressed respect for their mothers' competence in fulfilling multiple roles. Since the only grown men represented in this study are Lyn's, and they are not yet married, only the future will determine whether there will be substantial and lasting changes in these boys' attitudes toward women and the enactment of their roles as husbands and fathers. However, perhaps because they have experienced mothers who do not enact traditional models, these sons may prove to be the "new males" awaited by Dinnerstein (1976), Farrell (1972), and Levine (1992), who will rewrite the dictates of their gender roles, be more active in child rearing, and transmit their more equitable attitudes to *their* sons, in turn.

Redefining Gender Roles

The women in this study have learned to value themselves. Their gendered images have changed too. Judith pursued the Cinderella dream, but when she found that her life did not match that image, she adjusted and moved toward a new ideal that incorporated parenting alone. She encourages the young women she knows to expect the best for themselves and not to await a handsome prince who will rescue and take care of them.

Kathleen maintains many of the traditional domestic roles of "women on the cusp" of two generations, the 1950s mom from the "cult of domesticity" and the 1990s "do-both" mom. She has combined the breadwinner role with the domestic role, compressing both and sometimes feeling as if she leads two lives, one between 8:00 a.m. and 4:30 p.m., and the other after 5:00 p.m. Though she acknowledges that this dual role duty is stressful, she is content with her choices. When Michael joined her family, he and Kathleen settled into a division of labor that is still somewhat governed by old gender socialization patterns, but that she feels is "comfortable."

Shawna sees herself primarily as the athlete—strong, determined, a winner. Though momentarily lost in her relationship, Shawna has regained identity and is giving her daughter a strong role model to follow. She is helping William to examine his reinforcement of gender roles with his children, encouraging him not to reproduce in them the behaviors and attitudes that have led him to disappointment in his relationships.

The connection between Lyn's self-esteem and her gendered experiences is perhaps the most nontraditional. She was never one to succumb to either the "myth of motherly infallibility" or the "superwoman complex." Her close friendships with childless women, strong identification with her mother's nonjudgmental mothering style, and self-respectful protection of her individuality and privacy are hallmarks of a woman who does what she "chooses to do."

Sarah, though not fully recovered from the destructive relationships she endured as a child and wife, found the strength to break free from a harmful marriage. She sought to prevent her daughters from internalizing the negative images of males and females modeled by their parents: men harm women, and women take it.

WOMEN'S DEVELOPMENT: JOURNEYS THROUGH SELF AND RELATIONSHIP

Kaschak (1992) states, "The very sense of self is a metaphor, an organizing concept" (p. 156). In harmony with the fabric metaphor pertinent to this study, she adds:

Each person's experience is woven of a combination of the complex meanings of the culture and significant influences within it, filtered through personal experience, a degree of choice and change, and certain biological and genetic aspects and predispositions such as health, talents, abilities and perhaps temperamental disposition. (p. 149, citing Kagan, 1984, 1989)

Each of the women in this study has undergone a journey of self-discovery. Each has resolved the many issues that faced her in ways shaped by her personal history, cultural heritage and membership, the circumstances of her career, her family, and her growing awareness of what it means to be a woman in the American culture of the late twentieth century. This discussion presents the themes that emerged regarding each woman's self-image, her comfort with being single again, and what she has learned about herself in relationship.

Judith: Learning to Enjoy Her Own Company

Judith's story is representative of many women facing changes in their lives forced by circumstance. Although she did not seek "to be put in the situation or to take this test," she *has* taken it, and she feels she has passed. Judith emerged from a past in which socialization and self-image made her aspire to an unrealistic ideal, and her quest for that ideal damaged her self-esteem and led her to depression. She told of agonizing days when her thoughts centered on her pain and her fear of being left alone. She sought professional help to manage her depression and changed her direction from turning inward to "focusing outward," and feeling like she's regained her life, surprised at her own strength.

Judith is realistic about her losses and does not think that she actually chose to liberate herself through divorce. She believes marriage was a safety net for her, but now that it is gone, she is amazed that she does not feel as if she is missing something. Feeling refreshed, she plans to make the decisions that will serve her needs, now freed from having to worry about how her behavior or the family activities will please her husband, a freedom she finds exhilarating.

Such feelings of liberation and relief are reported by those who have studied women in postdivorce situations. Joy Rice (1994) writes that, for many women, divorce is a liberation. Llewelyn and Osborne (1990) report that beyond the "initial jolt" of the divorce, the women in their case studies reported gains in self-efficacy similar to those reported by a host of other researchers who have studied single women (Bem, 1974; Spence, 1979; Williams, 1984) and women beyond divorce (Gigy, 1980; Hafner, 1986; Hoeffer, 1987; Loewenstein et al., 1981).

Judith has reached a point in her self-imaging that allows her to be content picturing herself in "positive solitude" (Andre, 1991). She distinguishes between being alone and being lonely: one can choose to be alone, but loneliness comes when one does not want to be alone but is. Her busy life has kept her from getting lonely, but she thinks later life alone "in a house with a little dog or something" will not be "real satisfying." When asked how she would feel if she knew she would continue her life alone indefinitely, she said her first reaction would be fear, but that she would begin to build a network of friends to "ensure that I won't be a lonely person, and I'll have a full life then." This certainly supports Bequaert's (1976) observation that women are never alone; they are always in relationship with someone—children, friends, other relatives, social networks—even if they are not in spousal relationship with one man.

Being alone sometimes frightens Judith for other reasons. Kaschak (1992) attributes this fear to years of conditioning women to be afraid of the world and dependent on being in relationship with men (p. 125). However, Judith's fear comes from her awareness that she is the "sole support of her family." She worries that if she gets sick or is unable to work, she could lose her home. She likens this fear to what men must have experienced when they bore the sole responsibility of supporting large families whose life and health depended on their ability to provide.

From what she calls "years of conditioning" (and perhaps because she once experienced the emotional and physical benefits of a mutually beneficial couple relationship), she is still ambivalent about not being part of a couple, though she did say, "I'm learning slowly to enjoy my own company." She is strong in advising other young women to seek their own way in the world. If they end up in a relationship, they should do so because it is satisfying to them, not simply for the sake of being in one. She wonders now if marriage is even necessary because "it's not essential."

Psychologists who specialize in female psychotherapy note that divorced women often experience periods of gloom when they learn an ex-spouse has remarried (Llewelyn and Osborne, 1990). Judith commented on her resentment and anger over her ex-husband's ability to "get on with his life" after he had "put my life in total turmoil." She admitted being hurt when she saw him with his female companion (now his wife) so soon after their divorce because she felt he had not mourned for the death of their relationship.

However, she believes she herself is not ready for another relationship. She worries that "it will be painful . . . to be dating after so many years." She is concerned that she will lose herself in the romance again and puzzles over the way that introducing a boyfriend into her family would require a three-way dynamic from the start. Bequaert (1976) notes that single mothers in her study often postponed their social needs until their children were older or in school because "motherhood and dating are frequently in conflict." Anxious about upsetting their children, women who are socialized to defer their needs for others say that the disruption in their lives posed by an evening out is "too high a price to pay just for their own pleasure" (p. 96).

While Judith advises other women to "live your life according to what *you* want" and not to put their needs before all others, she still grapples with her emotional dependence on her son. Because her spouse did not return her love, her son, Ian, was "the only direction for all the love to flow." Her honest observation that Ian "is a momma's boy" registers her awareness of the problems attributed to boys whose mothers are strong influences. Psychoanalytic theory has pathologized this relationship (Bieber and Society of Medical Psychoanalysts, 1962; Farrell, 1972). However, feminist psychologists are reluctant to stigmatize women for this. They cite evidence that fear of dominance by mothers is rooted in accepting the myth of the omnipotence of motherhood, and in ignoring the agency of children who are not simply passive recipients of parenting pressures (Dinnerstein, 1976; Kaschak, 1992; Skolnick, 1978).

Judith has come a long way from longing for gifts given by a loving spouse at holidays. She is content and happy to be free from an emotionally unfulfilling relationship and faces life on her own with a sense of strength and pride.

Kathleen: A Euphoric Feeling

Reflecting on her life twelve years beyond her divorce, Kathleen said she enjoys a "euphoric feeling." She feels good about her present life, is happy, and proud of her daughters' growth and accomplishments, and believes that she is a good parent. She has not always felt good about herself. Kathleen described insecurities about her talents at work and needing Michael's encouragement. Her initial lack of confidence may have been a residual effect from living with her ex-husband who "would rather put me down, maybe because I was more educated than him."

Kathleen finds her career "self-fulfilling." She believes that increasing numbers of women in the workforce, especially those who have succeeded and act as mentors for others, are forcing the world to acknowledge a new, strong, independent image of womanhood. She attributes her rise to her current supervisory position to strong women mentors who recognized her potential before she did and encouraged her to move forward. Such changes are documented by historians who cite chronological evidence to point out that the Women's Liberation Movement was more a *result* of the movement of women into the workforce than a motivation for it (Coontz, 1992).

Kathleen is particularly sensitive to the stigma attached to single mothers and their children. Avoiding being labeled "deviant" was a powerful motivator for her (Schur, 1984). She took on all of the challenges posed by economics, school participation, employment, and domestic chores, sometimes crying from exhaustion. However, as she established her routines and her daughters grew up, she found more time for herself and for her relationship with Michael.

Her relationship with Michael has its ups and downs, especially as she copes with the practical problems posed by Michael's inability to obtain a legal divorce. Twice rejected in court because his wife opposed the divorce and the judge ruled there were insufficient grounds, Michael maintains a noncohabiting, but full-time relationship with Kathleen. Kathleen worries that her legal rights are shaky, but she can accept the duality of continual courtship and virtual marriage as "somehow part of the good relationship."

Shawna: Strong-Minded

Shawna's development has proceeded from childhood, when anger over her mother's prohibitions about her father made her act out in school, to adulthood, when she teaches her values to her daughter and faces the future with determination and a positive attitude. She attributes her metamorphosis to mentors in school who encouraged her to believe in herself, to work hard, and to persevere.

Shawna marvels at the way she lost her identity in her relationship with William but understands that his controlling manner of dealing with her drained all of her energy. She forgot the lessons she learned from her mother—to stand up for what she felt was right—until the day that William crossed the line from *controlling* to *assaulting* her body. That day she "lost it" in her response to William, but by her actions, she gained the opportunity to get herself back on track. Such angry resistance is what Levine (1992) traced in case studies of women who develop man-hating tendencies through their unhappy experiences with men. In contrast to many of the eighty women Levine interviewed, Shawna pulled no punches; she actually came to blows with William as her passive submission turned into blinding rage.

Resisting his pleas to come back, Shawna recognized that parenting her daughter apart from William was the only way for her to be happy and free from his control. Shawna is happy raising her daughter, and she is not reluctant to be a friend to William's son by his first marriage. She negotiates the tricky tasks of dealing with Thomas's mother and teaching William to be a better parent. She lives her life as an example for her daughter and encourages Tasha to be strong-minded, independent, honest, and confident in her ability to reach goals, qualities her daughter already exhibits, even at age three.

Worried about telling her mother about her pregnancy, Shawna struggled to make decisions for her future according to "what would make me happy." Her fear of confronting her mother extended from her own fear that she had failed her family by falling into a pattern that would not encourage her pursuit of *their* dreams. Recognizing that her personal plans for the future might be in conflict with her mother's was a turning point in her life. This is what Llewelyn and Osborne (1990) and Chodorow (1978) refer to as women's ambivalence, brought on by memories of their own childhoods. Women who recall the anger and sadness of unhappy relationships with their mothers are confused by their concurrent esteem for their mothers. In Shawna's case, her assessment of her mother's life and her dreams for her own are alternately in conflict and in harmony. As with other women who cope successfully with this dichotomy, her motivation was to provide a better life for Tasha (Llewelyn and Osborne, 1990, p. 161).

Shawna did not talk about a dating life or her desire to develop new relationships with men. She did refer to wanting more time to herself, wishing that William would have more visitation hours during the times when she was not at work. Shawna's relationships with her daughter, William, William's son, her mother, her brothers and sisters, and her niece provide evidence of a young woman who knows her mind, who is breaking cycles of behavior she has seen enacted in her family, and who works hard to be successful so that she will never "let her team down," because "*I* [am] my only team."

Lyn: Selfishness, An Antidote for Guilt

Lyn's self-integration was quite different from those of the other four cases. Lyn described herself as an introvert, "a private person," something I considered surprising because her public image is quite the opposite. She stated, "My inner life is much more real to me," and suggested that it is perhaps not the life most people would want to lead because of the minimal social contact. She mused that her introversion might not have provided a good role model for her sons, observing that the youngest, Rich, went through a "hermit stage," withdrawing from the social world. However, she believes that they now have "found their own way."

She never hesitated to assert her needs in her family, from the time of her divorce through the raising of her sons to her negotiations with the men in her relationships. She does not believe that mothers should purchase their children's love by sacrificing their own autonomy. She said that parenting was a central priority when her children were young, but that they were not central to her life: "I feel that kind of self*ish*ness is important and not to feel guilty about it. You've got to meet your own needs if you're going to be able to meet the kids' needs."

Kaschak (1992) encourages women to meet their own needs for "nondriven caring and closeness" in their relations with their children—that is, women should seek closeness from their children because it is desirable and mutually satisfying, not because it is a woman's *obligation* to provide such care (p. 128). Bennett, Wolin, and McAvity (1988) agree that "it is healthy for a woman to refuse to be nurturant at times," to resist social pressure to be the "emotional fixers" of needy men and boys (p. 243). Lyn called this attitude an "antidote to guilt," a metaphor described by Markson (1993), who contrasted "a healthy or ordinary sense of entitlement" to the martyrdom of the moral masochists. To achieve this "requires a belief in the legitimacy of one's own needs and a right to pursue their gratification" (p. 934). Without such a healthy selfishness, moral masochists feel that they are unworthy and have no right to a life of their own. This is alarmingly similar to traditional assumptions about women's development; "the primacy of nurturance" theory, for example, assumes that sacrifice is what a woman must do to keep the family running smoothly, and "if she focuses on her own development, she is viewed as selfish and narcissistic" (Bennett, Wolin, and McAvity, 1988, p. 236).

Lyn's relationships with men were conducted with respect for their compatibility or incompatibility with her family. She did not desire to "divorce her kids" to remarry someone she believed would not be good for them, so she maintained some of her relationships apart from her family, never "imposing" them on her sons or forcing herself to make a choice she could not make.

She does not exalt single parenting because she believes that two-parent families are more troublesome. Rather, she says that having two adults can provide a "healthy skepticism and balance." For herself, however, single parenting, with its unilateral decisions, has been so much more peaceful. She does not know whether it is advantageous for the children, but she asserts that it is certainly easier. Unlike the suffering, lonely, time-starved women the self-help books portray, Lyn is similar to a young, divorced, professional woman whom Bequaert (1976) quoted: "I love it. . . . I have enough time for myself, enough time for friends, enough time to take care of my work, enough time to be with my children. It works" (p. 1).

She talked about what happens to women when they become involved in relationships with men, and she laughed about her tendency to become needy. She added that sexual relations certainly complicate matters, and that she tends to invest too much "emotional energy and worry" in her relationships with men. Levine (1992) notes, "As long as there is intimacy, there are expectations and disappointments, terror and rage, and as long as there is sex, there is power—which all add up to conflict" (p. 386).

Lyn described her relationships with women friends, especially those who did not have children, and asserted that women can "get in touch" with their womanhood without being in relationship with a man. Kaschak (1992) uses that very argument to dispute Gilligan's (1982) conclusions that women's moral development is relational, and that women define their self-worth through relationship. This is not to say that women do not experience joy from relationships. Indeed, Lyn had many satisfying relationships with other women friends and with her sons, but more than the other women in this study, Lyn found her "inner world most real."

Lyn never lost her identity on her journey through self as her fellow participants did, but she did not escape the effects of depression. She described her chronic depression as something she felt was an inherited tendency exacerbated by the long winters in the North. Symptomatically, it was never debilitating for her, but it made everything an extra effort, exhausting her with each decision and action. Similar to Judith and Sarah, she sought help through counseling and medication, convinced that depression is more physiological than psychological. She described it as similar to being a diabetic; medication allows the sufferer to feel normal again.

Lyn's closing interview highlighted construction of a new narrative for her life in which her newly adopted myth is an image of a graceful, older woman. She sees herself in a bright, beautiful place, rejecting the woman's nightmare of "growing old with no children to look after you"—the renewed infantilism so often the unfortunate result for mothers who sacrificed themselves for their families only to find they have no self-definition or direction after their children are gone (Dinnerstein, 1976).

Sarah: A Collage of Many Sarahs

The most eloquent narrative of Sarah's journey through self was the collage of pictures she showed me during her last interview. In it she included a multiplicity of images she has described in her life narrative that portray the ways she has come to accept the many pieces that make up the whole woman. The barefoot, feisty little girl; the ancient stone frieze of a woman's ample, "lumpy," middle-aged figure; and the serene tableaus of mothers and daughters catalog Sarah's coming to peace with her family history, and the many versions of herself: "buffaloed Sarah," "spiritual Sarah," "sexual Sarah," "Maine Sarah," "nightmare Sarah," and "dancing Sarah," to name a few.

Feelings of powerlessness and the "insidious effect that categorical devaluation can have on women's self-conceptions," as described by Schur (1984, p. 38), may have contributed to Sarah's confessed desire to overeat. The many reasons for eating disorders in women have been discussed at length by psychologists and sociologists who study women's development. The blatant devaluing of fat women in society elevates the young, thin, taut body as the ideal, making women especially vulnerable to self-definition through their bodies. Kaschak (1992) devotes an entire chapter of her book *Engendered Lives* to "Identity Embodied," in which she describes the many ways a woman measures herself against images of female perfection, always coming up deficient (pp. 89-113). Sarah dislikes her body image and has sought therapy and tried dieting to cope with her "problem," but she admits to eating binges when under stress.

Sarah has baggage from which she must free herself; one of the pictures she chose to represent herself was a woman at a train station laden with bags. Her self-image was severely damaged by her childhood experiences and her marriage. However, her pride in her intellect and her success as a student survived even her mother's attempts to downplay her successes and her husband's insults. She has made progress through therapy (she notes that her therapist is also a single mother), through support groups in her church, through her very ego-fulfilling work as a teacher of older students, and through her continuing life as a student. (Since this book was compiled, she completed her PhD.) Despite her daughters' actions that force her to focus on their needs, Sarah is determined to pursue her life goals.

She faced a crisis after the death of her parents and her sister, when she found herself the new matriarch of her family and the only surviving adult. This realization, added to the announcement of her older daughter's pregnancy, sent her into a serious depression: "I was biologically, emotionally, and spiritually depressed." Medication and therapy helped her to see how much she had accomplished and to regain her feeling of control over her life. Markson (1993) recognizes this type of depression in the children of "moral masochists" such as Sarah's mother. The children of "martyrs" try in vain to elicit pleasure or comfort from their parents and eventually internalize their inability to have an impact, lowering self-esteem and making them feel powerless to change their adult environments as well (p. 934).

Currently, Sarah's self-image is in flux. She alternates between feelings of pride and guilt—exultant about her competence and achievements, but worried about her failures and her part in "causing all my own and all my children's grief." Mother blaming is a chronic result of the many mythologies that venerate *and* castigate a mother for controlling or failing to control her children, assuming that she alone is responsible for the actions or mistakes of her family (Bennett, Wolin, and McAvity, 1988; Boss and Weiner, 1988; Dinnerstein, 1976). Sarah, however, laughed as she discussed this, and her final collage represents, not guilt and despair, but happy images, a distinct change from the one she constructed at the beginning of her therapy.

Sarah is not pessimistic about relationships with men, despite the many ways that the men in her life have hurt her. She believes that it "makes sense to have two adults to share the responsibility" of a family, and she can envision an ideal sort of mate who would be more wife than husband, a male companion who nurtures, supports, and shares. This should not require that person to "live for and through other people," but she hopes there is a happy medium between being entirely self-centered—her husband and father—or entirely sacrificial—her mother.

Synthesis of Common Themes
Concerning Women's Development

Being Alone and in Relationships

The women spoke about making their peace with singleness. Judith, perhaps, had the hardest time because she had developed a myth for her life that always included a loving couple relationship, one her parents never had. However, as she faced her divorce and fears of being alone, she learned that she was stronger than she thought. She described the many relationships and networks of which she is a part, and how she learned to enjoy her own company. She worried about how dating again would upset the emotional balance of the dyad between herself and her son, something her ex-husband did not seem to worry about. She expressed some residual fear of life alone after her son leaves, but she is determined to maintain her connections to friends and a social network so that she will never be lonely.

Kathleen did not talk about being alone, since she is already in a full-time relationship with Michael. She enjoys the benefits in her nonmarital relationship with Michael because it allows her to play the role of wife and girlfriend, to have companionship and support in times of stress, while keeping the excitement of the courtship alive.

Shawna's strong character dominated her journey through self. She did not even mention being alone or dating again. She and her daughter make each other happy, and she is involved in community work, giving of herself in relationships with others. She has learned to confront her identity apart from her mother, and to regain it after losing it in her relationship with William.

Lyn, an introvert, is most comfortable alone. Her singleness has been peaceful, though she has not avoided relationships with men. She can see the benefits of building a history with someone and of having two parents to offer different life perspectives, but she has found that being single is easier. She acknowledges a tendency to become needy when she is in a relationship and is happy affirming her womanhood as a friend of other women, not necessarily as part of a male-female couple.

Sarah became dramatically aware of being alone when her parents and sister died and she realized that she was the last surviving adult of her family, "the new matriarch." Doubts and fears coupled with depression over her teenage daughters' traumas brought her to a crisis point of temporary helplessness. Medication and therapy helped her regain her confidence in her ability to make it on her own.

Self-Esteem and Stigma

Each of the women expressed her individual awareness of the social stigmata associated with single parenting and with being a single woman. Judith had been socialized to measure herself against perfect images of families and loving couples. When she found herself without this safety net, she was surprised that she did not feel as if she was actually missing something. Her critical assessment of her close relationship with her son may be simply an honest assessment of their interactions, or it may reflect an internalization of the stigma associated with the effects of overbearing mothers on the sexual development of their sons. She is currently trying to change what she sees as their codependency. Researchers and psychologists who base their interpretations on Freudian theory conduct studies that establish support for the claim that overbearing mothers may damage their male children, some even offering evidence that homosexuality is related to this type of mother-son relationship. However, new evidence on the strength of genetic causes of homosexuality has fueled feminist claims that male fear and distrust of female sexuality is at the heart of mother blaming (Faludi, 1991).

Kathleen has been greatly affected by the stigmata about working single mothers and has worked ever harder to "prove them wrong." Unlike her sister-in-law, who follows a more traditional image of wifely satisfaction, Kathleen finds personal self-fulfillment in her work. An ego once destroyed by her husband has been rebuilt through the support of Michael and of women mentors. More than twelve years beyond her divorce, Kathleen feels euphoric; her self-esteem has reached an all-time high.

Shawna is a strong-minded woman raising a strong-minded daughter. Momentarily confused by the life course adjustments she had to make when she became pregnant, she faced her family's disappointment and disapproval to pursue what she believed was best for her. As she related the values she tried to instill in her daughter, she told her own story of growth out of anger and resentment into the discipline and hard work of the talented runner she is. Her self-image was strengthened by mentors at school, as she struggled to make her own way, determined never to lose to circumstance or family history.

Lyn, the most self-assured of all the women interviewed, was unafraid to assert that her needs often took priority over her children's. She refused to allow the central tasks of parenting to become the center of her life, and her sons learned about her many interests and relationships outside of their family. Though she copes with chronic depression, she is controlling it with medication and therapy and is facing her retirement with hopeful new imagery. She refuses to be overwhelmed by stigma or guilt, asserting that the "antidote to guilt" is respect for the value of satisfying one's own needs and the refusal to give up oneself entirely for others.

Surfacing from a crippling depression exacerbated by her husband's denigration, Sarah now holds many happier images of herself. The darkness of her childhood memories lives as motivation for her renewed determination to pursue goals that will give her self-confidence. She struggles most against the body image stigma placed on women who do not match the "thin ideal," and against the tendency to lay blame for children's behavior on the mother's inadequacies.

Depression

I am not an authority on depression, nor did I want to research it separately, but since it was an important part of the narratives of three of the women in this study, it has been discussed in several places with connection to other themes. Psychologists and medical doctors may be more authoritative in discussing the many reasons why depression manifests itself in both men and women, especially in times of severe stress. Certainly, the women in this study have experienced stressors of many kinds. Without hypothesizing about the ways that their depression is connected to their divorces and subsequent single motherhood, it is sufficient to note that at least three of the five women remarked that they had experienced severe enough depression to seek therapy: Judith, before and during her divorce, and Lyn and Sarah, at times throughout their lives. Lyn also reported that her son, Paul, experienced what she recognized as depression during his high school years. It appears that the depression experienced by women in this study may be related to genetic tendency, as both Sarah and Lyn explained; to weather, as Lyn explained; and to the shock of a traumatic life change, as Judith explained. Based on the women of this study, it safe to say that depression is often related to divorce and single parenting.

Divorce As Resistance

Joy Rice (1994) has suggested that divorce may be considered a form of "resistance to the oppression of women in families" and a "marker of societal and historical change and transformation" (p. 560). It appears from the women in this study that this may be an accurate assessment. Five of the women divorced and one chose to not marry her long-term companion, with all but Judith initiating the process of separation. All of the women expressed their resistance against the oppression of gender ideals imposed by intergenerational transmission and societal pressure. They rebelled against the expectations of mothers, the oppression of mates, the myths of motherhood, and the stigma associated with being single women.

Judith did not "ask for this test," but she passed it with pride. Kathleen was the first one of her peer group to get divorced, but she resisted guilt by proving to all that she could make it on her own as a good person and a good parent. Shawna literally fought her way out of the oppression that made her submissive, a state in which she hardly recognized the winning spirit she prized. Lyn saw her divorce as an assertion of her primacy of parenting, believing that she could do alone the same parenting she did while married. She viewed her husband as another child to raise and asserted that fulfilling her own needs was important to the healthy functioning of her family. Sarah finally mobilized her internal resources to leave an abusive husband, something she had been unable to do with abusive parents.

Some of the women expressed it in words, some in action, but divorce was liberating for all of them. All feel that they are leading happier, more fulfilling lives. They are optimistic about their futures and their children's development. All have respect for relationships with friends, children, *and* men, acknowledging the benefits of having a helpmate, but none have found those benefits in their past couple relationships, and only Kathleen is currently involved in another full-time relationship with a man.

THE CHILDREN OF DIVORCE: BEFORE AND AFTER

One consistent area of concern for researchers who examine the relationship between families and schools is the effects of divorce and single parenting on children's functioning in school. Though my first question, "What is life like for single mothers?" was the most compelling reason for writing these women's narratives, they provided important information for educators and policymakers who most often stigmatize their homes and expect deviance from their children. Since it is impossible to separate the experiences of their children from the women's stories, much information about them has already been presented and discussed; however, this discussion will highlight particular references to these mothers' interactions with schools that may provide surprising and important information to educators.

Judith: A Matter of Personality

Judith's son, Ian, has a close relationship with his mother. She credits him with having taught her how to communicate better. Their conversations before school and in the evenings lead to insightful problem solving and comforting warmth. Judith is trying to encourage him to be more independent, but she does not want to push him to do things that may make him insecure until some time has passed and his family has settled into its new rhythms.

Judith and Mike were aware of the possibility that their divorce might affect Ian's school performance; they were sensitive to the dire warnings of researchers (Hetherington, Cox, and Cox, 1978; Wallerstein and Kelly, 1980; Wallerstein and Blakeslee, 1989). Ian's response when his parents announced their impending divorce was fear that he would be forced to choose between them, so Judith vowed to keep their personal differences from making Ian feel he had to take sides.

To be certain that Ian suffered no ill effects in adjustment, Judith and Mike had him evaluated by two counselors. The first counselor assured them that they did "a hell of a divorce" because Ian was "doing just fine." The school psychologist who observed Ian's interactions in school told them nothing more than they already knew; Ian was an unusual child who exhibited unchildlike behaviors, such as complimenting other children. Judith described Ian as always having been sensitive, "a worrier, perfectionist," insecure in school. His personality sometimes clashed with teachers who preferred more independent children who asked fewer questions. Developing long before the divorce, Ian's personality has remained unchanged. Ian still "frets the details" and is sensitive to the disapproval of others. He does well in school but is not outstanding. He is a very creative child with great imagination and many surprising observations on life and people for one so young.

As a teacher, Judith expressed a change in her attitude toward children from single-parent homes. She, similar to many others, once had a vision of the "troubled children" of single-parent homes, that is, before she realized the kind of people who become single parents. Many authors who investigate school behavior and achievement use teacher ratings as a measurement (Cooper and Moore, 1995; Featherstone and Cundick, 1992; Grymes et al., 1993; Wanat, 1993). Such ratings, however, are often affected by many factors other than the one the teachers *perceive* affects the students' performance. For example, Dornbusch and Gray (1988) reviewed data from the National Health Examination Survey to determine the effects of single-parent family structures on measures of deviance in schoolchildren. They found that, rather than parental configuration, social class exerted a greater influence on teacher's assessments of discipline problems. Though IQ and achievement tests found little difference between children from single-parent homes and those from two-parent homes, teachers rated adolescents from single-parent homes lower on intellectual ability and performance primarily when such adolescents exhibited deviant behaviors associated with their social class (p. 288).

This is not a criticism of the use of subjective ratings. After all, I have identified my own subjectivity in this study in many places, but when a rating scale is used as a quantitative measure, it is important to acknowledge the qualitative ways that teacher judgment is formed before drawing conclusions or making generalizations upon which decisions about children are based. Even now, Judith is afraid to check "Divorced" on an application form because "I'm afraid people will think less of me." She explained that she usually does not know or care much about the family backgrounds of her students, but she has noticed that many of her brightest students just *happen* to be from single-parent homes. This might be attributable to the "halo effect"; that is, because she herself is a single mother, she now sees *all* children of single mothers in a positive light. However, this supports the assertion that social stigma affects teacher's perceptions and illustrates how stereotypical expectations can change when an individual has personal contact with a formerly stigmatized experience.

Kathleen: Expensive Education

Kathleen's stories about her daughters' school highlighted the many ways that schools expect homes to contribute to expenses and curriculum that may create a wide disparity between the "haves" and the "have-nots." In their public high school, Kathleen's daughters can participate in field trips that range from expensive cruises to theater excursions. Despite her limited finances, she has always found a way to pay so that her daughters would not miss out on these opportunities, but she wonders about the many children from less resourceful homes who cannot go and are thus unfairly disadvantaged.

Kathleen's sensitivity about the effect that day care might have on her daughters reflects her knowledge of widely publicized studies on maternal work adversely affecting child development (Mischel and Fuhr, 1988) and her acceptance of the "primacy of nurturance" theory—that is, the assumption that the mother is the best companion for young children (Boss and Weiner, 1988; Farrell, 1972). However, in their Montessori day care center, the girls learned many skills and attitudes that Kathleen believes actually gave them an advantage over their non-nursery school peers. This is a conclusion also reached by Kagan (1984) and Rutter (1977), who point out that children may benefit from attachments to other caregivers without damaging their special bonds with their parents.

Kathleen's observations about the volume of homework that her daughters must do and the nature of assignments that cannot be done alone are important. In summarizing the findings of research on single parents, even feminist researchers paint the picture of the single mother as an overtasked woman with too many roles, who is unable to provide quality time for homework help or pay sufficient attention to her children's academic development. Typical of many similar studies, Mulkey, Crian, and Harrington (1992) studied standardized test scores and grades in connection with parents' and students' behavior and economic status and concluded that adolescents from single-parent homes were less willing or able to meet academic demands.

Kathleen's family, similar to Judith's, certainly does not represent this picture. Kathleen's oldest daughter was the valedictorian of her high school. Kathleen's hard work for and with her girls, including marathon sessions with complicated projects such as the one she related in the "cat story," are evidence of her stated desire that her daughters get good grades. She secured tutors, attended all school functions, communicated often with teachers, and acted as chauffeur to the neighborhood to ensure her daughters had every opportunity. Though the intensity of her involvement did indeed strain her many roles and her family time, Kathleen was certainly not unable to find time to help her daughters. Their outstanding performance in school is truly unlike the sample of single-parent homes Mulkey, Crian, and Harrington (1992) studied.

Shawna: Communication and Values

Shawna's story actually provides three examples of children from single-parent homes—her daughter's, her niece's, and her own. Shawna was the stereotypical angry, acting-out, low achiever represented in studies of single-parent children. She described herself as a "cocky somethin'." However, through involvement in the discipline of sports, discovery of her talents, the setback of becoming temporarily disabled, and the patient attention and encouragement of mentors who looked beyond her attitude and recognized her potential, Shawna turned her life around.

Her niece, Vanessa, was not as lucky. Sent to an institution for adolescents by her mother, who felt she could not control her, and "rescued" from it by Shawna, who hoped to give her a fighting chance to change, Vanessa was unable to break out of the patterns of behavior that got her into trouble in school. Despite Shawna's urging her to make friends who would benefit her, Vanessa continued to hang out with people whom Shawna considered losers. A bright young woman, Vanessa lost herself in teenage rebellion and eventually was expelled for a violent outburst in school. Fear for her own family's well-being made Shawna concede defeat and send Vanessa back to her mother.

Vanessa certainly typifies the studies correlating the deviance in children at risk for school failure with single-parent homes (e.g., Davis and McCaul, 1991; Galston, 1993; Mintzies and Hare, 1985). Vanessa's behavior seemed strongly influenced by her racial identity and socioeconomic peer group, having learned to distance herself from her teenage mother, who did not attend to Vanessa's growth and development.

The third example of a child in a single-parent home in Shawna's narrative is her daughter, Tasha. Unlike the developmental delays experienced by the preschool child of divorced parents described by Wallerstein and Kelly (1974, 1976) and those cited in numerous sources on family research (e.g., Carter and McGoldrick, 1980; Dornbusch and Strober, 1988), Shawna's three-year-old is a precocious, independent little girl whose mother is very popular with her classmates. Shawna described a typical day as full of talk and sharing, educational activities done together, and rituals that surround Tasha with love and stability. Tasha imitates her mother in dress and attitude, standing up for what she feels is right, even to children twice her age.

The day care facility where Tasha goes each morning is close to her mother's workplace, making it convenient for Shawna to steal some extra time with her daughter, especially on days when their quality time has been reduced. William, too, can visit Tasha while she is in day care, and he finds quality time with his daughter when they share breakfast or lunch in a restaurant. Tasha feels affirmed and special on these days, but disappointed on the days when William's work schedule will not allow him to see her. At such times, Tasha uses the telephone to maintain contact with him and her stepbrother.

Tasha's day care providers are helpful with her medications when she has trouble with her asthma, and they reinforce behaviors Shawna is trying to develop in her daughter. All caregivers work together for Tasha's benefit, and she expresses her satisfaction with the love she receives from, and gives to, many people in her life.

Tasha's early childhood has not been inhibited by her mother being overstressed, nor by a lower quantity or quality of interaction with her parents, nor by a decrease in parental control, fewer demands for mature behavior, or less rational and explanatory communication with her parents. Tasha and Shawna are cases who contrast with the claims of early family researchers that the quality and quantity of maternal interactions with children were less than those of intact families (Carter and McGoldrick, 1980).

Lyn: Launched

Few studies of single parenting follow children into adulthood. Those which do often report the grown children's satisfaction with their parental relationships and healthy gender role enactments

(Aquilino, 1994; Kennedy, 1992). Lyn's story provides some insight into the ways that children who are not particularly successful in school may ultimately end up "finding their niche" later in life, turning mediocre secondary school records into postsecondary educational achievement.

Lyn's descriptions of her boys in school are informative from a practitioner's perspective. She explained how their different personalities contributed to their differing responses to the divorce. Rich, emotionally dramatic, beat his mother with his fists when she left him at school, but Paul, the quieter and more adaptable one, needed only the assurance that she would be there after they moved away. Their personality differences were accompanied by differential treatment in school. Rich, the model child who was charming and sweet, was the kind of student every teacher wanted. Paul, the loner, was polite and quiet, content to disappear in the background. Teachers recognized that both boys had more potential than their work demonstrated, and Lyn stated that her only regret about her child-rearing style was her policy of noninterference in what she considered were her sons' responsibilities for their school success.

Lyn's story about Paul's encounter with a counselor provides some very important information about the practice of assessment and prescription. The counselor who saw Paul at Lyn's request concluded that Paul's suspected depression was really lack of ability. This he shared with Paul, to Lyn's chagrin. Discouraged by what he felt was his own lack of ability, Paul did not aspire any higher than what he was told he could achieve. Leaving high school with lackluster grades, Paul was lucky to gain admission to a state college under its regular admissions quota. Once in college, Paul began to "feel smart," to see evidence of how capable he really was, and applied himself to his studies with excellent results. He became a dean's list student with a dual major in a challenging program. With the assistance of mentors who encouraged and inspired them, both Paul and Rich found academic fulfillment in college. Rich has completed his teacher certification, moved into graduate study, and landed a job as a teacher—no small accomplishment in a poor market.

The potential damage of pigeonholing a child through psychological testing and overzealous prescription cannot be underestimated. The "sifting and sorting" function of schools leads to what Henslin, Henslin, and Keiser (1976) call the "cooling out" of students who fail. Children who learn early in school that they are "stupid and higher education is meant for others" are selected out and often fulfill exactly what little is expected of them (p. 311). Fortunately, Paul's mother, herself an educator, helped to push him at least to apply for college admission. This proved to be a turning point. Others who did not know or care about his IQ testing results encouraged Paul to recognize his abilities until he learned to "feel smart" again.

Sarah: School Interference in the Home

Similar to Kathleen, Sarah noted the many ways that the school intrudes into home life through unrealistic expectations for homework and poor teacher understanding of the cognitive complexity of some of the tasks they assume children can perform without help. Sarah took the time to explain how much she resented the many ways that the school, especially the high school, dominated her family time.

Despite their adolescent rebellions, Sarah assessed that, except for Annie's late paper in English causing her to fail and repeat the subject in summer school, both of her daughters were very successful in school. She had encouraged them to be curious and to share her love of learning through her many activities with her daughters even before they entered school. These mother-child interactions, however, which were centered on trips and mutual activities, lessened as the girls became more involved in schoolwork. Homework demanded more and more of the little time they had in the evenings, and Sarah refused to cut out the extracurricular activities that she believed helped her daughters learn and grow every bit as much as their academics.

As a teacher herself, Sarah criticizes the school for a lack of respect for parents' educational contributions. Some forms of homework are little more than "busy work," imposing on time that might be better spent in parent-child interactions such as reading, playing games, taking trips, and other social activities. She believes the imposition of homework on the home is "an affront to women as mothers, to their adulthood, to their responsibility to their children."

She expressed some guilt about communicating that attitude to her daughters, but asserted that if schools cannot do what they must do in the six hours of contact time they have with children, they shouldn't expect the home to extend the school day. She stated, "I love to learn. I love to study. . . . But I don't think it owns your life. And when it starts trying to own the evening hours . . . it's just too much."

This provides a different angle on the "homework question," which is most often viewed negatively in connection with single mothers. A commonly accepted explanation in research on school achievement patterns for children from single-parent homes is that task overload causes single parents to have less time to help their children with homework, and, thus, their children experience deficits in school achievement (Baca Zinn and Eitzen, 1990). Other researchers have disputed these claims (e.g., Marsh, 1990; Rice, 1994). Sarah's objections join Kathleen's protests that single mothers do *indeed* extend themselves to help with homework but regard it as an intrusion on their few valuable hours of quality contact time. These two mothers, however, may be contrasted with Lyn, who did not provide homework assistance. Shawna's daughter is too young for homework, and Judith did not comment on homework time specifically.

Synthesis of Common Themes Concerning Children of Divorce

The Only Similarity Is Difference

Even in this small set of case studies, children with greatly varying personalities are represented. Judith's son, always a perfectionist and a worrier, does well in school but is not "outstanding." Kathleen's older daughter was the valedictorian of her high school and is currently attending college on a full scholarship. Her younger daughter is doing very well also. Shawna and her niece Vanessa both acted out in school, yet the results of their school careers have been very different. Shawna's preschool-age daughter is bright and highly verbal. Lyn's sons, both mediocre performers in school, have found their stride in college. Sarah's daughters exhibit behaviors that are emotionally exhausting for her, but she reports that they have been very successful in school for most of their growing years. Differences in personality, living circumstances, financial resources, styles of adjustment, family tendencies toward depression, child-rearing practices, individual motivation, the presence of mentors, and schooling are represented in all of these children. In effect, the only *common* denominator for these five families is *difference*.

The mystery remains, then, why so many policymakers and public officials are willing to make assertions about children from single-parent homes, believing that the structure of the home overwhelms all other variables, even when multiple regressions factor out such strong variables as socioeconomic status and the statistical influence of family configuration suddenly "disappears" (Finn and Owings, 1994). Though children's behaviors might be grouped as similar, on closer inspection, the reasons for these behaviors are as different as the children. Attributing causation, or even talking about a linear type of association between variables, oversimplifies what is obviously a complex interrelationship between human agency, environments, and culture. The element of choice and personality should be considered in studies of human behavior, but these are slippery concepts that are not easily factored out of multiple regressions or comparative analyses.

Judith's son might be viewed as growing up too fast, acting as a little adult because his mother depends on him. That this is the result of being in a single-mother-headed family is not consistent with the fact that Ian has always been this way, even when his father was present in the home. He is a worrier, and he exhibits the maturity and comfort with adultlike behaviors that is also attributed to only children.

Kathleen's daughters contrast with reports that the children of single mothers perform poorly in school; they have been shining stars. Yet Shawna and her niece Vanessa typify this observation. Because this study presents them in detail within their different socioeconomic, race, and family circumstances, we can see that their lives are different in more ways than they are similar, yet all four young women might be represented in demographic correlations or school survey data as "children from single-mother-headed households." These studies do not always account for such variables as socioeconomic level, race, marital status of the mother, or number of children in the household (Rice, 1994).

The importance of contrasting variables can be seen in the differences between the children in these case studies. Shawna's school behavior changed as she matured and found mentors who could see past her attitude, but Shawna's deliberate mentoring of Vanessa did not have the same effect. Though teachers said the same things about lack of academic achievement for Lyn's two sons—that they did not achieve their potentials—the two boys were very different in all of their interpersonal relationships, including the way they acted socially in school and were thus regarded by their teachers: Paul was quiet, shy, and virtually ignored; Rich was outgoing, pleasing, and well liked. Though Sarah's daughters both exhibited the most severe responses to adolescence (suicide, teen pregnancy, petty theft), they were quite different in their relationships with their mother and father. The girls were born within sixteen months of each other, but teenage pregnancy sent one daughter into her own home as a mother and left the other, the "peacemaker," alone to act out her adolescent rebellion on her mother. They are now light-years apart in terms of maturity and life course. However, both girls were mostly successful in school, with the exception of Annie's failure in twelfth-year English. Such differential results, then, are never simply attributable to single causes.

Consequently, even though aggregate data on achievement may place the children represented in this study in similar groups, ranging from poor (Shawna and Vanessa) to mediocre (Paul and Rich) to superior (Kathleen's daughters, Kim and Terry), their many differences in measures of adjustment, attitude, behavior, social skills, and motivation must be recognized.

Parent Participation

Of all the mothers studied, only Lyn expressed that she was less involved in her sons' schooling, but this was consistent with her child-rearing philosophy—to support their independence and self-efficacy in ways that did not necessarily include pushing them to achieve.

Judith, Kathleen, and Sarah spend as much time as is necessary—and in Kathleen's case, a maximum of time—helping to support their children's achievement in school. Though Shawna's daughter is not yet in school, Shawna mentioned that she often goes to Tasha's day care center at lunchtime, interacts with Tasha's friends, goes with the group on field trips, and works with the day care center staff to enforce Tasha's learning and help with her medications. As educated women, they talked about the importance of education, but they expressed an awareness of the stigmas associated with single-parent homes and were determined not to become statistics. Judith, Kathleen, Shawna, and Sarah are all involved in their children's schools through the Parent-Teacher Association (PTA), conferences, club activities, financial support, field trips, room-mothering (a voluntary mother-helper for a classroom), frequent communication, and homework support. (Lyn's sons are on their own, and her story about their childhoods was retrospective, so she did not talk about her involvement with school events except to say that PTA was *not* something she "chose to do.")

Though there is certainly evidence of work overload and time constraints in most of these cases, Kathleen, Judith, Shawna, and Sarah did not feel that their parental functioning was inhibited with regard to substantively and emotionally supporting and encouraging their children's success in school.

The Importance of Mentors

Kathleen, Shawna, Lyn, and Sarah all discussed mentors in their interviews. Kathleen herself was mentored by strong women in the workplace who encouraged and promoted her as well as providing her with psychological support. Shawna's mentors supported her in ways her mother could not. From sixth-grade teachers to women coaches to a collegiate mentoring program, Shawna was guided to reaffirm her strengths and talents. She, herself, is currently involved in her community as a mentor for the children of others. Lyn's sons both enjoyed the encouragement of mentors at the college level who helped them recognize their competence and make career choices. Sarah's daughter Julia was encouraged by a collegiate mentor to pursue her desire to be a doctor, a dream she must put on hold for awhile, but one she might never have dreamed on her own.

Parents cannot provide everything for their children, no matter how hard they try, or how much time they devote to them. In this, the children of single mothers are no different from the children of two-parent households. The influence of others in our lives is important from the time we emerge on the social scene. Role models come in every form, and it is certainly a narrow view that expects one person, or even two, to present children or young people with all of the variety of perspectives and personalities that frame their choices as adults. Perhaps the inward turning of the family during the mid-twentieth century led to an overemphasis on the family's responsibility for children's socialization and the transmission of values. It is clear from these cases that the caring support of others outside the family is welcome and effective in the lives of young men and women.

Schools Intrude on the Home

Studies of the relations between home and school constitute another entire agenda for scholarly investigation, but it is interesting to note that research on the effects of single-parent households on school achievement is often based on scores, behaviors, and attitudes usually measured in school. It seems that few researchers are interested in the home lives of their students. In discussing my research with colleagues, I was amazed when asked what my topic had to do with my doctoral area, learning and instruction. Educators who are not truly interested in parents and homes are those who focus their attention on the school day and expect that the home will simply provide the kind of environment that makes schools, not homes, more successful.

This attitude is evident in the stories told by the women in this study. *Home*work is an accepted artifact of school culture, yet educators do not understand the impact it has on the home where they expect the work to be done. Educators who criticize parents for not doing their part to support student success might look at the ways that homework itself structures and co-opts family time. Kathleen and Sarah were most forward about it, though Judith and Lyn both mentioned it. Kathleen described her sheer exhaustion as she tried to cope with supporting two daughters who had different learning styles, tackling the domestic chores around dinner time "because I would rather see them start their homework, get it over with, so I don't have to stay up or they're not up too late." When referring to helping her daughters take advantage of field trips, she said, "Education isn't only what they do in the classroom," but she noted the disadvantage for children whose home situations could not support many outside activities or extracredit projects, such as ferrying children to a school board meeting late at night or stripping the skeleton of a dead cat for Advanced Biology.

Sarah resents the intrusiveness of schools that assume they are solely responsible for the education of children and that they know better than parents just what types of homework might be educational. Sarah is angry about not having the chance to read to her daughters, as she once did when they were very young. As a teacher, she is sensitive to the conceptual framework that is represented in some of the work sent home, and she finds that teachers may have a poor concept of the intellectual levels necessary for work that even she finds challenging. She does not want her daughters to be disrespectful of their learning, but when homework "tries to own" the evening hours, she resists.

Parents as partners in education, an idea that has seen renewed interest in recent years, usually means parents who are willing to reinforce school policies and supervise school-assigned activities in their homes. This hegemony does not allow the partnership to function equally well in both directions. The schools themselves exhibit a patronizing attitude toward homes. In educational research concerning single-parent families, many references point to ways that schools can help by providing the "consistency and stability" that one-parent homes are expected to lack (Debusk and Leslie, 1991; Wanat, 1993). In Wanat's (1993) study of programs for single-parent children, principals surveyed expressed their belief that schools were more effective than parents in meeting their children's needs. Such a philosophy assumes that the school *can* and *should* exert its presence in the home to strengthen it, implying that school is strong and the home is weak.

Not one study of those I researched discussed the ways that the home may strengthen the school, other than in ways the school sponsors, such as homework, parental participation in its extracurricular activities, and the reinforcement of an American work ethic. The parents in this study provided much detail about the ways that school work and school expectations may interfere with family time and not allow parents to meet their children's needs as they see fit. These women's narratives provide information about the importance of mentors, the many ways literacy is supported at home, the value of educational experiences outside of the classroom, and their own hidden resources of talent and educational experience from which their children's schools might benefit.

Summary

The narratives of the five women in this study provide rich information about their lives as mothers, daughters, and women, in relationships and in solitude. They describe their lives as if they are journeys still in progress. They have experienced the strong effects of intergenerational gender role socialization. They have felt guilty about not fulfilling their mothers' ideals or the ideals for women and families they themselves were taught to prize. They have endured the indignities imposed by a culture that allows men to dominate and expects women to accommodate.

They work hard to overcome stigma, to balance the many responsibilities of working mothers, to stretch finances, to learn to value themselves for all that they are and can do, rather than what they are not and cannot do. They rebel against the unconscious generational repetitions of gender or family interaction patterns, and their lives often contrast with assumptions others may make based on their socioeconomic standing, gender, race, or marital status.

They promote their children's independence and encourage them directly and indirectly to adopt a more equitable view of gender roles than the ones they learned as they grew up. They are buffeted by the same storms as any mothers—adolescent rebellion, mother blaming, fear of loneliness, self-doubt. They recognize their strengths and speak positively about the benefits of their family structure. They seek networks of support from other women, join community-based efforts to support others, and express pride in their children's growth and accomplishments. Yet, they openly discuss their weaknesses and defeats. They have coped with depression—their own and their children's—and have sought help. Some have already emerged into peace and "normalcy"; others continue to fight. They are happy at times, sad at others, and often exhausted, yet able to take on new challenges.

They are neither paragons of virtue nor social pariahs. Their stories are rich with particular information about women, men, children, marriage, divorce, parenting, schools, and our culture. They have speculated about the meaning of their life experiences and have made honest and sometimes contradictory assessments of themselves and their children. I have tried to represent their words accurately, to summarize their meanings faithfully, and to add my own interpretive structure in answer to my research questions. I invite readers, now, to stand back and view the quilt for themselves.

CONCLUSIONS AND RECOMMENDATIONS

The Unbroken Home

It is obvious when one reads much of the literature on single parents that single mothers are stigmatized. American society habitually constructs normative examples of what, at any historical moment, may be suggested as the "ideal American family." Pursuing this ideal, measuring ourselves against it, longing for it from days gone past, and trying to advance it as a virtual truth for all ages have consumed much of the energy of research in the past several decades.

History, says Stephanie Coontz (1992), explodes that myth: "The idea that there is one single blueprint for parents to follow, one family form that always produces well-adjusted children, or one 'normal' set of family arrangements and interactions is not true now and never has been" (p. 228). Such nostalgic practices prevent us from learning the lessons of the past and effectively deter any movement toward innovations that will benefit *real* families' futures. *Real* American families, says Judith Stacey (1990), are a "multiplicity of family and household arrangements that we inhabit uneasily and reconstitute frequently to changing personal and occupational circumstances" (p. 17). Humorist Art Buchwald (1981) pokes satirical fun at politicians who insist on the nuclear family as the preferred image. He asks, "Whose family is this anyway?" and adds that policymakers who make plans and policies in accordance with this vision are doomed to fail: "That's why nothing they plan turns out to be right" (p. K1).

Historically, politically, socially, and psychologically, the home has been the focus of vilification as well as veneration. Politicians are fond of deflecting public focus on persistent social ills away from the more difficult dragons to slay, such as depressed economy, overgrown and ineffectual government, incoherent social policy, and racial and class intolerance, toward a personal realm where each individual is responsible and may feel in control—the family. Yet, as Lerner (1988) suggests, fixing the family does not fix the world.

Coontz (1992) claims that blaming the family gives the government an excuse for inactivity: "Why launch new school reforms when . . . the key to educational performance is whether a child comes from a two-parent family? Why experiment with a new anti-poverty program when the most important indicator of poverty is whether there are two parents at home?" (p. 256). Demos (1986) adds that policy response is needed to address the problems of real families, "but the need is obscured and the problems themselves denied by the presence of long-standing cultural myths." When Americans engage in useless comparisons of their families against these cultural myths, they almost always fail the test. Both personal and social consequences result from such comparisons. "When things go awry, the individual family members must somehow be at fault. The price of such beliefs is paid in guilt, in lessened self-esteem, and in disorganized, wholly inadequate programs of social services" (p. 196).

Life cycle theory may contribute to the stigmatization of families who break what is seen as an inevitable stage pattern of development. Carter and McGoldrick (1980) assert that family development has little to do with choice: "Many people act as though they can choose [membership and function in a family] when in fact there is very little choice," and "[w]hom we are related to in the complex web of family ties over all the generations is unalterable by us" (p. 13). The philosophy they espouse, and others accept, supports research and policymaking that privileges the two-parent normative model over all others and sets up all variants for failure, unless they can somehow scramble to realign their family system as close to the ideal as possible (Rice, 1994).

Other theorists welcome the insecurities represented by choice and change. Rice (1994) notes, "For the first time in our society, marriage is freely terminable, divorce normative and family form infinite. We lack psychological theory to understand these phenomena" (p. 578). She adds that to consider maintaining stability as a main function of the family "denies the essence of learning and evolution is openness and change" (p. 573). Women who choose to leave a nonbeneficial relationship could be considered as exhibiting adaptive rather than maladaptive behavior, and divorce as feminine resistance to oppression and a vehicle for liberation is a much less negative concept for women than divorce as the failure or "brokenness" of marriage (p. 577).

The systematic devaluing of women, as described by Schur (1984), is intimately connected to the stigmatization of the "failed" home. As the health of a family is considered to be primarily the woman's responsibility, when the home in which she is only a member is suddenly changed, she is blamed, and when the man leaves, the home is somehow broken. The many mythologies about motherhood focus blame heavily on women. Schur notes that by focusing on the deviance of women, once again we deflect attention from male culpability, and since stigma is often employed as a prelude to punishment, men's offenses against women go unpunished, but women are punishable for their own shortcomings and for those of their children. Stacey (1990) is stronger in shifting attention for family disruption to men by suggesting that "if there is a family crisis, it is a male family crisis" (p. 269).

Weitzman (1985) warns that even no-fault divorce laws claiming to treat both partners equally actually enforce gross inequalities in gender-related economic advantage and disadvantage and encourage the perpetuation of a system whereby "children and former wives are sentenced to bear the economic burden of divorce" (p. 322). Stacey (1990) points out that gains in "gender equality" have often been losses for women and gains for men. Some critics of efforts at women's liberation express the fear that women's liberation "frees men first" (p. 259).

Weitzman (1985) suggests that changing laws will not necessarily change social practice. Changing the material conditions of men's and women's lives will be needed to "overcome the pervasive weight of tradition" (p. 261). Farrell (1972) maintains that the only way for men to be able to choose to work for gender equity is to ensure that both men and women are internally secure enough to have the psychological freedom to control their lives, and for men to free themselves from self-definition through their jobs to become more child oriented in their families (pp. 8-11).

Though some authors, such as Levine (1992), contend that the single mother has lost most of the disapprobation she once faced, Coontz (1992) points to current research findings that show how "stereotypes and prejudices about broken families still prevail among teachers, psychologists and the general public, while no new values, guidelines or support systems have evolved to nourish the strengths that many [families] exhibit" (p. 280). However, Schur (1984) is optimistic about the possibilities of changing these entrenched patterns: "Since stigma is imposed, it can be deposed, [and] . . . women's currently perceived deviances are all subject to conscious efforts at change" (p. 241).

The women in this study are intensely aware of the stigmas attached to their status as women and to their family structures, and of the ideals they failed to achieve. All five mentioned the effects of stigma directly. Judith's life expectations were so unrealistic that she felt at first her dreams were shattered by divorce. Kathleen did not want anyone to say that her daughters had failed in any way because they came from a single-parent home, so she doubled her efforts to ensure their success and to show others that she was "a good person." Shawna mentioned that she thought it was ridiculous to believe that children from single-parent homes were more troubled than those from two-parent homes because her own experience of family life *before* her parents' divorce showed her that turmoil and trouble may come from conflict in an unhappy, *intact* family. Lyn, who came from a tradition of single mothers, expressed her feelings of guilt at "being the bitch," the one who left. Sarah currently struggles against blaming herself for her teenagers' behaviors and is saddened when she sees other families and believes they have what she wanted but could not achieve.

Thus, the normative privileging of two-parent families over single-parent families can foster a sense of deficiency in single parents, especially mothers, that is not necessarily a fair judgment of their abilities as parents and heads of household. This, instead, constructs an ideal that is rarely enacted in real families, serving only to stigmatize and punish those who fail to achieve it in their own families. Punishment is often leveled in the form of blame, and the target of that blame is most often mothers. Psychoanalysts such as Dinnerstein (1976) and Farrell (1972) attribute distrust of women in general to myths of omnipotence, dominance, and the infallibility of mothers. Always falling short of such godlike perfection, men distrust the women who might have such power over them, and women despair over their own imperfections. Such interactions are clearly evident in the couple relationships of at least four of these five women, and in their struggles to regain their lost identities and strengthen their self-esteem.

"Broken" Homes and School Achievement

Children from single-parent homes are expected to fail in their social arena, the school, simply because their families do not match society's ideal. Evidence of their failures is amassed mostly through statistical manipulation. The American public has come to expect that research is unaffected by bias or emotion, especially when results are presented as numbers supported by the impersonality of scientific method. Assumptions about children based on labels attached to them by scientific research and predictions that they are at risk for school failure may produce more damage than the characteristics themselves. The pejorative label so glibly applied to single-parent families, mostly those created by divorce, is "the broken home." Attached to this label is the assumption that persons living in such homes are themselves broken and need to be fixed. Thus, therapeutic advice and programs of intervention for single-parent families abound, right along with programs for other forms of deviance, such as alcoholism, drug abuse, teenage pregnancy, and violence.

What may be seen in the different children represented by this study are the many ways that their personalities, ages, circumstances, and contacts with people outside of their families create contexts for each of them that make predictions or generalizations about *all* of them problematic. An appreciation and celebration of their individuality, however, can be justified. The distinctly qualitative nature of this assertion is problematic for policymakers. How can one construct programs, evaluate achievement, and compare schools against each other and against a set of national standards if one cannot amass individuals in groups with certain consistent and shared attributes? This question can best be answered in a treatment of the application of qualitative research to policy and evaluation, a methodological discussion I cannot reconstruct here. For an expert discussion on the uses of qualitative information in educational policymaking, I refer the reader to D. M. Fetterman's (1984) *Ethnography in Educational Evaluation*, a compilation of essays suggesting multiple ways of using qualitative designs in educational evaluation.

Hansen (1986) reminds educators that children from any type of home can be relatively advantaged in some classrooms and disadvantaged in others. The tendency in educational and family research is to focus on attributes or traits of children, spending little time or energy examining the various ways that a single child may interact in different contexts. By placing the child at the center of his or her own problems, all other individuals and groups that are fully functioning parts of the educational milieu are of secondary or *contextual* importance only. Such a child-*concentrated* focus (not child-*centered*, as is often claimed) deflects attention from parents, teachers, programs, classrooms, and social contexts that are larger and more complex and, thus, more difficult to assess, manipulate, and control.

The prevalent practice of labeling students as at risk is an attempt at prediction and prevention of school failure. Predicting how a child may behave by describing his or her characteristics is dangerously simplistic. Coontz (1992) notes that researchers themselves often are not fully aware of what they are measuring. What may seem maladaptive at one stage of life may become a strength later on. She cites the findings of one longitudinal study that the predictions made about which kids would become troubled or successful as adults were wrong in *two-thirds* of the cases (MacFarlane, 1964, cited in Coontz, 1992, p. 227). Prevention of failure may be offered as a rationale for comparing all children against a single standard that is ill-suited for any of them, and an excuse for schools and social agencies to intervene in family life when few authentic opportunities exist for the family to change school functioning or policy.

Coontz (1992) suggests that a better agenda for research could easily shift focus from broad generalization to particularization, examining, not what categorical membership means for school performance, but what particular aspects of homes and home-school interactions produce positive or negative effects. Rice (1994) suggests a research agenda that focuses on dyads of people as they interact with the contexts of political, social, and economic conditions to "better their lives and the lives of their families" (p. 577). The women in this study would suggest that the schools become better aware of these interactions in a serious effort to understand how the school is only a part of the child's entire cultural context. Such an awareness might allow homework to reflect more of the unique and important contributions to literacy and learning made by the home, rather than simply being an extension of school curriculum.

Fixing the Family

Schools that make stereotypical assumptions about homes are also guilty of patronizing them. In a society that reveres and celebrates the independent American spirit, it is curious to see how research is used to support intrusions into human lives to prevent social disintegration, which actually means promoting conformity. Many such efforts are made in the ostensibly noble spirit of social reform.

Protests against the feminization of poverty, led to *equating* single mothers with poverty and blaming black matriarchal families for the results of economic and racial prejudices leveled against them. The financial loss resulting from halving a former two-income family cannot be underestimated, but neither is it the all-encompassing, overwhelming factor that leads Weitzman (1985) to assert, "Poverty begins with single parenthood" (p. 347). Coontz (1992) reminds critics that "single-parent poverty is not an equation," and that while poverty is concentrated, at 38 percent, in single-parent families, the remaining percentage is located in two-parent families (p. 259).

The women and children in this study do not suffer from the deprivations associated with poverty, primarily because they are fully employed professional women or, in Sarah's case, financially independent. None of the women in this study is rich; all are professional women whose salaries (or yearly income in Sarah's case) range from $28,000 to $80,000. Judith has been able to establish a new residence. Kathleen has paid off a mortgage. Shawna supports herself and her daughter on her full-time job. Lyn supports two sons in college. Sarah can help her daughters buy cars and can refurnish her home on income from an inherited trust. Father-paid child support has helped in four of the five cases but has not been the mainstay of the family income.

The concept of brokenness in families who have gone through divorce assumes that the family was *actually* intact beforehand. In all five cases, the women believe that this was not true of their families. The women of this study join the voices of those studied by Bequaert (1976), Llewelyn and Osborne (1990), Levine (1992), Rice and Rice (1986), and Stacey (1990), women who assured their interviewers that their lives were vastly improved after their divorces. Even Weitzman (1985), in her critique of no-fault divorce laws, admits that the divorced women she interviewed agreed that their lives were improved. She quotes them: "I am a whole person. I like myself better. The children like me better. I am happier. I learned how strong I am. I've been through hell and back and I know I can make it. I survived and am in control" (p. 347). Despite such optimistic data, in the paragraphs following, Weitzman persists in using metaphors of breakage that include phrases such as "financial disaster," and "drastic psychological effects on the children." She sees the laws as "forcing" mothers to work and "depriving" children of care and attention (pp. 347-377).

Intrusive therapeutic interventions for single-parent families are based on an assumption that the single-parent household is badly "off-cycle" (referring of course to the family life cycle theory underlying the therapy). In encouraging divorced persons to remarry, Carter and McGoldrick (1980) claim that remarriage helps the marrying spouse to make a better postdivorce adjustment (p. 252). This assumes that marriage is the norm to be desired and that singleness is a temporary aberration. The women of this study described the normalization of their homes as occurring when they learned to value their singleness. They do not necessarily reject the possible benefits of marriage or couple relationships, but all have arrived at various degrees of satisfaction with the lives they have constructed as single women. Even Kathleen, who is in a committed relationship, described the ways that maintaining their physical distance from each other was sometimes preferable to the continual contact of marriage.

Other prevailing stereotypical visions of single mothers include their depleted energy, isolation, loss of identity from losing their husbands, manic or chronic depression, lack of time to interact with their children, permissive parenting styles, disinterest in community activities or lack of time to establish support networks, and engagement in "behaviors that are not helpful to their children" (Dornbusch and Gray, 1988, p. 293). Schools and social agencies whose programs and intervention strategies build on these assumptions may simply accept this attitude:

> It will not be easy to inform single parents of these problems or of appropriate ways of dealing with them. It does not seem reasonable to expect that schools, faced with a relatively low rate of single-parent participation in school activities, might undertake special programs to attract their attendance. . . . Such programs might well focus on the problems that single parents have in common, and thus might improve family-school relations for this less-involved set of parents. (Dornbusch and Gray, 1988, p. 293)

The women in this study have honestly related that they have experienced depression, depleted energy, loss of identity, and the pressures of time to be both wage earners and parents. These characteristics, however, do not necessarily merit negative interpretations, nor do they make single parenting entirely unattractive.

Once again, examining more of the context surrounding these characteristics clarifies and extends the concepts as they are presented in individual lives. The women in this study are working women, and they experience role strain typical of working mothers, married or unmarried. This strain is especially heightened by their singular family responsibility; however, most of the women in this study employ wise time management, have established comfortable routines, and exhibit adaptability and flexibility in meeting the challenges of multitasking.

Of the three women who described experiences with depression, Judith's case was temporary—related to the stress of divorce—and Lyn and Sarah attributed their chronic depressions to a genetic predisposition exacerbated in periods of stress. Loss of identity was not expressed as loss of the relational self (although Judith did discuss her problems with adjusting to valuing herself outside of a relationship), but they did discuss loss of identity, self-pride, and self-efficacy *within* their couple relationships, feeling that self-esteem was strengthened after their divorces. Their parenting styles ranged from highly structured (Kathleen) to largely permissive (Lyn). Child-rearing philosophies or practices were certainly not consistent across all of the cases.

Finally, lack of interest in community or networking contacts and isolation do not describe these women. Shawna is particularly involved in community affairs. Kathleen, Sarah, and Shawna are (or were) highly involved with their daughters' many activities, both in and outside of school. Judith and Lyn maintain strong support networks of friends.

Thus, after closer analysis, what originally appears to be supportive of the stereotype of the overburdened single mother proves to be quite different from the dark picture painted by Dornbusch and Gray (1988). What appear to be common characteristics, when examined in a more detailed context, are not at all common in causation or uniformly enacted in the lives of real women. Therefore, Kissman and Allen (1993) and Rice (1994) encourage social service practitioners to take stock of their own value systems in analyzing the kind of therapeutic interventions they attempt with clients. Those who accept the notion of the overburdened, isolated, and neglectful single parent will most certainly be off the mark when they encounter women such as Judith, Kathleen, and Sarah, whose interactions with the schools are continual and who resent the patronizing way that schools assume mothers do not know what is good for their children. Even those assumptions made about teenage mothers must be qualified in assessing young women such as

Sarah's daughter, Julia, who is not entirely powerless, immature, or without means of support.

Coontz (1992) warns against a more insidious effect of family-based social reform movements. After tracing historically the many ways that families are affected by outside forces, she questions how many of the social ills blamed for the breakdown of American society can be solved by changing the form of the family. Major social problems such as poverty, crime, abuse, alcoholism, drug use, and suicide are macrosocial influences to which the family responds, but which have not proven responsive to the family. Coontz maintains that historical evidence lends support to the no-tion that "strengthening" the family to strengthen society is a futile struggle, since the forces *outside* of the family are much more effective at changing its members than the forces *within* the family are at changing the context in which they live. In other words, it is illogical to believe that instability outside the family can be changed by stability within it (pp. 257-278).

Any reader who approaches the women in this study from a problem orientation will certainly find problems. The women and families represented in this study have been touched by many of the major social problems previously mentioned: abuse, alcoholism, attempted suicide, financial constraints. They have also discussed personal problems with time squeezes, depression, children's ad-justment, and identity confusion, but this in-depth presentation and analysis of their stories offers more information than can be under-stood by simply categorizing their experiences and reporting them as numbers. It is important to reiterate that readers of research on single parents need to look *beyond* the descriptive adjectives that generalize to the contexts and meanings that particularize. What may be seen as negative characteristics by one theorist are consid-ered positive by another, and what is certain is uncertainty.

After we examine both the strengths and weaknesses that single mothers ascribe to their experiences as parents and as women, we can suggest that their lives exhibit some similar features, but that they are, at the same time, as different as their histories, their per-sonalities, their social contexts, and their outward and inner lives. To say, "they are this way because they are single parents," blurs the quality of the lives they live and does not serve to improve them.

Without ignoring the negative interpretations these women give to some of their life experiences or overdramatizing the positive aspects of being a single parent, the reader can see in their stories an emphasis on their feelings of efficacy in raising their children, their many strategies for coping with time constraints and multiple roles, the value of their connections with friends and their children, and their optimistic goals for the future.

An Agenda for Change

Because of the subtle ways social stigma can interfere with the formulation and conduct of research, it is potentially damaging to human subjects studied to assume that the behavior of *all* of the members of a particular social group is predictable and controllable simply because certain researchers describe and explain patterns observed in some members of the group. This seems particularly true in the case of single mothers. If the object of research is not to predict and control behavior by generalizing characteristics to a diverse population, what might be an alternative? Research employing the tenets of human agency and embracing the uncertainties it represents would include at its foundation a curiosity about the way that individuals and groups of humans construct their world, and respect for the local and personal truths revealed in such a search.

In an agenda for future research on families and schools there is a justifiable need to set aside standardization in favor of diversity. Linear models that attribute causation and predict the future functioning of children to prevent anomalies do not account for the many complexities of children's internal and external lives. *New* programs based on *new* conclusions from *new* data based on *old* assumptions will probably reach *old* conclusions. Families are not as they once were, nor are they what they will someday be. Schools will not change families until families are given the opportunities to change schools.

As Coontz (1992) maintains, burgeoning social problems require large-scale social solutions. The inward turning to the family for rescue from the "jungle out there" will not even make a dent in the enormity of global problems, just as the many personal bomb shelters constructed during the cold war did not contribute to disarmament peace treaties. Blaming families, parents, mothers, fathers, and children for the failures of society is as illogical as blaming a plant for withering in a pot of poor soil with no sunlight and no water. A more worthy endeavor would be a concentration on inter-actions where researchers and policymakers attempt to *discover* and *display,* not predict and control, the many ways families interact with each other, their environments, and their self-conceptions.

Single-parent families are only one of the many social groups that may be included in research whose mission is to better understand the meanings humans attribute to their lived experiences. The women and children in this study are best represented in their own words, valued for the information they bestow, and for the ways that their lived experiences help us to appreciate both their sorrows and struggles, their resilience and resourcefulness. Thus, as I have attempted to do in this study, researchers may gather the many squares of the quilt from the many hands that sewed them, but despite the collage of colors and patterns that will inevitably result, the quilt will assert its own unifying themes. Impressions of the quilt as a whole will *necessarily* be different for each viewer.

Finally, as I view the quilt represented in this study, what I have learned from its individual contributors has profoundly affected my own life experience. I have affirmed my conviction that the home I enjoy with my son has a solid foundation for growth and development for both of us. As I shared the lives of my female participants, surprisingly, too, I have learned to listen more acutely to my male acquaintances who have already or are currently experiencing divorce, to be curious about their struggles with gender role prescriptions, and to empathize with their frustrations over the limitations of their participation in their children's lives.

I emerge from this process hopeful, but reserved. All the while I was writing this book, news reports, advertisements, and casual discussions with teachers still echoed the widely held public belief that the rising divorce rate heralds the demise of the American family, and that the breakdown of the family is at the heart of all our social evils. Television sitcoms and high-budget movies reinforce gender role stereotypes and invent some new ones, and a campaign to raise standards and hold schools accountable that ignores the social context of education as if it does not exist will not be successful.

American educators should instead entertain a new vision of families that renounces blame and establishes mutually beneficial partnerships, challenging the unexamined axioms that inhibit their understanding of the families of the children whose well-being and advancement is central to their mission. As they become more willing to view the richly textured quilts of their students' *whole* lives, I am convinced that they will learn more than they might from any unidimensional images portrayed in grade reports and standardized tests. After all, one cannot look deeply into the lives of others without gaining some sense that, even in small measure, one is looking into one's own.

References

Alcott, L. M. (1924). *Little Women.* Fairfield, NJ: Wm. Morrow and Company.

Alessandri, S. M. (1992). Effects of maternal work status in single-parent families on children's perception of self and family and school achievement. *Journal of Experimental Child Psychology, 54*(3), 417-433.

Amato, P. A. and Keith, B. (1991). Parental divorce and child well-being: A meta-analysis. *Psychological Bulletin, 110,* 26-46.

Anderson, J. (Author of screenplay) (1995). Pillsbury, S. and Sanford M. (Producers). *How to make an American quilt* [Film]. (Available from Amblin Entertainment, MCA Universal Studios, Los Angeles, CA)

Andre, R. (1991). *Positive solitude.* New York: HarperCollins.

Aquilino, W. S. (1994). Impact of childhood family disruption on young adults' relationships with parents. *Journal of Marriage and the Family, 56*(2), 295-313.

Asmussen, L. and Larson, R. (1991). The quality of family time among young adolescents in single-parent and married-parent families. *Journal of Marriage and the Family, 53*(4), 1021-1030.

Astone, N. M. and McLanahan, S. S. (1994). Family structure, residential mobility, and school dropout: A research note. *Demography, 31,* 575-584.

Baca Zinn, M. and Eitzen, D. S. (1990). *Diversity in families,* Second edition. New York: Harper & Row.

Banyard, V. L. and Olson, S. L. (1991, April). *Intergenerational correlates of daily coping behavior in single-parent mothers of young children.* Paper presented at the Biennial Meeting of the Society for Research in Child Development, Seattle, WA. (ERIC Document Reproduction Service No. ED340 507)

Barnes, G. M., Farrell, M. P., and Banerjee, S. (1994). Family influences on alcohol abuse and other problem behaviors among black and white adolescents in a general population sample. *Journal of Research on Adolescence, 4*(2), 183-201.

Bayrakal, S. and Kope, T. M. (1990). Dysfunction in the single-parent and only-child family. *Adolescence, 25,* 1-7.

Belsky, J. (1986). Infant day care: A cause for concern? *Zero to Three: Bulletin of the National Center for Clinical Infant Programs.* Washington, DC: U.S. Government Printing Office.

Bem, S. (1974). The measurement of psychological androgyny. *Journal of Consulting and Clinical Psychology, 42,* 155-162.

Bennett, L. A., Wolin, S. J., and McAvity, K. J. (1988). Family identity, ritual and myth: A cultural perspective on life cycle transitions. In C. J. Falicov (Ed.), *Family transitions* (pp. 211-234). New York: Guilford Press.

Benson, P. L. and Roehlkepartian, E. C. (1993). *Youth in single-parent families: Risk and resiliency.* Background paper. Minneapolis, MN: Search Institute. (ERIC Document Reproduction Service No. ED360 462)

Bequaert, L. (1976). *Single women alone and together.* Boston, MA: Beacon Press.

Bernard, J. (1975). *Women, wives and mothers: Values and options.* Chicago: Aldine.

Bieber, I. and Society of Medical Psychoanalysts (1962). *Homosexuality: A psychoanalytic study.* New York: Basic Books.

Blake, J. (1974). Coercive pronatalism and American population policy. In E. Peck and J. Senderowitz (Eds.), *Pronatalism: The myth of mom and apple pie.* New York: Thomas Crowell.

Blum, H. M., Boyle, M. H., and Offord, D. R. (1988). Single-parent families: Child psychiatric disorder and school performance. *Journal of American Academy of Child and Adolescent Psychiatry, 27,* 214-219.

Boss, P. and Weiner, J. P. (1988). Rethinking assumptions about women's development and family therapy. In C. J. Falicov (Ed.), *Family transitions* (pp. 235-251). New York: Guilford Press.

Brady, J. (1990). I [still] want a wife. *Ms.,* July/August, 17.

Buchwald, A. (1981, March 8). Whose family is this anyway? *The Washington Post, 93,* K1.

Buck, N. and Scott, J. (1993). She's leaving home: But why? An analysis of young people leaving the parental home. *Journal of Marriage and the Family, 55(4),* 863-874.

Bumpass, L. L. and Raley, K. (1995). Redefining single-parent families: Cohabitation and changing family reality. *Demography, 32,* 97-109.

Burgoyne, J. (1987, April). Material happiness. *New Society, 10,* 12-14.

Carlson, M. B. (1992, June 1). Why Quayle has half a point. *Time, 139,* 30-31.

Carter, B. and McGoldrick, M. (1989). *The changing family life cycle: A framework for family therapy* (Second edition). Boston, MA: Allyn & Bacon.

Carter, E. A. and McGoldrick, M. (Eds.) (1980). *The family life cycle.* New York: Gardner Press, Inc.

Cashion, B. G. (1982). Female-headed families: Effects on children and clinical implications. *Journal of Marital and Family Therapy, 8,* 77-85.

Casper, L. and Bryson, K. (1998, March). Household and family characteristics. Current population reports: Population characteristics. Available from <www.census.gov/prod/3/98pubs/p20-515.pdf>.

Center for the Study of Social Policy (1993). *Kids count data book: State profiles of child well-being.* Washington, DC: Anne E. Casey Foundation. (ERIC Document Reproduction Service No. ED357 110)

Cherlin, A. (1991). Longitudinal studies of effects of divorce on children in Great Britain and the United States. *Science, 7,* 1386-1389.

Cherlin, A. and Furstenberg, F. (1989, March). Divorce doesn't always hurt the kids. *The Washington Post, 19,* C3.

Chinn, W. L. (1938). A brief survey of 1000 juvenile delinquents. *British Journal of Educational Psychology, 8,* 78-85.

Chodorow, N. (1978). *The reproduction of mothering: Psychoanalysis and the sociology of gender.* Berkeley: University of California Press.

Chodorow, N. and Contratto, S. (1976). The fantasy of the perfect mother. In N. Chodorow (Ed.), *Feminism and psychoanalytic theory.* New Haven, CT: Yale University Press.

Coffman, S. G. and Roark, A. E. (1992). A profile of adolescent anger in diverse family configurations and recommendations for intervention. *School Counselor, 39*(3), 211-216.

Committee for Economic Development (1991). *The unfinished agenda: A new vision for child development and education.* A statement by the Research and Policy Committee of the Committee for Economic Development, New York. (ERIC Document Reproduction Service No. ED336 444)

Cooley, W. W. (1993). *The difficulty of the educational task.* Pittsburgh, PA: Learning Research and Development Center of Pittsburgh University. (ERIC Document Reproduction Service No. ED358 527)

Coontz, S. (1992). *The way we never were: American families and the nostalgia trap.* New York: Basic Books, a Division of HarperCollins Publishers, Inc. Copyright 1992 by Basic Books.

Cooper, H. M. and Moore, C. J. (1995). Teenage motherhood, mother-only households, and teacher expectations. *The Journal of Experimental Education, 63,* 231-248.

Coughlin, E. K. (1988). Sociologists investigate the costs to children of growing up in a "mother-only" family. *The Chronicle of Higher Education, 34,* A5.

Daly, M. (1974). *Beyond God the father.* Boston, MA: Beacon Press.

Darrity, W. and Myers, S. (1984). Does welfare dependency cause female headship? *Journal of Marriage and the Family, 46*(4), 765-779.

Davies, B. (1989). *Frogs and snails and feminist tales: Preschool children and gender.* Sydney, Australia: Allen and Unwin.

Davies, B. (1993). *Shards of glass.* Cresskill, NJ: Hampton Press, Inc.

Davis, K. (1988). Wives and work: A theory of sex-role revolution and its consequences. In S. M. Dornbusch and M. H. Strober (Eds.), *Feminism, children and the new families* (pp. 67-86). New York: Guilford Press.

Davis, W. E. and McCaul, E. J. (1991). *The emerging crisis: Current and projected status of children in the United States.* Maine University, Oronoco Institute for the Study of At-Risk Students, Augusta, ME. (ERIC Document Reproduction Service No. ED348 434)

Demo, D. H. (1992). Parent-child relations: Assessing recent changes. *Journal of Marriage and the Family, 54*(1), 104-117.

Demos, J. (1986). *Past, present, and personal: The family and life course in American history.* New York: Oxford University Press.

Debusk, S. and Leslie, K. (1991). How can we help? *Momentum, 22*(3), 25-28.

Dinnerstein, D. (1976). *The mermaid and the minotaur: Sexual arrangements and human malaise.* New York: HarperCollins Publishers.

Dornbusch, S. M. and Gray, K. D. (1988). Single-parent families. In S. M. Dornbusch and M. H. Strober (Eds.), *Feminism, children and the new families* (pp. 274-296). New York: Guilford Press.

Dornbusch, S. M. and Strober, M. H. (1988). *Feminism, children, and the new families.* New York: Guilford Press.

Dulaney, C. and Banks, K. (1994). *Racial and gender gaps in academic achievement.* Report summary. Raleigh, NC: NC Department of Evaluation and Research. (ERIC Document Reproduction Service No. ED380 198)

Duxbury, L., Higgins, C., and Lee, C. (1994). Work-family conflict: A comparison by gender, family type, and perceived control. *Journal of Family Issues, 15,* 449-466.

Ehrenreich, B. (1983). *The hearts of men.* New York: Anchor Press/Doubleday.

Eichenbaum, L. and Orbach, S. (1982). *Outside in . . . inside out.* Harmondsworth: Penguin.

Eitzen, D. S. with Baca Zinn, M. (1988). *In conflict and order: Understanding society,* Fourth edition. Boston, MA: Allyn & Bacon.

Emery, K. J. (1993). *Position statement on youth violence prevention and recommended actions.* Dayton, OH: New Futures for Dayton Area Youth. (ERIC Document Reproduction Service No. ED357 091)

Falicov, C. J. (Ed.) (1988). *Family transitions.* New York: Guilford Press.

Faludi, S. (1991). *Backlash: The undeclared war against American women.* New York: Crown.

Farrell, E. (1994). *Self and school success. Voices and lore of inner-city students.* Albany, NY: State University of New York Press. (ERIC Document Reproduction Service No. ED368 829)

Farrell, W. (1972). *The liberated man.* New York: Berkley Books.

Featherstone, D. R. and Cundick, B. P. (1992). Differences in school behavior and achievement between children from intact, reconstituted, and single-parent families. *Adolescence, 27*(105), 1-12.

Fetterman, D. M. (Ed.) (1984). *Ethnography in educational evaluation.* Beverly Hills, CA: Sage.

Fine, M. (1994). Working the hyphens: Reinventing self and other in qualitative research. In N. K. Denzin and Y. S. Lincoln (Eds.), *Handbook of qualitative research* (pp. 70-82). Thousand Oaks, CA: Sage.

Finn, J. D. and Owings, M. F. (1994). Family structure and school performance in eighth grade. *Journal of Research and Development in Education, 27*(3), 176-187.

Firestone, S. (1971). *The dialectic of sex: The case for feminist revolution.* New York: Bantam Books.

Friedan, B. (1979, November 18). Feminism takes a new turn. *New York Times Magazine, 129*(44), 40-102.

―――― (1981). *The second stage.* New York: Summit Books.

Galston, W. A. (1993). Causes of declining well-being among U.S. children. *Aspen Institute Quarterly, 5*(1), 52-77.

Gergin, M. (1990). Finished at 40: Women's development within the patriarchy. *Psychology of Women Quarterly, 14*, 471-493.

Gigy, L. L. (1980). Self-concept of single women. *Psychology of Women Quarterly, 5*, 321-340.

Gilligan, C. (1982). *In a different voice: Psychological theory and women's development.* Cambridge, MA: Harvard University Press.

Gimenez, M. (1984). Feminism, pronatalism and motherhood. In J. Trebilcot (Ed.), *Mothering: Essays in feminist theory.* NJ: Rowman and Allanheld.

Glaser, D. (Ed.) (1974). *Handbook of criminology.* Chicago: Rand McNally.

Gornick, V. and Moran, K. (Eds.) (1972). *Women in sexist society.* New York: Signet Books.

Grove, W. (1976). The relationship between sex roles, marital status and mental illness. In A. Kaplan (Ed.), *Beyond sex-role stereotypes: Reading toward a psychology of androgyny.* Boston, MA: Little, Brown and Company.

Grymes, J. M., Cramer, M. K., Lawler-Prince, D., and Atwood, K. (1993, November). *Pre-service teachers' expectations for children from different family structures.* Paper presented at the Annual Meeting of the Mid-South Educational Research Association, New Orleans, LA. (ERIC Document Reproduction Service No. ED367 649)

Gutman, H. (1976). *Black family in slavery and freedom, 1750-1925.* New York: Pantheon.

Hafner, R. J. (1986). *Marriage and mental illness.* New York: Guilford Press.

Harrison, B. G. (1992, September). The unsinkable Murphy Brown. *Mademoiselle, 98*, 54.

Hattley, R. E. (1959, Winter). Children's concepts of male and female roles. *Merrill-Palmer Quarterly, 85.*

Henslin, J. M., Henslin, L. K., and Keiser, S. D. (1976). Schooling for social stability: Education in the corporate society. In J. M. Henslin and L. T. Reynolds (Eds.), *Social problems in American society* (pp. 311-312). Boston, MA: Allyn & Bacon.

Herzog, E. and Sudia, C. (1968). Fatherless homes: A review of research. *Children, 15*, 177-182.

Herzog, E. and Sudia, C. E. (1973). Children in fatherless families. In B. E. Cadwell and N. H. Riccuti (Eds.), *Review of child development research,* Volume 3 (pp. 141-233). Chicago: University of Chicago Press.

Hetherington, E. M., Cox, M., and Cox, R. (1977). The aftermath of divorce. In J. H. Stevens Jr. and M. Matthews (Eds.), *Mother-child, father-child relations.* Washington, DC: National Association for the Education of Young Children.

———— (1978). Stress and coping in divorce: A focus on women. In J. E. Gullahorn (Ed.), *Psychology and women: In transition* (1979), Washington, DC: Winston Holt.

Hirsch, J. and Ellis, J. B. (1995). Family support and other social factors precipitating suicidal ideation. *The International Journal of Social Psychiatry, 41*, 26-30.

Hoeffer, B. (1987). Predictors of life outlook of older single women. *Research in Nursing and Health, 10,* 111-117.

Holland, D. C. and Eisenhart, M. A. (1990). *Educated in romance.* Chicago: University of Chicago Press.

Hollon, W. E. (1974). *Frontier violence: Another look.* New York: Oxford University Press.

Holstein, J. A. and Gubrium, J. F. (1994). Phenomenology, ethnomethodology, and interpretive practice. In N. K. Denzin and Y. S. Lincoln (Eds.), *Handbook of qualitative research* (pp. 262-272). Thousand Oaks, CA: Sage.

Howe, D. (1994). *Single, African-American, low income mothers' child-rearing practices and stressors and their relationships to children's prosocial behavior and peer status.* Research Project, Wayne State University, Detroit, MI. (ERIC Document Reproduction Service No. ED373 877)

Howe, L. K. (1972). *The future of the family.* New York: Simon and Schuster.

Jenkins, J. E., Hedlund, D. E., and Ripple R. E. (1988). Parental separation effects on children's divergent thinking abilities and creativity potential. *Child Study Journal, 18,* 149-159.

Jing, J. and Mayer, L. (1995). Single parents: In need of a support network. *Community College Journal, 65,* 44-48.

Kagan, J. (1984). *The nature of the child.* New York: Basic Books.

Kagan, J. and Moss, H. (1962). *Birth to maturity.* New York: John Wiley.

Kanoy, K. W. and Cunningham, J. L. (1984). Consensus or confusion in research on children and divorce: Conceptual and methodological issues. *Journal of Divorce, 7,* 45-71.

Karraker, M. W. (1991, April). *Growing up in a single-parent family: Some not-so-negative effects on adolescent females' plans for the future.* Paper presented at The Troubled Adolescent: The Nation's Concern and Its Response, Milwaukee, WI. (ERIC Document Reproduction Service No. ED337 516)

Kaschak, E. (1992). *Engendered lives: A new psychology of women's experience.* New York: Basic Books, a Division of HarperCollins Publishers, Inc. Copyright 1992 by Basic Books.

Kennedy, G. E. (1992, November). *The value and commitment to work and family roles: Influence of gender and family background.* Paper presented at the Annual Conference of the National Council on Family Relations, Orlando, FL. (ERIC Document Reproduction Service No. ED358 383)

Kissman, K. (1991). Feminist-based social work with single-parent families. *Families in Society, 72,* 23-28.

Kissman, K. and Allen, J. (1993). *Single-parent families.* Newbury Park, CA: Sage.

Kotelchuck, M. (1976). The infant's relationship to the father: Experimental evidence. In M. E. Lamb (Ed.), *The role of the father in child development.* New York: Wiley.

Krantz, S. E. (1988). Divorce and children. In S. M. Dornbusch and M. H. Strober (Eds.), *Feminism, children and the new families* (pp. 249-268). New York: Guilford Press.

Kurdek, L. A. and Siesky, A. E. (1980). Children's perceptions of their parents' divorce. *Journal of Divorce, 3,* 339-378.

Kurtz, L., Derevensky, J. L., and Tarabulsky, G. (1993, August). *Access by non-custodial parents: Effects upon children's post divorce coping resources.* Paper presented at the Annual Meeting of the American Psychological Association, Toronto, Ontario, Canada. (ERIC Document Reproduction Service No. ED371 266)

Lamb, M. E. (1976). Interactions between 8-month old children and their fathers and mothers. In M. E. Lamb (Ed.), *The role of the father in child development.* New York: Wiley.

———— (1977). Father-infant and mother-infant interaction in the first year of life. *Child Development, 48,* 167-181.

Lather, P. (1988). Feminist perspectives on empowering research methodologies. *Women's Studies International Forum, 11*(6), 569-581.

Laws, J. and Schwartz, P. (1977). *Sexual scripts: The social construction of female sexuality.* Hinsdale, IL: Dryden Press.

LeCompte, M. D. and Preissle, J. (1993). *Ethnography and qualitative design in educational research.* San Diego, CA: Academic Press, Inc.

Lee, V. E., Burkham, D. T., Zimites, H., and Lasewski, B. (1994). Family structure and its effect on behavioral and emotional problems in young adolescents. *Journal of Research on Adolescence, 4*(3), 405-437.

Lenhart, T. L. and Chudzinski, J. (1994). *Children with emotional/behavioral problems and their family structures.* Washington, DC: U.S. Department of Education. (ERIC Document Reproduction Service No. ED377 634)

Lerner, B. (1996, Summer). Merlyn's magic . . . and ours. *American Educator, 20*(2), pp. 4-8.

Levine, J. (1992). *My enemy, my love: Man-hating and ambivalence in women's lives.* New York: Doubleday.

Lewis, J. K. (1992). Death and divorce: Helping students cope in single-parent families. *NASSP Bulletin, 76*(543), 55-60.

Llewelyn, S. and Osborne, K. (1990). *Women's lives.* New York: Routledge.

Loewenstein, S. F., Bloch, N. E., Campion, J., Epstein, J. S., Gale, P., and Salvatore, M. (1981). A study of satisfactions and stresses of single women in midlife. *Sex roles, 7,* 1127-1141.

Lund, D. W. (1995). Matrilineal descent and juvenile offender counseling. *International Journal of Offender Therapy and Comparative Criminology, 39,* 43-46.

MacFarlane, J. (1964). Perspectives on personality consistency and change from the guidance study. *Vita Humana, 7,* 123.

Markson, E. R. (1993). Depression and moral masochism. *International Journal of Psycho-Analysis, 74,* 931-939.

Marsh, H. W. (1990). Two-parent, stepparent, and single-parent families: Changes in achievement, attitudes, and behaviors during the last two years of high school. *Journal of Educational Pscyhology, 82*(2), 327-340.

Maslow, A. H. (1970). *Motivation and personality.* New York: Harper & Row.

McCord, J., McCord, W., and Thurber, E. (1962). Some effects of parental absence on male children. *Journal of Abnormal and Social Psychology, 64,* 361-369.

Milne, A. M., Myers, D. E., Rosenthal, A. S., and Ginsburg, A. (1986). Single parents, working mothers, and the educational achievement of school children. *Sociology of Education, 59,* 125-139.

Mintzies, P. and Hare, I. (1985). *The human factor: A key to excellence in education.* Silver Springs, MD: National Association of Social Workers. (ERIC Document Reproduction Service No. ED365 915)

Mischel H. N. and Fuhr, R. (1988). Maternal employment: Its psychological effects on children and their families. In S. M. Dornbusch and M. H. Strober (Eds.), *Feminism, children and the new families* (pp. 191-207). New York: Guilford Press.

Mitchell, B. A. (1994). Family structure and leaving the nest: A social resource perspective. *Sociological Perspectives, 37,* 651-671.

Mones, P. A. (1995, July 28). Life and death and Susan Smith. *The New York Times,* A27.

Mulkey, L. M., Crian, R. L., and Harrington, A. J. (1992). One-parent households and achievement: Economic and behavioral explanations of a small effect. *Sociology of Education, 65,* 48-65.

Nelson, E. A. and Maccoby, E. E. (1966). The relationship between social development and differential abilities on the SAT. *Merrill-Palmer Quarterly, 12,* 269-289.

Norton, A. J. and Glick, P. C. (1986). One parent families: A social and economic profile. *Family Relations, 35,* 9-17.

Nye, F. I. (1957). Child adjustment in broken and in unhappy unbroken homes. *Marriage and Family Living, 19,* 356-360.

Oakley, A. (1974). *Housewife.* London: Allen Lane.

————— (1976). *Women's work.* New York: Vintage Books.

————— (1986). Feminism, motherhood and medicine—Who cares? In J. Mitchell and A. Oakley (Eds.), *What is feminism?* Oxford: Basil Blackwell.

Obiakor, F. E. (1992, November). *At-risk youngsters: Methods that work.* Paper presented at the Annual Conference of the Tennessee Association on Young Children, Nashville, TN. (ERIC Document Reproduction Service No. ED352 175)

Otto, W. (1991). *How to make an American quilt.* New York: Ballentine Books.

Parish, T. S. and Necessary, J. R. (1994). Do attitudinal and behavioral ratings of family members vary across familial configurations? *Adolescence, 29,* 649-652.

Pearson, J. C. and Sessler, C. J. (1991, May). *Family communication and health: Maintaining marital satisfaction and quality of life.* Paper presented at the Annual Meeting of the International Communication Association, Chicago, IL. (ERIC Document Reproduction Service No. ED335 722)

Peng, S. S. and Lee, R. M. (1992, April). *Measuring student at-riskness by demographic characteristics.* Paper presented at the Annual Meeting of the

American Educational Research Association, San Francisco, CA. (ERIC Document Reproduction Service No. ED347 879)

Rankin, J. H. and Kern, R. (1994). Parental attachments and delinquency. *Criminology, 32,* 495-515.

Raphael-Leff, J. (1985). Facilitator and regulators: Vulnerability to post-natal disturbance. *Journal of Psychosomatic Obstetrics and Gynaecology, 4,* 151-168.

Reinhard, D. W. (1977). The reaction of adolescent boys and girls to the divorce of their parents. *Journal of Clinical Child Psychology, 6,* 15-20.

Rice, J. K. (1994). Reconsidering research on divorce, family life cycle, and the meaning of family. *Psychology of Women Quarterly, 18,* 559-584.

Rice, J. K. and Rice, D. G. (1986). *Living through divorce.* New York: Guilford Press.

Richards, L. N. and Schmiege, C. J. (1993). Problems and strengths of single-parent families: Implications for practice and policy. *Family Relations, 42,* 277-285.

Riger, S. (1992). Epistemological debates, feminist voices: Science, social values, and the study of women. *American Psychologist, 47,* 730-740.

Rosen, R. (1977). Children of divorce: What they feel about access and other aspects of the divorce experience. *Journal of Clinical Child Psychology, 6,* 15-20.

Rutter, M. (1977). *Maternal deprivation reassessed.* Harmondsworth, UK: Penguin.

Santrock, J. W. (1972). Relation and type of onset of father-absence of cognitive development. *Child Development, 43,* 455-469.

Schur, E. M. (1984). *Labeling women deviant: Gender, stigma, and social control.* New York: Random House.

Seidman, I. E. (1991). *Interviewing as qualitative research.* New York: Teachers College Press.

Shinn, M. (1978). Father absence and children's cognitive development. *Psychological Bulletin, 85,* 295-324.

Shreeve, W., Goetter, W. G. J., Bunn, A., Norby, J. R., Stueckle, F., Midgley, T. K., deMichele, B. (1986). Single-parents and students achievements—A national tragedy. *Early Child Development and Care, 23,* 175-184.

Sidey, K. H. (1992, July 30). The veep and the sitcom. *Christianity Today, 36,* 18.

Simon, P. (1996). State will issue report cards on schools. *Buffalo News,* January 21, A1.

Skolnick, A. (1978). The myth of the vulnerable child. *Psychology Today, 11,* 58.

Smith, J. K. and Heshusius, L. (1986). Closing down the conversation: The end of the quantitative-qualitative debate among educational inquirers. *Educational Researcher, 15* (1), 4-12.

Solomon, J. C. and Marx, J. (1995). To grandmother's house we go: Health and school adjustment of children raised solely by grandparents. *The Gerontologist, 35,* 386-394.

Spence, J. (1979). Traits, roles and the concept of androgyny. In J. E. Gullahorn (Ed.), *Psychology and women: In transition.* Washington, DC: Winston, Holt.

Stacey, J. (1990). *Brave new families: Stories of domestic upheaval in late twentieth century America.* New York: Basic Books.

Stake, R. E. (1994). Case studies. In N. K. Denzin and Y. S. Lincoln (Eds.), *Handbook of qualitative research* (pp. 236-247). Thousand Oaks, CA: Sage.

Stark, R. (1989). *Sociology,* Third edition. Los Angeles: Wadsworth.

Sullivan, V. (Ed.) (1994). Year of the family (Special issue). *California Agriculture, 48*(7), 1-49. (ERIC Document Reproduction Service No. ED380 260)

Swanson, J. W., Holzer, C. E., and Canavan, M. M. (1989). Psychopathology and economic status in mother-only and mother-father families. *Child Psychiatry and Human Development, 20,* 15-24.

Van Stone, N., Nelson, J. R., and Niemann, J. (1994). Poor single-mother college students' views on the effect of some primary sociological and psychological belief factors on their academic success. *The Journal of Higher Education, 65,* 571-584.

Van Wormer, K. (1989). Co-dependency: Implications for women and therapy. *Women and Therapy, 8*(4), 51-64.

Veevers, J. E. (1974). Voluntary childless wives. In A. Skolnick and J. Skolnick (Eds.), *Intimacy, family and society.* Boston, MA: Little Brown.

Walker, H. A. (1988). Black-white differences in marriage and family patterns. In S. M. Dornbusch and M. H. Strober (Eds.), *Feminism, children and the new families* (pp. 87-112). New York: Guilford Press.

Wallerstein, J. S. and Blakeslee, S. (1989). *Second chances: Men, women and children a decade after divorce.* New York: Ticknor and Fields.

Wallerstein, J. S. and Kelly, J. B. (1974). The effects of parental divorce: The adolescent experience. In A. Koupernick (Ed.), *The child in his family—Children at a psychiatric risk* (pp. 479-505). New York: John Wiley.

————— (1975). The effects of parental divorce: Experiences of the preschool child. *Journal of the American Academy of Child Psychiatry, 14*(4), 600-616.

————— (1976). The effects of parental divorce: Experiences of the child in later latency. *Journal of Orthopsychiatry, 46*(2), 256-269.

————— (1980). *Surviving the breakup.* New York: Basic Books.

Wanat, C. L. (1993). Programs for single-parent children: Principals and single parents disagree. *Journal of School Leadership, 3*(4), 427-448.

Wattenberg, E. and Reinhardt, H. (1981). Female-headed families. In E. Howell and M. Bayes, *Women and mental health* (pp. 357-372). New York: Basic Books.

Weitzman, L. J. (1985). *The divorce revolution.* New York: The Free Press.

White, L. (1994). Growing up with single parents and stepparents: Long-term effects on family solidarity. *Journal of Marriage and the Family, 56*(4), 935-948.

Whitehead, B. D. (1993, April). Dan Quayle was right. *Atlantic Monthly, 271*(4), 47-84.

Williams, J. (1984). Women and mental illness. In J. Nicholson and H. Beloff (Eds.), *Psychology Survey,* Volume 5. Leicester: British Psychological Society.

Wolfe, W. S., Campbell, C. C., and Frongillo, E. A. (1994). Overweight school-children in New York State: Prevalence and characteristics. *American Journal of Public Health, 84*, 807-813.

Wyoming State Department of Education. (1993). *Wyoming's education progress report*. Cheyenne, WY: Author. (ERIC Document Reproduction Service No. ED380 904)

Zimiles, H. and Lee, V. E. (1991). Adolescent family structure and educational progress. *Developmental Psychology, 27*(2), 314-320.

Index

Order Your Own Copy of
This Important Book for Your Personal Library!

UNBROKEN HOMES
Single-Parent Mothers Tell Their Stories

_____ in hardbound at $69.95 (ISBN: 0-7890-1139-5)

_____ in softbound at $27.95 (ISBN: 0-7890-1140-9)

COST OF BOOKS_____

OUTSIDE USA/CANADA/
MEXICO: ADD 20%_____

POSTAGE & HANDLING_____
(US: $4.00 for first book & $1.50
for each additional book
Outside US: $5.00 for first book
& $2.00 for each additional book)

SUBTOTAL_____

IN CANADA: ADD 7% GST_____

STATE TAX_____
(NY, OH & MN residents, please
add appropriate local sales tax)

FINAL TOTAL_____
(If paying in Canadian funds,
convert using the current
exchange rate. UNESCO
coupons welcome.)

☐ **BILL ME LATER:** ($5 service charge will be added)
(Bill-me option is good on US/Canada/Mexico orders only;
not good to jobbers, wholesalers, or subscription agencies.)

☐ Check here if billing address is different from
shipping address and attach purchase order and
billing address information.

Signature_____

☐ **PAYMENT ENCLOSED: $**_____

☐ **PLEASE CHARGE TO MY CREDIT CARD.**

☐ Visa   ☐ MasterCard   ☐ AmEx   ☐ Discover
☐ Diner's Club   ☐ Eurocard   ☐ JCB

Account # _____

Exp. Date _____

Signature _____

Prices in US dollars and subject to change without notice.

NAME _____

INSTITUTION _____

ADDRESS _____

CITY _____

STATE/ZIP _____

COUNTRY _____ COUNTY (NY residents only) _____

TEL _____ FAX _____

E-MAIL_____

May we use your e-mail address for confirmations and other types of information? ☐ Yes   ☐ No
We appreciate receiving your e-mail address and fax number. Haworth would like to e-mail or fax special
discount offers to you, as a preferred customer. **We will never share, rent, or exchange your e-mail
address or fax number.** We regard such actions as an invasion of your privacy.

Order From Your Local Bookstore or Directly From
The Haworth Press, Inc.
10 Alice Street, Binghamton, New York 13904-1580 • USA
TELEPHONE: 1-800-HAWORTH (1-800-429-6784) / Outside US/Canada: (607) 722-5857
FAX: 1-800-895-0582 / Outside US/Canada: (607) 772-6362
E-mail: getinfo@haworthpressinc.com
PLEASE PHOTOCOPY THIS FORM FOR YOUR PERSONAL USE.
www.HaworthPress.com

BOF00